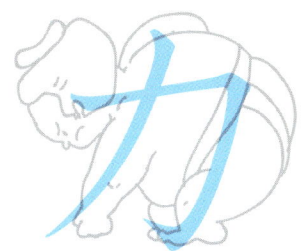

Understanding through pictures
1000 KANJI

イラストで覚える漢字 1000

Kamijima Fumiko
上島　史子

Takeuchi Yumiko
竹内夕美子

ナツメ社

◆ はじめに ◆

　外国語として日本語を学ぶうえで，漢字の学習は非常に重要です。日本語学習者のなかには，漢字学習にさほど抵抗を感じない人もいます。しかし，多くの学習者にとって，その習得は難しいものとなっています。

　この本は，日本語学習者，とりわけ非漢字圏の学習者が，漢字の形や意味を理解し，記憶するのに役立つ一書です。本書で扱う1000の漢字には，1字も漏れなく，漢字の読みと意味が挙げられており，さらに，漢字の形や意味を説明する短い文とイラストが添えられています。各章末には，漢字の読み・書きを復習することができるように練習問題を置いています。また，ミニ字典として機能するように，巻末には索引も備えています。

　学習者が漢字を楽しく効率的に習得するのに，この本が大きな手助けとなることを著者一同強く望んでいます。

Learning *Kanji* is a very important part of studying Japanese as a foreign language. Some learners of Japanese may not feel much resistance to studying *Kanji*; however, for many students, learning *Kanji* can be difficult.

This book will be useful for learners of Japanese, especially people from *non-Kanji* backgrounds. This book will help learners to understand and memorize the shape and meaning of *Kanji*. Among the 1,000 *Kanji* covered in this book, nothing has been omitted. The *Kanji* readings and meanings are cited, and there are short sentences and illustrations that explain the shape and meaning of the *Kanji*. At the end of each chapter, there are exercises so that learners can review and read *Kanji*. Furthermore, there is an index at the back of the book that can be used as a learning resource, and also a mini dictionary.

We strongly hope that this book will be a great resource for learners and enable them to learn *Kanji* efficiently and in a fun way.

◆ この本について

　この本は、ひらがな・カタカナを学び終えた学習者を対象に、1000字の漢字について、絵を用いて、効果的に、そして楽しく学びながら、読み・書きができるようになることを目的としています。

　漢字については、数が多いうえに字形が複雑であり、かつ、字そのものに多くの意味が含まれるなど、英語で使用されるアルファベットなどとは大きな違いがあります。

　したがって、漢字の一つ一つをそのまま暗記していくと考えると、膨大な手間が必要となります。それをできる限り防ぐために、この本では、漢字そのものの意味や形から連想されるような短い説明文を、全部の漢字に付しています。この短い説明文と、その文を漢字の字形とともに組み込んで図示化した絵とを、関連づけることで、漢字の字形だけを単独で覚える場合と違い、漢字の字形を自然と思い出すことができるようにしています。

主な学習の流れ

① 漢字の大まかな形を確認する。

② 短い説明文と絵を、漢字の字形と照らし合わせながら確認する。

Check
The sun appears from the horizon in the early morning.

③ 漢字そのものが持つ意味の代表的なものや、その漢字の読み方などを確認する。

いみ early, quick, to hasten
おんよみ ソウ・サッ
くんよみ はや(い)・はや(まる)・はや(める)

④ 字形を覚えるために、一画ごとに分かれている書き順を見ながら漢字をなぞって書く。次に、書き順を見ながら自分でマス目に漢字を書きこむ。

strokes 6画　

⑤ 漢字が用いられる熟語を覚える。

Remember
早起き　はやおき　getting up early
早期　　そうき　　early stage

　このように、まず漢字の字形と短い説明文・絵を確認し、それから実際に手を動かすという流れで学習することによって、記憶に残りやすくなるようにしています。

◆ About this book

This book is aimed at helping people who have finished learning *Hiragana* and *Katakana* to be able to read and write 1,000 *Kanji* characters with the help of illustrations. Its aim is to give learners an effective and fun way to learn *Kanji*.

There are a great number of *Kanji*, and the shape and strokes of these characters are very complicated. Furthermore, there can be multiple meanings for each character. As a result, learners may find *Kanji* to be very different from the alphabet, or other writing systems in their own native languages.

Therefore, when considering that each *Kanji* must be memorized, an enormous amount of effort is required to learn *Kanji*. This book adds a short phrase connected to the meaning and form of each *Kanji* character. By relating this short phrase with the character shape of the *Kanji* and associating it with an illustration, it is possible for people to remember the character shape and nature of the *Kanji*. This is different from just learning and trying to remember only the character form of the *Kanji* alone.

Steps to learning

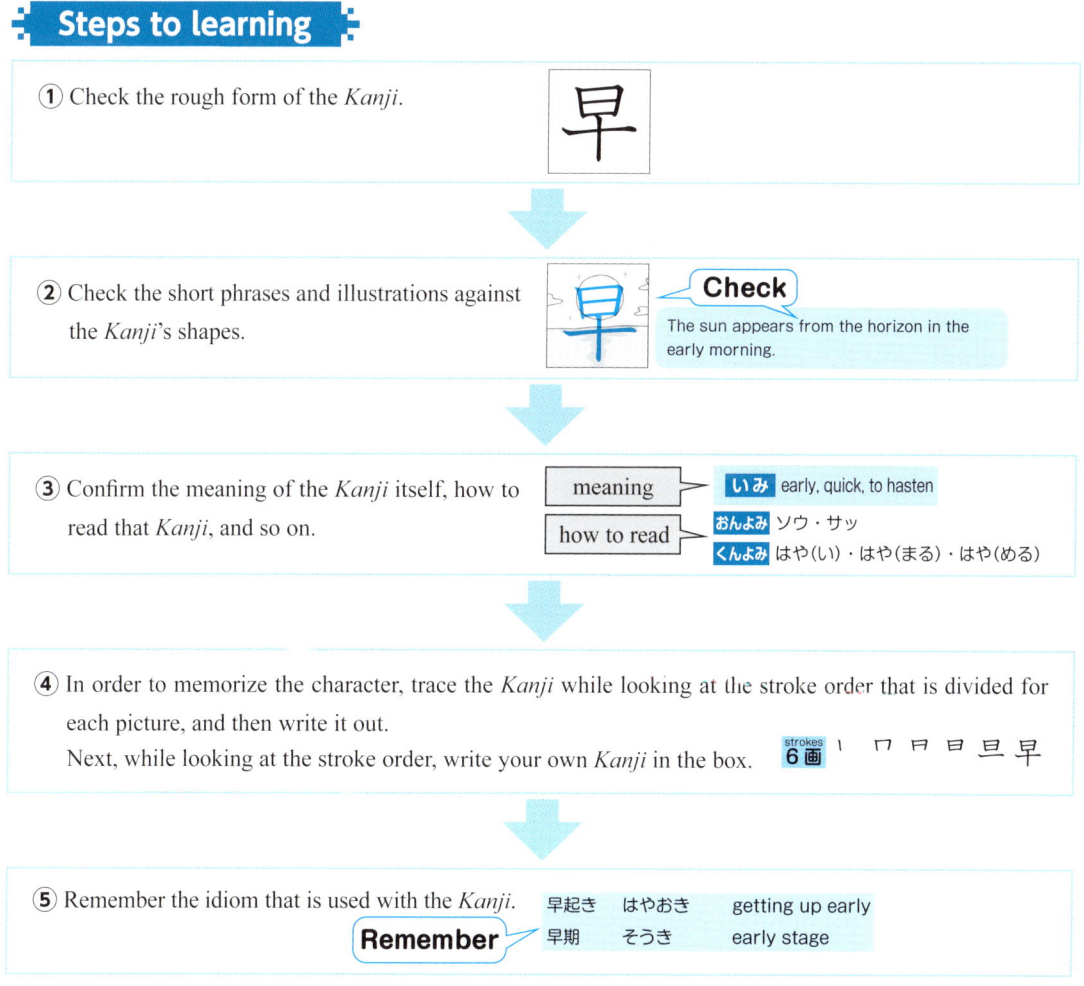

By following these steps, learners can first learn the shape of the *Kanji*, then the short phrase, and then confirm it with the illustration. Finally, learners can check their skills by actually writing the *Kanji*. Following these steps will enable people to easily remember the *Kanji*.

◆ この本の使い方

　この本では、1000字の漢字について、読み・書きができるように説明しています。
　それぞれの漢字は次のようにまとめた形で説明をしています。まずは、それぞれの部分が何を表しているのかを確認しましょう。

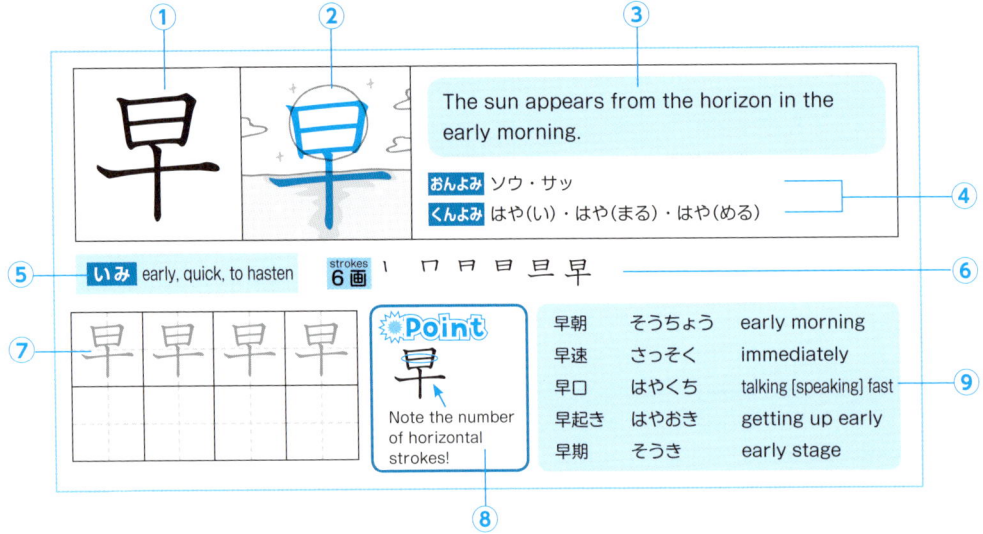

① 扱う漢字です。手書きに近い書体で表しています。
② 漢字の字形を覚えるためのイラストです。③とあわせて覚えます。
③ 漢字の字形をもとにした短い説明文です。イラストは、ある程度漢字の意味と関係のある内容にしていますが、あくまでも形を覚えるための説明文であるため、漢字の意味、成り立ちを正確に表すものではありません。
④ 漢字の読み方のうち、音読みをカタカナで示しています。読み方は常用漢字表に基づき、代表的なものを挙げています。
　漢字の読み方のうち、訓読みをひらがなで示しています。送り仮名は(　)で示しています。読み方は常用漢字表に基づき、代表的なものを挙げています。
⑤ 漢字そのものが持つ意味の代表的なものを英語で示しています。
⑥ 漢字の画数と、その漢字の書き順を示しています。
⑦ 練習として漢字を書く場所です。①の漢字の字形、⑥の書き順を見ながら書きます。最初の数文字は灰色の字をなぞって書き、そのあとは自力で正しく書きましょう。
⑧ 漢字を書くときに注意すべきポイントです。
⑨ 学んでいる漢字を使用した熟語を挙げています。左からその漢字を使った熟語や言葉、その読み方、代表的な意味、その熟語・言葉を使った例文を示しています（例文を省略しているページもあります）。熟語や言葉は、その漢字の読み方をできるだけ多く挙げられるように選んでいます。

　このほかに、各章の章末には練習問題のページがあります。漢字の読み、書きの復習ができる問題となっているので、それぞれのページの指示にしたがって、取り組みましょう。

◆ How to use this book

This book explains 1,000 *Kanji* characters so that people can learn to read and write them. Each *Kanji* is described in the way as summarized below. To see what each part represents, please look at the following.

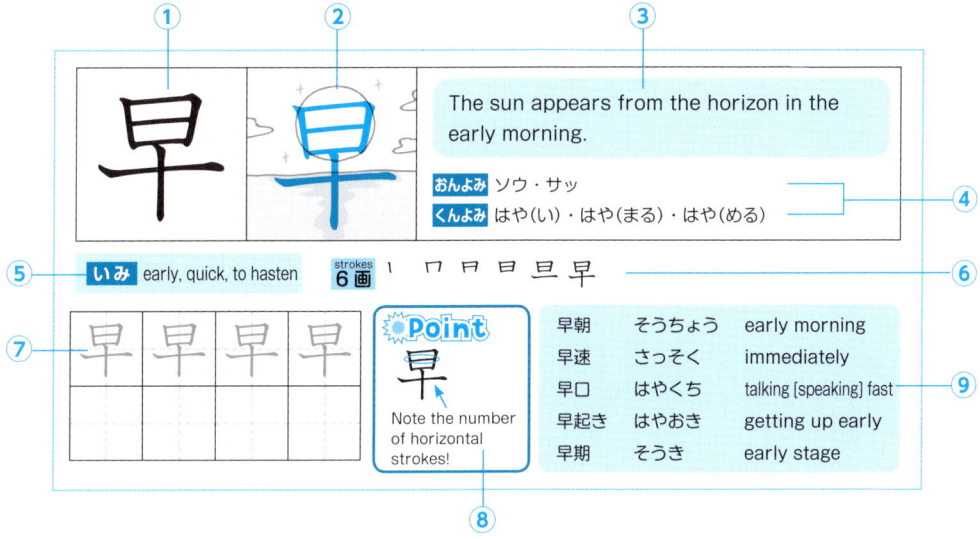

① This is the *Kanji* to be learned. It is represented by a handwritten typeface.

② This is an illustration to help remember the *Kanji* shape. It should be remembered together with ③.

③ This is a short phrase based on the shape of the *Kanji*. Illustrations have contents related to the meaning of the *Kanji* to some extent; however, because they are phrases to help remember the shape, it does not accurately represent the meaning of the *Kanji* or the formation.

④ Among the readings of *Kanji*, this indicates the "*On-yomi*" reading, which is the Chinese-style reading. These are the typical readings that based on a Chinese Characters commonly used list. These are shown in *Katakana*.

Among the readings of *Kanji*, this indicates the "*Kun-yomi*" reading, which is original to Japanese. These are shown in *Hiragana*. "*Okurigana*" (*Hiragana* to accompany *Kanji*) is shown in ( ).

⑤ This indicates the meaning of the *Kanji* itself in English.

⑥ This shows the number of strokes of the *Kanji* and the stroke order of that *Kanji*.

⑦ This is a place to practice writing the *Kanji*. Write while looking at the character shape in ① and the strokes in ⑥. Write the first few times by tracing over the gray characters, and then write it correctly on your own.

⑧ This is a cautionary note for points to be aware of when writing the *Kanji*.

⑨ This lists idioms that use the *Kanji* that you are learning. It shows idioms and words that use that *Kanji* from the left, the way to read it, the meaning, and an example sentence that uses the *Kanji*'s idioms and words (some examples are omitted). Idioms and words are chosen so that people can have a list of as many possible ways to read that *Kanji*.

In addition to this information, there is a page of exercises at the end of each chapter. Since they are quizzes for people to practice and review the *Kanji*, people should work on each page according to the instructions.

◆ 漢字の分け方について

この本で扱っている1000の漢字を、下のような段階に分けて配列しています。

N5：　日本語能力試験4級（＝N5相当）の漢字を中心に、扱っています。
N4：　日本語能力試験3級（＝N4相当）の漢字を中心に、扱っています。
N3：
N2：　｝日本語能力試験2級（＝N3～N2相当）の漢字を中心に、扱っています。

　各段階では、曜日に関係する、数に関係するなどのように、同じカテゴリーに属する漢字や、成り立ちが近い「へん」や「つくり」が同じ漢字、漢字の一部が同じ要素でできている漢字などを集めて配列しています。N3～N2相当の漢字では、「へん」「つくり」などがイメージしやすいものを優先的にN3で扱うようにしています。また、N3、N2の中を要素が切れる部分、かつ学習の目安となる半分程度をもって①・②に分割して構成しています。

◆ 漢字の書き方について

　この本では、漢字を書くときの順番（書き順）を示しています。
　漢字を書くときには、この書き順にしたがって書くとよいでしょう。書き順の基本的なルールを下で紹介します。

① 　線・部分は上から下へ

　　　一 → 丁 → 工

② 　線・部分は、左から右へ

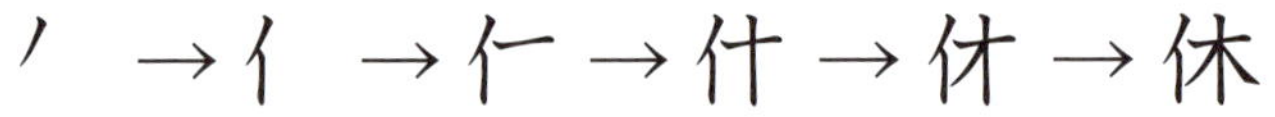

　　　丿 → 亻 → 仁 → 什 → 休 → 休

③ 　外側を先に、囲みの完成は最後に

　　　｜ → 冂 → 冂 → 冋 → 用 → 国 → 国 → 国

④ 　貫く画は最後に

　　　一 → 厂 → 戸 → 戸 → 亘 → 亘 → 車

　　　く → 夊 → 女

◆ How the *Kanji* have been divided

The 1,000 *Kanji* to be studied in this book are divided into levels of the Japanese Language Proficiency Test (JLPT). N1 is the highest level of the JLPT; N5 is the lowest level. N stands for *Nihongo* (Japanese) and also "new", as in the new version of the test.

- N5： contains the *Kanji* of the Japanese Language Proficiency Test Level 4
  (the equivalent of the new test level: N5).
- N4： contains the *Kanji* of the Japanese Language Proficiency Test Level 3
  (the equivalent of the new test level: N4).
- N3：
- N2： We deal mainly with *Kanji* for the Japanese Language Proficiency Test Level 2 (the equivalent of the new test level: N3 ~ N2).

At each stage, *Kanji* have been grouped with similar *Kanji* belonging to the same category, related to the days of the week, etc., that are close to each other, and are written with the same elements of the same *Kanji*. We arranged the *Kanji* that are equivalent to levels N3 ~ N2. We are trying to give preference to N3 and to things that are easy to have images of the same elements of the same *Kanji*. In addition, we have divided N3, N2 into sections ① and ②, and about half which is a guide for learning.

◆ How to write *Kanji*

This book shows learners the order (stroke order) for writing *Kanji*.
When writing *Kanji*, you should follow the correct stroke order. The basic rules of the "stroke order" are listed below.

① Write the line and part from top to bottom

一 → 丁 → 工

② Write the line and part from left to right

丿 → 亻 → 仁 → 什 → 休 → 休

③ Write the outside first, and finally complete the enclosure

丨 → 冂 → 冂 → 冋 → 用 → 国 → 国 → 国

④ Write strokes passing through other strokes last

一 → 厂 → 冂 → 冃 → 亖 → 亘 → 車

く → 女 → 女

もくじ：Contents of this book

N5 レベルに相当する漢字 —————————— P.11

N4 レベルに相当する漢字 —————————— P.43

N3 レベルに相当する漢字① ————————— P.101

N3 レベルに相当する漢字② ————————— P.172

N2 レベルに相当する漢字① ————————— P.226

N2 レベルに相当する漢字② ————————— P.281

N5: contains the *Kanji* of the Japanese Language Proficiency Test Level 4 — P.11

N4: contains the *Kanji* of the Japanese Language Proficiency Test Level 3 — P.43

N3①: contains the *Kanji* of the Japanese Language Proficiency Test Level 2 — P.101

N3②: contains the *Kanji* of the Japanese Language Proficiency Test Level 2 — P.172

N2①: contains the *Kanji* of the Japanese Language Proficiency Test Level 2 — P.226

N2②: contains the *Kanji* of the Japanese Language Proficiency Test Level 2 — P.281

N5

ここでは、日本語能力検定4級相当の漢字を掲載しています。

contains the *Kanji* of the Japanese Language Proficiency Test Level 4

I like lying in bed on Sunday morning.

おんよみ ニチ・ジツ
くんよみ ひ・か

いみ sun, day, Japan, Sunday
strokes 4画 １ 冂 日 日

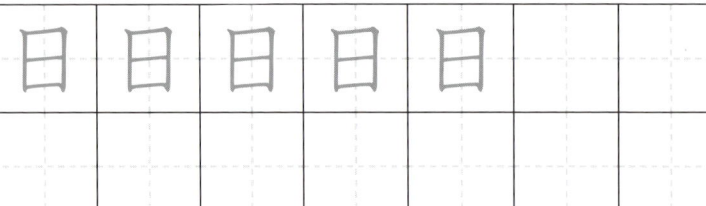

Point

Note the number of horizontal strokes!

日曜日	にちようび	Sunday	日曜日に友人に会う。
休日	きゅうじつ	holiday	休日は、家ですごす。
日米	にちべい	Japan and U.S.A.	日米の同盟がむすばれる。
日光	にっこう	sunlight, sunshine	外に出て、日光をあびる。
十日間	とおかかん	ten days	夏休みは十日間ある。
明日	あす・あした	tomorrow	明日は雨が降りそうだ。

On the way home on Monday, I looked at the moon.

おんよみ ゲツ・ガツ
くんよみ つき

いみ moon, month, Monday
strokes 4画 ） 冂 月 月

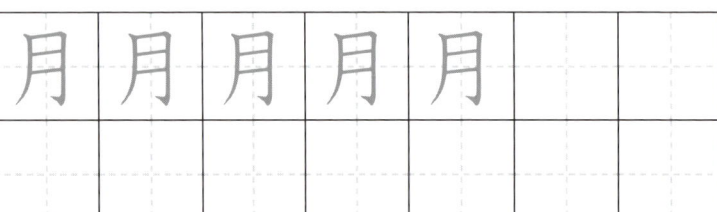

Point

Do not connect!

月曜日	げつようび	Monday	月曜日にプールで泳ぐ。
一月	いちがつ	January	一月の天気をよそくする。
一月	ひとつき	one month	一月先の予定を決める。
今月	こんげつ	this month	今月の売上を計算する。
月見	つきみ	moon viewing	庭で月見をする。
正月	しょうがつ	New Year holiday	正月は家族で過ごす。

I had a camp fire on Tuesday.

おんよみ カ
くんよみ ひ・ほ

いみ fire, Tuesday **strokes** 4画 丶 ⺂ ⺊ 火

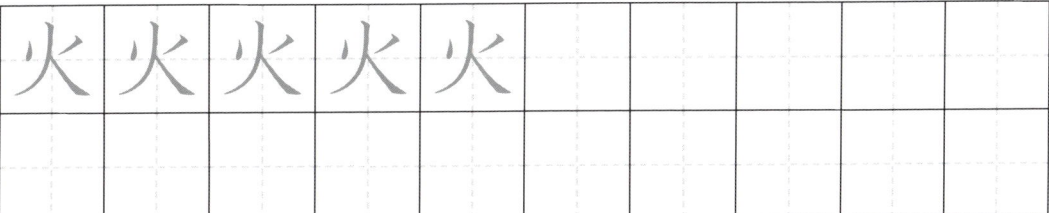

火曜日	かようび	Tuesday	今日は火曜日だ。
火災	かさい	a fire	火災にならないように、注意する。
火力	かりょく	heat	火力をあげる。
消火	しょうか	fire extinguishing	火災の消火に当たる。
火山	かざん	volcano	火山が煙を上げている。
防火訓練	ぼうかくんれん	a fire drill	学校で防火訓練を行う。

 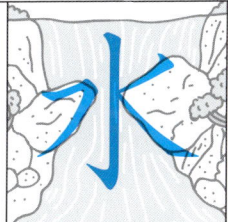

I looked at a waterfall on Wednesday where water hit the rocks and flowed down.

おんよみ スイ
くんよみ みず

いみ water, Wednesday **strokes** 4画 亅 ⺈ オ 水

 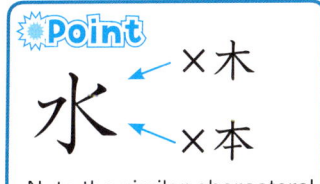

Note the similar characters!

水曜日	すいようび	Wednesday	水曜日の天気予報を見る。
水道	すいどう	water supply	水道が止まる。
防水	ぼうすい	waterproof	防水の靴をはく。
水色	みずいろ	light blue	水色のシャツを着る。
水平	すいへい	horizontal	棚を水平に取り付ける。
水位	すいい	water level	川の水位が上がる。

木

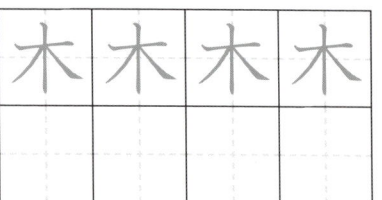

I have lunch under the tree on Thursday.

おんよみ ボク・モク
くんよみ き・こ

いみ wood, tree, Thursday　　strokes 4画　一 十 才 木

×水
×本
Note the similar characters!

木刀	ぼくとう	wooden sword
木材	もくざい	wood
植木	うえき	potted plant
木曜日	もくようび	Thursday
木陰	こかげ	shade of a tree

金

Every Friday, to save money, I put coins in my house-shaped money box.

おんよみ キン・コン
くんよみ かね・かな

いみ money, gold, Friday　　strokes 8画　

金額	きんがく	sum of money
黄金	おうごん・こがね	gold
料金	りょうきん	charge, fare, rate
金曜日	きんようび	Friday
金具	かなぐ	metal fittings

土

I practice yoga every Saturday.

おんよみ ド・ト
くんよみ つち

いみ soil, dirt, earth, Saturday　　strokes 3画　一 十 土

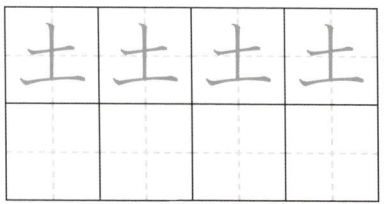

Do not protrude!

土地	とち	land
粘土	ねんど	clay
土台	どだい	foundation
土曜日	どようび	Saturday
赤土	あかつち	red soil

		There is one log.
一	(log)	おんよみ イチ・イツ くんよみ ひと・ひと(つ)

いみ one, ace, first　**stroke** 1画 一

一	一	一	一		

一月	いちがつ	January
一回	いっかい	once
一人	ひとり	one (person)
統一	とういつ	unity
一つ	ひとつ	one

		There are two logs.
二	(logs)	おんよみ ニ くんよみ ふた・ふた(つ)

いみ two, second　**strokes** 2画 一 二

二	二	二	二		

二月	にがつ	February
二つ	ふたつ	two
二人	ふたり	two (people)
二重	にじゅう	double
二次元	にじげん	two dimensions

		There are three logs.
三	(logs)	おんよみ サン くんよみ み・み(つ)・みっ(つ)

いみ three, third　**strokes** 3画 一 二 三

三	三	三	三		

三月	さんがつ	March
三日月	みかづき	crescent moon
三つ	みっつ	three
三角形	さんかくけい	triangle
三次元	さんじげん	three dimensions

四

I opened the curtains and looked outside through the window.

おんよみ シ
くんよみ よ・よ(つ)・よっ(つ)・よん

いみ four, fourth　　strokes 5画　一 冂 冂 四 四

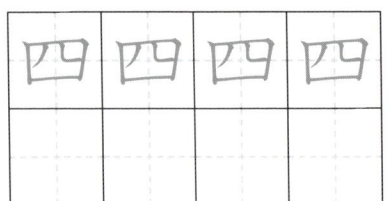

Point

Do not protrude!

四月	しがつ	April
四年	よねん	four years
四輪	よんりん	four wheels
四角形	しかくけい	quadrangle
四つ	よっつ	four

五

We are building a nice log cabin.

おんよみ ゴ
くんよみ いつ・いつ(つ)

いみ five, fifth　　strokes 4画　一 丆 五 五

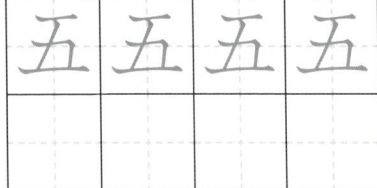

Point

Do not protrude!

五月	ごがつ	May
五日間	いつかかん	five days
五輪	ごりん	the Olympics
五角形	ごかくけい	pentagon
五つ	いつつ	five

六

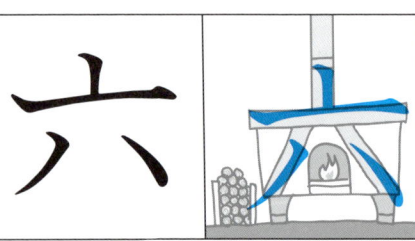

There is a wood-burning stove inside a cozy log cabin.

おんよみ ロク
くんよみ む・む(つ)・むっ(つ)・むい

いみ six, sixth　　strokes 4画　一 亠 六 六

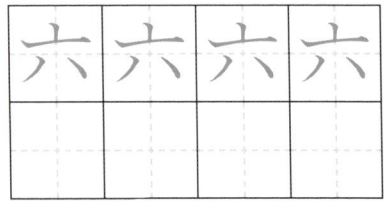

Point

Do not protrude!

六月	ろくがつ	June
六日間	むいかかん	six days
双六	すごろく	Japanese backgammon
六角形	ろっかくけい	hexagon
六つ	むっつ	six

七

I moved to the next city by sled.

おんよみ シチ
くんよみ なな・なな(つ)・なの

いみ seven, seventh **strokes** 2画 一 七

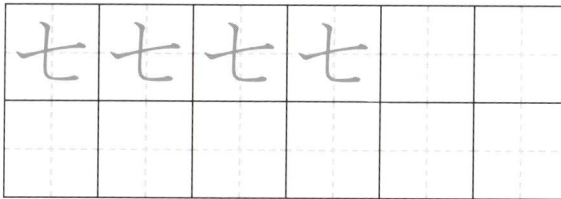

七月	しちがつ	July
七つ	ななつ	seven
七日間	なのかかん	seven days
七面鳥	しちめんちょう	turkey
北斗七星	ほくとしちせい	the Big Dipper

八

I can see the log cabin's big roof.

おんよみ ハチ
くんよみ や・や(つ)・やっ(つ)・よう

いみ eight, eighth **strokes** 2画 ノ 八

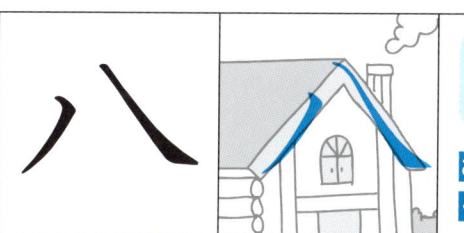

Point
Do not connect!

八月	はちがつ	August
八日間	ようかかん	eight days
八角形	はっかくけい	octagon
八百屋	やおや	greengrocer
八つ	やっつ	eight

九

I need more logs, so I will cut down a tree.

おんよみ キュウ・ク
くんよみ ここの・ここの(つ)

いみ nine, ninth **strokes** 2画 ノ 九

Point
九 ×丸
Note the similar character!

九月	くがつ	September
九州	きゅうしゅう	*Kyushu*
九日間	ここのかかん	nine days
九つ	ここのつ	nine

I can see inside the house through the big window.

おんよみ ジュウ・ジッ
くんよみ とお・と

いみ ten, tenth　strokes 2画 一十

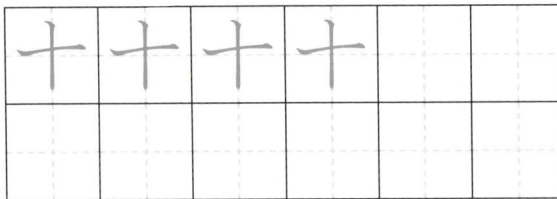

十月	じゅうがつ	October
十円玉	じゅうえんだま	ten-yen coin
十日間	とおかかん	ten days
十五夜	じゅうごや	night with a full moon
十分(な)	じゅうぶん(な)	enough, sufficient

I need one hundred pieces of firewood for the wood-burning stove.

おんよみ ヒャク
くんよみ ―

いみ hundred, hundredth　strokes 6画 一丆丆百百百

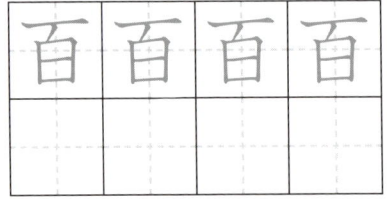

Point
百
Do not protrude!

百円玉	ひゃくえんだま	hundred-yen coin
二百	にひゃく	two hundred
百円ショップ	ひゃくえんしょっぷ	100-yen shop
百科事典	ひゃっかじてん	encyclopedia
百貨店	ひゃっかてん	department store

There are icicles hanging from the log cabin's roof.

おんよみ セン
くんよみ ち

いみ thousand, thousandth　strokes 3画 ノ二千

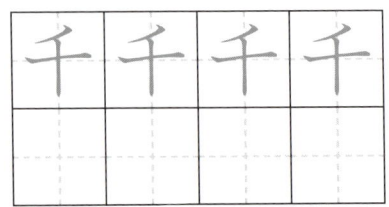

Point
千
Do not protrude!

千円	せんえん	thousand yen
三千	さんぜん	three thousand
千代紙	ちよがみ	Japanese paper with colorful patterns

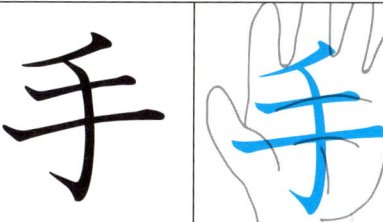

This is my left hand.

おんよみ シュ
くんよみ て・た

いみ hand, means, way, skill
strokes 4画 一ニ三手

Point
手 ← Do not protrude!

握手	あくしゅ	handshake	仲間たちと握手をする。
手袋	てぶくろ	glove	手袋をはめる。
手綱	たづな	reins	馬の手綱をにぎる。
手術	しゅじゅつ	operation, surgery	胃の手術を受ける。
手紙	てがみ	letter	友人に手紙を書く。
手段	しゅだん	means	交通手段を考える。

Stretch your legs well before playing sports.

おんよみ ソク
くんよみ あし・た(りる)・た(る)・た(す)

いみ leg, foot, to add, enough
strokes 7画 ノ口口甲甲甲足

Point
足 ← Do not protrude!

一足	いっそく	a pair of shoes	新しい靴を一足買う。
足首	あしくび	ankle	足首をくじく。
足し算	たしざん	addition	子供に足し算を教える。
足場	あしば	scaffold, foothold	足場を固める。
補足	ほそく	supplement	わかりにくい説明の補足をする。
満足(な)	まんぞく(な)	satisfied, contented	満足な結果をえる。

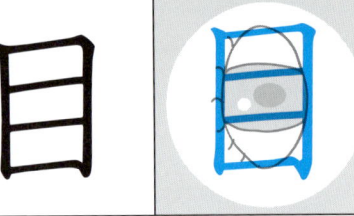

I looked in the small hole.

おんよみ モク・ボク
くんよみ め・ま

いみ eye, point　strokes 5画　｜ 冂 冃 目 目

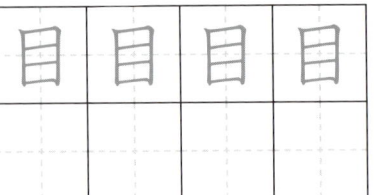

Note the number of horizontal strokes!

目薬	めぐすり	eye drops
目的	もくてき	purpose
役目	やくめ	job, part, role
目標	もくひょう	goal
科目	かもく	subject

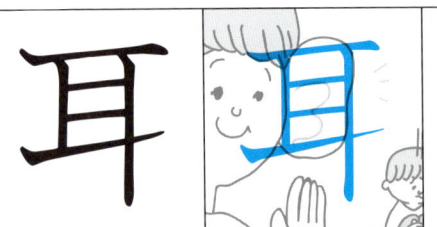

When my friends are feeling down, I always lend them a sympathetic ear.

おんよみ ジ
くんよみ みみ

いみ ear　strokes 6画　一 丅 Ŧ F 王 耳

Protrude!

右耳	みぎみみ	right ear
耳元	みみもと	one's ear
耳栓	みみせん	earplug
中耳炎	ちゅうじえん	otitis media

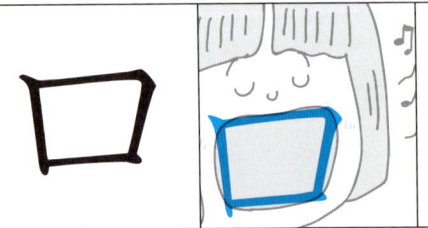

Open your mouth wide when you sing a song.

おんよみ コウ・ク
くんよみ くち

いみ mouth　strokes 3画　｜ 冂 口

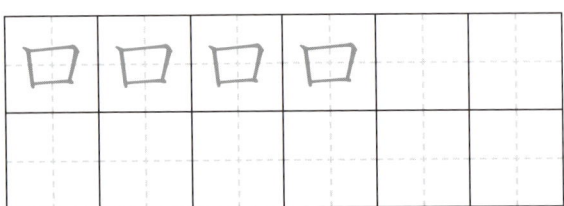

人口	じんこう	population
口調	くちょう	tone of voice, manner of talking
口紅	くちべに	lipstick
口論	こうろん	argument, quarrel
非常口	ひじょうぐち	emergency exit

林

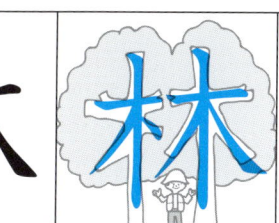

I am standing between the two trees.

おんよみ リン
くんよみ はやし

いみ woods, forest, grove

strokes 8画 一 十 オ 才 木 村 材 林

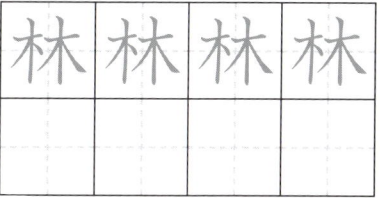

Note the similar characters!

林道	りんどう	forest road
植林	しょくりん	afforestation
杉林	すぎばやし	Japanese cedar forest
林間学校	りんかんがっこう	open-air school

森

You can see a lot of trees in the forest.

おんよみ シン
くんよみ もり

いみ big forest, grove

strokes 12画 一 十 オ 木 木 朩 オ 杰 森 森 森 森

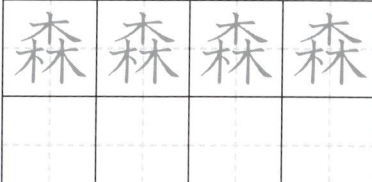

Note the similar character!

| 森林 | しんりん | forest, woods |
| 青森市 | あおもりし | *Aomori* City |

天

There are two staircases that lead you into the sky and into heaven.

おんよみ テン
くんよみ あめ・あま

いみ sky, space, weather, heaven

strokes 4画 一 二 チ 天

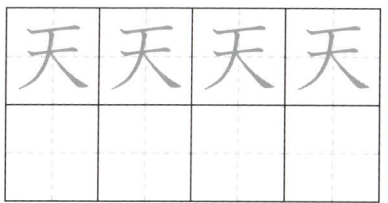

Do not protrude!

天気	てんき	weather
天井	てんじょう	ceiling
天の川	あまのがわ	the Milky Way
天使	てんし	angel
天才	てんさい	genius

気

I made a fire and simmered stew in a pot. Steam and a delicious smell soon came out of the pot.

おんよみ キ・ケ　　くんよみ —

いみ air, sign

strokes 6画　ノ ⺍ 气 气 気 気

気温	きおん	temperature
気分	きぶん	mood
気配	けはい	sign
空気	くうき	air

空

A propeller aircraft and two birds are flying under the clouds.

おんよみ クウ　　くんよみ そら・あ(く)・あ(ける)・から

いみ sky, empty

strokes 8画　ノ ⼍ 宀 宀 空 空 空 空

Point: 空 Do not protrude!

空港	くうこう	airport
夜空	よぞら	night sky
空手	からて	*karate*
空き家	あきや	vacant house, unoccupied house

夕

There is a bird sitting on the branch of a tree.

おんよみ セキ　　くんよみ ゆう

いみ evening

strokes 3画　ノ ク 夕

一朝一夕	いっちょういっせき	in a short time
夕方	ゆうがた	evening
夕食	ゆうしょく	supper
夕日	ゆうひ	setting sun

石

I saw a huge stone under the cliff.

おんよみ セキ・シャク・コク　　くんよみ いし

いみ stone, rock

strokes 5画　一 ア 丆 石 石

Point: 石 ←×右　Note the similar character!

石油	せきゆ	oil
磁石	じしゃく	magnet
宝石	ほうせき	jewel
石畳	いしだたみ	stone pavement

貝

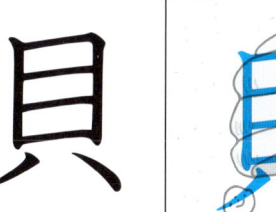

One spiral shell and two small pebbles are on the beach.

おんよみ —
くんよみ かい

いみ shellfish, shell

strokes 7画 １ 冂 冃 月 目 貝 貝

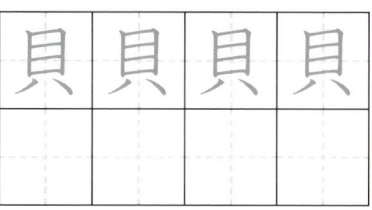

Point

貝 ←× 目
貝 ←× 見

Note the similar characters!

貝殻	かいがら	shell
帆立貝	ほたてがい	scallop
二枚貝	にまいがい	bivalve, clam
貝柱	かいばしら	adductor muscle

草

 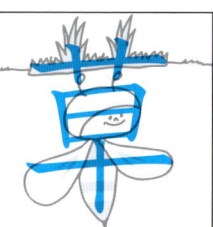

A honeybee is hiding in the weeds.

おんよみ ソウ
くんよみ くさ

いみ grass, weed

strokes 9画 一 十 艹 艹 艹 艹 苎 草 草

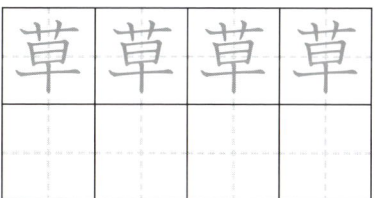

Point

草

Note the longest horizontal stroke!

草	くさ	grass
野草	やそう	wild grass
海草	かいそう	seagrass
草原	そうげん	grassland
牧草	ぼくそう	grass, pasture

花

I found a flower in the weeds.

おんよみ カ
くんよみ はな

いみ flower, blossom

strokes 7画 一 十 艹 艹 艹 花 花

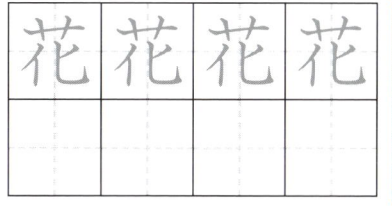

Point

花

Do not protrude!

花壇	かだん	flower bed
花瓶	かびん	vase
花束	はなたば	bouquet
花火	はなび	fireworks
花嫁	はなよめ	bride

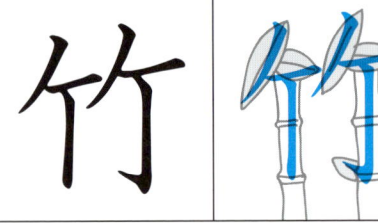

There are two bamboo trees.

おんよみ チク
くんよみ たけ

いみ bamboo strokes 6画 ノ 丨 ⺮ ⺮ 竹 竹

竹林	ちくりん	bamboo grove
竹馬	たけうま	bamboo stilts
竹垣	たけがき	bamboo fence
竹の子	たけのこ	bamboo shoots

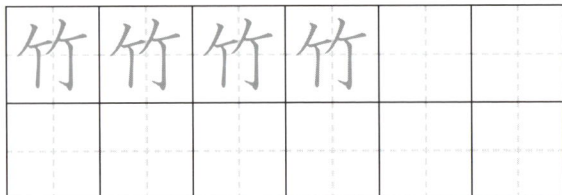

I am climbing to the three peaks of the mountain.

おんよみ サン
くんよみ やま

いみ mountain strokes 3画 丨 凵 山

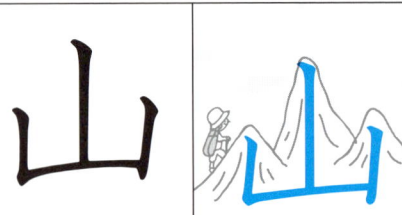 

Point
山
Do not protrude!

富士山	ふじさん	Mt. Fuji
登山	とざん	climbing
山火事	やまかじ	forest fire
火山	かざん	volcano
高山	こうざん	high mountain

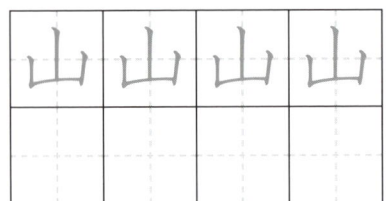  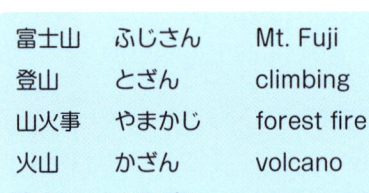

I am swimming in the river.

おんよみ セン
くんよみ かわ

いみ river strokes 3画 ノ 丿 川

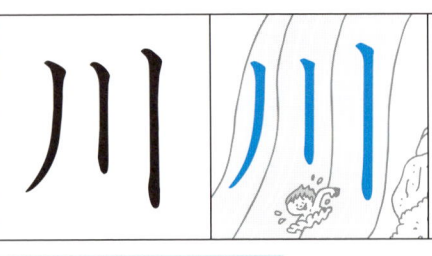

Point
川
Note the longest vertical stroke!

河川	かせん	river
川辺	かわべ	riverside
川上	かわかみ	the upper reaches of a river
小川	おがわ	brook, creek, stream
川岸	かわぎし	riverbank

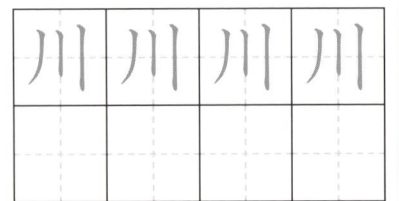 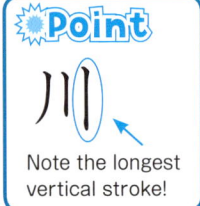 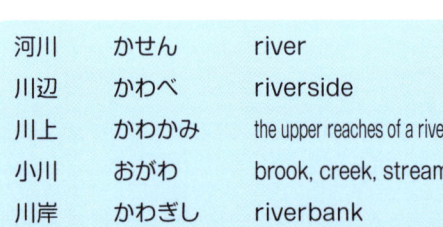

Rain falls from a big cloud.

おんよみ ウ
くんよみ あめ・あま

いみ rain   strokes 8画

Point — Do not connect!

雨	らいう	thunderstorm	夕方は雷雨になるらしい。
長雨	ながあめ	long rain	秋は長雨の季節だ。
雨具	あまぐ	rain gear	雨具を忘れる。
雨量	うりょう	rainfall	6月は雨量が多い。
豪雨	ごうう	heavy rain	豪雨のために、川が増水した。
雨水	あまみず	rainwater	雨水を活用する。

The rice paddy is laid out to be grid-shaped.

おんよみ デン
くんよみ た

いみ rice field, paddy   strokes 5画

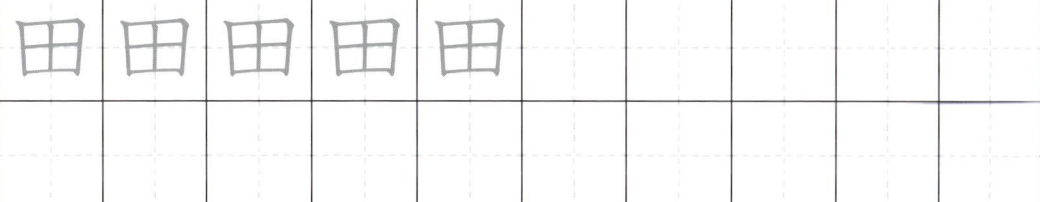

水田	すいでん	rice paddy	米は水田で作られる。
田畑	たはた	field, farmland	田畑を耕す。
油田	ゆでん	oil field	油田が見つかる。
田園	でんえん	the countryside	豊かな田園が広がっている。
田植え	たうえ	rice planting	家族みんなで田植えをする。

25

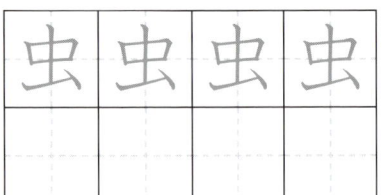

Someone is trying to catch a worm crawling on a leaf with a butterfly net.

おんよみ チュウ
くんよみ むし

いみ bug, worm, insect
strokes 6画 丨 口 日 中 虫 虫

Point
虫
Do not protrude!

昆虫	こんちゅう	insect, bug
毛虫	けむし	hairy caterpillar
虫歯	むしば	bad tooth
弱虫	よわむし	wimp, coward
殺虫剤	さっちゅうざい	insecticide

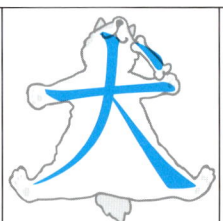

A dog is lying on his back and stretching his legs. There is a bone next to him.

おんよみ ケン
くんよみ いぬ

いみ dog, hound
strokes 4画 一 ナ 大 犬

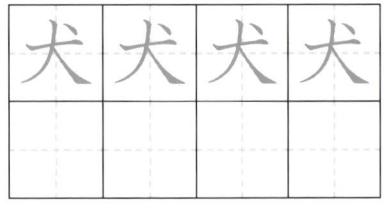

Point
犬 ×大
犬 ×太
Note the similar characters!

愛犬	あいけん	pet dog
番犬	ばんけん	guard dog
猟犬	りょうけん	hound
野良犬	のらいぬ	stray dog
犬小屋	いぬごや	doghouse

Music is coming out of the speaker.

おんよみ オン・イン
くんよみ おと・ね

いみ sound, tone
strokes 9画 丶 亠 ナ 立 产 音 音 音

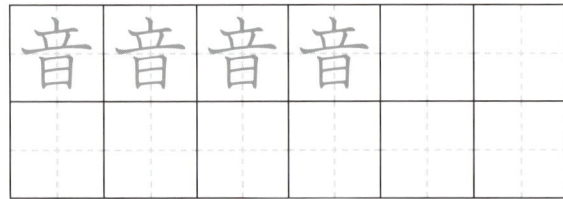

音楽	おんがく	music
足音	あしおと	footstep
音色	ねいろ	sound, tone
騒音	そうおん	noise
子音	しいん	consonant

 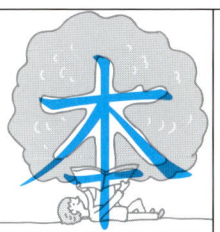

I am lying under a tree reading a book.

おんよみ ホン
くんよみ もと

いみ root, important part, book   strokes 5画   一 十 才 木 本

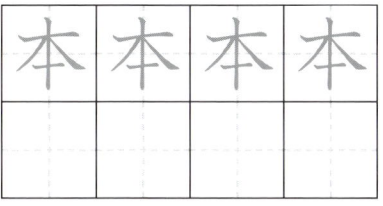

本 ←×木
Note the similar character!

本屋	ほんや	bookstore
本音	ほんね	real feelings
熊本市	くまもとし	*Kumamoto* City
基本	きほん	basis, basics
資本	しほん	capital

A man is carrying two heavy straw rice bags.

おんよみ ダン・ナン
くんよみ おとこ

いみ man, gentleman, male   strokes 7画   丨 口 罒 田 甲 男 男

男
Protrude!

男性	だんせい	man
長男	ちょうなん	the eldest son
男女	だんじょ	men and women
男前	おとこまえ	handsome man

 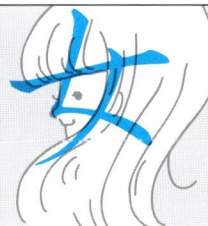

I see a woman's profile. Her long hair is fluttering in the wind.

おんよみ ジョ・ニョ・ニョウ
くんよみ おんな・め

いみ woman, lady, female   strokes 3画   く 夂 女

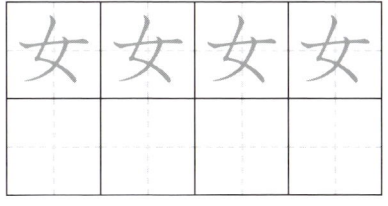

女
Protrude!

女性	じょせい	woman
乙女	おとめ	young girl
少女	しょうじょ	girl
女神	めがみ	goddess
女王	じょおう	queen

27

The boy studies at the school.

おんよみ ガク
くんよみ まな(ぶ)

いみ to study, to learn　strokes 8画　

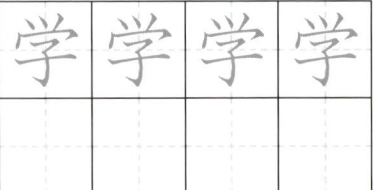

Point 学 — Note the position of the dots!

学ぶ	まなぶ	to learn
学校	がっこう	school
留学	りゅうがく	studying abroad
学習	がくしゅう	learning, study
学生	がくせい	student

Two children are holding hands together near the big tree.

おんよみ コウ
くんよみ ―

いみ school, to compare　strokes 10画　一 十 オ 木 木 杧 杧 校 校 校

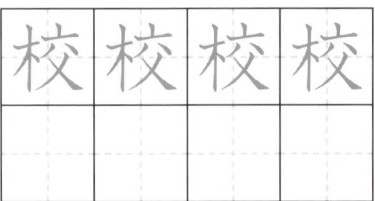

Point 校 — Note the position of the dots!

校庭	こうてい	playground
校舎	こうしゃ	school building
校長	こうちょう	principal
校正	こうせい	proofreading
校歌	こうか	school song

 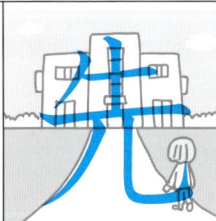

There is a building at the end of the road.

おんよみ セン
くんよみ さき

いみ preceding, pointed end　strokes 6画　ノ 一 丄 生 牛 先

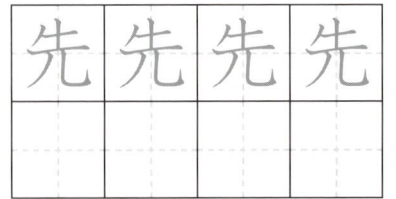

Point 先 — Protrude!

先生	せんせい	teacher
先輩	せんぱい	one's senior
先程	さきほど	a little while ago
先頭	せんとう	the front, the head
先月	せんげつ	last month

生

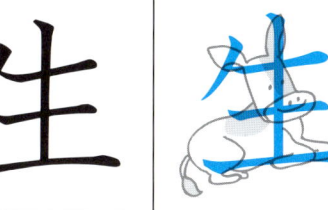

A cow is resting on the ground.

おんよみ セイ・ショウ　**くんよみ** い(きる)・い(かす)・い(ける)・う(まれる)・う(む)・お(う)・は(える)・は(やす)・き・なま

いみ to live, life, birth, to create　**strokes** 5画　ノ 一 牛 牛 生

Note the longest horizontal stroke!

生命	せいめい	life, existence
一生	いっしょう	one's whole life
生き物	いきもの	living thing
生徒	せいと	student

子

 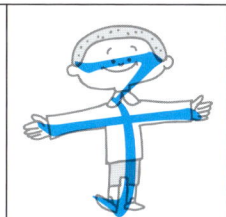

A child is spreading both his arms.

おんよみ シ・ス
くんよみ こ

いみ child　**strokes** 3画　フ 了 子

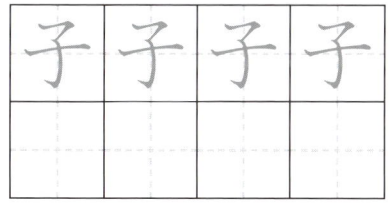

Connect!

帽子	ぼうし	cap, hat
椅子	いす	chair
子供	こども	child
調子	ちょうし	condition
男子	だんし	boy, man

入

I am going into the tent.

おんよみ ニュウ
くんよみ い(る)・い(れる)・はい(る)

いみ to enter, to join　**strokes** 2画　ノ 入

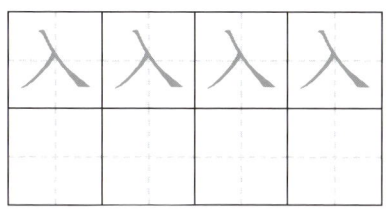

Do not protrude!

入学	にゅうがく	admission to a school
入国	にゅうこく	entry into a country
侵入	しんにゅう	invasion
輸入	ゆにゅう	import
入り口	いりぐち	entrance

A child is going to write a word with a pencil.

おんよみ ジ
くんよみ あざ

いみ letter, script, character   strokes 6画

Note the similar characters!

文字	もじ	letter, character
数字	すうじ	number
字数	じすう	the number of characters
字幕	じまく	subtitles
大文字	おおもじ	capital (letter)

A man is standing with his legs spread wide.

おんよみ ジン・ニン
くんよみ ひと

いみ person, people   strokes 2画

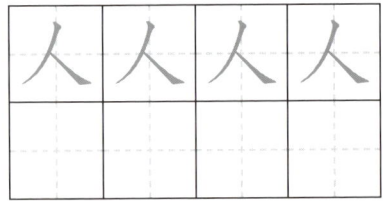  

Note the similar character!

人生	じんせい	one's (whole) life
人間	にんげん	human being
人柄	ひとがら	personality
友人	ゆうじん	friend
個人	こじん	individual

A lizard is moving towards the exit.

おんよみ シュツ・スイ
くんよみ で(る)・だ(す)

いみ to appear, to leave, to go out   strokes 5画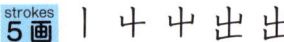

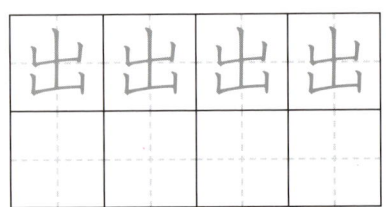 

Do not connect!

外出	がいしゅつ	going out
出納	すいとう	cashier
出口	でぐち	exit, way out
出国	しゅっこく	departure from a country
出現	しゅつげん	emersion, appearance

右

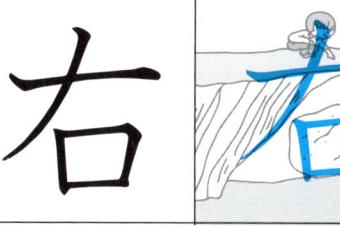

There is a huge stone on the right side under the cliff, on which a man is looking at the stone.

おんよみ ウ・ユウ
くんよみ みぎ

いみ right　**strokes** 5画　ノ ナ オ 右 右

右折	うせつ	right turn	次の角は右折禁止だ。
左右	さゆう	right and left	左右をよく確認する。
右手	みぎて	right hand	右手ではしを持つ。
右側	みぎがわ	the right (side)	道路の右側を歩く。
右利き	みぎきき	right-handed	私は右利きです。
右岸	うがん	the right bank of a river	右岸に花を植える。

左

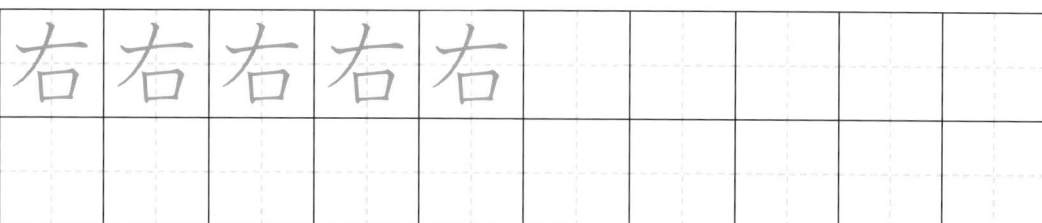

A pilot saw a big bird flying towards the light airplane from the left side.

おんよみ サ
くんよみ ひだり

いみ left　**strokes** 5画　一 ナ オ 左 左

左折	させつ	left turn	交差点で左折をする。
左手	ひだりて	left hand	左手を痛める。
左側	ひだりがわ	the left (side)	日本では、車は左側通行だ。
左利き	ひだりきき	left-handed	左利き用のゴルフクラブを使う。
左岸	さがん	the left bank of a river	左岸にわたる。

A sprout grows above the soil.

おんよみ ジョウ・ショウ **くんよみ** うえ・うわ・かみ・あ(げる)・あ(がる)・のぼ(る)・のぼ(せる)・のぼ(す)

いみ top, surface, over, to go up, to raise **strokes** 3画 丨 卜 上

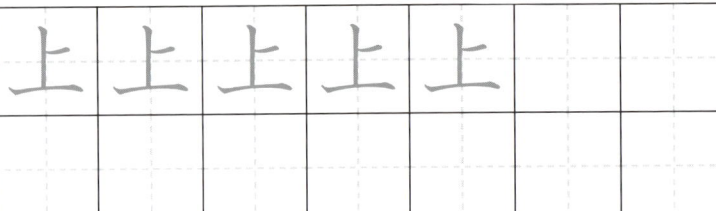

Point 上 ← Do not protrude!

屋上	おくじょう	roof floor	屋上からは、花火がよく見える。
年上	としうえ	older, senior	兄は私よりも四つ年上だ。
上半期	かみはんき	the first half of the year	上半期の決算が報告された。
上昇	じょうしょう	rise	気温の上昇をおさえる。
向上	こうじょう	improvement	質の向上が大切だ。
上着	うわぎ	coat, jacket	上着を着る。

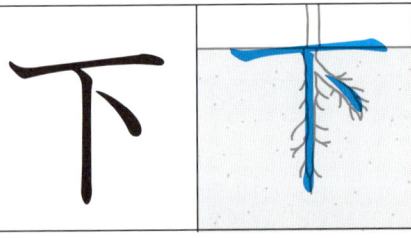

Roots grow under the soil.

おんよみ カ・ゲ **くんよみ** した・しも・もと・さ(げる)・さ(がる)・くだ(る)・くだ(す)・くだ(さる)・お(ろす)・お(りる)

いみ bottom, under, to go down, to lower **strokes** 3画 一 丅 下

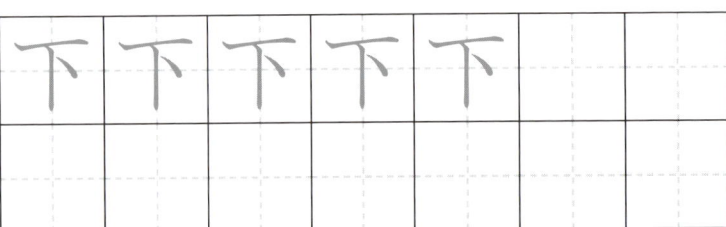

Point 下 ← Do not protrude!

地下	ちか	underground	地下一階におりる。
下車	げしゃ	getting off	次の駅で下車をする。
下半期	しもはんき	the latter half of the year	下半期の売上をよそくする。
下り坂	くだりざか	downward slope	下り坂にさしかかる。
上下	じょうげ	top and bottom, up and down	頭を上下に動かす。
下着	したぎ	underwear	下着を替える。

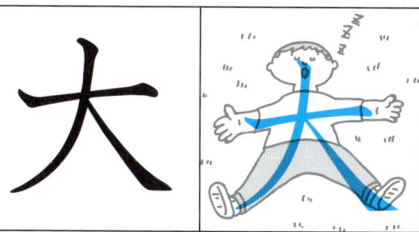

A big man is sleeping on the grass with his arms and legs stretched widely.

おんよみ ダイ・タイ
くんよみ おお・おお（きい）・おお（いに）

いみ big, large, adult, very　strokes 3画　一ナ大

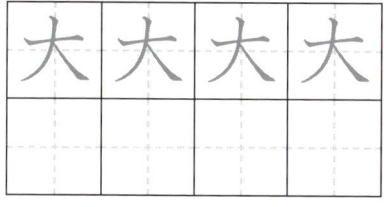

Note the similar characters!

大学	だいがく	college, university
大切(な)	たいせつ(な)	important
大型	おおがた	big, large
拡大	かくだい	expansion
大事(な)	だいじ(な)	important

A worm is crawling in the middle of the leaf.

おんよみ チュウ・ジュウ
くんよみ なか

いみ middle, center, central　strokes 4画　丨 ㇆ 口 中

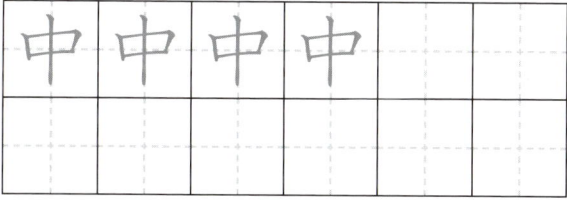

中学校	ちゅうがっこう	junior high school
世界中	せかいじゅう	all over the world
背中	せなか	back
中止	ちゅうし	canceling
中央	ちゅうおう	center

A mother holds her children's hands.

おんよみ ショウ
くんよみ ちい（さい）・こ・お

いみ small, little, child　strokes 3画　亅 小 小

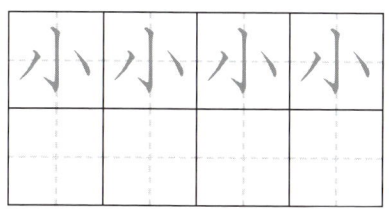

Note the position of the dots!

小学校	しょうがっこう	elementary school
小雨	こさめ	light rain
小川	おがわ	brook, creek, stream
小鳥	ことり	little bird
小説	しょうせつ	novel

青

By the moon the astronaut of the Saturn-shaped spaceship sees the blue earth.

- おんよみ セイ・ショウ
- くんよみ あお・あお(い)

いみ blue, green, young
strokes 8画 一 十 キ 主 キ 青 青 青

Point

Note the longest horizontal stroke!

青年	せいねん	young people
群青色	ぐんじょういろ	ultramarine
青空	あおぞら	blue sky
青春	せいしゅん	youth
青信号	あおしんごう	green light

赤

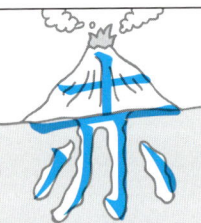

Volcanic eruptions are caused by the activity of red magma burning underground then rising.

- おんよみ セキ・シャク
- くんよみ あか・あか(い)・あか(らむ)・あか(らめる)

いみ red, to redden
strokes 7画 一 十 土 キ 方 赤 赤

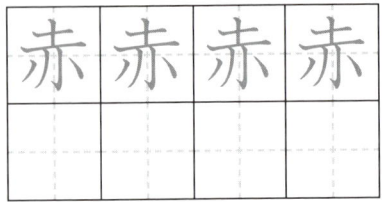

Point

Protrude!

赤潮	あかしお	red tide
赤字	あかじ	in the red, deficit
赤道	せきどう	equator
赤外線	せきがいせん	infrared (rays)
赤面	せきめん	blushing

白

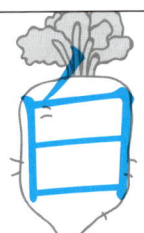

A radish is light green on top and white at the roots.

- おんよみ ハク・ビャク
- くんよみ しろ・しら・しろ(い)

いみ white, to say
strokes 5画 ノ イ 白 白 白

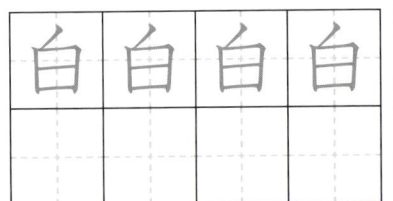

Point

×日
×百
Note the similar characters!

白衣	はくい	white coat
白熊	しろくま	polar bear
白黒	しろくろ	black and white
告白	こくはく	confession
白髪	しらが	gray hair

立

I am standing on the table.

おんよみ リツ・リュウ
くんよみ た(つ)・た(てる)

いみ to stand, to rise **strokes** 5画 丶 亠 ナ 立 立

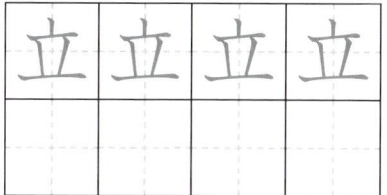

立 ×土
 ×辛
Note the similar characters!

国立の	こくりつの	national
建立	こんりゅう	erection (of a temple)
立つ	たつ	to stand
立体	りったい	solid, 3-D
立派(な)	りっぱ(な)	fine, splendid

見

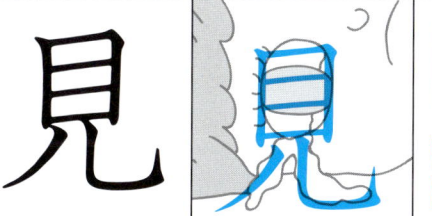

I lay and continued crying.

おんよみ ケン
くんよみ み(る)・み(える)・み(せる)

いみ to look, to see, to show **strokes** 7画 丨 冂 冃 月 目 目 見

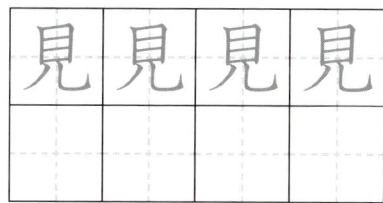

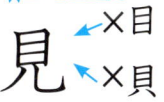

見 ×目
 ×貝
Note the similar characters!

見物	けんぶつ	sightseeing
意見	いけん	opinion
花見	はなみ	cherry-blossom viewing
見学	けんがく	visit, field trip
発見	はっけん	discovery

休

A woman is resting while leaning against the tree.

おんよみ キュウ
くんよみ やす(む)・やす(まる)・やす(める)

いみ to rest, to relax **strokes** 6画 丿 イ 仁 什 休 休

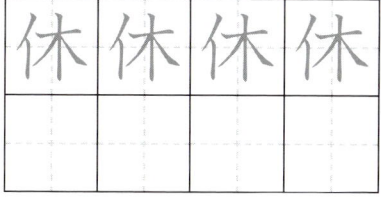

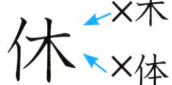

休 ×木
 ×体
Note the similar characters!

休暇	きゅうか	vacation
連休	れんきゅう	consecutive holidays
夏休み	なつやすみ	summer vacation
定休日	ていきゅうび	regular day off

The sun appears from the horizon in the early morning.

おんよみ ソウ・サッ
くんよみ はや(い)・はや(まる)・はや(める)

いみ early, quick, to hasten　strokes 6画　一 口 日 日 旦 早

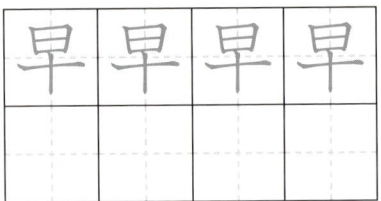 

Note the number of horizontal strokes!

早朝	そうちょう	early morning
早速	さっそく	immediately
早口	はやくち	talking [speaking] fast
早起き	はやおき	getting up early
早期	そうき	early stage

I am standing and looking to find the right direction.

おんよみ セイ・ショウ
くんよみ ただ(しい)・ただ(す)・まさ

いみ right, proper, to correct　strokes 5画　一 丁 下 正 正

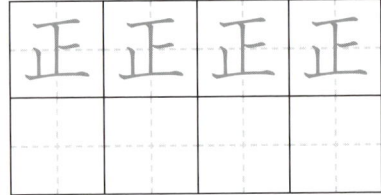 

Do not protrude!

正確	せいかく	accuracy
正月	しょうがつ	New Year holiday
正しい	ただしい	correct, right
正解	せいかい	correct answer
訂正	ていせい	correction

This village has a big tree, a scarecrow, and dragon flies flying around.

おんよみ ソン
くんよみ むら

いみ village　strokes 7画　一 十 才 木 朩 村 村

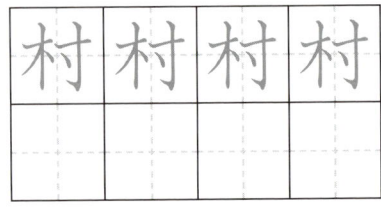 

×林
×材

Note the similar characters!

農村	のうそん	farming village
漁村	ぎょそん	fishing village
村里	むらざと	village
村人	むらびと	villager
市町村	しちょうそん	cities, towns and villages

町

My town is next to the rice paddy, and it has two main streets.

おんよみ チョウ
くんよみ まち

いみ town, city

strokes 7画 一 丁 丌 刑 用 田 町 町

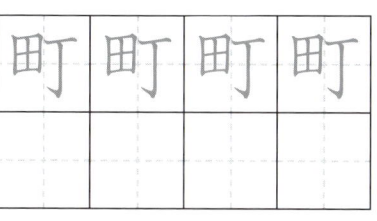

Connect!

町営の	ちょうえいの	municipal
港町	みなとまち	port town
町長	ちょうちょう	town mayor

年

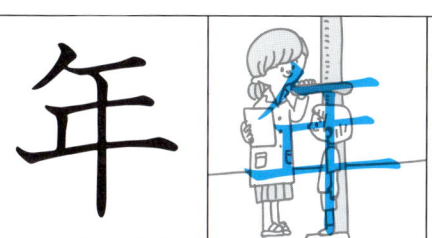

A teacher checks a student's height. As children get older, they grow taller.

おんよみ ネン
くんよみ とし

いみ year, age

strokes 6画 ノ ヒ ヒ 午 年 年

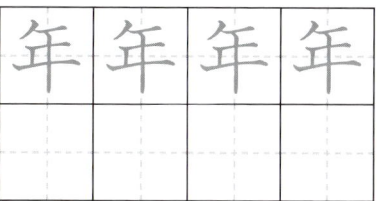

Do not protrude!

年齢	ねんれい	age
学年	がくねん	educational stage
今年	ことし	this year
一年	いちねん	one year
年収	ねんしゅう	annual income

文

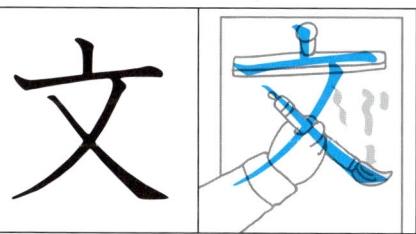

I put a long paper weight on the paper and write sentences with a brush.

おんよみ ブン・モン
くんよみ ふみ

いみ letter, book, mail, script

strokes 4画 、 一 ナ 文

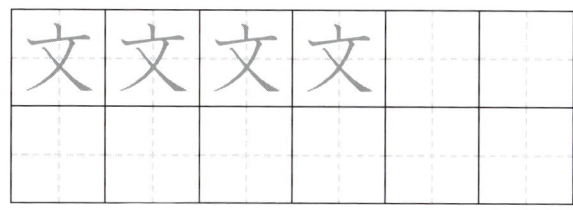

文化	ぶんか	culture
注文	ちゅうもん	order, request
恋文	こいぶみ	love letter
文房具	ぶんぼうぐ	stationery
論文	ろんぶん	treatise

名

I am writing my name with a pen on a piece of paper.

おんよみ メイ・ミョウ　　**くんよみ** な

いみ name, reputation　　**strokes** 6画　ノ ク タ タ 名 名

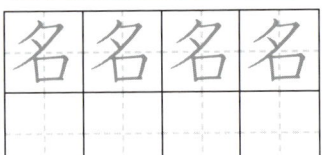

Point 名 ← Connect!

氏名	しめい	(full) name
名字	みょうじ	family name
名前	なまえ	name
有名(な)	ゆうめい(な)	famous

円

Runners are running around the track toward the goal.

おんよみ エン　　**くんよみ** まる(い)

いみ circle, round, Japanese yen　　**strokes** 4画　１ 冂 円 円

Point 円 ← Do not protrude!

十円	じゅうえん	ten yen
円満(な)	えんまん(な)	peaceful
円い	まるい	round
円形	えんけい	round, circle

王

The king is wearing a gorgeous crown.

おんよみ オウ　　**くんよみ** ―

いみ king　　**strokes** 4画　一 T 千 王

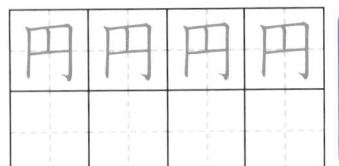

Point 王 ← Note the longest horizontal stroke!

国王	こくおう	king
女王	じょおう	queen
王宮	おうきゅう	royal palace
王冠	おうかん	crown

玉

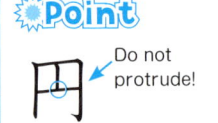

The king wearing a gorgeous crown is holding a scepter with a beautiful ball on top.

おんよみ ギョク　　**くんよみ** たま

いみ ball, jewel　　**strokes** 5画　一 T 千 王 玉

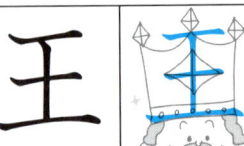

Point 玉 ×王 ×土　Note the similar characters!

珠玉	しゅぎょく	gem
玉葱	たまねぎ	onion
百円玉	ひゃくえんだま	hundred-yen coin
目玉商品	めだましょうひん	eye catching items

糸

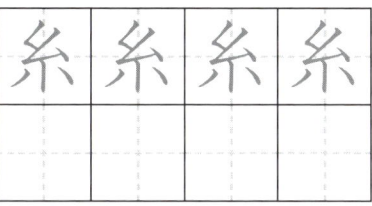

The thread spool is holding scissors and has needles on each side of it.

- おんよみ シ
- くんよみ いと

いみ thread, string **strokes** 6画 く 幺 幺 糸 糸 糸

Point 糸 ← Do not protrude!

製糸	せいし	spinning
毛糸	けいと	knitting wool
糸口	いとぐち	clue
生糸	きいと	raw silk
抜糸	ばっし	suture removal

車

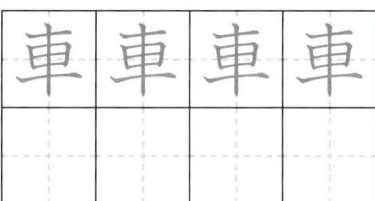

Before the car was invented, people rode in carriages.

- おんよみ シャ
- くんよみ くるま

いみ car, wheel **strokes** 7画 一 ニ 亓 亘 車 車 車

Point 車 ← Protrude!

自動車	じどうしゃ	car
列車	れっしゃ	train
肩車	かたぐるま	riding on one's shoulders
台車	だいしゃ	dolly, cart
駐車場	ちゅうしゃじょう	parking lot

力

Before the match begins, the *sumo* wrestler puts a hand on the ground.

- おんよみ リョク・リキ
- くんよみ ちから

いみ strength, power **strokes** 2画 フ 力

Point 力 ← Protrude!

努力	どりょく	effort
人力車	じんりきしゃ	rickshaw
力持ち	ちからもち	strong person
能力	のうりょく	ability
体力	たいりょく	physical strength

1 Below the *Kanji*, write the Japanese reading of *Kanji* in *Hiragana*.

① 日　　② 月　　③ 火　　④ 水　　⑤ 木
(　　)　(　　)　(　　)　(　　)　(　　)

⑥ お金　⑦ 手　　⑧ 足　　⑨ 空　　⑩ 雨
(　　)　(　　)　(　　)　(　　)　(　　)

2 Choose the correct reading.

① 森林　(a　しんりん　b　りんしん　c　ぼくりん)　(　　)

② 男女　(a　だんせい　b　じょせい　c　だんじょ)　(　　)

③ 先生　(a　せいせん　b　せんせい　c　せんにん)　(　　)

④ 空気　(a　くうき　　b　そうき　　c　ゆうき)　　(　　)

⑤ 左右　(a　じょうげ　b　くさばな　c　さゆう)　　(　　)

3 Write down the correct reading of the underlined part of the sentence.

① <u>赤</u>い信号(しんごう)は「とまれ」です。(　　　　　)

② <u>十円玉</u>を拾(ひろ)った。　　(　　　　　)

③ <u>耳</u>をすましてみましょう。(　　　　　)

④ <u>文字</u>で書(か)いてあります。　(　　　　　)

⑤ まず<u>下</u>を<u>見</u>てください。(　　　)(　　　)

4 After reading the *Hiragana* and English, write the *Kanji* that applies to the word in the box.

① さん (three) ☐   ② ろく (six) ☐

③ はち (eight) ☐   ④ むし (bug) ☐

⑤ かわ (river) ☐   ⑥ こども (child) ☐ ども

⑦ あおいろ (blue) ☐ いろ   ⑧ はやい (early) ☐ い

5 Choose the correct *Kanji* that corresponds to the *Hiragana* reading.

① かい (a 目　b 見　c 貝)　　( )

② じ　(a 子　b 字　c 学)　　( )

③ むら (a 村　b 林　c 材)　　( )

④ しろ (a 日　b 白　c 百)　　( )

⑤ だい (a 大　b 太　c 犬)　　( )

6 In the boxes, write the *Kanji* that applies to the *furigana* reading.

① いつのまにか ☐(いち)☐(ねん)が過(す)ぎた。

② あの ☐(ひと)は、とても ☐(ちから)持(も)ちだ。

③ 服の [じょう][げ] をかう。

④ 思い切って [みず] の [なか] に [た] った。

⑤ [ゆう] 方になってから [あめ] がふるらしい。

⑥ 向こうから歩いてくる [いぬ] を [み] た。

⑦ [くさ] がゆれる [おと] をきく。

⑧ [くるま] がのっている [ほん] を買う。

⑨ [たけ] が [は] えている [やま] に行く。

⑩ [やす] んだら、 [で][ぐち] をさがそう。

答え（answers）

❶ ①ひ（か） ②つき ③ひ ④みず ⑤き ⑥かね ⑦て ⑧あし ⑨そら ⑩あめ
❷ ①a ②c ③b ④a ⑤c
❸ ①あか ②じゅうえんだま ③みみ ④もじ ⑤した, み
❹ ①三 ②六 ③八 ④虫 ⑤川 ⑥子 ⑦青 ⑧早
❺ ①c ②b ③a ④b ⑤a
❻ ①一年 ②人, 力 ③上下 ④水, 中, 立 ⑤夕, 雨 ⑥犬, 見 ⑦草, 音 ⑧車, 本 ⑨竹, 生, 山 ⑩休, 出口

N4

ここでは、日本語能力検定3級相当の漢字を掲載しています。

contains the *Kanji* of the Japanese Language Proficiency Test Level 3

朝

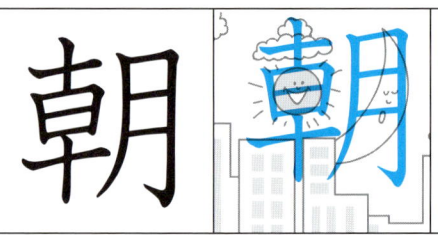

The sun is rising in the morning while the moon sets behind the skyscrapers.

- おんよみ チョウ
- くんよみ あさ

いみ morning

strokes 12画 一 十 十 亡 古 古 古 卓 朝 朝 朝 朝

Point
朝
Do not protrude!

朝	あさ	morning
朝食	ちょうしょく	breakfast
早朝	そうちょう	early morning
朝日	あさひ	the morning sun
朝焼け	あさやけ	morning glow

昼

I am taking a nap in the tent.

- おんよみ チュウ
- くんよみ ひる

いみ noon, daytime

strokes 9画 一 コ ア 尺 尺 尽 昼 昼 昼

Point
昼
Do not protrude!

昼食	ちゅうしょく	lunch
昼間	ひるま	daytime
昼寝	ひるね	(afternoon) nap
真昼	まひる	midday
昼時	ひるどき	lunchtime

夜

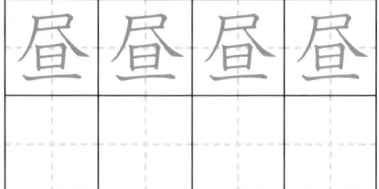

A boy held a lantern aloft and the moon was there to greet him.

- おんよみ ヤ
- くんよみ よ・よる

いみ night, evening

strokes 8画 一 亠 广 疒 夜 夜 夜 夜

深夜	しんや	midnight
夜中	よなか	the middle of the night
夜間	やかん	night time
昼夜	ちゅうや	day and night
夜景	やけい	night view

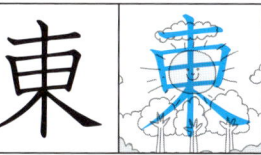

The sun is rising in the east behind the woods under a cloud.

おんよみ トウ　　**くんよみ** ひがし

いみ east　　**strokes** 8画　一 ｒ 冃 百 亘 車 東 東

Point: Protrude!

東洋	とうよう	the Orient
関東	かんとう	the Kanto district
東風	ひがしかぜ	east wind
北東	ほくとう	northeast

I am going to travel west with my nice suitcase.

おんよみ セイ・サイ　　**くんよみ** にし

いみ west　　**strokes** 6画　一 ｒ 冂 丙 西 西

Point: Do not protrude!

西洋	せいよう	the West
関西	かんさい	the Kansai district
西風	にしかぜ	west wind
大西洋	たいせいよう	the Atlantic Ocean

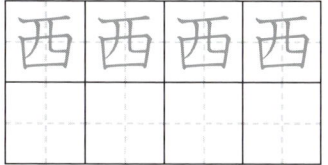

The souvenir in the box from the southern island is a cactus.

おんよみ ナン・ナ　　**くんよみ** みなみ

いみ south　　**strokes** 9画　一 十 广 内 内 丙 甬 南 南

南極	なんきょく	the South Pole
南下	なんか	southward movement
南風	みなみかぜ	south wind
南米	なんべい	South America

I ran toward the north while jumping.

おんよみ ホク　　**くんよみ** きた

いみ north　　**strokes** 5画　一 ｆ ｊ 北 北

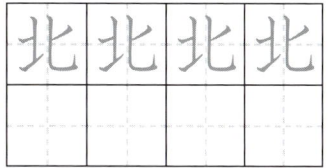

Point: Do not protrude!

北極	ほっきょく	the North Pole
北上	ほくじょう	northward movement
北風	きたかぜ	north wind
北米	ほくべい	North America

45

The father has two sticks for hunting.

おんよみ フ
くんよみ ちち

いみ father

strokes 4画 ノ ハ ケ 父

お父さん	おとうさん	dad	お父さんとあそぶ。
祖父	そふ	grandfather	祖父の誕生日を祝う。
義父	ぎふ	father-in-law	義父に話を聞く。
父親	ちちおや	father	父親と釣りに行く。
父方	ちちかた	paternal	正月に父方のしんせきが集まった。
神父	しんぷ	father, priest	ブラウン神父に会う。

My mother got two stains on her apron while cooking.

おんよみ ボ
くんよみ はは

いみ mother

strokes 5画 ㄑ 口 口 口 母

Point

Note the position of the dots!

お母さん	おかあさん	mom	お母さんはやさしい。
祖母	そぼ	grandmother	祖母の家へ遊びに行く。
義母	ぎぼ	mother-in-law	義母と食事をする。
母親	ははおや	mother	母親の手料理を食べる。
母国	ぼこく	mother country	母国へ帰る。
母語	ぼご	mother tongue, native language	私の母語は日本語だ。

46

My older sister is very fashionable, and she is thinking about buying a hat or scarf, or both.

おんよみ シ **くんよみ** あね

いみ older sister

strokes 8画 　く　丬　女　女'　女亠　妒　妒　姉

 Do not connect!

お姉さん	おねえさん	older sister, young lady
姉妹	しまい	sisters
義姉	ぎし	sister-in-law
姉婿	あねむこ	older sister's husband

My younger sister remembers the time when she climbed a tree.

おんよみ マイ **くんよみ** いもうと

いみ younger sister

strokes 8画 　く　丬　女　女'　女=　妡　妹　妹

 Protrude!

妹分	いもうとぶん	junior female peer
姉妹都市	しまいとし	sister city
義妹	ぎまい	sister-in-law

My older brother has a square-shaped face, and he always stands with his legs wide open.

おんよみ ケイ・キョウ **くんよみ** あに

いみ older brother

strokes 5画 　丨　冂　口　尸　兄

 Do not protrude!

お兄さん	おにいさん	older brother, young man
兄弟	きょうだい	brothers
義兄	ぎけい	brother-in-law
兄嫁	あによめ	older brother's wife

My younger brother is good at picking up a snake with a stick.

おんよみ テイ・ダイ・デ **くんよみ** おとうと

いみ younger brother, disciple

strokes 7画 　丶　丷　丷丷　当　当　弟　弟

 Do not protrude!

弟分	おとうとぶん	junior male peer
子弟	してい	young child
義弟	ぎてい	brother-in-law
弟子	でし	disciple

春

In the spring, a sprout has started to bud, and an underground worm has become active.

おんよみ シュン　　**くんよみ** はる

いみ spring

strokes 9画　一 一 三 三 夫 表 春 春 春

Point: Protrude!

春分	しゅんぶん	the vernal equinox
早春	そうしゅん	early spring
春一番	はるいちばん	the first spring gale
青春	せいしゅん	youth

夏

In the sizzling hot summer, I wear a cotton *yukata* and carry a parasol.

おんよみ カ・ゲ　　**くんよみ** なつ

いみ summer

strokes 10画　一 一 丁 丙 丙 百 頁 夏 夏 夏

Point: Note the longest horizontal stroke!

夏至	げし	the summer solstice
夏季	かき	summer
真夏	まなつ	midsummer
初夏	しょか	early summer

秋

In fall, trees become bare when the leaves fall. I rake the fallen leaves and burn them.

おんよみ シュウ　　**くんよみ** あき

いみ fall, autumn

strokes 9画　一 二 千 千 禾 禾 秒 秋 秋

秋分	しゅうぶん	the fall equinox
晩秋	ばんしゅう	late fall
秋晴れ	あきばれ	nice fall weather
秋風	あきかぜ	fall breeze

冬

A bear hibernates in a cave during the winter.

おんよみ トウ　　**くんよみ** ふゆ

いみ winter

strokes 5画　ノ ク 冬 冬 冬

Point: ×各　×名　Note the similar characters!

冬至	とうじ	the winter solstice
冬季	とうき	winter
真冬	まふゆ	midwinter
冬眠	とうみん	hibernation

 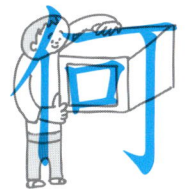

A man is looking into the box to see what is inside.

おんよみ カ
くんよみ なに・なん

いみ what, how, why　strokes 7画　ノ イ イ 仁 仃 何 何

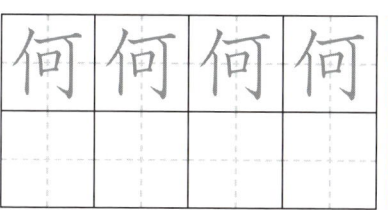 

Note the similar characters!

何か	なにか	something
何時	なんじ	what time
何回	なんかい	how many times
幾何学模様	きかがくもよう	geometric pattern

A farmer carrying a hoe has tilled the field.

おんよみ サク・サ
くんよみ つく(る)

いみ to make, to work　strokes 7画　ノ イ イ 乍 乍 作 作

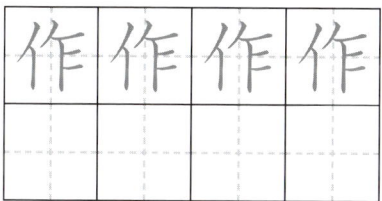 

Note the longest horizontal stroke!

作る	つくる	to make
作者	さくしゃ	author, maker
作業	さぎょう	working
作り話	つくりばなし	made-up story
動作	どうさ	movement

My body needs a rest. I would like to read under a tree.

おんよみ タイ・テイ
くんよみ からだ

いみ body, main part　strokes 7画　ノ イ 亻 什 休 体 体

Note the similar characters!

体	からだ	body
体重	たいじゅう	body weight
体裁	ていさい	looks, format
体験	たいけん	experience
体制	たいせい	(political) system

行

Whichever road I take, they are dead ends.

おんよみ コウ・ギョウ・アン
くんよみ い(く)・ゆ(く)・おこな(う)

いみ to go, to act, action   **strokes** 6画   ノ ノ イ 彳 行 行

Point
行 ← Do not protrude!

行く	いく	to go	母が買い物に行く。
行動	こうどう	action	行動をおこす。
行事	ぎょうじ	event	学校の行事にさんかする。
行く先	ゆくさき	destination	行く先を決めずに旅に出る。
飛行機	ひこうき	airplane	飛行機にのる。
流行	りゅうこう	fashion, trend	チェック柄が流行している。

後

 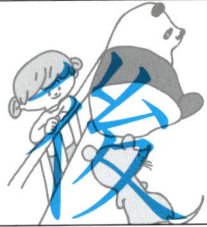

A girl is watching a mouse stepping toward a panda that has its back turned toward it.

おんよみ ゴ・コウ
くんよみ のち・うし(ろ)・あと・おく(れる)

いみ back, later, to be delayed   **strokes** 9画   ノ ノ イ 彳 彳 後 後 後 後

Point
後 ← ×係
Note the similar character!

後ろ	うしろ	behind	弟は母の後ろにかくれている。
後日	ごじつ	afterward	後日ごれんらくいたします。
後輩	こうはい	one's junior	後輩のそうだんにのる。
後程	のちほど	later	後程お会いしましょう。
午後	ごご	afternoon	午後から晴れた。
最後	さいご	last	最後まであきらめない。

来

There are three sets of tracks lying ahead of the train that is coming through the trees.

おんよみ ライ
くんよみ く(る)・きた(る)・きた(す)

いみ to come, future

strokes 7画 一 ｒ ｒ ｒ 平 来 来

Point: Note the position of the dots!

来る	くる	to come	友達が日本に来る。
来客	らいきゃく	guest, visitor	明日は来客がある。
来年	らいねん	next year	来年の予定をたてる。
未来	みらい	future	未来を守る。
本来	ほんらい	originally	彼は本来は優しい。
来週	らいしゅう	next week	来週の金曜日に会いましょう。

楽

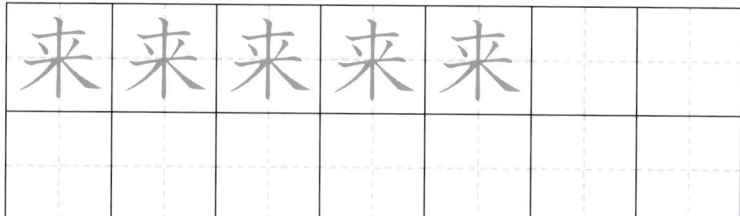

It is great fun to play the guitar on the top of a tree with two birds flying around.

おんよみ ガク・ラク
くんよみ たの(しい)・たの(しむ)

いみ to enjoy, joyful, music

strokes 13画 ｒ ｒ ｎ 甪 白 白 泊 泊 汨 楽 楽 楽 楽

Point: Note the position of the dots!

楽しい	たのしい	happy	楽しい時間をすごした。
楽器	がっき	musical instrument	楽器を演奏する。
気楽(な)	きらく(な)	easy	彼とは気楽なつきあいだ。
能楽	のうがく	Noh and Kyogen	能楽を見に行った。
安楽(な)	あんらく(な)	comfort	安楽な暮らしがしたい。
楽勝	らくしょう	easy victory	試合は楽勝だった。

51

弓

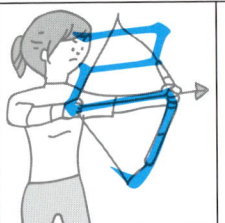

I draw a bow.

おんよみ キュウ
くんよみ ゆみ

いみ bow, archery
strokes 3画 　フ　コ　弓

弓道	きゅうどう	Japanese archery
弓術	きゅうじゅつ	Japanese archery
弓矢	ゆみや	bow and arrow
弓形	ゆみなり	arched shape

引

I aim for the center of the target and shoot an arrow from a bow.

おんよみ イン
くんよみ ひ(く)・ひ(ける)

いみ to pull, to lead
strokes 4画 　フ　コ　弓　引

引く	ひく	to pull, to lead
引用	いんよう	quotation
引き算	ひきざん	subtraction
強引(な)	ごういん(な)	pushy

羽

A bird flies, flapping its wings.

おんよみ ウ
くんよみ は・はね

いみ wing, feather
strokes 6画 　丁　刁　习　羽　羽　羽

Point

Note the position of the dots!

羽毛	うもう	feather
羽織	はおり	Japanese coat
羽田空港	はねだくうこう	Haneda Airport
羽根	はね	wing, feather
合羽	かっぱ	raincoat

強

There is one man drawing a bow, and there is another man wearing a helmet and armor and holding a shield. They are strong.

おんよみ キョウ・ゴウ
くんよみ つよ(い)・つよ(まる)・つよ(める)・し(いる)

いみ strong, powerful, to force
strokes 11画 フ ユ 弓 弓' 弓ハ 弓ハ 弓ム 弓ム 強 強 強

Point: Do not protrude!

強い	つよい	strong, powerful	強い体をつくる。
勉強	べんきょう	study	彼女は勉強がよくできた。
強引(な)	ごういん(な)	pushy	強引なやり方だ。
心強い	こころづよい	reassuring	家族の支えが心強い。
強敵	きょうてき	strong enemy	強敵を負かした。
強化	きょうか	strengthening	チームを強化する必要がある。

弱

When I feel weak, tears run down my cheeks.

おんよみ ジャク
くんよみ よわ(い)・よわ(る)・よわ(まる)・よわ(める)

いみ weak, young, to weaken
strokes 10画 フ コ 弓 弓 弓' 弓ハ 弓ハ 弱 弱 弱

Point: Note the position of the dots!

弱い	よわい	weak	彼は気が弱い。
弱点	じゃくてん	weak point	彼の弱点は短気なところだ。
弱気(な)	よわき(な)	weak-spirited	つい弱気なことを言ってしまう。
弱み	よわみ	weakness	人の弱みにつけこむ。
貧弱(な)	ひんじゃく(な)	poor, meager	貧弱な体をきたえる。
弱者	じゃくしゃ	weak people	弱者に優しい社会であってほしい。

電

If it starts to thunder, you must pull the plug out from the outlet.

おんよみ デン　　**くんよみ** —

いみ electricity, lightning　　**strokes** 13画　一 厂 戸 币 币 币 雨 雨 雨 雪 雪 雪 電

Point 電　Do not protrude!

電気	でんき	electricity
電話	でんわ	telephone
電車	でんしゃ	electrical train
電光	でんこう	lightning

雲

A propeller airplane that is flying under a rain cloud is producing vapor trails.

おんよみ ウン　　**くんよみ** くも

いみ cloud　　**strokes** 12画　一 厂 戸 币 币 币 雨 雨 雨 雪 雪 雲

Point 雲　Do not protrude!

雲海	うんかい	a sea of clouds
雨雲	あまぐも	rain cloud
雲間	くもま	break in the clouds
積乱雲	せきらんうん	thunderhead

雪

A child is enjoying riding on a sled on a snowy day.

おんよみ セツ　　**くんよみ** ゆき

いみ snow　　**strokes** 11画　一 厂 戸 币 币 币 雨 雨 雨 雪 雪

Point 雪　Do not connect!

積雪	せきせつ	accumulated snow
雪国	ゆきぐに	snowy country
大雪	おおゆき	heavy snow
吹雪	ふぶき	snowstorm

当

The person who picked the longest potato has been elected.

おんよみ トウ　　**くんよみ** あ(たる)・あ(てる)

いみ to hit, to win, to take charge, rightful　　**strokes** 6画　丨 ⺌ ⺌ 当 当 当

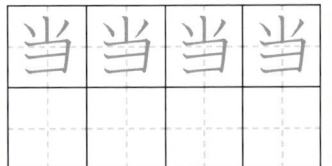

Point 当　Note the position of the dots!

当たる	あたる	to hit, to win
担当	たんとう	taking charge
当日	とうじつ	that day
当社	とうしゃ	our company

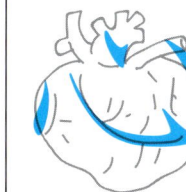

The heart is one of the most important organs.

おんよみ シン
くんよみ こころ

いみ heart, spirit, center **strokes** 4画 心心心心

Point Note the position of the dots!

心臓	しんぞう	heart (organ)	心臓がどきどきする。
心配	しんぱい	concern	親に心配をかける。
心細い	こころぼそい	uneasy	ひとりだと心細い。
安心	あんしん	peace of mind	彼になら、安心して任せられる。
初心者	しょしんしゃ	beginner	ゴルフは初心者だ。
中心	ちゅうしん	center	町の中心に広場がある。

A farmer is always thinking of his crops in the rice paddy.

おんよみ シ
くんよみ おも(う)

いみ to think, idea, thought **strokes** 9画 丨 冂 冂 甲 田 甲 思 思 思

Point ×男 ×恩 Note the similar characters!

思う	おもう	to think	世界が平和になればよいと思う。
思案	しあん	consideration	これからどうするか思案を重ねる。
不思議(な)	ふしぎ(な)	mysterious	不思議なできごとがあった。
思い出	おもいで	memory	思い出がよみがえる。
意思	いし	thought, mind	会議で意思決定がされた。
思考	しこう	thinking, thought	その問題について思考をめぐらす。

55

 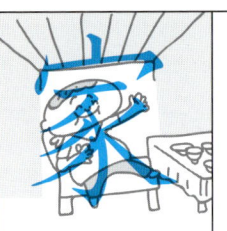

There is a happy child in the house who was fed well.

おんよみ カ・ケ
くんよみ いえ・や

いみ house, home, family

strokes 10画 　丶丶宀宀宀宇宇家家家

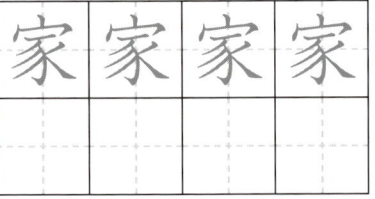 

Do not protrude!

家族	かぞく	family
家路	いえじ	one's way home
家賃	やちん	(house) rent
農家	のうか	farmer
国家	こっか	nation, state

A person is practicing yoga in a room with a window.

おんよみ シツ
くんよみ むろ

いみ room

strokes 9画 　丶丶宀宀宀宀宕宕室

Note the longest horizontal stroke!

教室	きょうしつ	classroom
和室	わしつ	Japanese-style room
氷室	ひむろ	icehouse
室内	しつない	indoor
室温	しつおん	room temperature

The girl in a triangle-shaped hat is picking tea at the tea plantation; she is sweating heavily.

おんよみ チャ・サ
くんよみ ―

いみ tea, tea ceremony

strokes 9画 　一十サ艹艾芢茶茶

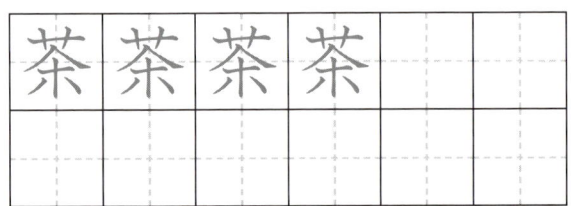

緑茶	りょくちゃ	green tea
紅茶	こうちゃ	tea
茶道	さどう	tea ceremony
茶色	ちゃいろ	(light) brown
茶会	ちゃかい	tea ceremony party

算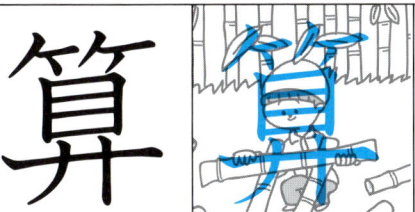

I am counting how many bamboo trees have been cut down.

おんよみ サン
くんよみ —

いみ to calculate, to figure strokes 14画 ノ ⺃ ⺌ ⺮ 竹 竹 笁 笁 筲 筲 筧 算 算

Point 算
Note the number of horizontal strokes!

計算	けいさん	calculation
予算	よさん	budget
掛け算	かけざん	multiplication
算出	さんしゅつ	computation

答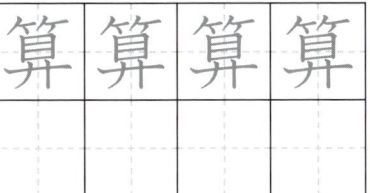

A hermit living in a bamboo forest may have an answer for your questions about life.

おんよみ トウ
くんよみ こた(える)・こた(え)

いみ to respond, to answer strokes 12画 ノ ⺃ ⺌ ⺮ 竹 竹 笒 笒 答 答 答

答える	こたえる	to respond, to answer
返答	へんとう	reply
応答	おうとう	response
口答え	くちごたえ	back talk
答弁	とうべん	rejoinder

海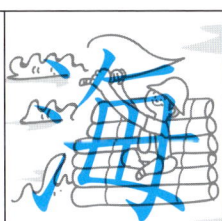

I am enjoying fishing on a raft while floating on the sea.

おんよみ カイ
くんよみ うみ

いみ sea, ocean strokes 9画 丶 氵 氵 汇 汇 海 海 海

Point 海
Protrude!

海岸	かいがん	seashore, seaside
海水浴	かいすいよく	swimming in the sea
海辺	うみべ	beach, seashore
深海	しんかい	the deep sea
航海	こうかい	voyage

活

A fisherman harpooned a big lively fish.

おんよみ カツ
くんよみ —

いみ to exist, to come alive, vigor

strokes 9画 ` ゙ ⺡ ⺡ 汙 汗 汗 活 活

Do not Protrude!

生活	せいかつ	life, living
活動	かつどう	activity
活発(な)	かっぱつ(な)	active
食生活	しょくせいかつ	eating habits
活躍	かつやく	(remarkable) activity, success

池

A tortoise bumped into a snake on the rock in the pond.

おんよみ チ
くんよみ いけ

いみ pond, pool

strokes 6画 ` ゙ ⺡ ⺡ 汕 池

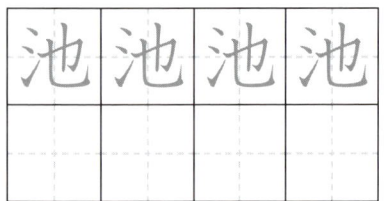

Note the longest vertical stroke!

貯水池	ちょすいち	reservoir
電池	でんち	battery
古池	ふるいけ	old pond
ため池	ためいけ	reservoir
太陽電池	たいようでんち	solar battery

汽

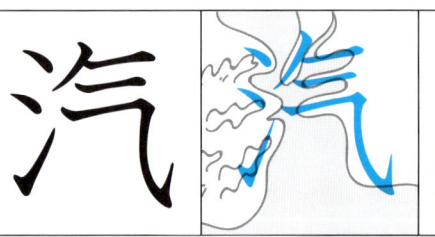

There is often a mixture of fresh water and salt water in the area where the river flows into the sea.

おんよみ キ
くんよみ —

いみ steam, moisture

strokes 7画 ` ゙ ⺡ ⺡ 氵 汽 汽

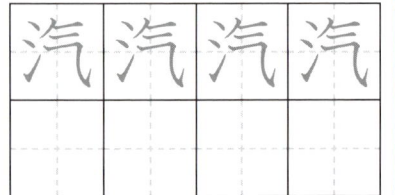

汽 ← ✕気
Note the similar character!

汽車	きしゃ	(steam) train
汽船	きせん	steamship
汽笛	きてき	steam whistle
汽水	きすい	brackish water

道

I am walking down the way carrying a bag with horizontal stripes.

おんよみ ドウ・トウ
くんよみ みち

いみ road, way, logic　**strokes** 12画　、 ソ 丷 厶 艹 芢 首 首 首 首 道 道

Point
道 ← Note the position of the dots!

道路	どうろ	road, street	道路がこんでいる。
道理	どうり	logic, reason	世の中の道理にしたがう。
近道	ちかみち	shortcut	ここを右に曲がると近道だ。
道場	どうじょう	training place	道場に通う。
道具	どうぐ	tool	彼はつりの道具を大切にしている。
街道	かいどう	highway	大きな街道をたどる。

遠

While I was running on the road, I saw somebody practicing yoga in the distance.

おんよみ エン・オン
くんよみ とお(い)

いみ far, distant, remote　**strokes** 13画　一 十 土 士 吉 吉 声 冑 宣 袁 袁 遠 遠

Point
遠 ← Do not protrude!

遠い	とおい	far	祖母の家までは、まだ遠い。
永遠	えいえん	eternity, permanence	永遠の愛をちかう。
遠足	えんそく	excursion	遠足で、水族館に行った。
遠出	とおで	outing	遠出はやめておこう。
遠隔の	えんかくの	remote	パソコンを遠隔操作する。
望遠鏡	ぼうえんきょう	telescope	望遠鏡をのぞく。

59

近

Until I came closer, I didn't realize that my friend had been on the road waving at me.

おんよみ キン
くんよみ ちか(い)

いみ near, close, almost **strokes** 7画

近い	ちかい	near, close	ここから一番近いレストランに入ろう。
近所	きんじょ	neighborhood	近所のスーパーへ買い物に行った。
最近	さいきん	lately, recently	最近、テレビを買い替えた。
近道	ちかみち	shortcut	駅までの近道を見つけた。
接近	せっきん	approach	台風が日本へ接近している。
近郊	きんこう	the outskirts	東京近郊で家をさがしている。

週

I practice yoga, and I sing once a week.

おんよみ シュウ
くんよみ ―

いみ week **strokes** 11画

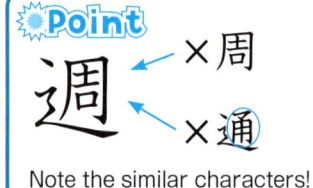

Note the similar characters!

一週間	いっしゅうかん	a week	病院で一週間分の薬をもらった。
今週	こんしゅう	this week	今週はずっと忙しかった。
週末	しゅうまつ	weekend	週末の天気が気になる。
週刊誌	しゅうかんし	weekly magazine	週刊誌を読んだ。
来週	らいしゅう	next week	来週も忙しくなりそうだ。
隔週	かくしゅう	every other week	この会議は隔週で開かれる。

I am walking along the way carrying a present.

おんよみ ツウ・ツ
くんよみ とお(る)・とお(す)・かよ(う)

いみ to pass through, street **strokes** 10画

Point
通 — Note the number of horizontal strokes!

通る	とおる	to go through	彼は毎日この道を通る。
交通	こうつう	traffic	交通じこに気をつける。
通り雨	とおりあめ	shower	通り雨なので、もうすぐ止むだろう。
通行	つうこう	traffic	この道路は通行できない。
直通	ちょくつう	direct (connecting)	このエレベーターはおくじょうまで直通だ。
通勤	つうきん	going to one's office	バスで通勤している。

I run.

おんよみ ソウ
くんよみ はし(る)

いみ to run **strokes** 7画

Point
走 — Do not protrude!

走る	はしる	to run	全力で走る。
走行	そうこう	running	車の走行距離がのびない。
滑走路	かっそうろ	runway	飛行機が滑走路から飛び立った。
走り高跳び	はしりたかとび	the high jump	走り高跳びで新記録を出した。
徒競走	ときょうそう	footrace	徒競走をすると、いつも負ける。
助走	じょそう	approach run	助走をつけて高く飛び上がる。

地

A person saw a tortoise that was on a rock on the ground encountered a snake.

おんよみ チ・ジ
くんよみ ―

いみ the ground, land, earth
strokes 6画　一 十 土 圵 坩 地

Point
地 ×池
地 ×他
Note the similar characters!

地球	ちきゅう	the Earth	地球を宇宙から見てみたい。
地下鉄	ちかてつ	subway	地下鉄にのる。
地面	じめん	the ground	地面に穴をほる。
遊園地	ゆうえんち	amusement park	遊園地が好きだ。
裏地	うらじ	lining	この上着にはよい裏地が付いている。
心地よい	ここちよい	comfortable	このタオルは心地よいはださわりだ。

場

When the sun rises, people gather at a place to practice yoga.

おんよみ ジョウ
くんよみ ば

いみ place, scene, space
strokes 12画　一 十 土 圵 圯 圫 圱 坦 場 場 場

Point
場 ← Do not protrude!

劇場	げきじょう	theater	ミュージカルを見に劇場へ行った。
職場	しょくば	workplace	新しい職場になれてきた。
場所	ばしょ	place	この場所で、初めて彼女と出会った。
市場	いちば・しじょう	market	市場で魚を買う。
会場	かいじょう	venue	会場はにぎわっていた。
場面	ばめん	scene	感動的な場面でなみだを流す。

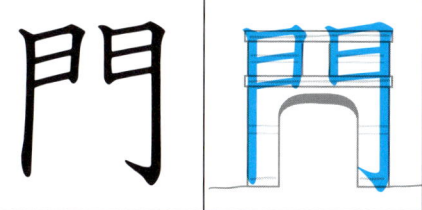

There is a gate.

おんよみ モン
くんよみ かど

いみ gate, clan　**strokes 8画**　丨 冂 冂 冂 門 門 門 門

門	門	門	門

Point
門
Do not connect!

正門	せいもん	the main gate
鬼門	きもん	unlucky direction
門番	もんばん	doorkeeper
一門	いちもん	clan, family
門出	かどで	departure

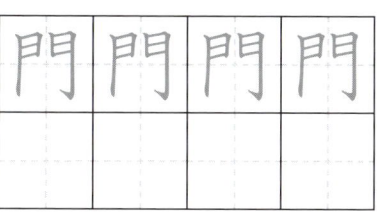 

There is music coming out of the speaker that is placed on the ground at the middle of the gate.

おんよみ カン・ケン
くんよみ あいだ・ま

いみ interval, period　**strokes 12画**　丨 冂 冂 冂 門 門 門 門 閂 問 間 間

間	間	間	間

Point
間 ←×問
　←×聞
Note the similar characters!

期間	きかん	period
世間	せけん	the world
手間	てま	time and effort
間隔	かんかく	interval
間接的(な)	かんせつてき(な)	indirect

I am listening to music that is coming through the gate.

おんよみ ブン・モン
くんよみ き(く)・き(こえる)

いみ to hear, to listen, rumor　**strokes 14画**　丨 冂 冂 冂 門 門 門 門 閂 問 間 間 聞 聞

聞	聞	聞	聞

Point
聞
Note the number of horizontal strokes!

聞く	きく	to hear, to listen
新聞	しんぶん	newspaper
聴聞	ちょうもん	hearing
見聞	けんぶん	experience
聞き覚える	ききおぼえる	to learn by hearing

同

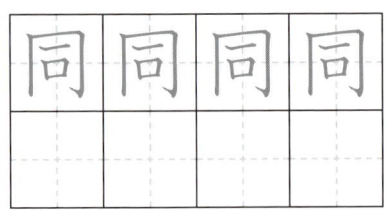

The robots on the conveyor belt all have the same face.

- おんよみ ドウ
- くんよみ おな(じ)

いみ equal, same **strokes** 6画 １ 冂 冂 冋 同 同

Do not connect!

同じ	おなじ	equal, same
同居	どうきょ	living together
同級生	どうきゅうせい	classmate
同い年	おないどし	the same age
賛同	さんどう	approval

内

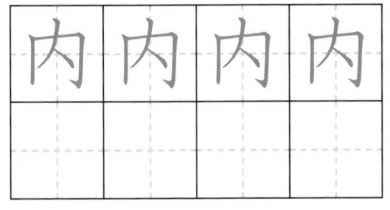

Two praying mantises inside the cage are trying to escape.

- おんよみ ナイ・ダイ
- くんよみ うち

いみ inside **strokes** 4画 １ 冂 内 内

×四 ×肉
Note the similar characters!

内容	ないよう	content(s)
境内	けいだい	precincts of a temple
身内	みうち	one's relatives
内面	ないめん	inside, mentality
場内で	じょうないで	in the hall

肉

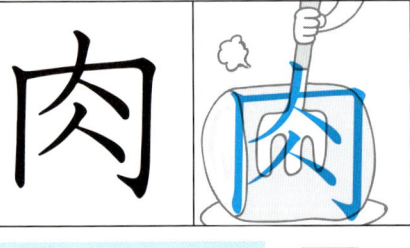

I pierce a big block of meat with a fork.

- おんよみ ニク
- くんよみ ―

いみ flesh, meat, body **strokes** 6画 １ 冂 内 内 肉 肉

Do not connect!

焼き肉	やきにく	grilled meat
肉屋	にくや	butcher's shop
筋肉	きんにく	muscle
牛肉	ぎゅうにく	beef
肉体	にくたい	body, physique

岩

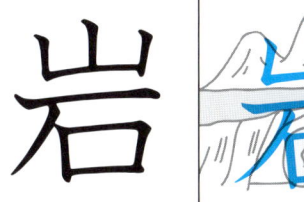

The rock that I saw rolling down the mountain is now lying under a cliff.

- おんよみ ガン
- くんよみ いわ

いみ rock

strokes 8画 　 丨 山 山 屵 屵 岩 岩 岩

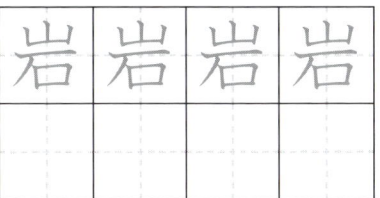

Point

岩

Note the longest vertical stroke!

岩石	がんせき	rock
岩盤	がんばん	bedrock
岩場	いわば	rocky tract
一枚岩	いちまいいわ	monolith, solidarity

言

A long time ago, information was passed down through generations by oral tradition.

- おんよみ ゲン・ゴン
- くんよみ い(う)・こと

いみ to speak, to tell, word

strokes 7画 　 丶 二 三 言 言 言 言

Point

言

Note the longest horizontal stroke!

言う	いう	to speak
方言	ほうげん	dialect
言葉	ことば	word
言語	げんご	language
言動	げんどう	one's words and deeds

記

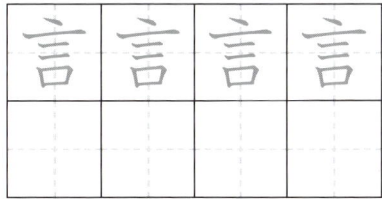

When writing was invented, people started recording information by writing it down.

- おんよみ キ
- くんよみ しる(す)

いみ to write, description

strokes 10画 　 丶 二 三 言 言 言 訁 訁 記 記

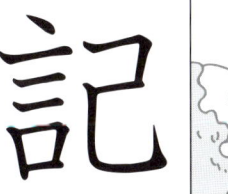

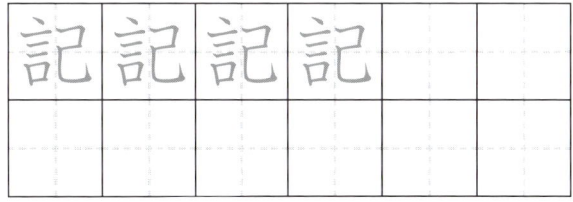

記す	しるす	to inscribe, to write
日記	にっき	diary
記念	きねん	commemoration
記憶	きおく	remembrance
記号	きごう	sign, symbol

65

計

We measured both the height and width according to the instructions.

おんよみ ケイ　　**くんよみ** はか(る)・はか(らう)

いみ to count, to measure, measure　　**strokes** 9画　　丶　亠　二　三　言　言　言　計　計

Point

 ←×記

Note the similar character!

計る	はかる	to measure
合計	ごうけい	the total
計画	けいかく	plan
腕時計	うでどけい	watch

読

I am lying and reading a book about the lecture I heard.

おんよみ ドク・トク・トウ　　**くんよみ** よ(む)

いみ to read　　**strokes** 14画　　丶　亠　二　三　言　言　言　計　計　詰　詰　読　読

Point

 Do not connect!

読む	よむ	to read
読書	どくしょ	reading books
読点	とうてん	(Japanese) comma
読者	どくしゃ	reader

語

I dozed off in front of my teacher when he was talking.

おんよみ ゴ　　**くんよみ** かた(る)・かた(らう)

いみ to talk, to tell, language　　**strokes** 14画　　丶　亠　二　三　言　言　言　計　詰　語　語　語　語

Point

 ←×話
 ←×記

Note the similar characters!

語る	かたる	to speak, to talk
語学	ごがく	the study of languages
日本語	にほんご	Japanese language
物語	ものがたり	story

話

I am having a conversation with my friend.

おんよみ ワ　　**くんよみ** はな(す)・はなし

いみ to speak, story　　**strokes** 13画　　丶　亠　二　三　言　言　言　計　計　話　話　話　話

Point

 Do not protrude!

話す	はなす	to speak, to talk
会話	かいわ	conversation
昔話	むかしばなし	old story
話題	わだい	subject, topic

The country is surrounded to protect the king who has a crown and scepter.

おんよみ コク
くんよみ くに

いみ country, nation **strokes** 8画   丨 冂 冂 冂 国 国 国 国

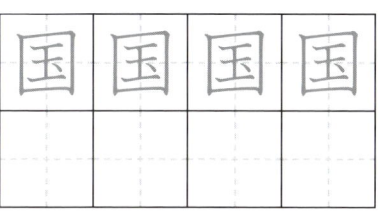 

Point
国
Connect!

国際的（な）	こくさいてき（な）	global, international
帰国	きこく	return to one's country
国柄	くにがら	national character
母国	ぼこく	mother country
他国	たこく	other countries

 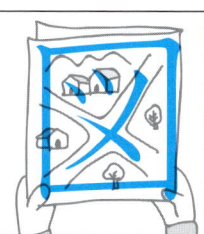

I read a map to look up my friend's house.

おんよみ ズ・ト
くんよみ はか（る）

いみ to plan, to think, drawing **strokes** 7画 丨 冂 冂 冈 図 図 図

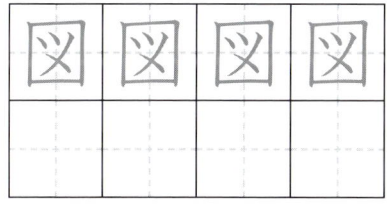 

Point
図
Note the position of the dots!

図る	はかる	to plan, to plot
地図	ちず	map
図書館	としょかん	library
図鑑	ずかん	illustrated reference book
意図	いと	intention

 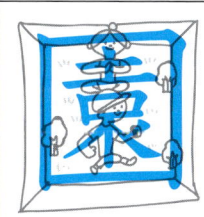

The park is surrounded. Inside the park, someone is practicing yoga and someone else is jogging.

おんよみ エン
くんよみ その

いみ yard, garden **strokes** 13画 丨 冂 冂 冂 門 門 門 周 周 園 園 園 園

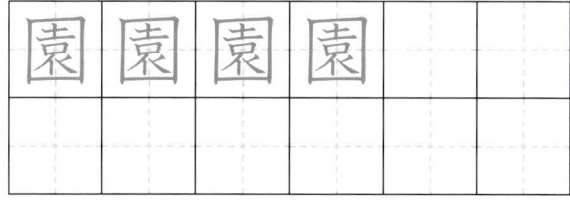

公園	こうえん	park
保育園	ほいくえん	nursery school
花園	はなぞの	flower garden
庭園	ていえん	garden
動物園	どうぶつえん	zoo

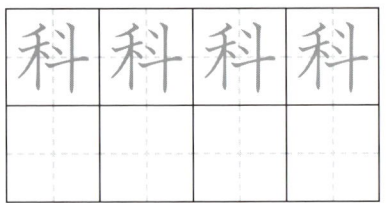 

I made a birds' nest with tree branches when all the leaves fell off them.

おんよみ カ
くんよみ —

いみ department, course, guilt

strokes 9画 　ノ 二 千 禾 禾 禾 禾 科 科

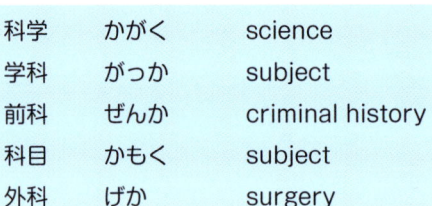

Point
科
Note the position of the dots!

科学	かがく	science
学科	がっか	subject
前科	ぜんか	criminal history
科目	かもく	subject
外科	げか	surgery

There is a market that sells rolls of cloth.

おんよみ シ
くんよみ いち

いみ market, fair, city

strokes 5画 　丶 亠 市 市 市

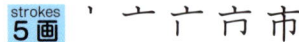

Point
市
Do not connect!

市役所	しやくしょ	city office
都市	とし	city
朝市	あさいち	morning market
市場	いちば・しじょう	market
市民	しみん	citizen

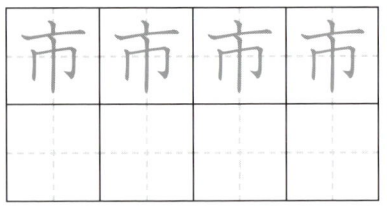 

After traveling around with a backpack, I finally came back home.

おんよみ キ
くんよみ かえ(る)・かえ(す)

いみ to return

strokes 10画 　丨 丿 丿刂 刂ヨ 刂ヨ 归 帰 帰 帰

Point
帰
Do not connect!

帰る	かえる	to come back, to return
帰宅	きたく	going home
復帰	ふっき	comeback, return
帰国	きこく	return to one's country

黄

A yellow flame was blazing up from the bonfire.

おんよみ コウ・オウ　　**くんよみ** き・こ

いみ yellow　　**strokes** 11画　一 十 艹 土 艹 芊 芎 苗 苗 黄 黄

Point: Note the position of the dots!

黄砂	こうさ	yellow sand
卵黄	らんおう	yolk
黄色	きいろ	yellow
黄金	おうごん・こがね	gold

元

A boy pumped his fists to show that he had a lot of energy.

おんよみ ゲン・ガン　　**くんよみ** もと

いみ root, cause, basis former　　**strokes** 4画　一 二 テ 元

Point: Do not protrude!

元気(な)	げんき(な)	energetic, lively
元日	がんじつ	New Year's Day
身元	みもと	identity
元祖	がんそ	founder, originator

光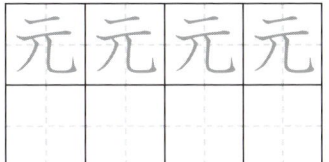

I saw a shining light at the end of the road.

おんよみ コウ　　**くんよみ** ひか(る)・ひかり

いみ light, to shine, to flash　　**strokes** 6画　丨 ⺌ ⺌ 平 平 光

Point: Note the position of the dots!

光る	ひかる	to flash, to shine
月光	げっこう	moonlight
光線	こうせん	beam
採光	さいこう	lighting

売

I sold ice cream to a mother and her child.

おんよみ バイ　　**くんよみ** う(る)・う(れる)

いみ to sell　　**strokes** 7画　一 十 士 䒑 声 声 売

Point: Do not protrude!

売る	うる	to sell
商売	しょうばい	business
売人	ばいにん	seller
売買	ばいばい	buying and selling

半

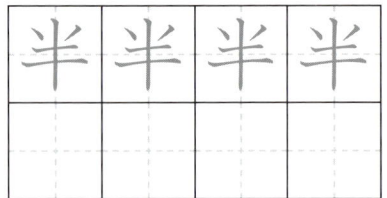

I used a knife to cut an apple in half.

おんよみ ハン
くんよみ なか(ば)

いみ half **strokes** 5画 丶 ヽ ソ ニ 半

Note the position of the dots!

半分	はんぶん	half
前半	ぜんはん	the first half
半ば	なかば	half, middle
半額	はんがく	half (the) price
半円	はんえん	half circle

切

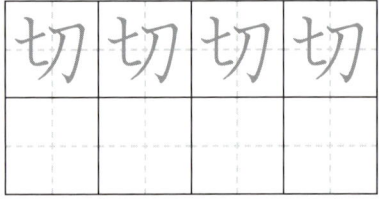

A *samurai* is practicing swordsmanship by cutting a tree stump.

おんよみ セツ・サイ
くんよみ き(る)・き(れる)

いみ to cut, to chop, to slice **strokes** 4画 一 七 切 切

Do not protrude!

切る	きる	to cut
切断	せつだん	cutting
一切	いっさい	all
大切(な)	たいせつ(な)	important, precious
切符	きっぷ	ticket

分

A *samurai* split the wood in two with his sword.

おんよみ ブン・フン・ブ
くんよみ わ(ける)・わ(かれる)・わ(かる)・わ(かつ)

いみ to divide, to share, minute **strokes** 4画 ノ 八 分 分

Do not protrude!

分ける	わける	to divide
部分	ぶぶん	part
五分間	ごふんかん	five minutes
分業	ぶんぎょう	the division of labor

番

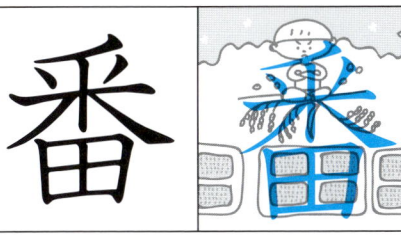

I was in front of the rice paddy to keep a vigil over the rice stalks.

おんよみ バン
くんよみ ー

いみ one's turn, order

strokes 12画 ノ ヽ 爫 平 平 来 来 乑 番 番 番 番

番号	ばんごう	number
順番	じゅんばん	order, one's turn
交番	こうばん	police box
欠番	けつばん	missing number
当番	とうばん	duty

米

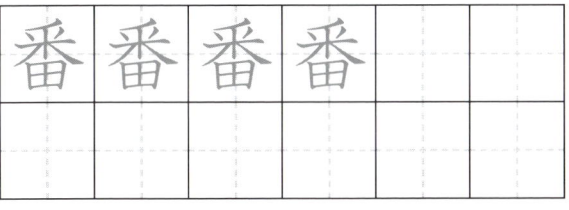

When the farmer harvested the rice stalks with a sickle, a lot of rice grains fell out.

おんよみ ベイ・マイ
くんよみ こめ

いみ rice, America, meter

strokes 6画 ヽ ソ 二 半 米 米

Point
米
Note the position of the dots!

米国	べいこく	U.S.A
玄米	げんまい	brown rice
米粒	こめつぶ	grain of rice
平米	へいべい	square meter
白米	はくまい	polished rice

絵

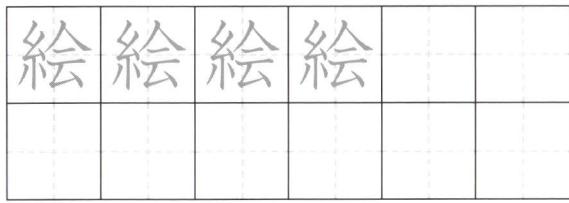

This spool stores scissors on the top. I used string and a needle from it to embroider a tapestry with a picture.

おんよみ カイ・エ
くんよみ ー

いみ picture, painting

strokes 12画 ノ ㄠ ㄠ 幺 糸 糸 糸 紣 紣 給 絵 絵

絵画	かいが	picture, painting
浮世絵	うきよえ	*ukiyo-e*
絵本	えほん	picture book
絵心	えごころ	artistic taste
下絵	したえ	rough sketch

細

This spool stores scissors on the top. I wrapped a present with a thin string from the spool.

おんよみ サイ
くんよみ ほそ(い)・ほそ(る)・こま(か)・こま(かい)

いみ thin, fine, small, detailed　**strokes 11画**　く 纟 幺 夂 糸 糸 糽 紭 細 細 細

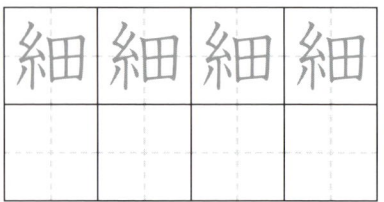

Do not protrude!

細かい	こまかい	detailed, fine, small
細工	さいく	artifice, trick, workmanship
詳細	しょうさい	details
細切り	こまぎり	slicing up finely

線

I unwind a thin thread like a line.

おんよみ セン
くんよみ ―

いみ line　**strokes 15画**　く 纟 幺 夂 糸 糸 糸' 糾 紵 綌 絎 線 線

線路	せんろ	railroad
曲線	きょくせん	curve
電線	でんせん	electric wire
子午線	しごせん	meridian
車線	しゃせん	traffic lane

紙

This spool stores scissors on the top. There is a woman making paper.

おんよみ シ
くんよみ かみ

いみ paper　**strokes 10画**　く 纟 幺 夂 糸 糸 紅 紙 紙

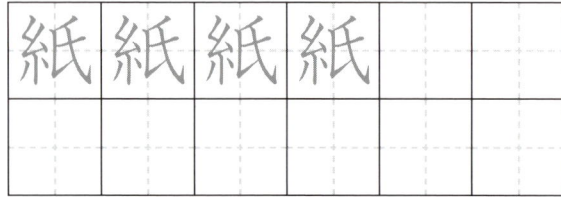

紙幣	しへい	paper money
手紙	てがみ	letter
紙袋	かみぶくろ	paper bag
新聞紙	しんぶんし	newspaper
用紙	ようし	form, paper

組

The spool and scissors are used to make a braided rug.

おんよみ ソ
くんよみ く(む)・くみ

いみ pair, class, to put together
strokes 11画　く 幺 幺 糸 糸 糸 糽 細 絈 組

Point
組
Do not protrude!

組織	そしき	organization, system
組む	くむ	to cross, to fold
番組	ばんぐみ	program
組曲	くみきょく	suite
組成	そせい	composition

外

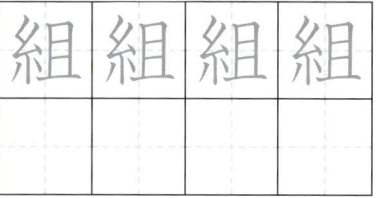

I opened the door and found a bird knocking on the outside of it.

おんよみ ガイ・ゲ
くんよみ そと・ほか・はず(す)・はず(れる)

いみ outside, to remove
strokes 5画　ノ ク タ 夘 外

外食	がいしょく	eating out
外科	げか	surgery
外側	そとがわ	outside
外貨	がいか	foreign currency
意外(な)	いがい(な)	surprising

角

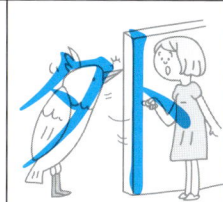

The Triceratops is a dinosaur with three big horns.

おんよみ カク
くんよみ かど・つの

いみ horn, corner, edge
strokes 7画　ノ ク ⺈ 角 角 角 角

Point
角
Do not protrude!

角度	かくど	angle
角部屋	かどべや	corner room
角	つの	horn
三角形	さんかくけい	triangle
四角形	しかくけい	quadrangle

73

歌

A singer held a microphone and sang a song while people in the audience were sitting in their seats.

- おんよみ カ
- くんよみ うた・うた(う)

いみ song, poem, to sing

strokes 14画　一 ｢ 冂 冂 可 可 丂 哥 哥 哥 哥 歌 歌 歌

歌手	かしゅ	singer
歌声	うたごえ	singing voice
歌う	うたう	to sing
和歌	わか	Japanese poetry
国歌	こっか	national anthem

牛

This is a cow.

- おんよみ ギュウ
- くんよみ うし

いみ cattle, cow

strokes 4画　ノ ヒ 二 牛

Point

Protrude!

牛乳	ぎゅうにゅう	cow milk
牛肉	ぎゅうにく	beef
牡牛座	おうしざ	Taurus
乳牛	にゅうぎゅう	milk cow, dairy cow
牛舎	ぎゅうしゃ	cowshed

午

The clock hands indicate that it is exactly noon.

- おんよみ ゴ
- くんよみ ―

いみ horse, noon

strokes 4画　ノ ヒ 二 午

Point

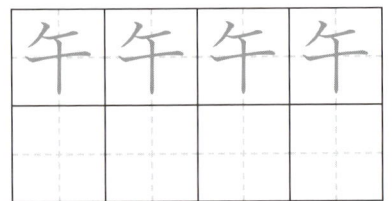

Do not protrude!

午前	ごぜん	morning, a.m.
午後	ごご	afternoon, p.m.
正午	しょうご	noon
子午線	しごせん	meridian

74

点

This is a device that discharges water when I push the button on the top.

おんよみ テン
くんよみ —

いみ dot, point, to turn on
strokes 9画

丶 丨 卜 占 占 占 卢 点 点 点

Point
点
Note the position of the dots!

得点	とくてん	score
欠点	けってん	defect, fault
終点	しゅうてん	terminal
点火	てんか	ignition
点字	てんじ	Braille

黒

Four black frogs were watching a man meditating in front of a rice paddy.

おんよみ コク
くんよみ くろ・くろ(い)

いみ black, guilty
strokes 11画

丨 冂 冃 日 甲 甲 里 里 黒 黒 黒

Point
黒
Note the longest horizontal stroke!

黒板	こくばん	blackboard
黒字	くろじ	surplus
黒い	くろい	black
黒潮	くろしお	the Japan Current
黒幕	くろまく	backroom fixer

魚

Four fish jumped out of the rice paddy when they saw a snake slithering into it.

おんよみ ギョ
くんよみ うお・さかな

いみ fish
strokes 11画

丿 ク 冫 匀 甪 角 角 魚 魚 魚 魚

Point
魚
Do not protrude!

金魚	きんぎょ	goldfish
魚河岸	うおがし	fish market
魚屋	さかなや	fish shop
鮮魚	せんぎょ	fresh fish
熱帯魚	ねったいぎょ	tropical fish

75

馬

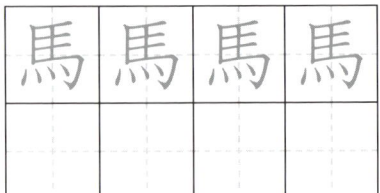

This is a horse with a gorgeous mane fluttering.

おんよみ バ
くんよみ うま・ま

いみ horse

strokes 10画 ｜ 厂 匚 乍 두 丐 馬 馬 馬 馬

Do not protrude!

乗馬	じょうば	horseback riding
馬小屋	うまごや	stable
絵馬	えま	*ema* (votive wooden plaque)
牛馬	ぎゅうば	horse and cattle
馬車	ばしゃ	carriage, coach

鳥

This is a bird on the grass.

おんよみ チョウ
くんよみ とり

いみ bird

strokes 11画 ′ 亻 丆 户 白 鳥 鳥 鳥 鳥 鳥

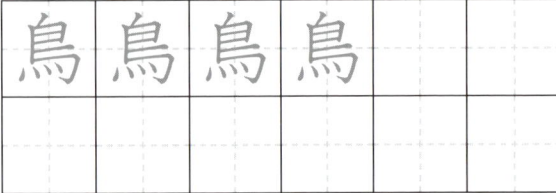

白鳥	はくちょう	swan
小鳥	ことり	little bird
鳥居	とりい	*torii* gate
鳥小屋	とりごや	aviary, birdhouse
鳥類	ちょうるい	birds

京

There is a beautiful temple in *Kyoto*.

おんよみ キョウ・ケイ
くんよみ ―

いみ capital city

strokes 8画 ′ 亠 亠 宁 市 吉 京 京

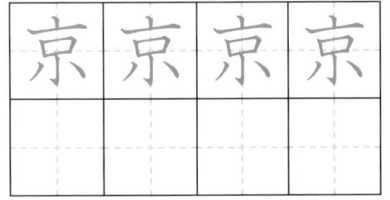

Note the position of the dots!

京都	きょうと	*Kyoto*
東京	とうきょう	*Tokyo*
京浜	けいひん	the *Keihin* region
帰京	ききょう	return to *Tokyo*
京菓子	きょうがし	*Kyoto* confectionery

I am a trader who sells weapons such as axes.

おんよみ コウ
くんよみ まじ(わる)・まじ(える)・ま(じる)・ま(ざる)・ま(ぜる)・か(う)・か(わす)

いみ to mix, to cross, to exchange　**strokes 6画**　丶 亠 六 亠 亠 交

交差点	こうさてん	intersection	交差点を直進してください。
交換	こうかん	exchanging	友人との意見の交換を楽しむ。
交ざる	まざる	to mix	友人に交ざって遊びに行く。
交通	こうつう	traffic	交通のルールを守る。
外交	がいこう	diplomacy	他の国と外交を行う。
交易	こうえき	commerce, trade	古くから、交易が行われていた。

I used some logs to create the form of a gate to the shrine; it is called *torii*.

おんよみ ケイ・ギョウ
くんよみ かた・かたち

いみ shape, figure, form　**strokes 7画**　一 二 テ 开 开 形 形

Point
 Note the position of the dots!

図形	ずけい	diagram, figure	図形の大きさをはかる。
人形	にんぎょう	doll	よく人形で遊んだ。
形見	かたみ	keepsake, memento	祖父の形見を大切にする。
形式	けいしき	form, formality	形式にとらわれすぎてもいけない。
形勢	けいせい	situation	試合の形勢が変わった。
円形	えんけい	round shape, circle	円形の舞台の上に立つ。

 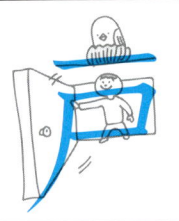

When I opened the door, I discovered a bird looking down from his nest on top of the door.

おんよみ コ
くんよみ と

いみ door　strokes 4画　一ラヨ戸

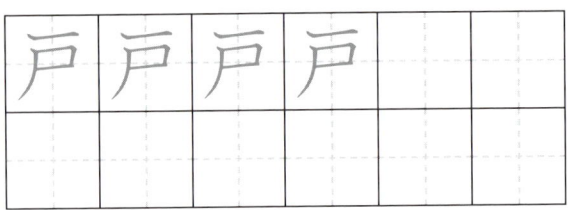

戸籍	こせき	family register
戸口	とぐち	doorway
戸棚	とだな	cupboard
雨戸	あまど	shutter, sliding door
江戸	えど	Edo (now Tokyo)

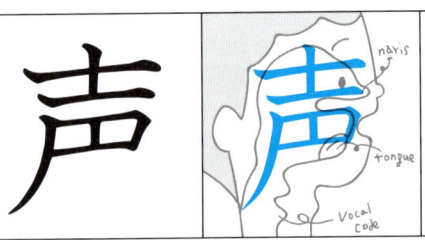

The vocal mechanism is very complicated; it has vocal cords, a larynx, a tongue and other parts.

おんよみ セイ・ショウ
くんよみ こえ・こわ

いみ voice, reputation　strokes 7画　一十士吉吉吉声

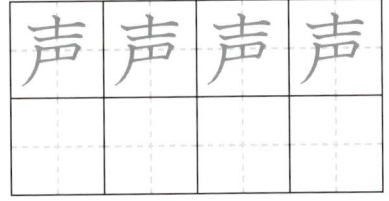 

Point
声
Do not protrude!

美声	びせい	beautiful voice
歌声	うたごえ	singing voice
声色	こわいろ	feigned voice
声優	せいゆう	voice actor (actress)
声援	せいえん	cheer, encouragement

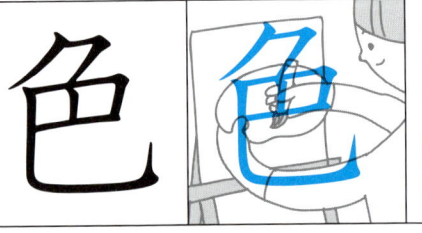

I used a palette and a brush to put some color on the canvas.

おんよみ ショク・シキ
くんよみ いろ

いみ color, look, love affair　strokes 6画　ノクク名名色

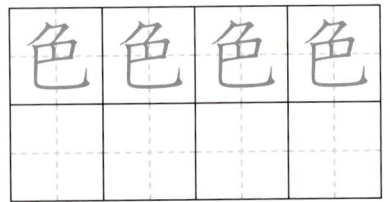 

Point
色
Do not protrude!

染色	せんしょく	dyeing
色彩	しきさい	color, hue
桃色	ももいろ	pink
色素	しきそ	pigment
青色	あおいろ	blue

 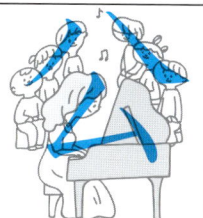

A pianist was playing the piano in public.

おんよみ コウ
くんよみ おおやけ

いみ public, government, fair **strokes** 4画 ノ 八 公 公

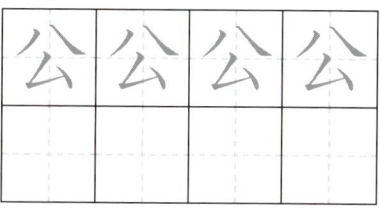

Do not connect!

公式	こうしき	official
公平(な)	こうへい(な)	fair
公	おおやけ	public
公開	こうかい	opening to the public
公園	こうえん	park

A pianist was playing the piano on the stage.

おんよみ ダイ・タイ
くんよみ ー

いみ stand, hill, height **strokes** 5画 ㇀ ㇅ 台 台 台

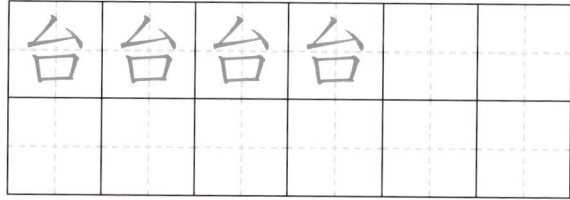

台所	だいどころ	kitchen
灯台	とうだい	lighthouse
台風	たいふう	typhoon
高台	たかだい	upland
台紙	だいし	a mount

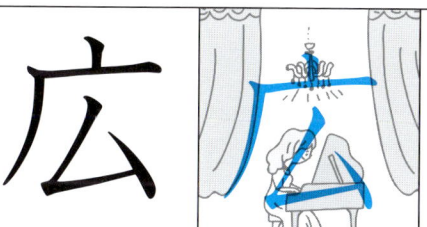

A pianist was playing the piano in the spacious hall.

おんよみ コウ
くんよみ ひろ(い)・ひろ(まる)・ひろ(める)・ひろ(がる)・ひろ(げる)

いみ large, to spread, wide **strokes** 5画 ㇀ 亠 广 広 広

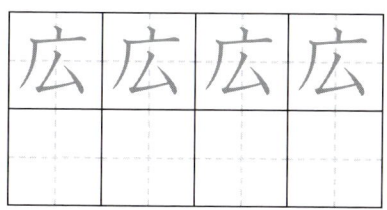

Do not connect!

広告	こうこく	advertisement
広場	ひろば	plaza, square
広い	ひろい	broad, large, wide
広域	こういき	wide area
背広	せびろ	business suit

店

A cat is trying to steal something nice from a food stand.

おんよみ テン
くんよみ みせ

いみ store, shop

strokes 8画 　丶 亠 广 广 庐 庐 店 店

Point
店 ×点
　 ×古
Note the similar characters!

売店	ばいてん	stall, stand	売店でポップコーンを買う。
店員	てんいん	(sales) clerk	店員にすすめられた服を買った。
店先	みせさき	shop front	店先の行列にならぶ。
店主	てんしゅ	storekeeper	店主においしさの工夫を聞いた。
閉店	へいてん	closing up shop	今日はもうすぐ閉店するらしい。
代理店	だいりてん	agency, agent	代理店で予約をした。

古

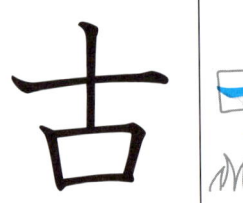 

The grave looked very old.

おんよみ コ
くんよみ ふる(い)・ふる(す)

いみ old, past

strokes 5画 　一 十 十 古 古

中古	ちゅうこ	used, secondhand	この車は中古で入手した。
古本	ふるほん	used book	読みたかった本を古本で見つけた。
古着	ふるぎ	used clothing	彼は古着をじょうずに着こなしている。
古代	こだい	ancient times	古代からここには人が住んでいたらしい。
古典	こてん	classic	日本の古典を研究する。
古風(な)	こふう(な)	antique, old-fashioned	若いわりに古風な考え方をしている。

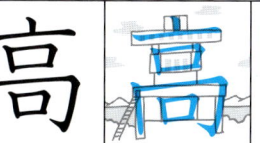

There is a tall observation deck on the hill so you can see beautiful views.

おんよみ コウ　　**くんよみ** たか(い)・たか・たか(まる)・たか(める)

いみ high, tall

strokes 10画　　丶 亠 亡 宁 古 亨 高 高 高 高

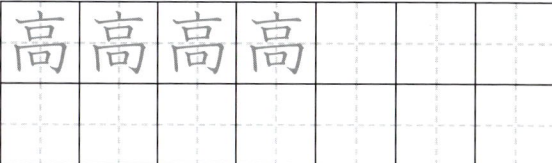

高い	たかい	high, tall
高値	たかね	high price
高校	こうこう	senior high school
高温	こうおん	high temperature

A small village in the valley has been formed between two mountains.

おんよみ コク　　**くんよみ** たに・や

いみ valley, trough, hollow

strokes 7画　　丿 ハ ク 父 公 谷 谷

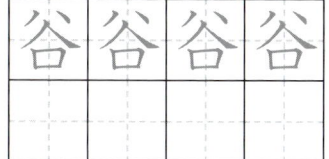

Point  ← Note the position of the dots!

渓谷	けいこく	gorge, ravine
谷間	たにま	valley
谷川	たにがわ	mountain stream
谷底	たにぞこ	the bottom of a ravine

You can gain knowledge by having a lot of experiences, or by reading books.

おんよみ チ　　**くんよみ** し(る)

いみ to know, knowledge, information

strokes 8画　　丿 ト 匕 チ 矢 知 知 知

知識	ちしき	knowledge
知人	ちじん	acquaintance
知り合い	しりあい	acquaintance
未知	みち	unfamiliar, unknown

A ship floating down the river nearly reached the pier.

おんよみ セン　　**くんよみ** ふね・ふな

いみ boat, ship

strokes 11画　　丿 丬 凢 月 舟 舟 舟 舩 舩 船 船

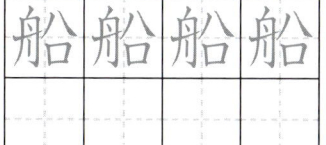

Point 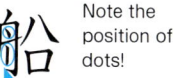 Note the position of the dots!

船	ふね	boat, ship
乗船	じょうせん	boarding
船便	ふなびん	sea mail
漁船	ぎょせん	fishing boat

A boy is sitting by a river wishing to see his friend who moved to the village on the mountain.

おんよみ カイ・エ
くんよみ あ(う)

いみ to meet, meeting, point **strokes** 6画 ノ 人 入 会 会 会

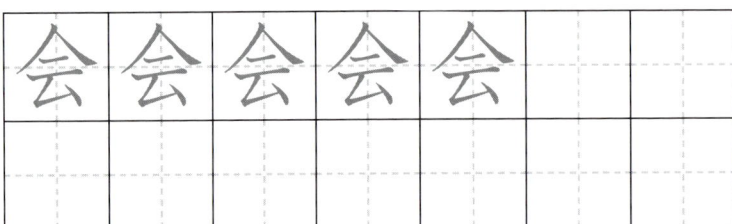

Point
会 ← Do not protrude!

会社	かいしゃ	company, corporation	東京の会社ではたらく。
会得	えとく	learning, understanding	技術を早く会得したい。
会う	あう	to meet, to see	待ち合わせ場所で、友人と会う。
会議	かいぎ	conference	今日の会議は長くなりそうだ。
会期	かいき	period, session	国会の会期が延びた。
宴会	えんかい	banquet, party	友人と宴会に参加した。

 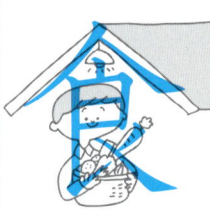

It is nice to have a roof over your head, to have electricity, and to have something to eat.

おんよみ ショク・ジキ
くんよみ た(べる)・く(う)・く(らう)

いみ food, to eat **strokes** 9画 ノ 人 入 今 今 今 食 食 食

Point
食 ←×良
食 ←×昼
Note the similar characters!

食事	しょくじ	meal	友人といっしょに食事に行った。
食べ物	たべもの	food	食べ物には気をつけている。
食べる	たべる	to eat	彼は細身だが、よく食べる。
定食	ていしょく	set meal	日替わり定食を食べる。
食堂	しょくどう	eating place	この食堂はいつも行列ができる。
夕食	ゆうしょく	supper	スーパーで夕食の材料を買う。

 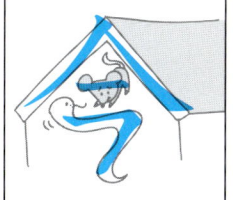

Right now, a snake is about to attack a mouse in the attic.

おんよみ キン・コン
くんよみ いま

いみ now, present **strokes 4画** ノ 人 今 今

Point 今 ← Connect!

今回	こんかい	this time	今回は、日本に一週間います。
今後	こんご	from now on	今後のことは、まだ決めていません。
今頃	いまごろ	around this time	今頃なにをしているだろう。
今月	こんげつ	this month	いつもより、今月はお金を使った。
今週	こんしゅう	this week	今週には日本に向かいます。
今夜	こんや	tonight	今夜は雨が降るらしい。

Let's sing a song in chorus.

おんよみ ゴウ・ガッ・カッ
くんよみ あ(う)・あ(わす)・あ(わせる)

いみ to fit, to match, to adapt **strokes 6画** ノ 人 合 合 合 合

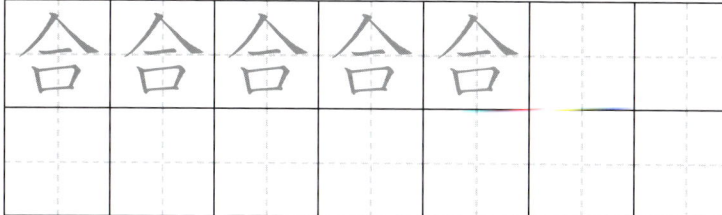 

Point 合 ←×台 ←×会
Note the similar characters!

合う	あう	to fit, to match, to suit	自分の考えと答えが合う。
合計	ごうけい	the total	そのバスには合計40人が乗っていた。
合唱	がっしょう	chorus	彼女は合唱をしている。
合格	ごうかく	passing (an exam)	娘が大学に合格した。
集合	しゅうごう	gathering, meeting	集合する時間は9時です。
連合	れんごう	alliance, union	いくつかの国が連合して新しく国ができた。

顔

My face turned pale when I saw a big spiral shell waving at me from the bottom of the cliff.

おんよみ ガン
くんよみ かお

いみ face　strokes 18画

Point: Note the position of the dots!

洗顔	せんがん	face washing		めざめるとすぐに洗顔をする。
顔色	かおいろ	complexion		彼の顔色が良くない。
笑顔	えがお	smile, smiling face		むりに笑顔を作ることはない。
朝顔	あさがお	morning glory		朝顔の花がさいていた。
顔面	がんめん	face		転んで顔面を打った。

頭

Since I saw a big spiral shell waving at me, my head has been full of it.

おんよみ トウ・ズ・ト
くんよみ あたま・かしら

いみ head, hair, beginning　strokes 16画

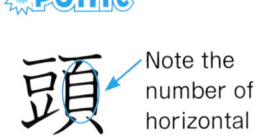

Point: Note the number of horizontal strokes!

頭部	とうぶ	head		頭部に少しだけけがをした。
頭痛	ずつう	headache		熱はないが、頭痛がする。
石頭	いしあたま	hard headed		彼は石頭だから、話してもむだだ。
頭上	ずじょう	overhead		頭上に注意してください。
冒頭	ぼうとう	the beginning		本の冒頭からおもしろかった。
台頭	たいとう	gaining power		若い選手たちが台頭してきた。

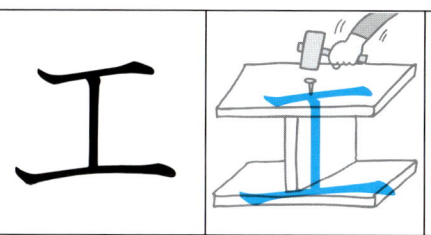

I made a shelf by jointing two boards with tools for weekend carpenters.

おんよみ コウ・ク
くんよみ —

いみ skill, to make, worker   **strokes** 3画   一 T 工

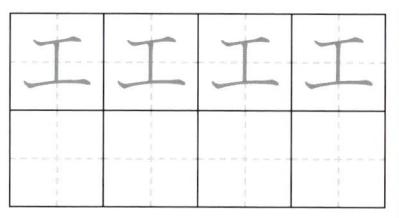

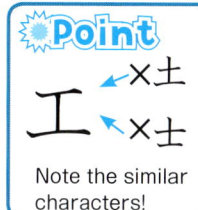

Note the similar characters!

工場	こうじょう	factory, plant
工事	こうじ	construction (work)
大工	だいく	carpenter
工業	こうぎょう	industry
工作	こうさく	handicraft

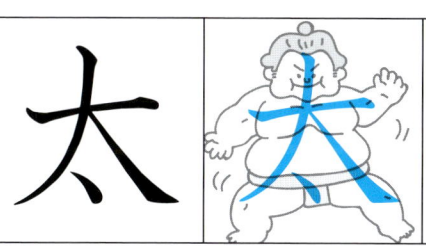

Although *sumo* wrestlers are very large, their movements are surprisingly quick.

おんよみ タイ・タ
くんよみ ふと(い)・ふと(る)

いみ thick, fat, greatly   **strokes** 4画   一 ナ 大 太

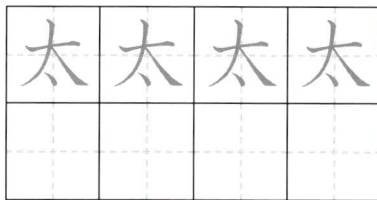

Note the similar characters!

太い	ふとい	fat, thick
太鼓	たいこ	drum
丸太	まるた	log
太陽	たいよう	the sun
太平洋	たいへいよう	the Pacific Ocean

A plot of land by the river was developed, and a residential area and a road were built.

おんよみ ガ・カク
くんよみ —

いみ to draw, painting, boundary   **strokes** 8画   一 T 〒 币 币 面 画 画

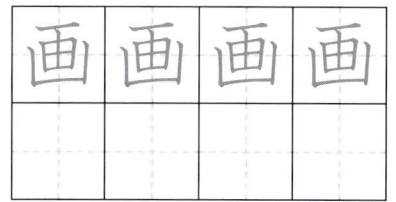

Do not connect!

映画	えいが	movie
漫画	まんが	cartoon, comic
企画	きかく	planning
画策	かくさく	maneuver, scheme
画数	かくすう	the number of strokes

85

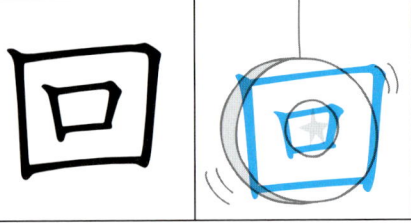

A yo-yo is spun by a child.

おんよみ カイ・エ
くんよみ まわ(る)・まわ(す)

いみ to turn, to spin   strokes 6画

回転	かいてん	revolution, rotation, turn
回復	かいふく	recovery
回り道	まわりみち	detour, roundabout
回数	かいすう	frequency
毎回	まいかい	every time

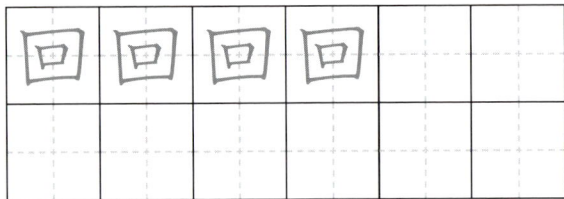

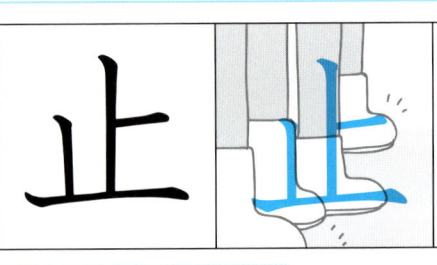

The marchers in the parade completely stopped with a shout of "Halt!".

おんよみ シ
くんよみ と(まる)・と(める)

いみ to stay, to stop, to end   strokes 4画

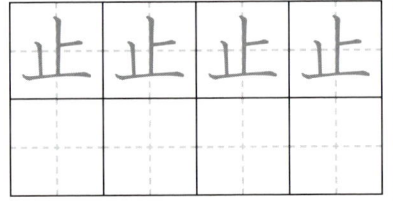

Point
止
Do not protrude!

停止	ていし	stop, suspension
中止	ちゅうし	cancel
止める	とめる	to stop
防止	ぼうし	prevention
静止	せいし	standstill

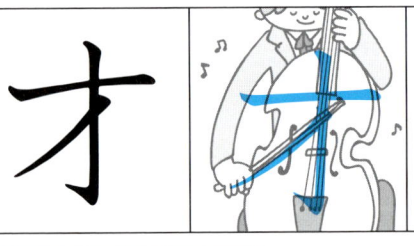

He is a genius at playing the cello.

おんよみ サイ
くんよみ —

いみ talent, aptitude, age   strokes 3画

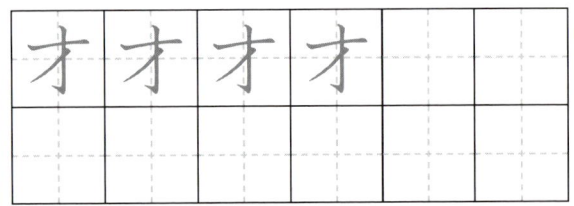

才能	さいのう	ability, gift, talent
天才	てんさい	genius
才覚	さいかく	resourcefulness
才気	さいき	brilliance
英才	えいさい	gifted person

寺

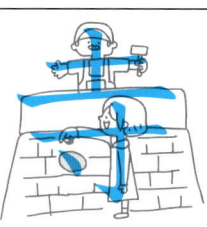

I told the person about the hole in the wall at the temple so he could repair it.

- おんよみ ジ
- くんよみ てら

いみ temple
strokes 6画 一 十 土 𠆢 寺 寺

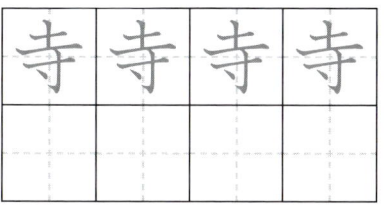

Note the longest horizontal stroke!

寺院	じいん	temple, monastery
寺子屋	てらこや	private elementary school
尼寺	あまでら	convent
禅寺	ぜんでら	zen temple
山寺	やまでら	mountain temple

自

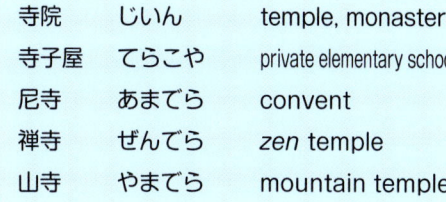

In Japan, when you want to refer to yourself, you often point at your nose with your index finger.

- おんよみ ジ・シ
- くんよみ みずか(ら)

いみ oneself, by oneself
strokes 6画 ′ ⺊ 冂 白 自 自

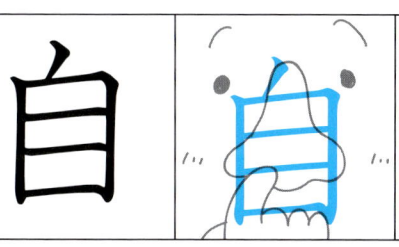

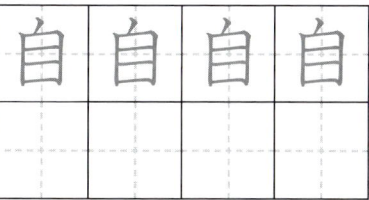

Note the similar characters!

自分	じぶん	oneself
自然	しぜん	nature
自ら	みずから	oneself
自由	じゆう	freedom, liberty
各自	かくじ	each (person)

時

I plan to repair the hole in the temple wall at the time when the sun rises.

- おんよみ ジ
- くんよみ とき

いみ time, period, hour
strokes 10画 １ 冂 月 日 日̄ 日⁺ 昨 昨 時 時

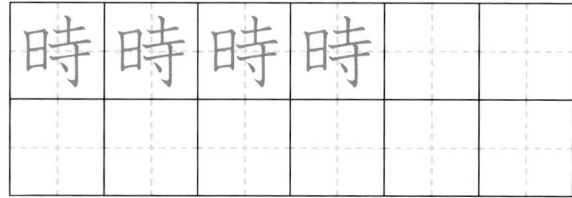

時間	じかん	time, hour
時代	じだい	age, epoch, period
潮時	しおどき	the right time
時給	じきゅう	hourly wage
同時に	どうじに	simultaneously

Two birds were flying on Sunday morning while I was enjoying a DIY project.

おんよみ ヨウ
くんよみ ―

いみ shine, day of the week
strokes 18画 丨 冂 日 日 日́ 日͞ 日͞ヨ 日͞ヨ 日͞ヨ 日͞ヨ 日͞ヨ 日ヨ 暐 暐 暉 曜 曜 曜

Point
曜
Do not connect!

曜日	ようび	day of the week
日曜日	にちようび	Sunday
火曜日	かようび	Tuesday
水曜日	すいようび	Wednesday
土曜日	どようび	Saturday

It was so sunny that I could enjoy sun bathing on the moon.

おんよみ セイ
くんよみ は(れる)・は(らす)

いみ to clear up, fine, sunny
strokes 12画 丨 冂 日 日̄ 日̄ 日͡ 晴 晴 晴 晴

Point
晴
Note the longest horizontal stroke!

晴れる	はれる	to clear up
快晴	かいせい	clear weather
晴天	せいてん	fair weather
晴れ着	はれぎ	one's best clothes
晴れ間	はれま	a break in the rain

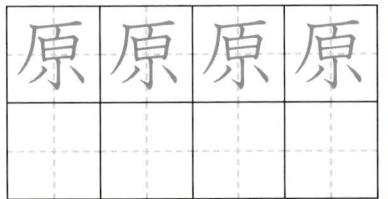

Primitive people lived in caves and made their own fire and took care of all of their needs.

おんよみ ゲン
くんよみ はら

いみ field, plain, root
strokes 10画 一 厂 厂 厈 厉 盾 盾 原 原 原

Point
原
Note the position of the dots!

原因	げんいん	cause
高原	こうげん	highlands
野原	のはら	field
原始	げんし	primitive
原価	げんか	first cost

書

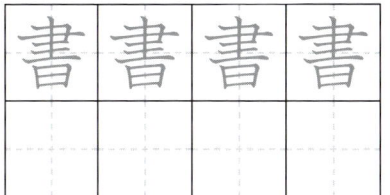

I was writing a letter.

おんよみ ショ
くんよみ か(く)

いみ to write, book　**strokes** 10画　フ コ ヨ ヨ 三 聿 聿 書 書 書

Note the number of horizontal strokes!

書く	かく	to write
書類	しょるい	document, papers
読書	どくしょ	reading
書道	しょどう	Japanese calligraphy
聖書	せいしょ	the (Holy) Bible

星

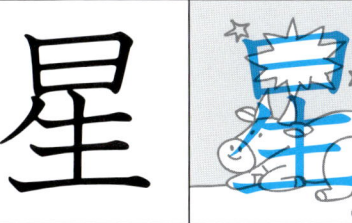

A cow lying on the ground saw something shining; it was a big star.

おんよみ セイ・ショウ
くんよみ ほし

いみ star, planet　**strokes** 9画　丨 冂 日 日 戸 尸 曰 星 星

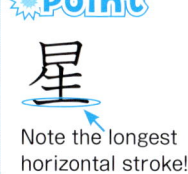
Note the longest horizontal stroke!

星座	せいざ	constellation
明星	みょうじょう	Venus
星空	ほしぞら	starry sky
火星	かせい	Mars
土星	どせい	Saturn

明

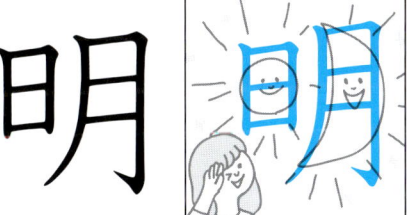

It would be really bright if the sun and the moon shine at the same time.

おんよみ メイ・ミョウ　**くんよみ** あ(かり)・あか(るい)・あか(るむ)・あか(らむ)・あき(らか)・あ(ける)・あ(く)・あ(くる)・あ(かす)

いみ bright, to brighten, dawn　**strokes** 8画　丨 冂 月 日 日' 明 明 明

照明	しょうめい	lighting
明朝	みょうちょう	tomorrow morning
星明かり	ほしあかり	starlight
明暗	めいあん	light and shade
明細	めいさい	details

社

When you are busy with work, you should pause and stretch yourself at the office.

- おんよみ　シャ
- くんよみ　やしろ

いみ shrine, company　**strokes** 7画　`ヽ ラ ネ ネ ネ 社 社`

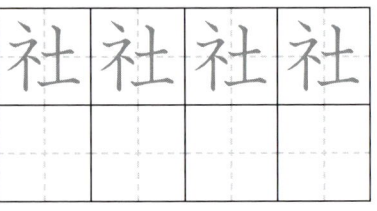

Point

Do not protrude!

社員	しゃいん	(company) employee
神社	じんじゃ	shrine
社	やしろ	(shinto) shrine
社長	しゃちょう	president of a company
社屋	しゃおく	office building

首

The neck is the part of the body that joins the trunk with the head.

- おんよみ　シュ
- くんよみ　くび

いみ neck, head, leader　**strokes** 9画　`ヽ ソ 亠 並 艹 苎 首 首 首`

首都	しゅと	capital city
首輪	くびわ	collar
手首	てくび	wrist
首	くび	neck
党首	とうしゅ	party leader

直

Soldiers marched lifting their legs at a right angle.

- おんよみ　チョク・ジキ
- くんよみ　ただ(ちに)・なお(す)・なお(る)

いみ straight, immediately, to mend　**strokes** 8画　`一 十 广 卉 肯 肯 直 直`

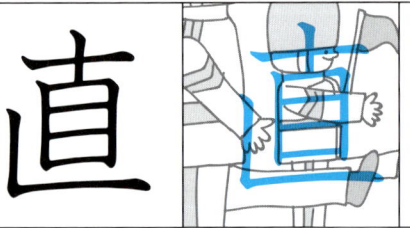

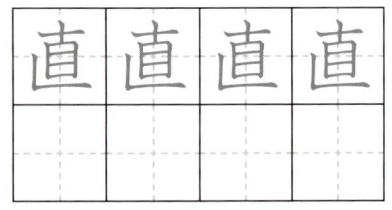

Point

Do not connect!

直線	ちょくせん	straight line
直筆	じきひつ	one's own handwriting
素直(な)	すなお(な)	obedient
実直(な)	じっちょく(な)	honest and sincere
直営	ちょくえい	direct management

新

I saw my new house when I was flying above the tree.

おんよみ シン
くんよみ あたら(しい)・あら(た)・にい

いみ new, fresh
strokes 13画 ` 丶 亠 ナ 立 立 辛 辛 亲 亲 新 新 新 `

Point: 新 ← Do not protrude!

新幹線	しんかんせん	the *Shinkansen*	新幹線で北海道へ行った。
新宿	しんじゅく	*Shinjuku*	新宿駅から電車に乗る。
新しい	あたらしい	new	新しいコートを買う。
新鮮(な)	しんせん(な)	fresh	新鮮なやさいを買う。
最新	さいしん	the latest	インターネットで最新のニュースを読む。
新説	しんせつ	a new idea, a new theory	新説を発表する。

親

I saw one of my parents looking for me when I was flying above the tree.

おんよみ シン
くんよみ おや・した(しい)・した(しむ)

いみ parent, to be friendly, friendly
strokes 16画 ` 丶 亠 ナ 立 立 辛 辛 亲 亲 新 新 新 親 親 親 `

Point: 親 ← Note the number of horizontal strokes!

両親	りょうしん	parents	両親といっしょに旅行にいく。
親子	おやこ	parent and child	親子で出かける。
親しい	したしい	friendly	親しい友人と、パーティーをする。
親切(な)	しんせつ(な)	kind	彼女はだれに対しても親切だ。
親近感	しんきんかん	a sense of closeness	彼にはなぜか、親近感を覚える。
親友	しんゆう	best friend	彼は子どものころからの親友だ。

数

We danced together while counting floral art.

- おんよみ　スウ・ス
- くんよみ　かず・かぞ(える)

いみ　number, to count
strokes 13画　丶丷丬半米米米娄娄娄娄数数

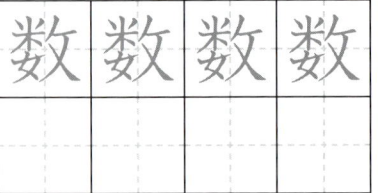

Do not protrude!

数学	すうがく	mathematics
数寄(な)	すうき(な)	checkered, varied
頭数	あたまかず	the number of people
数値	すうち	numerical value
整数	せいすう	integer

教

The teacher told the child to take a seat in front of the desk for studying so he can teach him.

- おんよみ　キョウ
- くんよみ　おし(える)・おそ(わる)

いみ　to teach, teaching
strokes 11画　一十土耂耂孝孝孝孝教教

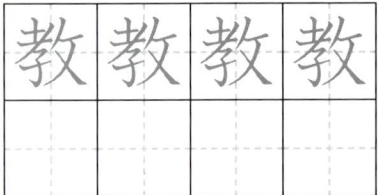

×数
×政
Note the similar characters!

教える	おしえる	to teach
教育	きょういく	education
教師	きょうし	teacher
教会	きょうかい	church
宗教	しゅうきょう	religion

買

Children used shellfish as money to buy items.

- おんよみ　バイ
- くんよみ　か(う)

いみ　to buy
strokes 12画　丨冂冂罒罒罒買買買買買買

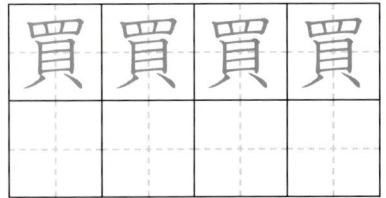

Do not protrude!

買う	かう	to buy
買収	ばいしゅう	buyout, takeover
購買	こうばい	purchase
買い物	かいもの	shopping

前

Two children discovered the moon sitting in front of the wall.

おんよみ ゼン
くんよみ まえ

いみ front, before

strokes 9画 　丶 ソ 寸 寸 竹 竹 肯 前 前

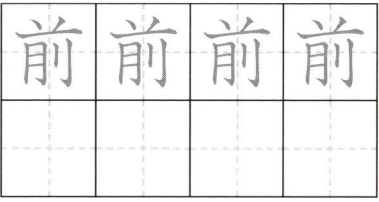

Do not connect!

前回	ぜんかい	the last time
前進	ぜんしん	advance, progress
前払い	まえばらい	advance payment
前方	ぜんぽう	front
食前に	しょくぜんに	before a meal

多

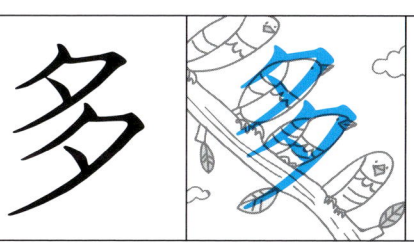

There were many birds on the branch of a tree.

おんよみ タ
くんよみ おお(い)

いみ many, much

strokes 6画 　ノ ク タ タ 多 多

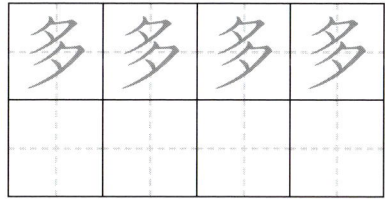

Note the similar characters!

多い	おおい	many, much
多数	たすう	a large number
多様(な)	たよう(な)	various
多量	たりょう	in large quantities
最多	さいた	the most

長

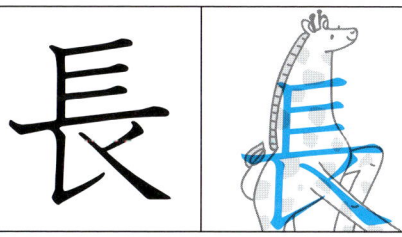

A giraffe with a long neck put out his front hoof.

おんよみ チョウ
くんよみ なが(い)

いみ long, to grow, leader

strokes 8画 　｜ 厂 厂 F 乍 巨 長 長 長

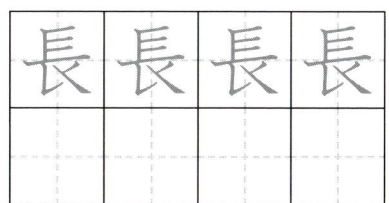

Note the longest horizontal stroke!

長期	ちょうき	long time
長所	ちょうしょ	good point, merit
長雨	ながあめ	long rain
店長	てんちょう	shop manager
年長者	ねんちょうしゃ	senior

少

There was only a little snow left on the ski slopes.

- おんよみ　ショウ
- くんよみ　すく(ない)・すこ(し)
- いみ　few, little, young
- strokes 4画　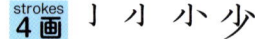

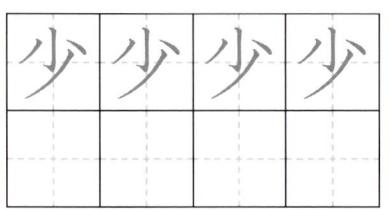

Point

Note the similar characters!

少数	しょうすう	small number
少量	しょうりょう	small quantity
少女	しょうじょ	girl
少年	しょうねん	boy
年少	ねんしょう	young

歩

There was a little snow left on the ski slopes, so I started walking.

- おんよみ　ホ・ブ・フ
- くんよみ　ある(く)・あゆ(む)
- いみ　walk, step
- strokes 8画　

歩行	ほこう	walking
歩合	ぶあい	rate
散歩	さんぽ	walking, stroll
進歩	しんぽ	progress
歩道	ほどう	sidewalk

毎

A mother wearing her apron cooks meals every day.

- おんよみ　マイ
- くんよみ　—
- いみ　every
- strokes 6画　

Point

Protrude!

毎回	まいかい	every time
毎日	まいにち	every day
毎年	まいとし	every year
毎時	まいじ	every hour
毎晩	まいばん	every night

方

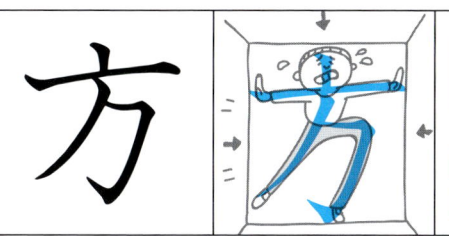

Walls from every direction pressed in on me.

おんよみ ホウ
くんよみ かた

いみ square, direction, means
strokes 4画 　丶　亠　方　方

Point
方 ×万 ×互
Note the similar characters!

方向	ほうこう	direction, way
方法	ほうほう	means, method, way
味方	みかた	ally
方角	ほうがく	direction
方針	ほうしん	policy

理

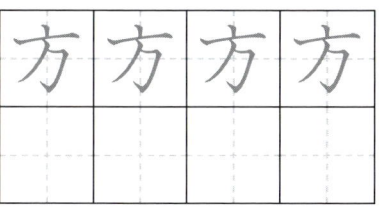

The king was wondering about the reason why the person was meditating in front of the rice paddy.

おんよみ リ
くんよみ ―

いみ reason, logic, truth
strokes 11画 　一　ｒ　Ｆ　Ｆ　王　玎　玎　玎　玾　理　理

Point
理
Note the longest horizontal stroke!

理由	りゆう	reason
理解	りかい	understanding
代理	だいり	agent
料理	りょうり	cooking
論理	ろんり	logic

友

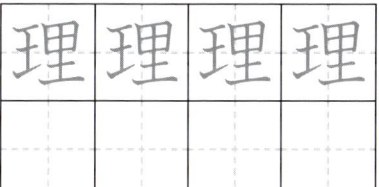

A real friend is somebody who always opens his or her arms wide and welcomes me when I am in trouble.

おんよみ ユウ
くんよみ とも

いみ friend
strokes 4画 　一　ナ　方　友

Point
友
Protrude!

友人	ゆうじん	friend
友情	ゆうじょう	friendship
友達	ともだち	friend
親友	しんゆう	best friend
級友	きゅうゆう	classmate

95

野

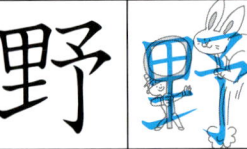

In the field, there was a person and a rabbit jumping high.

おんよみ ヤ **くんよみ** の

いみ field, wild, unexplored

strokes 11画 一 口 日 日 甲 甲 里 野 野 野 野

Point
野
Do not protrude!

野外	やがい	the open air
野球	やきゅう	baseball
野原	のはら	field
視野	しや	field of vision

風

I was trying to catch the worm resting on the leaf while the wind was blowing outside.

おんよみ フウ・フ **くんよみ** かぜ・かざ

いみ wind

strokes 9画 ノ 几 凡 凡 凨 風 風 風

風雨	ふうう	wind and rain
風情	ふぜい	taste, elegance
潮風	しおかぜ	sea breeze
暴風	ぼうふう	storm

丸

I used a knife to cut the whole chicken at dinner time.

おんよみ ガン **くんよみ** まる・まる(い)・まる(める)

いみ circle, whole, round

strokes 3画 ノ 九 丸

Point
丸
Protrude!

一丸	いちがん	all together as a group
丸見え	まるみえ	can see everything in ~
弾丸	だんがん	bullet
丸暗記	まるあんき	rote learning

毛

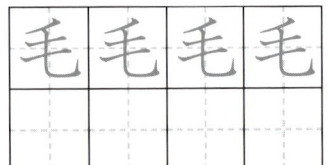

The princess's hair was tied up nicely.

おんよみ モウ **くんよみ** け

いみ hair, fur

strokes 4画 一 二 三 毛

Point
毛 ×手
  ×去
Note the similar characters!

毛布	もうふ	blanket
毛髪	もうはつ	hair
毛虫	けむし	hairy caterpillar
毛糸	けいと	knitting wool

96

考

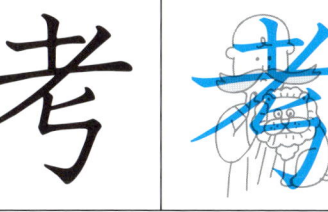

The mountain hermit was thinking about whether the animal is a lion or a dog.

おんよみ コウ
くんよみ かんが(える)

いみ to think, to consider **strokes** 6画

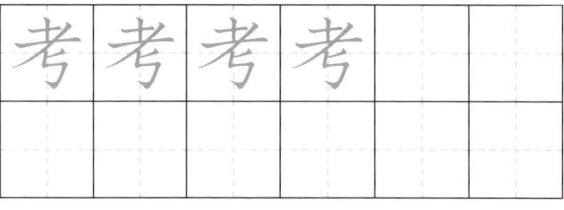

考える	かんがえる	to consider, to think
思考	しこう	consideration
参考	さんこう	reference
熟考	じゅっこう	careful consideration
選考	せんこう	selection

万

There were 10,000 people in the audience to watch her skate.

おんよみ マン・バン
くんよみ —

いみ ten thousand **strokes** 3画

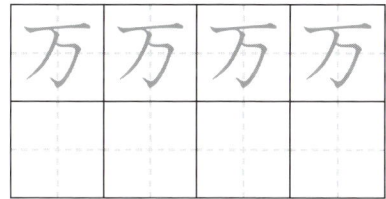 

Point
万 ← Do not protrude!

十万	じゅうまん	a hundred thousand
万年筆	まんねんひつ	fountain pen
万能(な)	ばんのう(な)	all-purpose, almighty
百万	ひゃくまん	million
万全	ばんぜん	perfection

用

One of my tasks today was to put a blanket on a cow.

おんよみ ヨウ
くんよみ もち(いる)

いみ to use, task, work **strokes** 5画

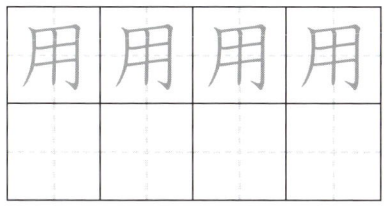 

Point
用 ← Do not protrude!

用事	ようじ	business
用意	ようい	preparation
用いる	もちいる	to use
急用	きゅうよう	urgent business
応用	おうよう	application

1 Below the *Kanji*, write the Japanese reading of *Kanji* in *Hiragana*.

① 父　　② 朝　　③ 弟　　④ 姉　　⑤ 北
（　　）（　　）（　　）（　　）（　　）

⑥ 雲　　⑦ 池　　⑧ 鳥　　⑨ 国　　⑩ 風
（　　）（　　）（　　）（　　）（　　）

2 Choose the correct reading.

① 昼夜　（a ちょうよ　b ちゅうや　c しょうゆ）（　　）

② 通行　（a つうこう　b とおぎょう　c つうさく）（　　）

③ 牛馬　（a ぎゅうば　b きゅうじ　c ごば）（　　）

④ 工作　（a こうさ　b こうさく　c くさく）（　　）

⑤ 前方　（a まえほう　b ぜんかた　c ぜんぽう）（　　）

3 Write down the correct reading of the underlined part of the sentence.

① 黒い羽を見つける。　（　　）（　　）

② 場内では禁止(きんし)されている。（　　）

③ 午後になりました。　（　　）

④ 星明かりで過(す)ごす。　（　　）

⑤ 顔を見せてください。　（　　）

4 After reading the *Hiragana* and English, write the *Kanji* that applies to the word in the box.

① いろ (color) ☐
② ひかり (light) ☐
③ にし (west) ☐
④ ふゆ (winter) ☐
⑤ おや (parent) ☐
⑥ せん (line) ☐
⑦ かく (to write) ☐く
⑧ うたう (to sing) ☐う

5 Choose the correct *Kanji* that corresponds to the *Hiragana* reading.

① かず (a 数　b 教　c 政)　　（　）
② うち (a 四　b 内　c 肉)　　（　）
③ あいだ (a 門　b 聞　c 間)　（　）
④ みせ (a 店　b 古　c 点)　　（　）
⑤ た (a 名　b 多　c 各)　　　（　）

6 In the boxes, write the *Kanji* that applies to the *furigana* reading.

①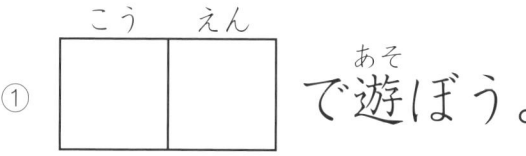

②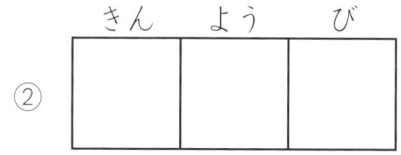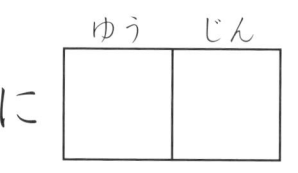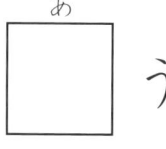

③ [どう][じ]に[ある]きはじめる。

④ [なつ]の[あいだ]に[はし]るれんしゅうをした。

⑤ [いえ]でゆっくりと[かんが]えようと[おも]う。

⑥ いろいろな[げん][ご]を[はな]す。

⑦ [あき]になってから[うみ]へ[い]く。

⑧ [なん]でも[たの]しむ[こころ]が大事だ。

⑨ [きょう][しつ]で本を[よ]む。

⑩ [ひろ][ば]への[ちか][みち]を[とお]る。

答え (answers)

❶ ①ちち ②あさ ③おとうと ④あね ⑤きた ⑥くも ⑦いけ ⑧とり ⑨くに ⑩かぜ
❷ ①b ②a ③a ④b ⑤c
❸ ①くろ，はね ②じょうない ③ごご ④ほしあ ⑤かお
❹ ①色 ②光 ③西 ④冬 ⑤親 ⑥線 ⑦書 ⑧歌
❺ ①a ②b ③c ④a ⑤b
❻ ①公園 ②金曜日，友人，会 ③同時，歩 ④夏，間，走 ⑤家，考，思 ⑥言語，話 ⑦秋，海，行 ⑧何，楽，心 ⑨教室，読 ⑩広場，近道，通

N3①

ここでは、日本語能力検定2級相当の漢字を掲載しています。

contains the *Kanji* of the Japanese Language Proficiency Test Level 2

使

We used a broom and dustpan to sweep our garden.

おんよみ シ
くんよみ つか(う)

いみ to use, to spend, to make, messenger
strokes 8画　ノ　イ　イ　仁　仁　使　使　使

使う	つかう	to use	新鮮な野菜を使う。
使用	しよう	use	パソコンを使用する。
使命	しめい	mission	彼は使命を果たした。
使者	ししゃ	messenger	使者を立てて、協力を求めた。
天使	てんし	angel	子供たちは天使のようにかわいい。
大使	たいし	ambassador	イギリス大使に会う。

他

I felt it was another person's business to notice that the tortoise was going to be attacked by a snake.

おんよみ タ
くんよみ ほか

いみ other, except
strokes 5画　ノ　イ　イ　他　他

Point: 他　×池　×地
Note the similar characters!

他人	たにん	others	他人の言うことを信じる。
他国	たこく	other countries	他国の文化に触れる。
他の	ほかの	other, another	他の意見はありますか。
他社	たしゃ	other companies	他社の商品の売れ行きが気になる。
排他的(な)	はいたてき(な)	exclusive	排他的な態度を示す。
他日	たじつ	some day	他日の再会を約束する。

I saw a dove flying over the ancestral grave while I was praying.

おんよみ ダイ・タイ　　**くんよみ** か(わる)・か(える)・よ・しろ

いみ to represent, age　　**strokes 5画** ノ イ 亻 代 代

Point 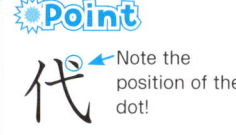 Note the position of the dot!

代わる	かわる	to represent
代理	だいり	agent
交代	こうたい	rotation
千代田区	ちよだく	*Chiyoda* ward

A wolf turned itself into a beautiful girl to bewitch people.

おんよみ カ・ケ　　**くんよみ** ば(ける)・ば(かす)

いみ to disguise, to bewitch　　**strokes 4画** ノ イ 亻 化

Point  Do not protrude!

化学	かがく	chemistry
化粧	けしょう	make-up
化け物	ばけもの	ghost, monster
変化	へんか	change

A man kneeled down in front of the king and showed his intention to serve him.

おんよみ シ・ジ　　**くんよみ** つか(える)

いみ to serve　　**strokes 5画** ノ イ 亻 什 仕

Point  ×化 ×位 Note the similar characters!

仕える	つかえる	to serve
仕事	しごと	job, work
給仕	きゅうじ	waiter, waitress
仕方	しかた	way, method

I pointed out where I live; it is the house with the chimney.

おんよみ ジュウ　　**くんよみ** す(む)・す(まう)

いみ to live, house　　**strokes 7画** ノ イ 亻 亻 仁 住 住

Point  Note the longest horizontal stroke!

住む	すむ	to live, to reside
住所	じゅうしょ	address
住居	じゅうきょ	house, residence
住民	じゅうみん	resident

位

I thought that the man giving a speech at the podium must be a person of high rank.

おんよみ イ　　**くんよみ** くらい

いみ position, rank, approximately

strokes 7画　ノ　イ　イ'　仁　什　位　位

Point
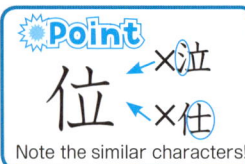
位 ×泣
　 ×仕
Note the similar characters!

位置	いち	position
単位	たんい	unit
順位	じゅんい	ranking

仲

I have a good relationship with the worm on the leaf.

おんよみ チュウ　　**くんよみ** なか

いみ terms, relationship

strokes 6画　ノ　イ　亻　仃　仲　仲

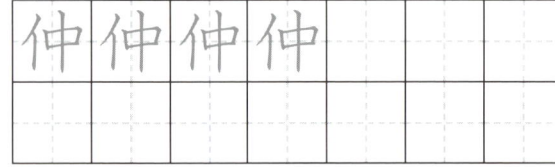

仲介	ちゅうかい	mediation
仲裁	ちゅうさい	arbitration
仲間	なかま	companion, friend
不仲	ふなか	discord

任

The king gave the soldier a sword and appointed him commander of the troops.

おんよみ ニン　　**くんよみ** まか(せる)・まか(す)

いみ duties, job, to entrust

strokes 6画　ノ　イ　イ'　仁　仟　任

Point

任 ×仕
　 ×住
Note the similar characters!

責任	せきにん	responsibility
任務	にんむ	duties
任命	にんめい	appointment, commission
任意(な)	にんい(な)	optional, voluntary

仏

People kneeled down and showed their respects to the Buddha.

おんよみ ブツ　　**くんよみ** ほとけ

いみ Buddha, France, the dead

strokes 4画　ノ　イ　仏　仏

仏像	ぶつぞう	Buddhist statue
大仏	だいぶつ	great image of Buddha
仏教	ぶっきょう	Buddhism
仏日	ふつにち	France and Japan

件

The police officer was confused to learn the suspect in the incident was a cow.

おんよみ ケン
くんよみ ー

いみ matter, case　　**strokes 6画**　ノ　イ　亻　仁　件　件

Point: 件 ← Protrude!

条件	じょうけん	condition, requirement	仕事をするための条件がある。
物件	ぶっけん	object, property, thing	不動産屋で物件を探す。
用件	ようけん	(matter of) business	彼女は用件をメールで送った。
件名	けんめい	subject matter	彼はメールの件名を書き忘れた。
件数	けんすう	the number of cases	交通事故の件数が発表された。
事件	じけん	case, event, incident	その事件はまだ解決していない。

伝

Buddha gave his disciples some scrolls in order to pass down his teachings.

おんよみ デン
くんよみ つた（わる）・つた（える）・つた（う）

いみ to tell, to pass down, biography　　**strokes 6画**　ノ　イ　仁　仁　伝　伝

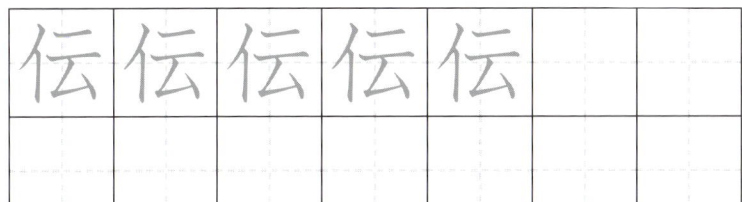

Point:  伝 ← Do not protrude!

伝える	つたえる	to tell, to pass down	このことを彼に直接伝える。
伝言	でんごん	message	彼に伝言をお願いしたいのですが。
伝統	でんとう	tradition	日本には、正月に餅を食べる伝統がある。
伝説	でんせつ	legend	伝説では、この山に財宝があるという。
遺伝	いでん	heredity	短気なのは父からの遺伝だ。
自伝	じでん	autobiography	人気歌手が自伝を書いた。

価

There is something valuable in this trunk.

おんよみ カ
くんよみ あたい

いみ value, price, cost
strokes 8画　ノ　イ　仁　仁　仃　価　価　価

Point
価 ← Do not protrude!

価格	かかく	price	野菜の価格が上がる。
価値	かち	value	この絵の価値を調べてもらった。
価	あたい	value	この商品には高めの価がつけられた。
評価	ひょうか	evaluation	彼の作品は高く評価されている。
安価	あんか	low price	この品物は安価だが、質がよい。
株価	かぶか	stock price	株価を予測する。

値

I was surprised when I saw the price of the plant standing on the table.

おんよみ チ
くんよみ ね・あたい

いみ value, price, cost
strokes 10画　ノ　イ　仁　仁　佇　佇　佶　佶　値　値

Point
値 ← Do not connect!

数値	すうち	numeral value	血圧の数値が高めだ。
値段	ねだん	price	この値段では高くて買えない。
値	あたい	value	彼の決断はほめるに値する。
偏差値	へんさち	deviation value	今回のテストで偏差値が上がっていた。
安値	やすね	low price	他の店よりも安値で買えた。
値引き	ねびき	discount	テレビを30％の値引きで買う。

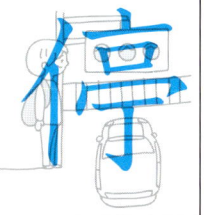

I confirmed that the car was stopped at the red traffic light, then I crossed the crosswalk.

おんよみ テイ
くんよみ —

いみ to stop, to stagnate strokes 11画 ノ イ 亻 亠 广 庐 庐 庐 庐 停 停

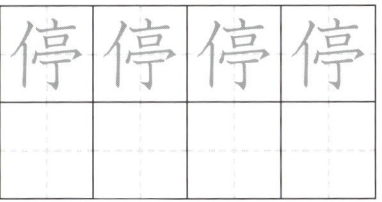 

Point
停
Do not connect!

停車	ていしゃ	stopping a car(train)
停滞	ていたい	stagnation
停電	ていでん	blackout
停止	ていし	stopping
停戦	ていせん	ceasefire

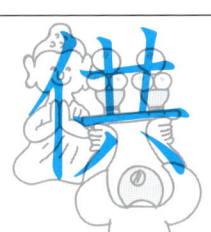

Buddha's believers delivered offerings to the Buddha.

おんよみ キョウ・ク
くんよみ そな(える)・とも

いみ to offer, to provide, attender strokes 8画 ノ イ 亻 什 什 供 供 供

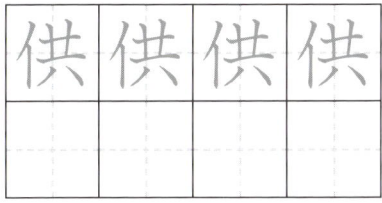 

Point
供
Note the number of horizontal strokes!

供える	そなえる	to offer
供給	きょうきゅう	supply
供養	くよう	oblation
試供品	しきょうひん	sample
提供	ていきょう	provision

低

A man crawled low toward the door so that the security guard couldn't see him.

おんよみ テイ
くんよみ ひく(い)・ひく(める)・ひく(まる)

いみ low, deep, to lower strokes 7画 ノ イ 亻 仁 任 低 低

Point
低 ×依
低 ×伝
Note the similar characters!

低い	ひくい	low
低速	ていそく	low speed
低温	ていおん	low temperature
低気圧	ていきあつ	low pressure
低地	ていち	lowlands

保

I placed the box containing my valuable things on the tree.

おんよみ ホ
くんよみ たも(つ)

いみ to keep, to maintain　strokes 9画　ノ イ イ 仁 仁 仔 仔 但 保 保

保つ	たもつ	to keep, to maintain
保存	ほぞん	preservation
保護	ほご	protection
保管	ほかん	custody
保育	ほいく	childcare

借

I borrowed a hat from the sun.

おんよみ シャク
くんよみ か(りる)

いみ to borrow, to use　strokes 10画　ノ イ 亻 仁 仕 併 併 借 借 借

Point

借
Note the longest horizontal stroke!

借りる	かりる	to borrow
借家	しゃくや	rented house
借金	しゃっきん	debt
借用	しゃくよう	borrowing, loan
借地	しゃくち	leased land

信

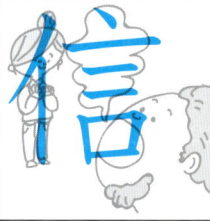

I believed what my teacher said.

おんよみ シン
くんよみ ―

いみ to believe, belief, correspondence　strokes 9画　ノ イ 亻 仁 仁 信 信 信 信

Point

信
Note the longest horizontal stroke!

信じる	しんじる	to believe
信頼	しんらい	trust
自信	じしん	confidence
信号	しんごう	signal
信仰	しんこう	faith

倍

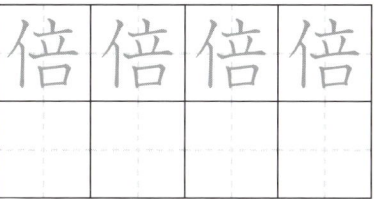

The magician took a bear out of a box, which was many times larger than the box.

おんよみ バイ
くんよみ ―

いみ twice, double

strokes 10画　ノ　イ　イ'　广　伫　佇　佇　倅　倍　倍

Note the longest horizontal stroke!

二倍	にばい	twice
倍増	ばいぞう	doubling
倍率	ばいりつ	magnification
倍額	ばいがく	double the price
人一倍	ひといちばい	more than others

個

This is an individually-owned hot dog shop.

おんよみ コ
くんよみ ―

いみ each, individual

strokes 10画　ノ　イ　イ　们　们　佣　個　個　個　個

Note the similar characters!
×固
×倍

個人	こじん	an individual
個性	こせい	individuality
個室	こしつ	private room
個数	こすう	the number
個別	こべつ	individual

便

I received a letter from the mailman.

おんよみ ベン・ビン
くんよみ たよ(り)

いみ convenience, news, excreta

strokes 9画　ノ　イ　イ'　广　仁　佢　佢　便　便

Protrude!

便利(な)	べんり(な)	convenient
郵便	ゆうびん	mail, postal service
便り	たより	letter, news
便所	べんじょ	lavatory, restroom
不便(な)	ふべん(な)	inconvenient

係

It is my turn to look after my grandmother today.

おんよみ ケイ　**くんよみ** かか(る)・かかり

いみ person in charge, to be involved

strokes 9画 ノ イ 亻 亻 伊 伊 係 係 係

Point 係 Do not protrude!

関係	かんけい	relation
係留	けいりゅう	mooring
係員	かかりいん	attendant, clerk
係長	かかりちょう	subsection chief

依

I asked a dancer with a big hat to show me how to dance.

おんよみ イ・エ　**くんよみ** —

いみ to depend, still

strokes 8画 ノ イ 亻 亻 术 佈 依 依

Point 依 Do not protrude!

依頼	いらい	request
依存	いそん・いぞん	dependence
依然	いぜん	still, yet
帰依	きえ	devotion

優

A kind person is somebody who can place a blanket on a depressed person.

おんよみ ユウ　**くんよみ** やさ(しい)・すぐ(れる)

いみ kind, good, to excel

strokes 17画 ノ イ 亻 亻 仃 伊 佢 佢 俥 俥 傳 傳 傳 優 優 優 優

Point 優 Note the number of horizontal strokes!

優しい	やさしい	kind, gentle
優れた	すぐれた	good, excellent
優秀(な)	ゆうしゅう(な)	excellent
俳優	はいゆう	actor

億

A wad of one billion yen in a trunk completely stole my heart.

おんよみ オク　**くんよみ** —

いみ a hundred million

strokes 15画 ノ イ 亻 亻 仁 亻 佇 佇 倍 倍 倍 倍 億 億 億

Point 億 Note the position of the dots!

一億	いちおく	a hundred million
千億	せんおく	a hundred billion
億万長者	おくまんちょうじゃ	billionaire
巨億	きょおく	billions

偉

I heard that the great man was granted a crown, a certificate of achievement, and a trophy.

おんよみ イ
くんよみ えら(い)

いみ great, important, excellent
strokes 12画 ノ亻亻亻゛伊伊伊偉偉偉偉

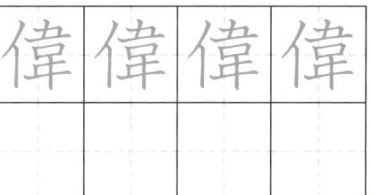

Point
偉
Do not protrude!

偉い	えらい	great
偉人	いじん	great person, hero
偉大(な)	いだい(な)	great
偉業	いぎょう	a great achievement
偉材	いざい	exceptional talent

備

Soldiers built up defenses at fortifications and stood ready for the enemy.

おんよみ ビ
くんよみ そな(える)・そな(わる)

いみ to prepare, to provide, to equip
strokes 12画 ノ亻亻゛゛伊伊伊伊備備備

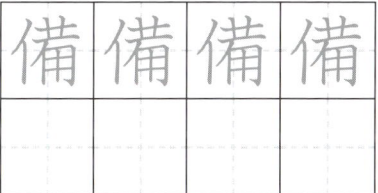

Point
備
Note the number of horizontal strokes!

備える	そなえる	to prepare
備品	びひん	equipment, furniture
準備	じゅんび	preparation
警備	けいび	guard
設備	せつび	facility

偶

I chanced to see my friend who was carrying many shopping bags.

おんよみ グウ
くんよみ —

いみ figure, chance, accident
strokes 11画 ノ亻亻゛伊伊伊偶偶偶

Point
偶
Do not protrude!

配偶者	はいぐうしゃ	spouse
偶然	ぐうぜん	chance
偶発	ぐうはつ	accidental occurrence
偶数	ぐうすう	even number
偶像	ぐうぞう	idol

111

側

I was standing by the armored knight who was holding a big spear.

おんよみ ソク
くんよみ がわ

いみ side, one side
strokes 11画 ノ　イ　イ　イ𠆢　但　但　俱　俱　俱　側

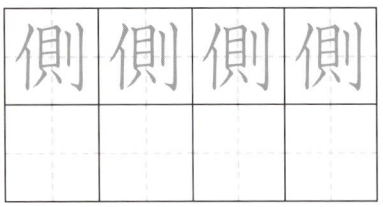

Note the similar characters!
×則
×測

側面	そくめん	side
縁側	えんがわ	veranda
内側	うちがわ	inside
裏側	うらがわ	backside
片側	かたがわ	one side

傾

I put both my arms forward to stop the building from tilting.

おんよみ ケイ
くんよみ かたむ(く)・かたむ(ける)

いみ to lean, to slant, to decline
strokes 13画 ノ　イ　イ　化　化　化　仟　佰　佰　佰　傾　傾　傾

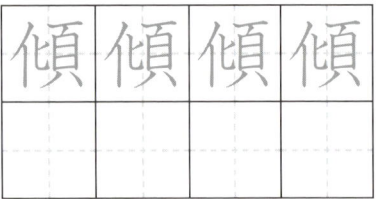

Note the similar characters!
×化
×頃

傾く	かたむく	to lean, to slant, to tilt
傾斜	けいしゃ	inclination, slant
傾向	けいこう	tendency, trend
傾聴	けいちょう	listening attentively
傾倒	けいとう	commitment

徒

Children started to dash in a footrace as soon as they heard the signal-gun.

おんよみ ト
くんよみ ―

いみ walk, fruitless, person
strokes 10画 ノ　ク　イ　彳　彳　𢓅　彷　徒　徒　徒

Do not protrude!

生徒	せいと	student
徒歩	とほ	walk, going on foot
徒競走	ときょうそう	footrace
徒労	とろう	fruitless effort
暴徒	ぼうと	mob

従

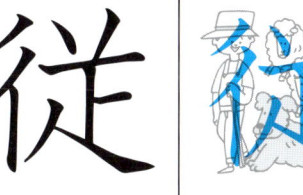

Sheep formed a flock by following a shepherd and a sheep dog.

おんよみ ジュウ・ショウ・ジュ
くんよみ したが(う)・したが(える)

いみ to obey, to follow, from
strokes 10画　ノ ク 彳 彳 彳' 彴 従 徉 従 従

Point
従
Note the position of the dots!

従う	したがう	to follow, to obey
従業員	じゅうぎょういん	employee
従容	しょうよう	calm
従事	じゅうじ	engagement
服従	ふくじゅう	submission

律

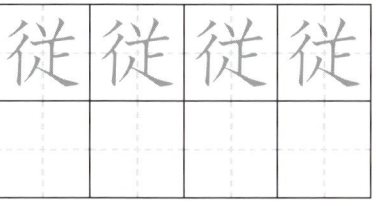

The soldier raised the flag according to regulations.

おんよみ リツ・リチ
くんよみ —

いみ to regulate, law
strokes 9画　ノ ク 彳 彳' 彴 彳白 律 律 律

Point
律
Protrude!

規律	きりつ	discipline, rule, regulation
自律	じりつ	autonomy
律儀(な)	りちぎ(な)	dutiful, honest
法律	ほうりつ	law
律動的(な)	りつどうてき(な)	rhythmic

術

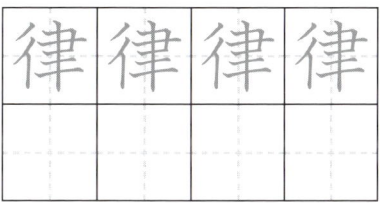

The surgery was performed by two surgeons.

おんよみ ジュツ
くんよみ —

いみ art, skill, way, means, trap
strokes 11画　ノ ク 彳 彳 彳' 彴 休 休 術 術 術

Point
術
Note the position of the dot!

技術	ぎじゅつ	technique
芸術	げいじゅつ	art
手術	しゅじゅつ	operation, surgery
武術	ぶじゅつ	martial art
話術	わじゅつ	narrative skill

113

得

I have got a good opportunity to lie in the sun under a sunshade.

おんよみ トク
くんよみ え(る)・う(る)

いみ to get, to acquire, to understand　**strokes** 11画　ノ ク 彳 彳 犭 犭 犭 得 得 得 得

Point 得 ← Do not protrude!

得る	える	to get	京都の情報を得る。
得意(な)	とくい(な)	proud, good	彼は料理が得意だ。
所得	しょとく	income	所得に対する税を払う。
納得	なっとく	understanding	その説明だけでは納得がいかない。
説得	せっとく	persuasion	病院に行くように、父を説得した。
得点	とくてん	mark, score	テストの得点が上がった。

待

The Buddhist priest waits for daybreak, chanting a sutra.

おんよみ タイ
くんよみ ま(つ)

いみ to wait, to depend　**strokes** 9画　ノ ク 彳 彳 彳 社 待 待 待

Point 待 ← ×特　← ×得　Note the similar characters!

待つ	まつ	to wait	次の電車まで30分待つ。
期待	きたい	expectation	父の期待に応えようと、勉強する。
招待	しょうたい	invitation	友人の結婚式に招待された。
待機	たいき	standing by	雨が止むまで自宅で待機する。
待望の	たいぼうの	long-awaited	待望の赤ちゃんが生まれる。
接待	せったい	reception	取引先から接待を受ける。

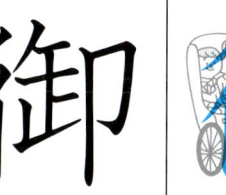 

A coachman on the box seat drove two passengers, handling the reins of the horse well.

おんよみ ギョ・ゴ
くんよみ おん

いみ to control, to govern, noble
strokes 12画 ノ ノ ィ ィ ィ ㇓ ㇓ ㇓ ㇓ 御 御 御

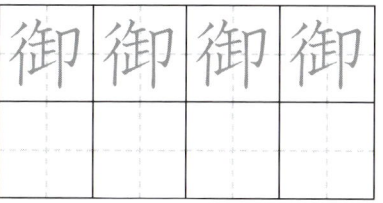

Point
御
↑
Do not protrude!

制御	せいぎょ	control
御者	ぎょしゃ	coachman
御社	おんしゃ	your company
御中	おんちゅう	dear
防御	ぼうぎょ	defense

My husband who is carrying a hoe is a very hard working man.

おんよみ フ・フウ
くんよみ おっと

いみ husband, man
strokes 4画 一 二 ヲ 夫

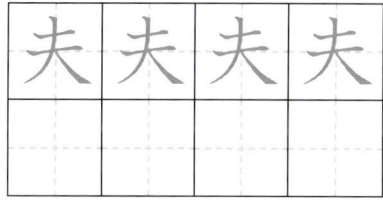

Point
夫
Protrude!

夫妻	ふさい	husband and wife
夫婦	ふうふ	husband and wife
夫	おっと	husband
大丈夫	だいじょうぶ	all right, OK
工夫	くふう	ingenuity, idea

My husband has a name tag tied to his hoe so as not to lose it.

おんよみ シツ
くんよみ うしな(う)

いみ to lose, to miss
strokes 5画 ノ ノ 二 ヲ 失

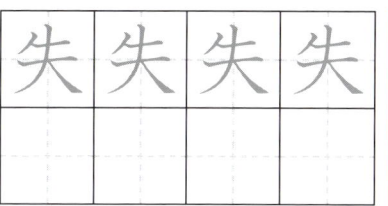

Point
失 ×天
  ×矢
Note the similar characters!

失う	うしなう	to lose
失業	しつぎょう	unemployment
失恋	しつれん	lost love
紛失	ふんしつ	loss
失望	しつぼう	disappointment

The *samurai* stood at the center of the enemy with a sword and a spear.

おんよみ オウ
くんよみ ―

いみ center, middle　strokes 5画　丨 冂 冂 央 央

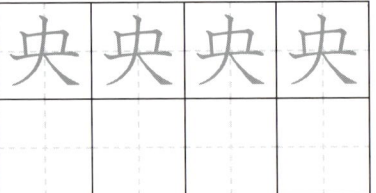

央
Protrude!

| 中央 | ちゅうおう | center |
| 震央 | しんおう | epicenter |

I decided what to wear and what to carry according to the weather.

おんよみ コウ
くんよみ そうろう

いみ to wait, to ask, sign, season　strokes 10画　丿 亻 亻 仁 𠂉 亻𠂉 侯 侯 候 候

天候	てんこう	weather
候補	こうほ	candidate
兆候	ちょうこう	sign
気候	きこう	climate
測候所	そっこうじょ	weather station

A monk holding a candle found a nun wearing a veil.

おんよみ シュウ・シュ
くんよみ おさ(める)・おさ(まる)

いみ to master, to learn, to regulate　strokes 10画　丿 亻 亻 亻 𠂉 攸 攸 修 修 修

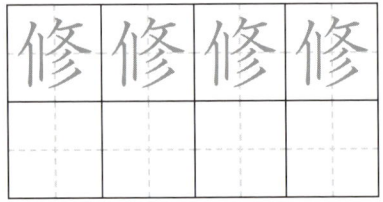

修
Note the position of the dots!

修める	おさめる	to master
修理	しゅうり	fixing, repair
修行	しゅぎょう	training
修道士	しゅうどうし	monk
改修	かいしゅう	improvement

砂

There was little snow left on the ground at the ski resort; it was mostly sand.

おんよみ サ・シャ　　**くんよみ** すな

いみ sand

strokes 9画　一 ア ア 石 石 石 砂 砂 砂

砂漠	さばく	desert
土砂	どしゃ	earth and sand
砂浜	すなはま	sandy beach
砂場	すなば	sandbox

研

I put a stone in front of a *shinto* shrine's gate to wish myself good luck.

おんよみ ケン　　**くんよみ** と(ぐ)

いみ to sharpen, to wash, to polish

strokes 9画　一 ア ア 石 石 石 研 研 研

Point  Do not protrude!

研ぐ	とぐ	to grind, to sharpen
研究	けんきゅう	research
研磨	けんま	grinding, polishing
研修	けんしゅう	study, training

収

The man pushed his stuff into a closet forcefully to store everything.

おんよみ シュウ　　**くんよみ** おさ(める)・おさ(まる)

いみ to store, to put

strokes 4画　丨 丩 収 収

Point 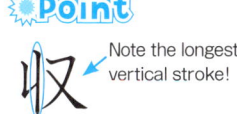 Note the longest vertical stroke!

収める	おさめる	to put, to store
収穫	しゅうかく	crop, harvest
収入	しゅうにゅう	income
回収	かいしゅう	callback, collection

取

I got information by bending my ear toward the people.

おんよみ シュ　　**くんよみ** と(る)

いみ to take, to get

strokes 8画　一 丆 丆 F 耳 耳 取 取

取る	とる	to take, to get
取得	しゅとく	acquisition
取材	しゅざい	collecting material
採取	さいしゅ	picking

枚

A girl sitting on a chair saw one leaf floating away from the tree.

おんよみ マイ　　**くんよみ** —

いみ sheet, piece, slice　　**strokes** 8画　　一 十 オ 木 朳 朾 枚 枚

枚数	まいすう	the number of sheets
十枚	じゅうまい	ten sheets
枚挙	まいきょ	enumeration
大枚	たいまい	a large sum (of money)

柱

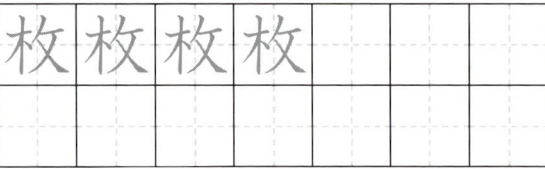

We cut down the tree next to our house and created a solid pillar.

おんよみ チュウ　　**くんよみ** はしら

いみ pillar, post　　**strokes** 9画　　一 十 オ 木 朴 村 杧 桂 柱

Point 柱 Note the longest horizontal stroke!

柱	はしら	pillar
電柱	でんちゅう	utility pole
門柱	もんちゅう	gatepost
大黒柱	だいこくばしら	the mainstay

杯

I drink a glass of liquor while looking at a beautiful tree.

おんよみ ハイ　　**くんよみ** さかずき

いみ cup, glass　　**strokes** 8画　　一 十 オ 木 朴 村 杯 杯

Point 杯 Do not protrude!

祝杯	しゅくはい	celebratory drink
乾杯	かんぱい	toast
杯	さかずき	cup for alcoholic drink
苦杯	くはい	bitter cup

枯

The tree that I put in the flowerpot died immediately.

おんよみ コ　　**くんよみ** か(れる)・か(らす)

いみ to die, to dry out　　**strokes** 9画　　一 十 オ 木 朴 村 村 枯 枯

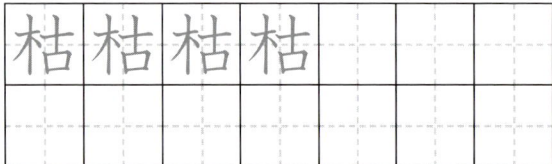

枯れる	かれる	to die, to dry out
栄枯	えいこ	rise and fall
枯れ木	かれき	dead tree
枯渇	こかつ	depletion

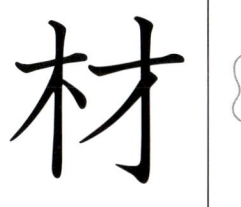 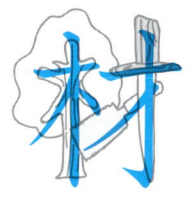

I made a knife using a tree branch that I sawed as material.

おんよみ ザイ
くんよみ —

いみ wood, lumber, material strokes 7画 一 十 才 木 村 材

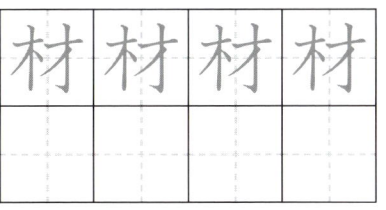

Point
材 ←×林
　 ←×杯
Note the similar characters!

材木	ざいもく	lumber
材料	ざいりょう	material
素材	そざい	raw material
資材	しざい	stuff
人材	じんざい	person of talent

A girl had talks with the tree, with her eyes wide open.

おんよみ ソウ・ショウ
くんよみ あい

いみ phase, each other, Minister strokes 9画 一 十 才 木 札 机 相 相 相

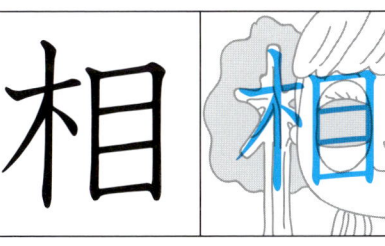

Point
相
Note the number of horizontal strokes!

相談	そうだん	consultation, talks
首相	しゅしょう	the Prime Minister
相手	あいて	companion, partner
世相	せそう	social conditions
真相	しんそう	the truth

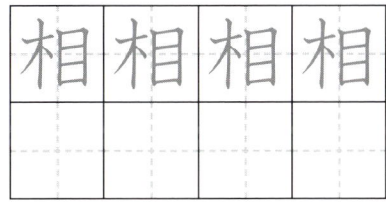 

Roots that spread underground support the tree.

おんよみ コン
くんよみ ね

いみ root strokes 10画 一 十 才 木 朷 朾 柜 根 根 根

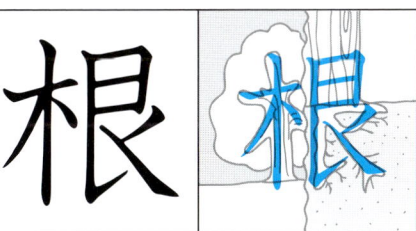

Point
根
Do not protrude!

根拠	こんきょ	ground, evidence
根菜	こんさい	root vegetables
屋根	やね	roof
球根	きゅうこん	bulb
根底	こんてい	basis, foundation

119

株

I cut down a tree and thrust an ax into the stump.

おんよみ かぶ　**くんよみ** —

いみ stump, stock

strokes 10画 一 十 オ 木 木 朴 朴 杵 株 株

Point 株 ← Protrude!

株式	かぶしき	stock
株価	かぶか	stock price
古株	ふるかぶ	old stump, old-timer
切り株	きりかぶ	stump

格

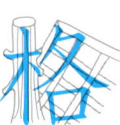

I cut down a tree and crossed it into the form of a lattice.

おんよみ カク・コウ　**くんよみ** —

いみ rule, status, grammatical case

strokes 10画 一 十 オ 木 木 杦 柊 枚 格 格

Point 格 ←×枯　←×洛　Note the similar characters!

性格	せいかく	character
資格	しかく	qualification
格子	こうし	grid, lattice
主格	しゅかく	nominative case

極

A witch was by a tree studying how to fly on a snowboard instead of on a broomstick.

おんよみ キョク・ゴク　**くんよみ** きわ(める)・きわ(まる)・きわ(み)

いみ to peak, top, peak, extremely

strokes 12画 一 十 オ 木 木 杠 杯 杯 柯 極 極 極

Point 極 Do not protrude!

極める	きわめる	to reach the top
極力	きょくりょく	as much as possible
極上	ごくじょう	best
極限	きょくげん	(the utmost) limit

械

Heavy machinery was used to cut down the tree.

おんよみ カイ　**くんよみ** —

いみ mechanism, device

strokes 11画 一 十 オ 木 木 杦 杯 栻 械 械 械

Point 械 Do not connect!

機械	きかい	machine, machinery
器械	きかい	instrument, tool

橋

There was a nice bridge by the tree.

おんよみ キョウ　　**くんよみ** はし

いみ bridge

strokes 16画　一 十 オ 木 木 杧 杧 杯 杯 栌 棒 棒 橋 橋 橋 橋

Point Do not protrude!

橋	はし	bridge
橋梁	きょうりょう	bridge
陸橋	りっきょう	overbridge, overpass
桟橋	さんばし	pier

標

A traveler put his trunk down and looked at the signpost by the tree.

おんよみ ヒョウ　　**くんよみ** ―

いみ sign, guide

strokes 15画　一 十 オ 木 木 杧 杧 枦 杯 枦 栖 標 標 標 標

標識	ひょうしき	sign, signpost
標準	ひょうじゅん	standard
目標	もくひょう	goal
指標	しひょう	index, indicator

機

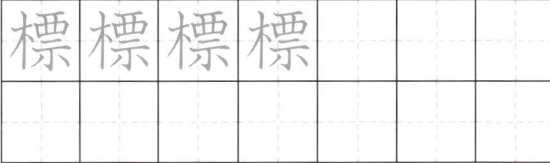

I had a chance to come across the beautiful design that was made of trees.

おんよみ キ　　**くんよみ** はた

いみ loom, machine, opportunity

strokes 16画　一 十 オ 木 木 杧 杧 杙 杙 榜 榜 橀 橀 機 機 機

Point  Note the position of the dots!

機能	きのう	function
飛行機	ひこうき	airplane
機織り	はたおり	weaving
機会	きかい	chance, opportunity

構

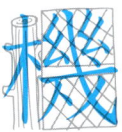

People cut down the trees and built a castle.

おんよみ コウ　　**くんよみ** かま(える)・かま(う)

いみ to construct, to get ready, structure

strokes 14画　一 十 オ 木 木 杧 杧 栉 構 構 構 構 構 構

Point Note the number of horizontal strokes!

構える	かまえる	to get ready
構造	こうぞう	structure
構成	こうせい	formation
構築	こうちく	construction

横

I collected firewood and made a bonfire by a tree.

おんよみ オウ
くんよみ よこ

いみ width, side, horizontall, violent
strokes 15画 一十才木木朾朾栟栟栟構構横横横

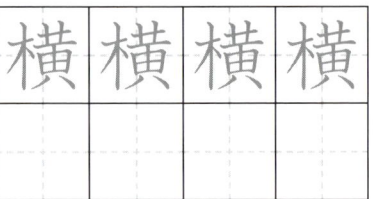

Point
横
Do not protrude!

横断	おうだん	crossing
縦横	じゅうおう	length and width
横綱	よこづな	(sumo) grand champion
横暴(な)	おうぼう(な)	oppressive
横顔	よこがお	profile

植

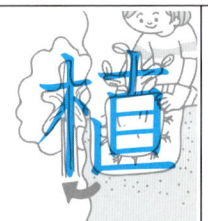

The garden tree that had been planted years ago has been growing very healthily.

おんよみ ショク
くんよみ う(える)・う(わる)

いみ to plant
strokes 12画 一十才木木朾朾柿柿植植植

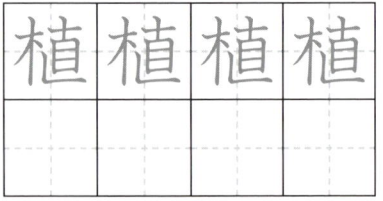

Point
植
Do not connect!

植える	うえる	to plant
植物	しょくぶつ	plant
植樹	しょくじゅ	planting a tree
植林	しょくりん	afforestation
移植	いしょく	transplantation

果

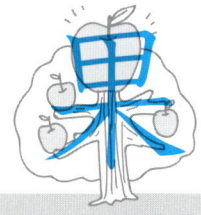

The tree bore a lot of fruit.

おんよみ カ
くんよみ は(たす)・は(てる)・は(て)

いみ fruit, to achieve, to be over
strokes 8画 一口日旦早果果

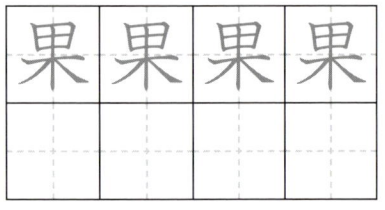

Point
果
Do not protrude!

果たす	はたす	to achieve, to fulfill
果てる	はてる	to be over
果樹	かじゅ	fruit tree
結果	けっか	result
効果	こうか	effect

Above the tree, there was a housing complex for birds.

おんよみ シュウ
くんよみ あつ（まる）・あつ（める）・つど（う）

いみ to gather, to collect, to meet **strokes** 12画 ノ 亻 イ 亻 什 什 隹 隹 隹 集 集 集

Point
集 ← Note the position of the dots!

集まる	あつまる	to gather	正月に家族全員が集まる。
集合	しゅうごう	assembly, gathering	集合する場所を確認する。
集中	しゅうちゅう	concentration	集中して、彼の話を聞いた。
募集	ぼしゅう	recruitment	店員を募集する。
集団	しゅうだん	group	集団に分かれて行動する。
詩集	ししゅう	collection of poems	図書館で詩集を借りる。

I stood on the tree and leaned over the wall.

おんよみ ジョウ
くんよみ の（る）・の（せる）

いみ to ride, to board, multiplication **strokes** 9画 ノ 二 三 千 乒 乒 乖 乖 乗

Point
乗 ← Note the longest horizontal stroke!

乗る	のる	to board, to ride	タクシーに乗る。
乗車	じょうしゃ	ride	駆け込んで乗車することは危険だ。
搭乗	とうじょう	boarding	飛行機の搭乗のための手続きをする。
乗馬	じょうば	horseback riding	旅先で乗馬をした。
乗客	じょうきゃく	passenger	夜行バスの乗客はみんな眠っていた。
便乗	びんじょう	getting a lift	友人の車に便乗させてもらう。

123

I stood on the tree and held the treaty document high.

おんよみ ジョウ
くんよみ ―

いみ twig, treaty, logic　strokes 7画　ノ ク タ 冬 冬 条 条

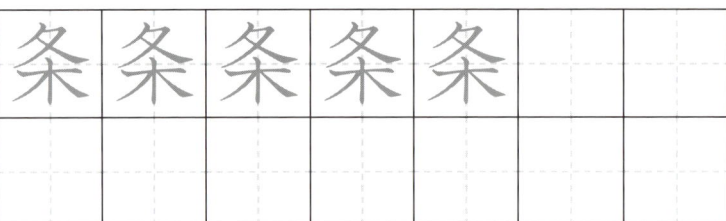

Point

条 ← Do not connect!

条件	じょうけん	condition, terms	条件のよい仕事を探す。
条約	じょうやく	treaty	条約を締結する。
箇条書き	かじょうがき	itemization	文章の一部を箇条書きに直す。
条理	じょうり	logic, reason	彼のやり方は条理に反している。
条文	じょうぶん	provision	条文を読んで法律を学ぶ。
条例	じょうれい	ordinance	条例を制定する。

We needed many workers and pieces of heavy equipment to construct the building.

おんよみ チク
くんよみ きず(く)

いみ to build, to construct　strokes 16画　ノ ト 亇 竹 竹 竹 竹 竺 笁 筑 筑 筑 築 築 築

Point

築 ← Do not connect!

築く	きずく	to build	幸せな家庭を築く。
建築	けんちく	construction	近所にマンションが建築される。
新築	しんちく	new construction	新築の家を買う。
修築	しゅうちく	repair of a building	寺の修築のための工事をする。
改築	かいちく	rebuilding	両親の家を改築することにした。
構築	こうちく	construction	データベースを構築する。

I did stretching exercises on the tree.

おんよみ ジュウ・ニュウ
くんよみ やわ(らか)・やわ(らかい)

いみ soft, flexible　**strokes** 9画　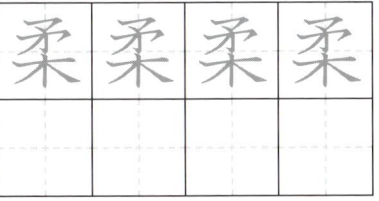

Note the longest horizontal stroke!

柔道	じゅうどう	judo
柔和(な)	にゅうわ(な)	gentle
柔らかい	やわらかい	soft
柔軟(な)	じゅうなん(な)	flexible
柔順	じゅうじゅん	obedience

 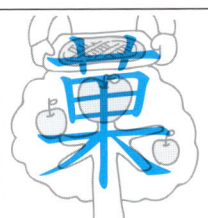

I baked a pie using fruits that were produced by the tree.

おんよみ カ
くんよみ ―

いみ fruit, confectionery　**strokes** 11画　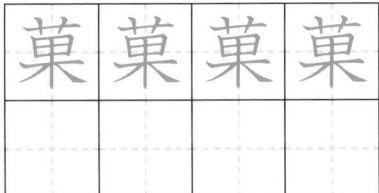

Point
菓
Do not protrude!

菓子	かし	confectionery
製菓	せいか	confectionery, production
氷菓	ひょうか	ice cream
冷菓	れいか	frozen dessert
茶菓	さか・ちゃか	refreshments

There was a restaurant located beyond the tree that was run by squirrels.

おんよみ ギョウ・ゴウ
くんよみ わざ

いみ action, study, karma　**strokes** 13画　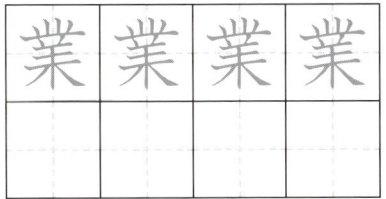

Point
業
Note the position of the dots!

業務	ぎょうむ	business
業績	ぎょうせき	achievement
業	ごう	karma
授業	じゅぎょう	class, lesson
卒業	そつぎょう	graduation

125

府

I decided to display a scarecrow in front of the government office.

おんよみ フ
くんよみ —

いみ prefecture, public office
strokes 8画 `丶 亠 广 广 广 庁 府 府`

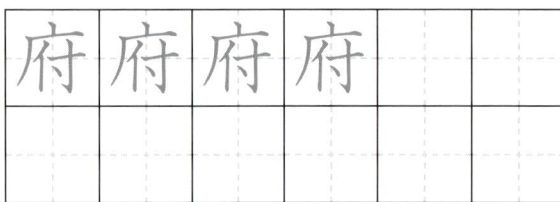

政府	せいふ	government
内閣府	ないかくふ	the Cabinet Office
大阪府	おおさかふ	*Osaka* Prefecture
京都府	きょうとふ	*Kyoto* Prefecture
府知事	ふちじ	prefectural governor

付

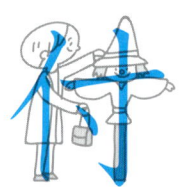

I put an accessory on the scarecrow.

おんよみ フ
くんよみ つ(ける)・つ(く)

いみ to stick, to add
strokes 5画 `ノ 亻 仁 什 付`

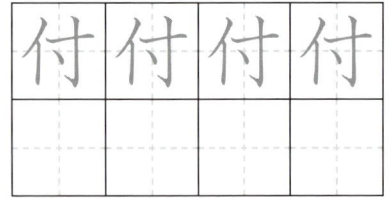

Point ×府 ×村
Note the similar characters!

付ける	つける	to put
交付	こうふ	issue
付属物	ふぞくぶつ	attachment
付録	ふろく	appendix, supplement
寄付	きふ	donation

符

A girl played the piano by reading musical notes.

おんよみ フ
くんよみ —

いみ mark, check, match
strokes 11画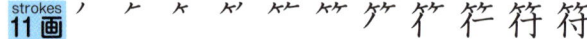

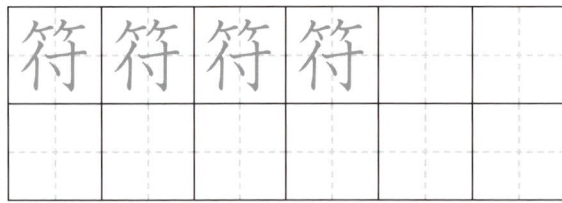

符号	ふごう	mark
音符	おんぷ	musical note
切符	きっぷ	ticket
符合	ふごう	accord
疑問符	ぎもんふ	question mark

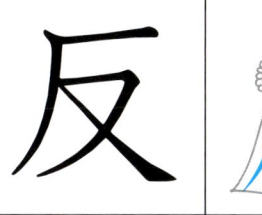 

A shop assistant showed a roll of cloth.

おんよみ ハン・ホン・タン
くんよみ そ(る)・そ(らす)

いみ to oppose, to bend, contrary
strokes 4画 一 厂 反 反

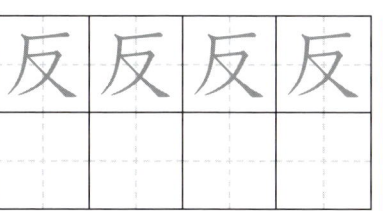

Point
反
Do not protrude!

反る	そる	to warp
反応	はんのう	reaction, response
反物	たんもの	roll of cloth
謀反	むほん	rebellion
反対	はんたい	objection, opposition

People practiced yoga on the bottom of the slope.

おんよみ ハン
くんよみ さか

いみ slope
strokes 7画 一 十 土 扌 坂 坂 坂

急坂	きゅうはん	steep slope
坂道	さかみち	slope
登り坂	のぼりざか	upward slope
坂路	はんろ	slope

A boy made a print from a wood block by pressing paper with ink, a roller and a rubbing pad.

おんよみ ハン
くんよみ ―

いみ version, board, to publish, to print
strokes 8画 丿 ㇉ 片 片 片 版 版 版

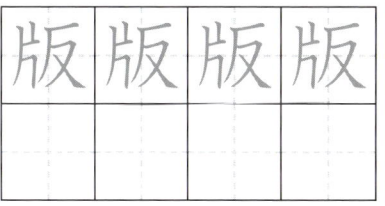

Point
版
Do not connect!

版画	はんが	woodcut, print
映画版	えいがばん	movie version
出版	しゅっぱん	publication
初版	しょはん	the first edition
版権	はんけん	copyright

板

A boy made a print from a wood block that he carved.

- おんよみ ハン・バン
- くんよみ いた

いみ board, plate, plank **strokes** 8画 一 † オ オ 朽 朽 板 板

合板	ごうはん	plywood
看板	かんばん	signboard
羽子板	はごいた	Japanese battledore
黒板	こくばん	blackboard
回覧板	かいらんばん	circular notice

販

A shop assistant showed a roll of cloth in order to make a sale.

- おんよみ ハン
- くんよみ ―

いみ business, trade **strokes** 11画 丨 冂 冃 月 目 貝 貝 貯 販 販 販

販売	はんばい	sale
直販	ちょくはん	direct sales
通信販売	つうしんはんばい	mail-order
市販品	しはんひん	goods on the market
販路	はんろ	market (for goods)

仮

My appearance during the daytime is a temporary identity; I am actually a Superhero.

- おんよみ カ・ケ
- くんよみ かり

いみ temporary, fictitious **strokes** 6画 ノ 亻 仁 仮 仮 仮

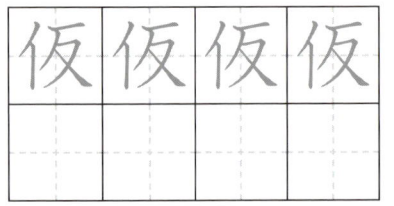

Point — 仮 Do not protrude!

仮定	かてい	supposition
仮病	けびょう	feigned illness
仮免許	かりめんきょ	temporary license
仮面	かめん	mask
仮眠	かみん	doze, nap

The woman was wearing a fur coat and a fur hat.

おんよみ ヒ
くんよみ かわ

いみ skin, surface　strokes 5画　ノ 厂 广 卢 皮

Point

皮
Protrude!

皮革	ひかく	leather
皮膚	ひふ	skin
毛皮	けがわ	fur
皮脂	ひし	sebum
樹皮	じゅひ	bark

The woman's fur coat was torn by a stone rolling down the cliff.

おんよみ ハ
くんよみ やぶ(る)・やぶ(れる)

いみ to tear, to break, to beat　strokes 10画　一 厂 プ 石 石 矴 矿 砕 破 破

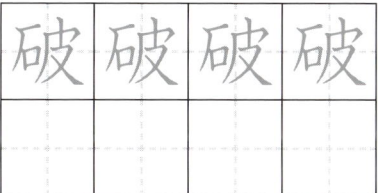

Point

破
Protrude!

破る	やぶる	to break, to tear
破壊	はかい	destruction
破片	はへん	fragment
破産	はさん	bankruptcy
破綻	はたん	breakdown

The woman wearing a fur coat found out that a man was standing far away.

おんよみ ヒ
くんよみ かれ・かの

いみ he, it, that, boyfriend　strokes 8画　ノ ク イ 彳 狩 狩 彼 彼

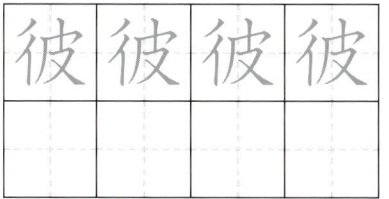

Point

彼 ×仮
彼 ×波
Note the similar characters!

彼岸	ひがん	the equinoctial week
彼氏	かれし	boyfriend
彼女	かのじょ	she, girlfriend
彼ら	かれら	they
彼我	ひが	he and I, they and we

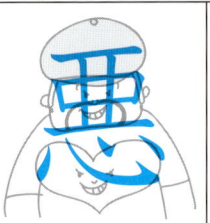

A bad mind makes a thief.

おんよみ アク・オ
くんよみ わる(い)

いみ bad, wrong, vice, to hate

strokes 11画 一 ァ ア 戸 亜 亜 亜 悪 悪 悪 悪

Point
 ← Do not protrude!

悪い	わるい	bad	体調が悪いので帰ります。
悪意	あくい	malice	悪意のある言葉に傷つけられた。
嫌悪	けんお	hatred, hate, disgust	自分を嫌悪してしまう。
悪質(な)	あくしつ(な)	malicious	悪質な犯罪が増えている。
罪悪	ざいあく	crime, sin	嘘をついたことに罪悪感を覚える。
憎悪	ぞうお	hatred	自分を裏切った仲間を憎悪する。

Although my heart was pounding, I stood up to give my opinion.

おんよみ イ
くんよみ ―

いみ feelings, mind, think

strokes 13画 丶 亠 一 亠 立 产 音 音 音 音 音 意 意

意志	いし	will	自分の意志を貫く。
意味	いみ	meaning	言葉の意味を調べる。
意外(な)	いがい(な)	unexpected	ここで彼と会うとは意外だ。
意見	いけん	opinion	彼の意見はとても参考になった。
意欲	いよく	volition, desire	働く意欲が高まる。
誠意	せいい	sincerity	彼の言葉に誠意は感じられなかった。

感

 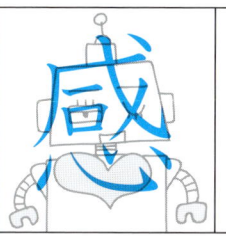

Indeed, this robot has feelings.

おんよみ カン
くんよみ ―

いみ to feel, feeling, sense

strokes 13画 ノ 厂 厂 厂 斤 后 咸 咸 咸 咸 感 感 感

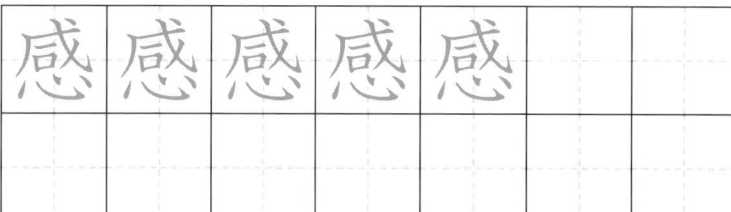

Point

 Note the position of the dots!

感じる	かんじる	to feel	親の愛情を感じる。
感情	かんじょう	feeling, emotion	彼女は感情をおさえきれずに泣き出した。
感想	かんそう	impression	映画の感想を語り合った。
感覚	かんかく	sense	寒くて指の感覚がなくなる。
感謝	かんしゃ	gratitude, thanks	親切にしていただき、感謝しています。
実感	じっかん	real feeling	優勝した実感がわいてきた。

急

 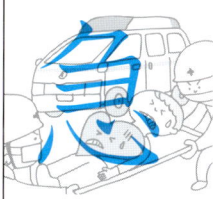

People carried the patient to the ambulance in a hurry.

おんよみ キュウ
くんよみ いそ(ぐ)

いみ to hurry, to rush, suddenly

strokes 9画 ノ ク 々 刍 刍 刍 急 急 急

Point

  Note the number of horizontal strokes!

急ぐ	いそぐ	to hurry	旅の準備を急ぐ。
急行	きゅうこう	express	急行電車に乗る。
至急	しきゅう	urgent	至急ご連絡いたします。
緊急	きんきゅう	emergency, urgency	緊急会議を開く。
急用	きゅうよう	urgent business	急用ができたので、予約をキャンセルした。
急病	きゅうびょう	sudden illness	急病人が出たので、救急車を呼ぶ。

The rice paddy with a scarecrow produced a rich harvest.

- おんよみ ケイ・エ
- くんよみ めぐ(む)

いみ to bless, to give, blessing, benefit

strokes 10画 一 一 一 戸 百 申 申 恵 恵 恵

恵む	めぐむ	to have mercy
恩恵	おんけい	benefit
知恵	ちえ	wisdom
恵方	えほう	lucky direction
互恵	ごけい	reciprocity

It was heart breaking when the two had to separate and go their separate ways.

- おんよみ ヒ
- くんよみ かな(しい)・かな(しむ)

いみ sad, to lament

strokes 12画 ノ 丿 彐 彐 彐 非 非 非 非 悲 悲 悲

Note the number of horizontal strokes!

悲哀	ひあい	sorrow
悲観	ひかん	pessimism
悲しい	かなしい	sad
悲劇	ひげき	tragedy
悲鳴	ひめい	scream, shriek

In the attic, the mouse wished from the heart that the snake would go away right now.

- おんよみ ネン
- くんよみ 一

いみ feeling, to think, to wish

strokes 8画 ノ 人 人 今 今 念 念 念

Do not connect!

念願	ねんがん	one's heart's desire
残念	ざんねん	regret
断念	だんねん	giving up
記念	きねん	commemoration
信念	しんねん	belief

 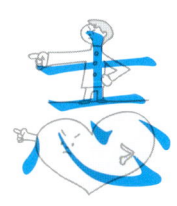

I stood my ground and confirmed my firm intention.

おんよみ シ
くんよみ こころざ(す)・こころざし

いみ to wish, ambition, goal **strokes** 7画 一 十 土 士 志 志 志

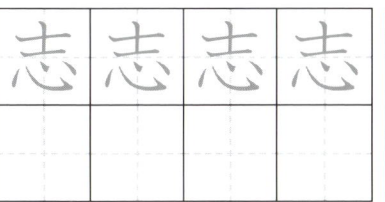 

Point
志
Protrude!

志す	こころざす	to aspire
志望	しぼう	desire, wish
初志	しょし	original intention
意志	いし	will, intention
大志	たいし	ambition

 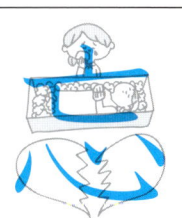

When I lost somebody I loved, I felt so sad as though I had left my heart somewhere else.

おんよみ ボウ
くんよみ わす(れる)

いみ to forget **strokes** 7画 ` 亠 亡 忘 忘 忘

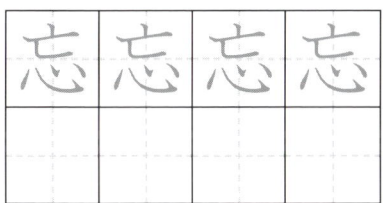 

Point
忘
Do not protrude!

忘却	ぼうきゃく	oblivion
忘年会	ぼうねんかい	year-end party
忘れ物	わすれもの	thing left behind
忘恩	ぼうおん	ingratitude
備忘録	びぼうろく	memorandum

The woman got so fiercely angry from the bottom of her heart that she held up her fist.

おんよみ ド
くんよみ いか(る)・おこ(る)

いみ angry, offended **strokes** 9画 く タ 女 奴 奴 怒 怒 怒

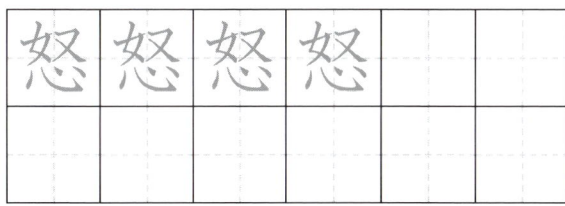

怒る	いかる・おこる	to get angry
怒気	どき	anger
激怒	げきど	fury
怒号	どごう	angry roar
喜怒哀楽	きどあいらく	emotions, feelings

窓

There was a moose with big antlers looking into the house through the window.

おんよみ ソウ
くんよみ まど

いみ window
strokes 11画 `ゝ ヽ 宀 宀 宀 宛 宛 宛 窓 窓 窓`

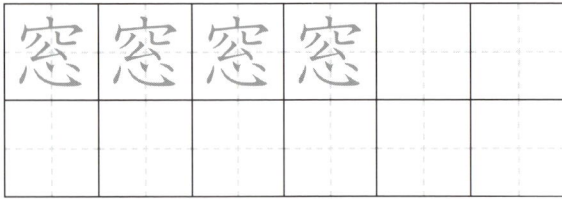

車窓	しゃそう	train window
同窓会	どうそうかい	alumni association
窓口	まどぐち	desk, window
窓辺	まどべ	by the window
出窓	てまど	bay window

恋

Taking shelter from rain under the eaves, a man and a woman fell in love with each other.

おんよみ レン
くんよみ こ(う)・こい・こい(しい)

いみ love, to miss, beloved
strokes 10画 `ゝ 亠 ナ 亦 亦 亦 恋 恋 恋 恋`

Point
恋 ←
Note the position of the dots!

恋愛	れんあい	love affair
恋人	こいびと	lover
恋しい	こいしい	beloved
初恋	はつこい	one's first love
失恋	しつれん	lost love

恐

The boy was scared by the earthquake and got under the desk for safety.

おんよみ キョウ
くんよみ おそ(れる)・おそ(ろしい)

いみ to fear, horrible, terrific
strokes 10画 `一 丁 工 功 巩 巩 巩 恐 恐 恐`

Point
恐 ←
Note the position of the dot!

恐怖	きょうふ	fear
恐喝	きょうかつ	blackmail
恐ろしい	おそろしい	horrible, terrible
恐縮(な)	きょうしゅく(な)	feeling obliged
恐慌	きょうこう	panic

恥

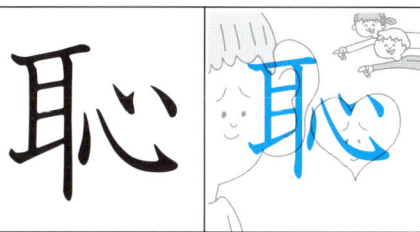

I could hear my heart beating that feel ashamed.

おんよみ チ
くんよみ は(じる)・はじ・は(じらう)・は(ずかしい)

いみ ashamed, shame, to feel ashamed
strokes 10画   一 T F F 耳 耳 耳 恥 恥 恥

Point
恥
Do not protrude!

恥じる	はじる	to feel ashamed
恥辱	ちじょく	humiliation
赤恥をかく	あかはじをかく	to be put to shame
羞恥心	しゅうちしん	a sense of shame
厚顔無恥(な)	こうがんむち(な)	impudent

息

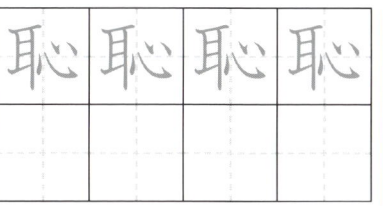 

Your mind feels relaxed when you take a slow breath through your nose.

おんよみ ソク
くんよみ いき

いみ breath, to cease
strokes 10画   ノ 亻 白 白 自 自 自 息 息 息

Point
息
Note the number of horizontal strokes!

息	いき	breath
休息	きゅうそく	rest
寝息	ねいき	sleeper's breathing
消息	しょうそく	one's information, one's news
子息	しそく	son

想

 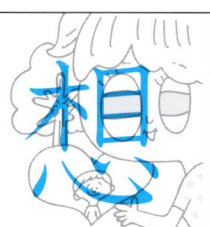

The girl opened her eyes and told a tree about her feelings towards a boy.

おんよみ ソウ・ソ
くんよみ ―

いみ to think, to feel
strokes 13画   一 十 才 木 朷 枊 相 相 相 想 想 想

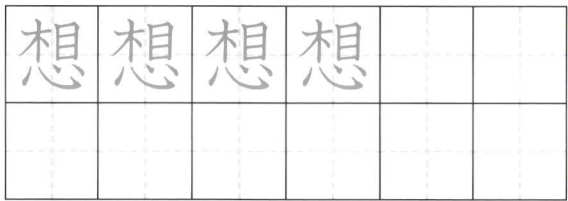

想像	そうぞう	imagination
理想	りそう	ideal
愛想	あいそ	friendliness
思想	しそう	thought, ideology
空想	くうそう	imagination, fantasy

135

忙

When I was extremely busy, I felt as though my mind had gone outside of the box.

おんよみ ボウ
くんよみ いそが(しい)

いみ busy, hectic
strokes 6画 　丶 丶 忄 忄 忙 忙

Point
忙
Do not protrude!

多忙(な)	たぼう(な)	(very) busy
繁忙期	はんぼうき	busy season
忙しい	いそがしい	busy
忙殺	ぼうさつ	being very busy

快

When I sleep well with a good quality pillow, my mind feels refreshed.

おんよみ カイ
くんよみ こころよ(い)

いみ pleasant, happy, rapid
strokes 7画 　丶 丶 忄 忄 忄 快 快

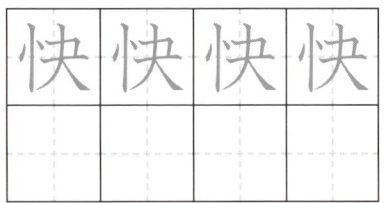

Point
快
Do not connect!

快感	かいかん	pleasure
全快	ぜんかい	complete recovery
快い	こころよい	pleasant
爽快(な)	そうかい(な)	refreshing
快速列車	かいそくれっしゃ	rapid train

怖

My mind froze with horror when I saw a ghost standing under the willow tree.

おんよみ フ
くんよみ こわ(い)

いみ horrible, frightening
strokes 8画 　丶 丶 忄 忄 忙 忙 怖 怖

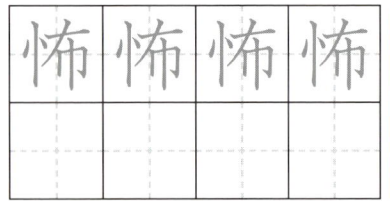

Point
怖
Do not protrude!

恐怖	きょうふ	fear
畏怖	いふ	awe
怖い	こわい	horrible, terrible

情

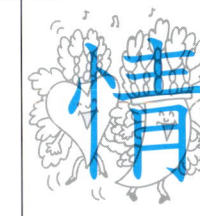

The moon wore a costume and passionately danced the samba.

- おんよみ ジョウ・セイ
- くんよみ なさ(け)

いみ feeling, pity, situation
strokes 11画

丶 丷 忄 忄 忄 忄 佳 佳 情 情 情

Point
情
Note the longest horizontal stroke!

人情	にんじょう	human feelings, humanity
情況	じょうきょう	situation, condition
情け	なさけ	pity, sympathy
情熱	じょうねつ	passion
友情	ゆうじょう	friendship

性

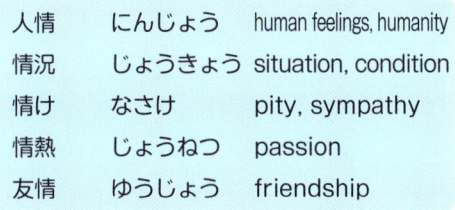

The cow lying on the ground has a very generous character.

- おんよみ セイ・ショウ
- くんよみ ―

いみ nature, disposition, sex, gender
strokes 8画

丶 丷 忄 忄 忄 性 性 性

Point
性
Note the longest horizontal stroke!

性格	せいかく	personality, character
性別	せいべつ	sex, gender
性分	しょうぶん	nature
性能	せいのう	performance
知性	ちせい	intellect

慣

Brushing your teeth after every meal is good for your teeth and heart.

- おんよみ カン
- くんよみ な(れる)・な(らす)

いみ practice, to get used, to habituate
strokes 14画

丶 丷 忄 忄 忄 忄 忄 忄 慣 慣 慣 慣 慣 慣

Point
慣
Protrude!

習慣	しゅうかん	custom, habit
慣例	かんれい	convention, custom
慣れる	なれる	to get used
慣用	かんよう	usage
慣行	かんこう	customary practice

憎

If you start to hate someone, your face will become like a devil.

おんよみ ゾウ　　**くんよみ** にく(む)・にく(い)・にく(らしい)・にく(しみ)

いみ to hate, hateful, hatred　**strokes** 14画　丶丶忄忄忄忄忄忄忄憎憎憎憎憎

Point: Note the position of the dots!

憎悪	ぞうお	hatred
愛憎	あいぞう	love and hate
憎い	にくい	hateful
生憎	あいにく	unfortunately

悩

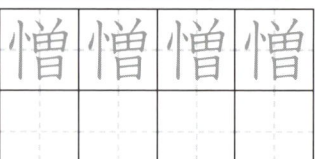

Worrying feels like someone is stabbing the bottom of the heart with a knife.

おんよみ ノウ　　**くんよみ** なや(む)・なや(ます)

いみ to worry, troubled　**strokes** 10画　丶丶忄忄忄忄忄悩悩悩

Point: Do not connect!

悩む	なやむ	to be worried, to worry
苦悩	くのう	agony
悩殺	のうさつ	bewitching

軍

A military tank marched courageously.

おんよみ グン　　**くんよみ** —

いみ army, armed forces, war　**strokes** 9画　丨冖冖冖冃冒宣軍

Point: Protrude!

軍隊	ぐんたい	armed forces
軍人	ぐんじん	soldier
軍事	ぐんじ	military affairs
将軍	しょうぐん	general

写

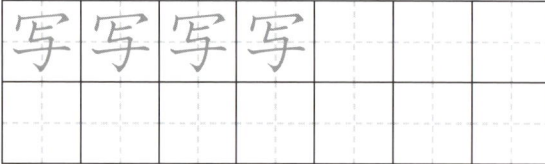

At the sketching event, I drew a landscape while holding a drawing board and a pen.

おんよみ シャ　　**くんよみ** うつ(す)・うつ(る)

いみ to copy, to trace　**strokes** 5画　冖冖写写

写す	うつす	to copy
写真	しゃしん	photograph
描写	びょうしゃ	description
複写	ふくしゃ	copy

138

安

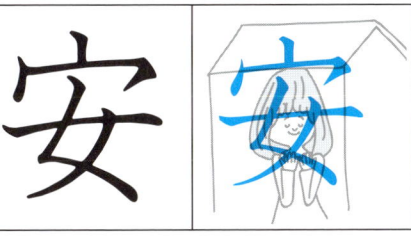

The woman felt safe in her house.

おんよみ アン
くんよみ やす(い)

いみ mild, relieved, cheap　**strokes** 6画　丶 丶 宀 灾 安 安

安全	あんぜん	safety, security
安心	あんしん	relief, security
格安	かくやす	bargain
安静	あんせい	repose
安易(な)	あんい(な)	easy

害

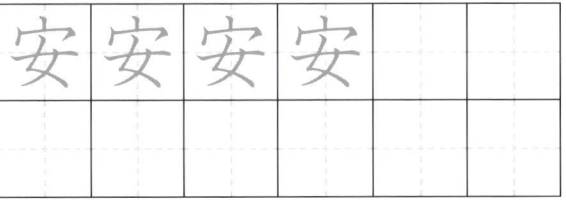

When I came back home, I found that my empty house had been broken into by a burglar.

おんよみ ガイ
くんよみ ―

いみ to harm, to spoil, damage　**strokes** 10画　丶 丶 宀 宀 宀 宇 宇 害 害 害

Point

Note the longest horizontal stroke!

危害	きがい	harm
災害	さいがい	disaster
侵害	しんがい	infringement
障害	しょうがい	barrier, defect
有害(な)	ゆうがい(な)	harmful

宙

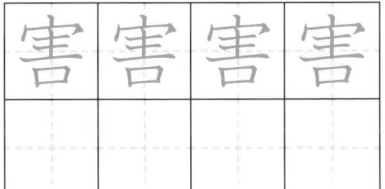

The spaceship took off to fly to space.

おんよみ チュウ
くんよみ ―

いみ space, sky　**strokes** 8画　丶 丶 宀 宀 宀 中 宙 宙

Point

Protrude!

宇宙	うちゅう	space, universe
宙吊り	ちゅうづり	hanging in midair
宙返り	ちゅうがえり	somersault
宇宙船	うちゅうせん	spaceship

宅

I enjoyed a relaxing time at home with my pet dog.

おんよみ タク　　**くんよみ** ―

いみ house, home

strokes 6画　丶丶宀宀宅宅

Point
宅
Do not protrude!

住宅	じゅうたく	housing
宅配	たくはい	home delivery
在宅	ざいたく	being home
帰宅	きたく	coming home

宇

The astronaut enjoyed a tethered space walk around the spaceship.

おんよみ ウ　　**くんよみ** ―

いみ roof, world

strokes 6画　丶丶宀宀宇宇

Point
宇
Do not protrude!

宇宙	うちゅう	space, universe

守

Inside the house, the mother sang a lullaby while holding her baby in her arms.

おんよみ シュ・ス　　**くんよみ** まも(る)・もり

いみ to protect, to defend, guard

strokes 6画　丶丶宀宀守守

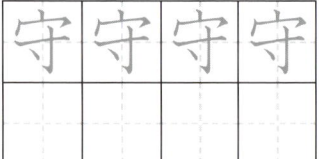

Point
守 ×寸 ×宇
Note the similar characters!

守る	まもる	to defend, to protect
守備	しゅび	defense
留守	るす	absence
子守歌	こもりうた	lullaby

富

That family must be wealthy because they have a large rice paddy and a box of treasures in their house.

おんよみ フ・フウ　　**くんよみ** と(む)・とみ

いみ rich, abound, richness

strokes 12画　丶丶宀宀宁宁官官宫富富富

富裕(な)	ふゆう(な)	wealthy
富む	とむ	to abound with, to be rich
富豪	ふごう	millionaire

容

When I opened the lid, steam came out of the container.

おんよみ ヨウ　**くんよみ** —

いみ shape, to contain

strokes 10画　丶宀宀宀宀宀宀宀容容

Point  Note the position of the dots!

容量	ようりょう	capacity
容姿	ようし	appearance, look
寛容	かんよう	generosity, tolerance
容器	ようき	container

客

I have a curtain in my doorway that visitors pass through when they enter my house.

おんよみ キャク・カク　**くんよみ** —

いみ visitor, guest, client

strokes 9画　丶宀宀宀宀宀客客

Point  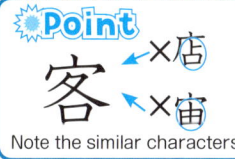 Note the similar characters!

客人	きゃくじん	guest, visitor
乗客	じょうきゃく	passenger
旅客	りょかく・りょきゃく	traveler
観客	かんきゃく	audience

宗

The students of *Ikebana* (flower arrangement) kneel and politely greet the head of their school.

おんよみ シュウ・ソウ　**くんよみ** —

いみ sect, head family, principle

strokes 8画　丶宀宀宀宀宗宗宗

Point   Do not protrude!

宗教	しゅうきょう	religion
宗派	しゅうは	sect, denomination
宗家	そうけ	the head family
宗旨	しゅうし	religious sect, taste

察

A police officer was patrolling the venue of the festival.

おんよみ サツ　**くんよみ** —

いみ to guess, to judge, to suppose

strokes 14画　丶宀宀宀宀宀宀宛宛宛察察察察

Point   Note the similar characters!

観察	かんさつ	observation
視察	しさつ	inspection
警察官	けいさつかん	police officer
推察	すいさつ	conjecture

It was so cold that I dug a hole under the building, and I found two bears hibernating there.

- おんよみ カン
- くんよみ さむ(い)

いみ cold **strokes** 12画 丶 冖 宀 宁 宀 宙 宙 実 実 寒 寒 寒

Point
寒
Note the longest horizontal stroke!

寒気	かんき	cold air
防寒	ぼうかん	protection against cold
寒い	さむい	cold
寒冷	かんれい	chilliness, cold
極寒	ごっかん	extreme cold

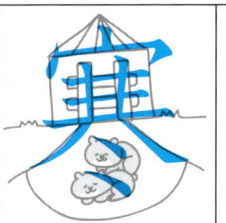

The *bonsai* plant in the house bore some pretty fruits.

- おんよみ ジツ
- くんよみ み・みの(る)

いみ fruit, true, to ripen **strokes** 8画 丶 冖 宀 宁 宁 実 実 実

Point
実
Protrude!

果実	かじつ	fruit
実家	じっか	one's parent's home
実る	みのる	to bear fruit
充実	じゅうじつ	enhancement
口実	こうじつ	excuse

One of the popular things about this hotel is that it has old chests in the rooms.

- おんよみ シュク
- くんよみ やど・やど(る)・やど(す)

いみ hotel, inn, to stay **strokes** 11画 丶 冖 宀 宁 宁 宁 宁 宿 宿 宿 宿

Point
宿
Do not protrude!

宿泊	しゅくはく	lodging, stay
宿屋	やどや	inn
宿る	やどる	to stay
宿題	しゅくだい	homework
合宿	がっしゅく	training camp

定

Through my school days and working experience, I got my own house and settled down there.

おんよみ テイ・ジョウ
くんよみ さだ(める)・さだ(まる)・さだ(か)

いみ to determine, to be fixed, rule **strokes** 8画 ｀ ｀ 宀 宀 宇 宇 定 定

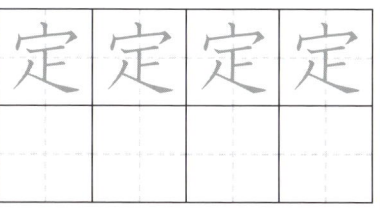

Point
定
Do not protrude!

指定	してい	designation
定規	じょうぎ	ruler
定める	さだめる	to determine
定価	ていか	list price
安定	あんてい	stability

案

When the girl wearing a big hat jumps, good thoughts seem to appear.

おんよみ アン
くんよみ —

いみ plan, proposal, to consider **strokes** 10画 ｀ ｀ 宀 宀 安 安 安 安 案 案

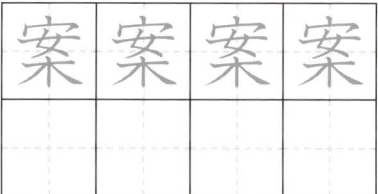

Point
案 ×条
案 ×柔
Note the similar characters!

案件	あんけん	item, matter
提案	ていあん	proposal, suggestion
案内	あんない	guide
名案	めいあん	good idea
発案	はつあん	invention, suggestion

完

It is perfect that I am so healthy at home.

おんよみ カン
くんよみ —

いみ perfect, full, to complete **strokes** 7画 ｀ ｀ 宀 宀 宇 宇 完

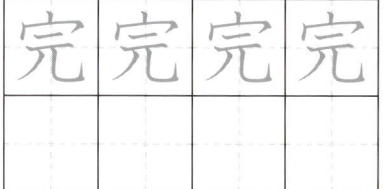

Point
完
Do not protrude!

完全(な)	かんぜん(な)	perfect
完備した	かんびした	fully equipped
完了	かんりょう	completion
完璧	かんぺき	perfection
完結	かんけつ	conclusion

官

A police officer was standing at the *Koban* (police box).

おんよみ カン   **くんよみ** ―

いみ official, officer

strokes 8画   ′ ″ ⇣ ⇡ 宀 宁 官 官

官庁	かんちょう	government office
警察官	けいさつかん	police officer
裁判官	さいばんかん	judge, the bench
器官	きかん	organ

寝

A girl and a dog were sleeping in the bedroom with a standing lamp.

おんよみ シン   **くんよみ** ね(る)・ね(かす)

いみ to go to bed, to lie

strokes 13画   ′ ″ ⇣ ⇡ 宀 宁 宇 宇 宇 宇 宇 寝 寝

Point — Do not connect!

寝室	しんしつ	bedroom
寝具	しんぐ	bedding
寝言	ねごと	talking in one's sleep
早寝	はやね	going to bed early

突

People panicked when a wild boar made a dash for the house.

おんよみ トツ   **くんよみ** つ(く)

いみ to thrust, suddenly

strokes 8画   ′ ″ ⇣ ⇡ 宀 空 突 突

Point — ×空 ×究 Note the similar characters!

衝突	しょうとつ	collision
突然	とつぜん	suddenly
突く	つく	to thrust
突風	とっぷう	gust, blast

究

Two scientists in the laboratory were engaging in their research late into the night.

おんよみ キュウ   **くんよみ** きわ(める)

いみ to master, to inquire into

strokes 7画   ′ ″ ⇣ ⇡ 宀 究 究

Point — Protrude!

研究	けんきゅう	study, research
探究	たんきゅう	inquiry, research
究める	きわめる	to master
究極	きゅうきょく	ultimate

管

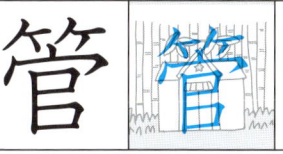

A bamboo forest is the area of jurisdiction for that *Koban* (police box).

おんよみ カン　**くんよみ** くだ

いみ tube, pipe, flute, to control　**strokes** 14画　ノ ㇑ ⺮ ⺮ ⺮ ⺮ 竹 竹 竹 竹 竺 管 管 管

Point 管 ×官 ×営 Note the similar characters!

血管	けっかん	blood vessel
管理	かんり	management
管	くだ	tube
管轄	かんかつ	jurisdiction

筆

I do calligraphy with a very large brush in the bamboo forest.

おんよみ ヒツ　**くんよみ** ふで

いみ writing brush, paint brush　**strokes** 12画　ノ ㇑ ⺮ ⺮ ⺮ ⺮ 竹 笁 笋 筆 筆 筆

Point 筆 ×書 ×律 Note the similar characters!

毛筆	もうひつ	writing brush
鉛筆	えんぴつ	pencil
筆箱	ふでばこ	pencil case
筆記	ひっき	writing

第

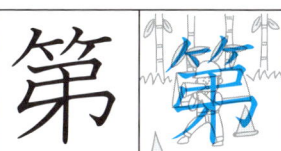

The construction work in the bamboo forest was carried out in the safety-conscious way.

おんよみ ダイ　**くんよみ** ―

いみ order, ordinal　**strokes** 11画　ノ ㇑ ⺮ ⺮ ⺮ ⺮ 竺 笃 第 第

Point 第 ×弟 ×易 Note the similar characters!

第一回	だいいっかい	the first
第二章	だいにしょう	chapter 2
及第	きゅうだい	passing an exam
落第	らくだい	flunk

節

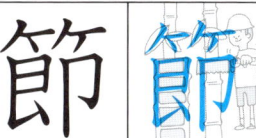

When you split a bamboo tree, you can see the joints inside as well.

おんよみ セツ・セチ　**くんよみ** ふし

いみ knot, joint, time, fidelity　**strokes** 13画　ノ ㇑ ⺮ ⺮ ⺮ ⺮ 竹 笁 笁 筲 節 節 節

節	ふし	knot, joint
関節	かんせつ	joint
季節	きせつ	season
調節	ちょうせつ	adjustment

箱

I sat by the tree and opened my *bento* box (lunch box) which was made of bamboo.

おんよみ — 　くんよみ はこ

いみ box, case, chest

strokes 15画　ノ ㇉ ㇏ ㇏ 竹 竹 竹 竹 竺 笁 笁 筲 箱 箱 箱

Point　箱 ×相　×想
Note the similar characters!

箱庭	はこにわ	miniature garden
巣箱	すばこ	birdhouse
弁当箱	べんとうばこ	lunch box
本箱	ほんばこ	bookcase

笑

The baby showed us a big smile.

おんよみ ショウ　くんよみ わら(う)・え(む)

いみ to laugh, to smile

strokes 10画　ノ ㇉ ㇏ ㇏ 竹 竹 竹 竺 笑 笑

Point　笑　Do not protrude!

爆笑	ばくしょう	explosion of laughter
笑い声	わらいごえ	laughter
微笑み	ほほえみ	smile
苦笑	くしょう	bitter smile

簡

It is easy to open a gate that is made of bamboo.

おんよみ カン　くんよみ —

いみ tag, label, to omit

strokes 18画　ノ ㇉ ㇏ ㇏ 竹 竹 竹 竺 笁 笁 筲 筲 簡 簡 簡 簡 簡

Point　簡 ×間　×問
Note the similar characters!

簡易(な)	かんい(な)	simple, easy
簡単(な)	かんたん(な)	brief, easy, simple
書簡	しょかん	letter
簡潔(な)	かんけつ(な)	brief, concise

居

I sat in front of the table and stretched myself out in the living room.

おんよみ キョ　くんよみ い(る)

いみ to live, to stay

strokes 8画　フ ユ 尸 尸 尸 居 居 居

Point　居　Do not connect!

居住	きょじゅう	residence
同居	どうきょ	living together
居間	いま	living room
転居	てんきょ	house-moving

屋

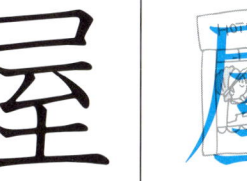

The hot dog vendor is preparing for the shop to open.

おんよみ オク
くんよみ や

いみ house, home, roof
strokes 9画 　一 コ ア 尸 尸 层 屋 屋 屋

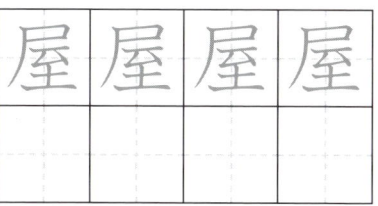

Point
屋
Do not protrude!

家屋	かおく	house
屋上	おくじょう	rooftop
屋根	やね	roof
部屋	へや	room
屋敷	やしき	mansion

層

 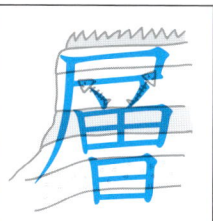

Geological strata are layers of rock or soil that form in stripes on top of one another.

おんよみ ソウ
くんよみ —

いみ layer, overlap, class, rank
strokes 14画 　一 コ ア 尸 尸 尸 层 层 屑 屑 層 層 層 層

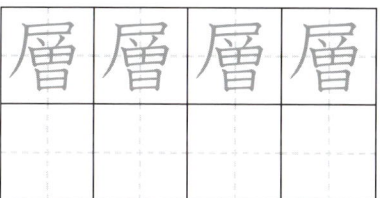 

Point
層
Do not connect!

断層	だんそう	fault
地層	ちそう	stratum
高層の	こうそうの	high-rise
階層	かいそう	class, rank
深層	しんそう	depth

届

In the room, I was going to open the parcel that was delivered.

おんよみ —
くんよみ とど(ける)・とど(く)

いみ to arrive, to reach, to offer
strokes 8画 　一 コ ア 尸 尸 吊 届 届

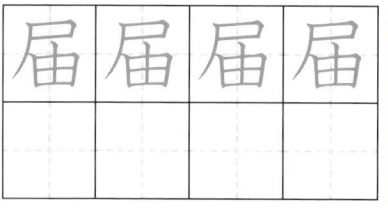 

Point
届 ×由
　 ×宙
Note the similar characters!

届く	とどく	to reach
出生届	しゅっしょうとどけ	birth registration
届け物	とどけもの	article to be delivered
婚姻届	こんいんとどけ	marriage registration

展

I visited the art show that was organized by my friend.

おんよみ テン
くんよみ —

いみ to stretch, to develop, show
strokes 10画 　一 ｺ ｱ ｱ 尸 屏 屏 屏 展 展

Point
展
Note the longest horizontal stroke!

展示	てんじ	exhibition
発展	はってん	development
展望	てんぼう	outlook, prospects
展開	てんかい	expansion
進展	しんてん	progress

労

At the construction site, the worker concentrated on his manual labor.

おんよみ ロウ
くんよみ —

いみ service, trouble, to work
strokes 7画 　、 、 ツ ビ 学 学 労

Point
労
Note the position of the dots!

労働	ろうどう	labor
労力	ろうりょく	effort, labor
苦労	くろう	hardships
心労	しんろう	anxiety
疲労	ひろう	fatigue

栄

The castle, which prospered in the old days, has been left on the other side of the trees.

おんよみ エイ
くんよみ さか(える)・は(え)・は(える)

いみ to prosper, to thrive, honor
strokes 9画 　、 、 ツ ツ 学 学 学 栄 栄

Point
栄 ×楽 ×労
Note the similar characters!

栄える	さかえる	to prosper
繁栄	はんえい	prosperity
栄光	えいこう	glory
栄誉	えいよ	honor
虚栄	きょえい	vanity

148

営

In order to manage a company well, you have to make use of the funds and human resources.

- おんよみ エイ
- くんよみ いとな(む)

いみ to conduct, to run, to manage
strokes 12画
、 ゛ ゛ ⺌ ⺍ 兴 営 営 営 営 営 営

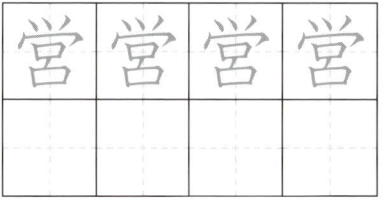 

Point: 営 Do not protrude!

営業	えいぎょう	business, sales
経営	けいえい	management
営む	いとなむ	to conduct, to run
運営	うんえい	management, operation
設営	せつえい	construction

覚

I remembered the faces of three people across the street with my eyes wide open.

- おんよみ カク
- くんよみ おぼ(える)・さ(ます)・さ(める)

いみ to memorize, to realize, to wake up
strokes 12画
、 ゛ ゛ ⺌ ⺍ 兴 学 営 営 覚 覚 覚

覚える	おぼえる	to memorize
錯覚	さっかく	illusion
目覚め	めざめ	waking
覚悟	かくご	resolution
自覚	じかく	(self-)awareness

挙

I raised my hand to ask the speaker some questions.

- おんよみ キョ
- くんよみ あ(げる)・あ(がる)

いみ to raise, to hold, to gather
strokes 10画
、 ゛ ゛ ⺍ 产 兴 兴 挙 挙 挙

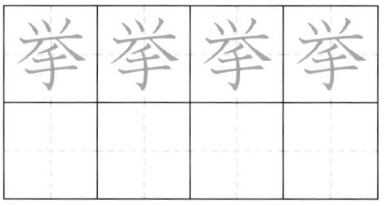 

Point: 挙 Do not protrude!

挙げる	あげる	to raise
挙手	きょしゅ	show of hands
選挙	せんきょ	election
挙式	きょしき	holding a ceremony
快挙	かいきょ	brilliant achievement

厳

The three diamonds were heavily guarded by a man with a spear at the security checkpoint.

- おんよみ ゲン・ゴン
- くんよみ おごそ(か)・きび(しい)

いみ strict, severe, solemn, grave

strokes 17画 　丶丷丷严严严严严严严严严严厳

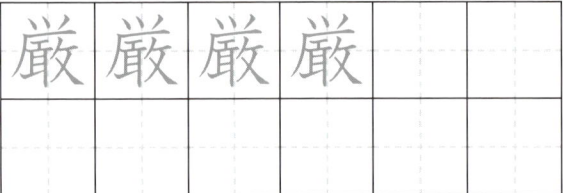

尊厳	そんげん	dignity
荘厳	そうごん	solemnity
厳しい	きびしい	severe, strict
厳正(な)	げんせい(な)	strict, fair
厳重(な)	げんじゅう(な)	strict, rigid

党

People who have a similar way of thinking form a political party.

- おんよみ トウ
- くんよみ ―

いみ party, circle

strokes 10画 　丶丷丷丷丷党党党党党

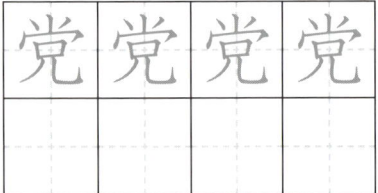

Point
党
Note the position of the dots!

与党	よとう	ruling party
野党	やとう	opposition party
徒党	ととう	faction, gang
政党	せいとう	political party
党首	とうしゅ	party leader

常

I enjoyed sun bathing among the palm trees at the endless summer island paradise.

- おんよみ ジョウ
- くんよみ つね・とこ

いみ always, constant(ly)

strokes 11画 　丶丷丷丷丷党常常常常常

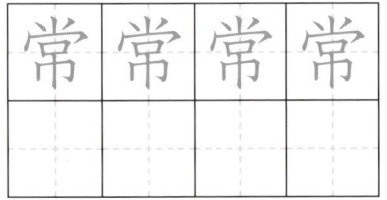

Point
常
Note the position of the dots!

通常の	つうじょうの	common, normal
常に	つねに	always, usually
常夏	とこなつ	endless summer
正常(な)	せいじょう(な)	normal
日常の	にちじょうの	daily

受

The woman opened both her hands to receive something from the man.

おんよみ ジュ　　**くんよみ** う(ける)・う(かる)

いみ to receive, to catch, to get　**strokes** 8画

ノ ノ ヽ ㄣ ㄣ 爫 爫 受 受

受け取る	うけとる	to receive
受信	じゅしん	reception, receipt
受験	じゅけん	taking an examination
受賞	じゅしょう	winning prize

愛

The man kneeled down and showed his devotion and love to the woman.

おんよみ アイ　　**くんよみ** ―

いみ to love, to cherish, to prize　**strokes** 13画

ノ ノ ヽ ㄣ ㄣ 爫 爫 爫 愛 愛 愛 愛 愛

愛情	あいじょう	affection, love, devotion
最愛の	さいあいの	most beloved
愛用	あいよう	favorite
溺愛	できあい	doting love

若

The young man sitting on the stone lifted a barbell with each of his arms.

おんよみ ジャク・ニャク　　**くんよみ** わか(い)・も(しくは)

いみ young, or, like　**strokes** 8画

一 十 艹 艹 艹 若 若 若

Point
若 ← Protrude!

若い	わかい	young
若年	じゃくねん	youth
老若男女	ろうにゃくなんにょ	men and women of all ages
若者	わかもの	young people

苦

I got hurt when I attached an elastic band to my head.

おんよみ ク　　**くんよみ** くる(しい)・くる(しむ)・くる(しめる)・にが(い)・にが(る)

いみ bitter, hard, to suffer　**strokes** 8画

一 十 艹 艹 艹 艹 苦 苦

Point
苦 ← Do not connect!

苦しい	くるしい	hard, painful
苦痛	くつう	pain
苦手	にがて	weak point
苦労	くろう	hardships

151

荷

The man lifted a package using a crane.

おんよみ カ　　くんよみ に

いみ load, cargo, to carry

strokes 10画　一 十 艹 艹 芢 芢 芢 荷 荷 荷

Point
荷 ←×何
荷 ←×可
Note the similar characters!

集荷	しゅうか	collecting cargo
荷物	にもつ	baggage, load
荷札	にふだ	shipping tag
入荷	にゅうか	arrival of goods

薄

Divers wearing thin but firm wet suits and oxygen tanks enjoyed scuba diving with fish.

おんよみ ハク　　くんよみ うす(い)・うす(める)・うす(まる)・うす(らぐ)・うす(れる)

いみ thin, light, to thin

strokes 16画　一 十 艹 艹 艹 芢 芢 芢 芦 蓮 蓮 薄 薄 薄 薄 薄

Point
薄
Note the position of the dots!

薄い	うすい	thin
薄氷	はくひょう	thin ice
薄情	はくじょう	heartlessness
薄着の	うすぎの	lightly dressed

著

I will go to the lecture by the author who wrote the book about *samurai* swords.

おんよみ チョ　　くんよみ あらわ(す)・いちじる(しい)

いみ to write, conspicuous

strokes 11画　一 十 艹 艹 芋 茅 茅 著 著 著 著

Point
著 ←Protrude!

著す	あらわす	to write
著者	ちょしゃ	author
顕著(な)	けんちょ(な)	remarkable
名著	めいちょ	masterpiece

蒸

When I put the steam cooker over the fire, hot steam came out.

おんよみ ジョウ　　くんよみ む(す)・む(れる)・む(らす)

いみ to steam, steam

strokes 13画　一 十 艹 艹 艹 艿 芽 芽 莁 茏 蒸 蒸 蒸

Point
蒸 ←Do not connect!

蒸気	じょうき	steam, vapor
蒸発	じょうはつ	evaporation
蒸し器	むしき	steam cooker
蒸留	じょうりゅう	distillation

菜

A bee was collecting honey in the field of rape blossoms that were spread around the tree.

おんよみ サイ　**くんよみ** な

いみ green vegetable, dish

strokes 11画　一 ｜ ｜ ｜ ｜ ｜ ｜ 苹 苹 菜 菜

Point 菜 — Note the position of the dots!

野菜	やさい	vegetable
山菜	さんさい	edible wild plants
菜の花	なのはな	rape blossoms
前菜	ぜんさい	appetizer

葉

The king who was sitting on the chair in the tree wore a crown made of leaves.

おんよみ ヨウ　**くんよみ** は

いみ leaf, blade

strokes 12画　一 ｜ ｜ ｜ ｜ ｜ ｜ ｜ 葉 葉 葉 葉

Point 葉 — Do not connect!

紅葉	こうよう	autumn colors
葉陰に	はかげに	under the leaves
葉書	はがき	postcard
言葉	ことば	word

夢

The boy was playing with an angel on a cloud in his dream.

おんよみ ム　**くんよみ** ゆめ

いみ dream, ambition, brief

strokes 13画　一 ｜ ｜ ｜ ｜ ｜ ｜ ｜ ｜ 夢 夢 夢 夢

Point 夢 — Do not protrude!

夢中	むちゅう	enthusiasm
悪夢	あくむ	nightmare
初夢	はつゆめ	first dream of the New Year
正夢	まさゆめ	dream that comes true

英

The armored *samurai* hero is standing with both his arms open.

おんよみ エイ　**くんよみ** ―

いみ petal, excellent, the United Kingdom

strokes 8画　一 ｜ ｜ ｜ ｜ ｜ 英 英

Point 英 ×央 ×決 — Note the similar characters!

英語	えいご	English
日英	にちえい	Japan and Britain
英雄	えいゆう	hero
英断	えいだん	wise decision

153

落

A man living on a deserted island opened his mouth and drank a drop of water from a leaf.

おんよみ ラク
くんよみ お(ちる)・お(とす)

いみ to fall, to drop **strokes** 12画 一 ナ ヰ ザ 芦 莎 莎 茨 落 落 落

落ちる	おちる	to drop, to fall
落下	らっか	fall
脱落	だつらく	dropping out
堕落	だらく	corruption

薬

Singing along with the guitar and birds in the trees is the best medicine for me.

おんよみ ヤク
くんよみ くすり

いみ medicine, drug **strokes** 16画 一 ナ ヰ ヰ 艹 甘 苩 苩 消 消 蓮 薬 薬 薬

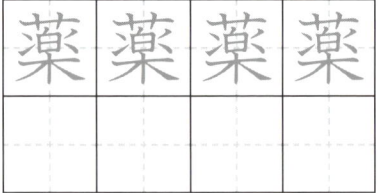
×楽 ×案
Note the similar characters!

薬草	やくそう	herb
薬局	やっきょく	pharmacy
薬指	くすりゆび	ring finger
風邪薬	かぜぐすり	cold medicine
火薬	かやく	gunpowder

病

I went to the hospital because I felt ill.

おんよみ ビョウ・ヘイ
くんよみ や(む)・やまい

いみ illness, disease, to suffer from **strokes** 10画 ` 亠 广 广 广 疒 疔 病 病 病

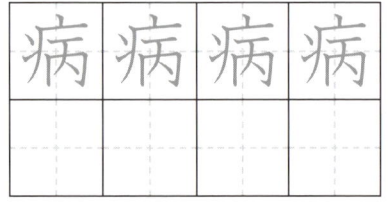
Do not protrude!

病気	びょうき	disease, illness
疾病	しっぺい	disease
病院	びょういん	hospital
看病	かんびょう	nursing
病人	びょうにん	sick person

 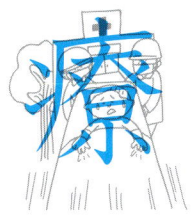

The patient was taken to hospital on a stretcher to receive treatment.

おんよみ リョウ
くんよみ —

いみ to heal, to cure, treatment
strokes 17画

丶亠广广广广疒疒疒疒疗疗疗疗療療療

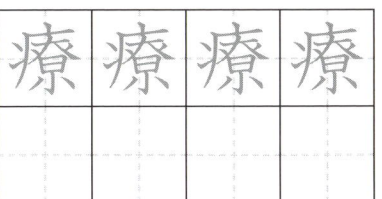

Note the position of the dots!

医療	いりょう	medical care
治療	ちりょう	treatment
診療	しんりょう	medical examination
療法	りょうほう	remedy, therapy
療養	りょうよう	recuperation

 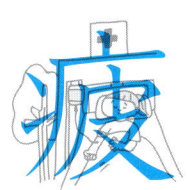

I was hooked up to an intravenous drip at the hospital when I came down with fatigue.

おんよみ ヒ
くんよみ つか(れる)

いみ to be tired, to weaken, fatigue
strokes 10画

丶亠广广广疒疒疒疲疲

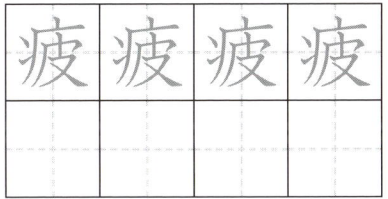

Protrude!

疲労	ひろう	fatigue
疲弊	ひへい	exhaustion
疲れる	つかれる	to be tired

I came to hospital on crutches because I was in pain due to my injury.

おんよみ ツウ
くんよみ いた(い)・いた(む)・いた(める)

いみ painful, sore, to feel pain, pain
strokes 12画

丶亠广广广疒疒疒痛痛痛痛

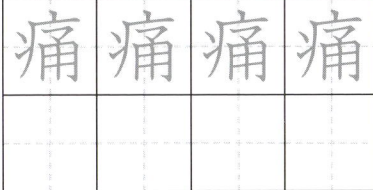

Note the similar character!

胃痛	いつう	stomach pain
苦痛	くつう	pain
痛い	いたい	painful, sore
激痛	げきつう	severe pain
悲痛(な)	ひつう(な)	grievous

155

温

I watered plants inside a greenhouse that was heated by the sun.

おんよみ　オン
くんよみ　あたた(か)・あたた(かい)・あたた(まる)・あたた(める)

いみ　warm, mild, to warm

strokes 12画　丶冫氵沪沪沪涡涡温温温温

温泉	おんせん	hot spring, spa	温泉につかる。
高温	こうおん	high temperature	高温注意報が出ている。
温かい	あたたかい	warm	温かいミルクを飲む。
温厚な	おんこう(な)	gentle	彼はとても温厚な人柄だ。
温室	おんしつ	greenhouse	このトマトは温室で栽培されている。
体温	たいおん	body temperature	体温を測る。

浅

A seagull got a surprise when the ship ran aground in the shallows.

おんよみ　セン
くんよみ　あさ(い)

いみ　shallow

strokes 9画　丶冫氵汁浅浅浅浅

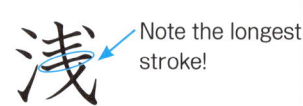

Note the longest stroke!

浅学	せんがく	shallow knowledge	浅学の身ですが、よろしくおねがいします。
浅瀬	あさせ	shallows	浅瀬に船が乗り上げる。
浅薄(な)	せんぱく(な)	superficial	浅薄な知識で話してしまった。
浅知恵	あさぢえ	shallow thought	まさに浅知恵とも言うべきだ。

There are a jellyfish and an octopus with bubbles in the deep sea.

おんよみ シン
くんよみ ふか(い)・ふか(まる)・ふか(める)

いみ deep, profound

strokes 11画

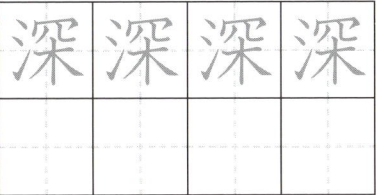

Point 深 ← Do not connect!

深海	しんかい	the deep sea
深夜	しんや	late at night
深手	ふかで	serious wound
深刻(な)	しんこく(な)	serious
水深	すいしん	water depth

 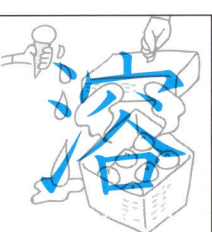

When I opened the lid of the container, hot steam came out and melted the ice cream.

おんよみ ヨウ
くんよみ と(ける)・と(かす)・と(く)

いみ to dissolve, to melt

strokes 13画

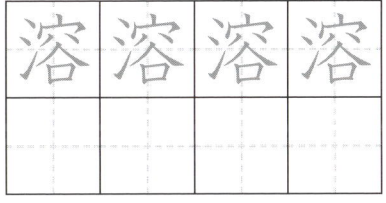

Point 溶 ← Do not connect!

溶液	ようえき	solution (liquid)
溶岩	ようがん	lava
溶ける	とける	to dissolve, to melt
溶解	ようかい	dissolution, melting
溶接	ようせつ	welding

 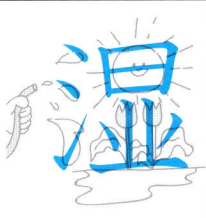

I moistened the soil because I saw flowers wilting under the sunshine.

おんよみ シツ
くんよみ しめ(る)・しめ(す)

いみ wet, to wet, to moisten

strokes 12画

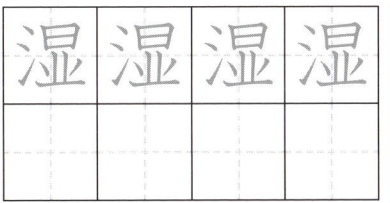

Point 湿 ← Do not protrude!

湿度	しつど	humidity
湿気	しっけ	moisture
湿る	しめる	to wet
除湿	じょしつ	dehumidification
湿地	しっち	marsh

測

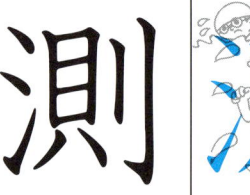 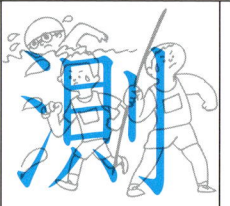

Physical fitness was measured through swimming, running and javelin throwing.

おんよみ ソク
くんよみ はか（る）

いみ to measure, to weigh　**strokes** 12画　丶 丶 丶 氵 泂 泂 泂 洞 浿 浿 測 測

Point

Note the longest vertical stroke!

測る	はかる	to measure	身長を測る。
計測	けいそく	measurement	体重を計測する。
予測	よそく	forecast, prediction	自然災害を予測する。
観測	かんそく	observation	月食を観測する。
憶測	おくそく	speculation	そのことは、彼の憶測にすぎない。
不測の	ふそくの	unexpected	不測の事態に備えておく。

決

A boy dived into the pool in the final race at the swimming competition.

おんよみ ケツ
くんよみ き（める）・き（まる）

いみ to decide, to fix　**strokes** 7画　丶 丶 氵 沪 沪 沖 決

Point

Do not connect!

決める	きめる	to decide	東京を離れることを決める。
決定	けってい	decision	全員一致で決定した。
解決	かいけつ	solution	その問題は、すでに解決した。
決意	けつい	determination	この決意は変わらない。
採決	さいけつ	vote	採決により法案は可決された。
決勝戦	けっしょうせん	final race	決勝戦まで勝ち進む。

消

A firefighter sprayed water to extinguish the fire that came out of the moon.

おんよみ　ショウ
くんよみ　き(える)・け(す)

いみ　to disappear, to extinguish

strokes 10画

Point
消 Do not connect!

消す	けす	to extinguish, to turn off	テレビを消す。
消火器	しょうかき	fire extinguisher	消火器の使い方を教わる。
消費	しょうひ	consumption	消費が落ち込む。
解消	かいしょう	resolution, reduction	ストレスを解消する。
消毒	しょうどく	disinfection	傷口を消毒する。
消滅	しょうめつ	disappearance	伝統文化が消滅する。

減

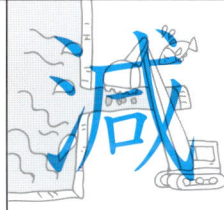

As reclamation of the waterfront continued, the habitat of the fish was reduced.

おんよみ　ゲン
くんよみ　へ(る)・へ(らす)

いみ　to decrease, to reduce

strokes 12画

Point
減 Note the position of the dots!

減る	へる	to decrease, to reduce	貯金が減った。
減少	げんしょう	decrease	売り上げが減少した。
減退	げんたい	decline	体力が減退している。
削減	さくげん	reduction	経費の削減に取り組む。
半減	はんげん	reduction by half	収入が半減した。
減量	げんりょう	loss in weight	減量のため、甘いものを控えている。

159

波

I caught a wave and enjoyed surfing.

- おんよみ ハ
- くんよみ なみ

いみ wave

strokes 8画 　丶　氵　氵　汁　沪　沪　波　波

Note the similar characters!

波浪	はろう	waves
電波	でんぱ	radio wave
津波	つなみ	tsunami
防波堤	ぼうはてい	breakwater
高周波	こうしゅうは	high frequency

泳

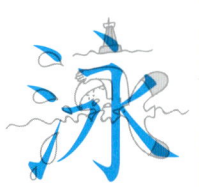

I swam towards the buoy being tossed about by waves.

- おんよみ エイ
- くんよみ およ(ぐ)

いみ to swim

strokes 8画 　丶　氵　氵　汁　汁　泳　泳　泳

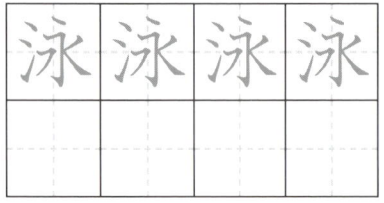

Note the position of the dot!

水泳	すいえい	swimming
競泳	きょうえい	swimming race
背泳ぎ	せおよぎ	backstroke
平泳ぎ	ひらおよぎ	breaststroke
泳法	えいほう	swimming technique

渡

A boy waved down at the person in the canoe while crossing the bridge over a river.

- おんよみ ト
- くんよみ わた(る)・わた(す)

いみ to cross, to go over

strokes 12画 　丶　氵　氵　汁　汁　沪　沪　沪　渡　渡　渡　渡

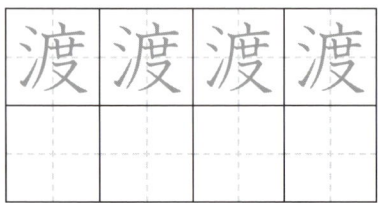

Connect!

渡る	わたる	to cross
渡航	とこう	voyage
譲渡	じょうと	transfer
渡り鳥	わたりどり	migratory bird
渡来	とらい	influx

漁

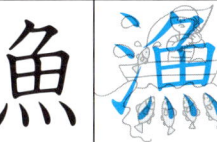

A fisherman caught one fish while the other four fish were watching it sadly.

おんよみ ギョ・リョウ　　**くんよみ** ―

いみ to fish, fishing　　**strokes** 14画　　丶丶冫冫氵汽汽汽渔渔渔漁漁漁

Point 漁 — Note the position of the dots!

漁港	ぎょこう	fishing port
漁業	ぎょぎょう	fishery
漁師	りょうし	fisherman
大漁	たいりょう	good catch of fish

流

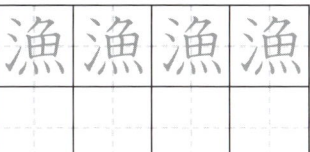 

I enjoyed canoeing going with the flow of the river.

おんよみ リュウ・ル　　**くんよみ** なが(れる)・なが(す)

いみ to flow, to run, through　　**strokes** 10画　　丶丶冫氵氵汘浐浐流流

Point 流 — Do not protrude!

流氷	りゅうひょう	drift ice, ice floe
流浪	るろう	wandering
流れる	ながれる	to flow
流行	りゅうこう	fashion, trend

湖

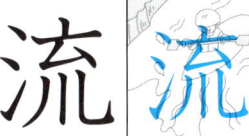

On a night when a big moon appeared in the sky, I rowed my boat out onto the lake.

おんよみ コ　　**くんよみ** みずうみ

いみ lake　　**strokes** 12画　　丶丶冫氵汁汁沽沽沽湖湖湖

湖	みずうみ	lake
湖畔	こはん	lakeside
湖底	こてい	the bottom of a lake
琵琶湖	びわこ	Lake *Biwa*

港

At the port, I tied a ship off with a knot.

おんよみ コウ　　**くんよみ** みなと

いみ port, harbor　　**strokes** 12画　　丶丶冫氵汁汁浐洪洪港港

Point 港 — Note the longest horizontal stroke!

港湾	こうわん	harbor
空港	くうこう	airport
港町	みなとまち	port town
出港	しゅっこう	departure from a port

滴

Water drops spattered when the boy drew water from the well.

おんよみ テキ　　**くんよみ** しずく・したた(る)

いみ drop, to drip　　**strokes** 14画　　丶丶氵氵汁汁汁泸涪涪滴滴滴滴

 Do not protrude!

滴る	したたる	to drip
水滴	すいてき	drop of water
一滴	いってき	one drop
点滴	てんてき	intravenous drip

混

The beach on a sunny day was crowded with people.

おんよみ コン　　**くんよみ** ま(じる)・ま(ざる)・ま(ぜる)・こ(む)

いみ to mix, to be crowded　　**strokes** 11画　　丶丶氵氵沪沪沪汨混混混

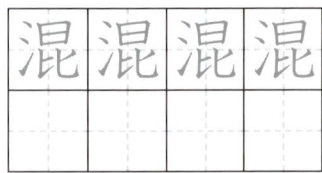

 Do not protrude!

混ざる	まざる	to mix
混雑	こんざつ	congestion
混乱	こんらん	confusion
混沌	こんとん	chaos

漢

The man had a float in a big Chinese river, and held out so that the air was not drained out of it.

おんよみ カン　　**くんよみ** —

いみ man, China　　**strokes** 13画　　丶丶氵氵汁汁汁淉淉淉漢漢漢

 Do not protrude!

漢字	かんじ	Chinese characters
漢方	かんぽう	Chinese medicine
巨漢	きょかん	giant
熱血漢	ねっけつかん	hot-blooded man

酒

I poured *sake* from the bottle into a cup.

おんよみ シュ　　**くんよみ** さけ・さか

いみ liquor, alcohol　　**strokes** 10画　　丶丶氵氵汀汀洒酒酒酒

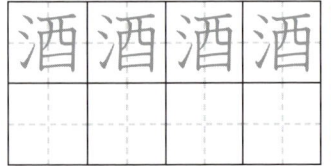

 Connect!

飲酒	いんしゅ	drinking alcohol
酒屋	さかや	liquor store
禁酒	きんしゅ	stopping drinking
日本酒	にほんしゅ	Japanese rice wine, *sake*

162

満

I felt full up to my throat because food and drinks were delivered one after another.

おんよみ マン　　**くんよみ** み(ちる)・み(たす)

いみ to fill, full, whole

strokes 12画　丶 丶 氵 氵 汁 汁 浐 浐 浐 淸 満 満

Point
満
Do not protrude!

満たす	みたす	to fill, to satisfy
満員の	まんいんの	crowded, packed
満足	まんぞく	satisfaction
不満	ふまん	complaint, discontent

湯

A crane was soaking in hot water while the sun was shining.

おんよみ トウ　　**くんよみ** ゆ

いみ hot water

strokes 12画　丶 丶 氵 氵 沪 沪 渭 渭 涓 湯 湯 湯

Point
湯　×場
　　×傷
Note the similar characters!

熱湯	ねっとう	boiling water
銭湯	せんとう	public bath
湯気	ゆげ	steam
湯治	とうじ	hot-spring cure

油

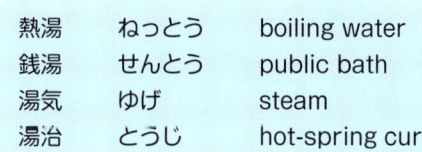

I poured the oil in the pan.

おんよみ ユ　　**くんよみ** あぶら

いみ oil

strokes 8画　丶 丶 氵 氵 汁 油 油 油

石油	せきゆ	oil
給油	きゅうゆ	refueling
油絵	あぶらえ	oil painting
醤油	しょうゆ	soy sauce

洋

A sheep swam in the ocean.

おんよみ ヨウ　　**くんよみ** ―

いみ ocean, large

strokes 9画　丶 丶 氵 氵 沪 沪 泮 洋 洋

Point
洋
Do not protrude!

海洋	かいよう	ocean
西洋	せいよう	the West
洋楽	ようがく	Western music
太平洋	たいへいよう	the Pacific Ocean

注

I filled a glass to the brim with Japanese *sake*.

おんよみ チュウ　　**くんよみ** そそ(ぐ)

いみ to pour, to concentrate　　**strokes** 8画　　丶丶氵氵汁汁注注

Point
注 ← Note the longest horizontal stroke!

注ぐ	そそぐ	to pour
注意	ちゅうい	attention, caution
注文	ちゅうもん	order
注射	ちゅうしゃ	injection

泣

A woman who had her heart broken stood on the cliff and cried hard.

おんよみ キュウ　　**くんよみ** な(く)

いみ to cry, to weep　　**strokes** 8画　　丶丶氵氵汁汁泣泣

Point
泣 ← Note the longest horizontal stroke!

泣く	なく	to cry
号泣	ごうきゅう	wailing
感泣	かんきゅう	being moved to tears
泣き虫	なきむし	crybaby

治

Thanks to a flood-control dam, we don't have to worry about floods even if it rains heavily.

おんよみ ジ・チ　　**くんよみ** おさ(める)・おさ(まる)・なお(る)・なお(す)

いみ to govern, to cure　　**strokes** 8画　　丶丶氵氵氵治治治

Point
治 ← Do not connect!

治める	おさめる	to govern, to reign
政治	せいじ	politics
治安	ちあん	public order
治水	ちすい	flood control

浴

I had a bath in the *onsen* (hot spring) that was welling up in the valley.

おんよみ ヨク　　**くんよみ** あ(びる)・あ(びせる)

いみ to bathe　　**strokes** 10画　　丶丶氵氵氵浴浴浴浴浴

Point
浴 ×容
浴 ×容
Note the similar characters!

浴びる	あびる	to bathe
浴室	よくしつ	bathroom
入浴	にゅうよく	bathing
海水浴	かいすいよく	sea bathing

泊

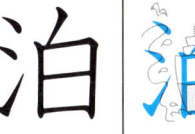 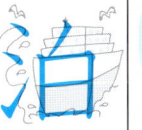

There was a luxury cruise ship lying at anchor in the port.

おんよみ ハク **くんよみ** と(まる)・と(める)

いみ to stay, to lodge

strokes 8画 丶 丶 氵 氵 汨 泊 泊 泊

泊まる	とまる	to stay
停泊	ていはく	anchoring, berthing
外泊	がいはく	staying out overnight
一泊	いっぱく	one overnight stay

汗

There was a rumor that it was so hot that a scarecrow was sweating.

おんよみ カン **くんよみ** あせ

いみ sweat

strokes 6画 丶 丶 氵 氵 汗 汗

Point 汗 ← Do not protrude!

汗腺	かんせん	sweat gland
発汗	はっかん	sweating
冷や汗	ひやあせ	cold sweat
寝汗	ねあせ	night sweat

済

She has finished getting herself ready to swim in the sea with her swimsuit, hat and swimming ring.

おんよみ サイ **くんよみ** す(む)・す(ます)

いみ to finish, to get off

strokes 11画 丶 丶 氵 氵 汀 汈 済 済 済 済

Point 済 Note the number of horizontal strokes!

済む	すむ	to finish
返済	へんさい	repayment
救済	きゅうさい	relief, help
経済	けいざい	economy, economics

洗

Take a shower and wash your body thoroughly with soap.

おんよみ セン **くんよみ** あら(う)

いみ to wash, to cleanse

strokes 9画 丶 丶 氵 氵 汁 汁 泮 洗 洗

Point 洗 ← Protrude!

洗う	あらう	to wash
洗顔	せんがん	washing one's face
洗剤	せんざい	detergent
洗練	せんれん	sophistication

沈

A diver looked at the ship that had sunk to the sea floor.

おんよみ チン　　**くんよみ** しず(む)・しず(める)

いみ to sink, to go down　　**strokes** 7画　　丶 冫 氵 汀 沈 沈

Point: 沈 Connect!

沈む	しずむ	to sink
沈没	ちんぼつ	sinking
沈黙	ちんもく	silence
沈痛(な)	ちんつう(な)	sad, sorrowful

汚

Letting household waste flow into the sea causes marine pollution.

おんよみ オ　　**くんよみ** けが(す)・けが(れる)・けが(らわしい)・よご(す)・よご(れる)・きたな(い)

いみ dirty, filthy, to dirty　　**strokes** 6画　　丶 冫 氵 汙 汚

Point: 汚 Do not protrude!

汚す	よごす	to dirty
汚染	おせん	pollution
汚点	おてん	blemish, blot, stain
汚名	おめい	stigma

涙

A mother shed tears of joy because she found her missing son standing on the doorstep.

おんよみ ルイ　　**くんよみ** なみだ

いみ tear　　**strokes** 10画　　丶 冫 氵 汀 沪 沪 沪 泸 涙 涙

涙腺	るいせん	lachrymal gland
感涙	かんるい	tears of gratitude
涙目	なみだめ	watery eye
涙声	なみだごえ	tearful voice

浮

A child was floating on the sea, clinging to a swim ring.

おんよみ フ　　**くんよみ** う(く)・う(かれる)・う(かぶ)・う(かべる)

いみ to float, careless　　**strokes** 10画　　丶 冫 氵 氵 汀 汀 浮 浮 浮

Point: 浮 Note the position of the dots!

浮く	うく	to float
浮沈	ふちん	ups and downs
浮上	ふじょう	surfacing
浮力	ふりょく	buoyancy

法

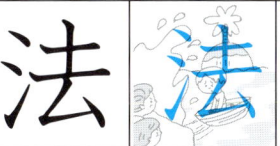

Those people who violated the country's law were deported to an island out in the sea.

おんよみ ホウ・ハッ・ホッ　　**くんよみ** —

いみ law, method, model, rule

strokes 8画　　丶　丶　氵　氵　泟　汢　法　法

法律	ほうりつ	law
作法	さほう	etiquette, manners
法度	はっと	prohibition
寸法	すんぽう	size

清

The moon wearing a night cap washed floors with a mop and kept them clean.

おんよみ セイ・ショウ　　**くんよみ** きよ(い)・きよ(まる)・きよ(める)

いみ pure, clear

strokes 11画　丶　丶　氵　氵　汁　汢　洼　清　清　清　清

Point 清 ← Do not connect!

清流	せいりゅう	clear stream
清潔	せいけつ	cleanliness
清い	きよい	clear, innocent, pure
清浄	せいじょう	cleanness

液

Liquid spattered out when the scientist opened the lid of the big bottle.

おんよみ エキ　　**くんよみ** —

いみ liquid, juice

strokes 11画　丶　丶　氵　氵　汀　汀　汁　沪　沪　液　液

Point 液 ← Do not protrude!

液体	えきたい	liquid
樹液	じゅえき	sap
液晶	えきしょう	liquid crystal
血液	けつえき	blood

演

A lecturer moved around speaking so strongly that the glass of water on the table spilt.

おんよみ エン　　**くんよみ** —

いみ to play, to act, to express

strokes 14画　丶　丶　氵　氵　氵　汀　汀　沪　浐　浐　渖　渖　演　演

Point 演 ← Do not protrude!

演説	えんぜつ	speech
演劇	えんげき	play, drama
演奏	えんそう	musical performance
上演	じょうえん	staging

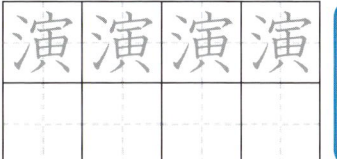 

激

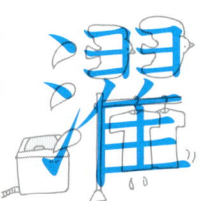

A ship and a surfer made their way forward on the violent wave.

おんよみ ゲキ
くんよみ はげ(しい)

いみ violent, intense, fierce　strokes 16画
丶　亠　氵　氵　氵　泊　泊　泊　泊　浔　湯　湯　激　激　激

激しい	はげしい	fierce, furious
激烈(な)	げきれつ(な)	fierce, furious
激励	げきれい	encouragement
急激(な)	きゅうげき(な)	abrupt, rapid
激流	げきりゅう	torrent

濯

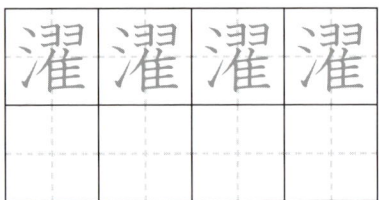

On a sunny day, I washed T-shirts and hung them out. There were two birds flying in the sky.

おんよみ タク
くんよみ ―

いみ to wash, to rinse　strokes 17画
丶　亠　氵　氵　氵　氵　洌　洌　潣　潣　濯　濯　濯　濯　濯　濯

Point
濯
Do not connect!

| 洗濯 | せんたく | washing |
| 洗濯機 | せんたくき | washing machine |

濃

A farmer milked a cow in the pasture with two silos, where I drank fresh, rich tasting milk.

おんよみ ノウ
くんよみ こ(い)

いみ dark, deep, thick　strokes 16画
丶　亠　氵　氵　氵　沪　浔　浔　浔　浔　浔　濃　濃　濃

Point
濃
Note the shortest horizontal stroke!

濃い	こい	dark, deep, thick
濃淡	のうたん	light and shade
濃厚	のうこう	richness
濃霧	のうむ	thick fog
濃縮	のうしゅく	condensation

1 Below the *Kanji*, write the Japanese reading of *Kanji* in *Hiragana*.

① 他 （　） ② 仏 （　） ③ 橋 （　） ④ 横 （　） ⑤ 恋 （　）

⑥ 筆 （　） ⑦ 夢 （　） ⑧ 宿 （　） ⑨ 波 （　） ⑩ 涙 （　）

2 Choose the correct reading.

① 性格 （a しょうかく　b せいかく　c せいかい）（　）

② 修理 （a しゅうり　b きゅうり　c そうり）（　）

③ 伝言 （a でんごん　b そうごん　c ちくごん）（　）

④ 構築 （a こうさ　b もうちく　c こうちく）（　）

⑤ 住宅 （a じょうちく　b じゅうたく　c そんたく）（　）

3 Write down the correct reading of the underlined part of the sentence.

① 店で販売する。　　　　　　（　　　　　）

② 天候に気をつける。　　　　（　　　　　）

③ 機械をつくる。　　　　　　（　　　　　）

④ よい目覚めの朝だ。　　　　（　　　　　）

⑤ 洗濯をするのに良い日だ。（　　　　　）

4 After reading the *Hiragana* and English, write the *Kanji* that applies to the word in the box.

① いき (breath) ☐

② かかり (person in charge) ☐

③ おっと (husband) ☐

④ ぐん (army) ☐

⑤ みずうみ (lake) ☐

⑥ あぶら (oil) ☐

⑦ あつまる (to gather) ☐まる

⑧ ねる (to go to bed) ☐る

5 Choose the correct *Kanji* that corresponds to the *Hiragana* reading.

① ざい (a 林　b 材　c 杯)　(　　)

② まも(る) (a 守　b 寸　c 宇)　(　　)

③ とど(く) (a 宙　b 由　c 届)　(　　)

④ くすり (a 案　b 薬　c 楽)　(　　)

⑤ ゆ (a 湯　b 場　c 傷)　(　　)

6 In the boxes, write the *Kanji* that applies to the *furigana* reading.

① 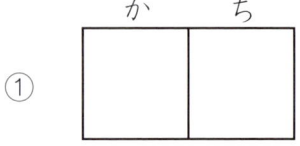が高い 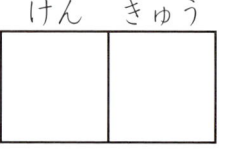を行う。

② ☐☐ があったわけではない。
　あく い

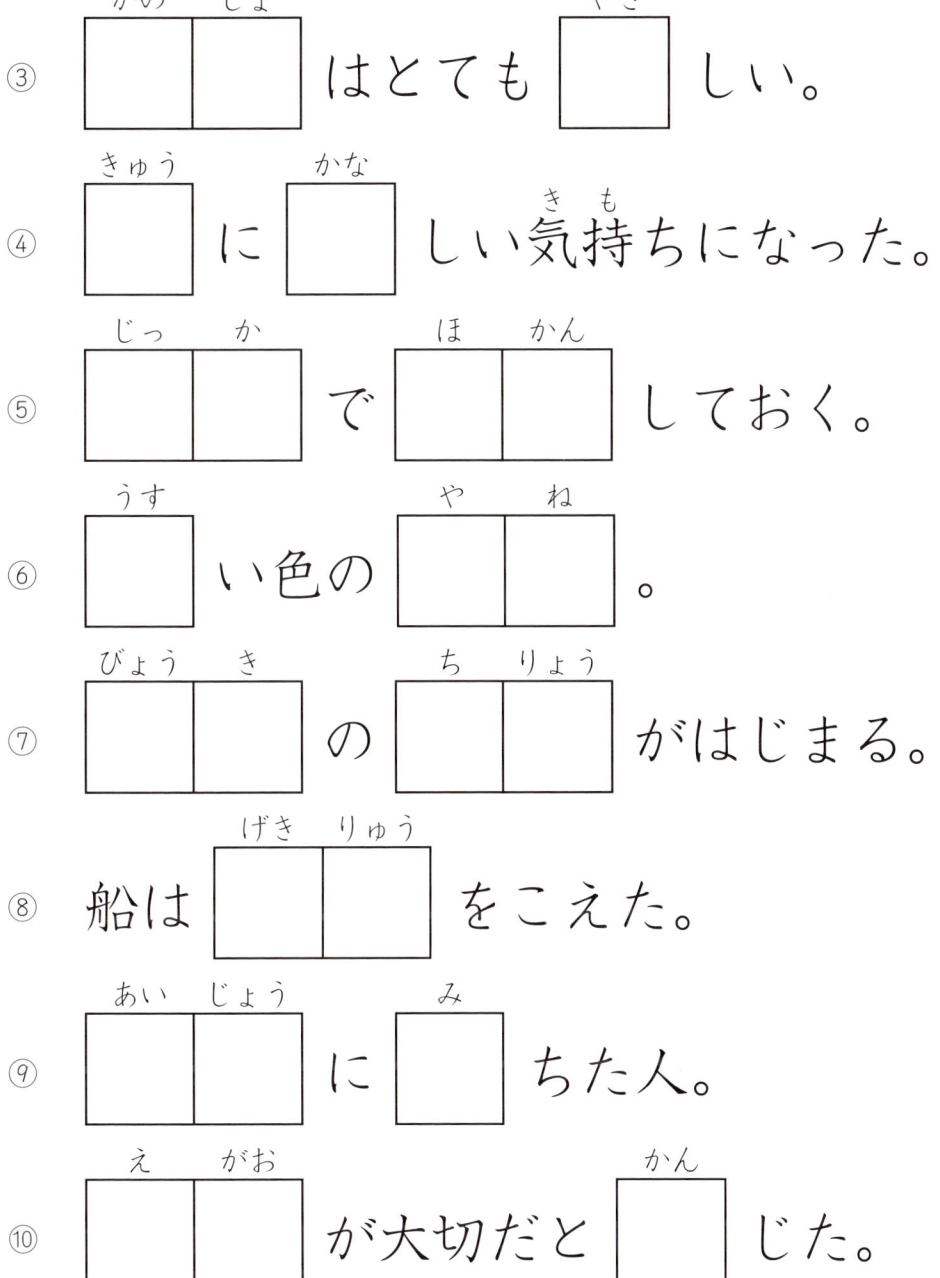

答え (answers)

❶ ①ほか ②ほとけ ③はし ④よこ ⑤こい ⑥ふで ⑦ゆめ ⑧やど ⑨なみ ⑩なみだ
❷ ①b ②a ③a ④c ⑤b
❸ ①はんばい ②てんこう ③きかい ④めざ ⑤せんたく
❹ ①息 ②係 ③夫 ④軍 ⑤湖 ⑥油 ⑦集 ⑧寝
❺ ①b ②a ③c ④b ⑤a
❻ ①価値, 研究 ②悪意 ③彼女, 優 ④急, 悲 ⑤実家, 保管 ⑥薄, 屋根 ⑦病気, 治療 ⑧激流
  ⑨愛情, 満 ⑩笑顔, 感

N3②

ここでは、日本語能力検定2級相当の漢字を掲載しています。

contains the *Kanji* of the Japanese Language Proficiency Test Level 2

次

A farmer planted the nursery plants one after another.

おんよみ ジ・シ　　**くんよみ** つ(ぐ)・つぎ

いみ next, order　　**strokes** 6画　　丶 冫 ソ 次 次 次

Note the position of the dots!

次	つぎ	next
次回	じかい	next time
目次	もくじ	table of contents
次男	じなん	the second son

凍

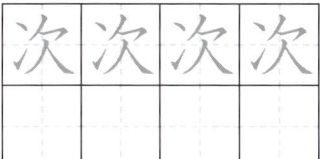 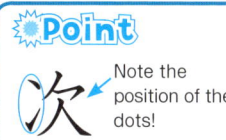

The Ice Queen froze a tree and birds when she touched them with both her hands.

おんよみ トウ　　**くんよみ** こお(る)・こご(える)

いみ to freeze, to be chilled　　**strokes** 10画　　丶 冫 冫 冫 厂 疒 汴 浐 凍 凍

Protrude!

凍る	こおる	to freeze
冷凍	れいとう	freezing
凍結した	とうけつした	frozen
解凍	かいとう	thawing

拾

I held the firewood gathered with both my hands and placed one log on the fire in the house.

おんよみ シュウ・ジュウ　　**くんよみ** ひろ(う)

いみ to pick up, to find, ten　　**strokes** 9画　　一 十 扌 扌 扲 扲 拎 拾 拾

拾う	ひろう	to pick up
拾得	しゅうとく	picking up
収拾	しゅうしゅう	control, settlement

捨

I threw away rubbish into the waste incinerator, holding on with both my hands.

おんよみ シャ　　**くんよみ** す(てる)

いみ to throw away, to dump, to discard　　**strokes** 11画　　一 十 扌 扌 扲 扲 捈 捈 捨 捨

Do not protrude!

捨てる	すてる	to throw away
取捨	しゅしゃ	choice, selection
捨て猫	すてねこ	abandoned cats

173

指

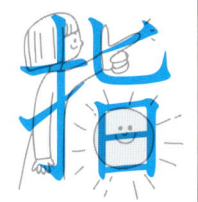

I raised my hand high and the sun smiled under my arm.

おんよみ シ
くんよみ ゆび・さ(す)

いみ finger, toe, to point　**strokes** 9画　一 十 才 扌 扩 护 指 指 指

指す	さす	to point	矢印の指す方角へ進む。
指示	しじ	instruction	上司に指示を仰ぐ。
親指	おやゆび	thumb	親指の爪を切る。
指摘	してき	indication	上司に書類の誤りを指摘された。
指圧	しあつ	acupressure	自分の足を指圧した。
指輪	ゆびわ	finger ring	彼女の誕生日に指輪を贈った。

持

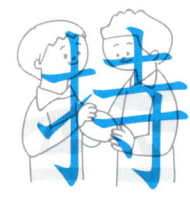

The team with the horizontally-striped uniform has the ball.

おんよみ ジ
くんよみ も(つ)

いみ to have, to keep　**strokes** 9画　一 十 才 扌 扩 扩 挂 持 持

Point
持
Protrude!

持つ	もつ	to have	重い荷物を持つ。
持病	じびょう	chronic disease	持病の腰痛が悪化してきた。
所持	しょじ	possession	所持品を検査する。
維持	いじ	maintenance	体形維持のために、ダイエットを始めた。
支持	しじ	support	反対派の支持にまわる。
持久走	じきゅうそう	endurance running	持久走は苦手だ。

打

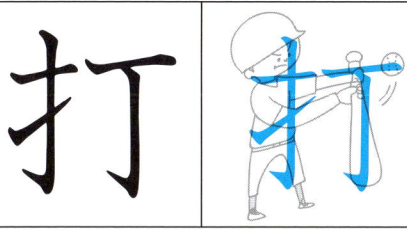

The batter hit the ball by strongly swinging the bat with both his hands.

- おんよみ ダ
- くんよみ う(つ)

いみ to hit, to strike, to beat **strokes 5画** 一 ナ 扌 扌 打

Do not protrude!

打つ	うつ	to hit, to strike, to beat
打撃	だげき	shock, blow
打開	だかい	breakthrough
打撲	だぼく	blow, stroke
強打	きょうだ	hard blow, whack

担

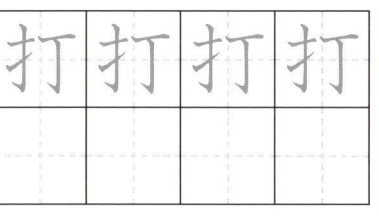

I held a stretcher with both my hands and carried a patient on it.

- おんよみ タン
- くんよみ かつ(ぐ)・にな(う)

いみ to carry, to shoulder, to undertake **strokes 8画** 一 ナ 扌 扌 扫 担 担 担

Do not connect!

担ぐ	かつぐ	to shoulder
担当者	たんとうしゃ	person in charge
負担	ふたん	burden
分担	ぶんたん	share, sharing
担架	たんか	stretcher

押

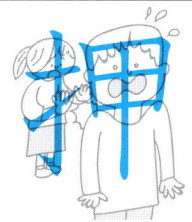

It is dangerous to push somebody's back suddenly.

- おんよみ オウ
- くんよみ お(す)・お(さえる)

いみ to push, to press **strokes 8画** 一 ナ 扌 扌 扣 押 押 押

Do not protrude!

押す	おす	to push
押印	おういん	sealing
押収	おうしゅう	seizure
押し花	おしばな	pressed flowers

175

授

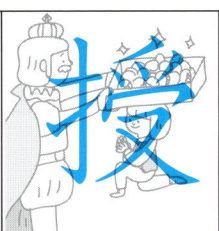

The king held a lot of gifts in his hands and granted them to the envoy who was kneeling down.

おんよみ ジュ
くんよみ さず(ける)・さず(かる)

いみ to grant, to give, to bestow
strokes 11画　一 十 扌 扩 扩 扩 扩 护 抬 授 授

授ける	さずける	to grant, to give
授業	じゅぎょう	class, lesson
授受	じゅじゅ	giving and receiving
伝授	でんじゅ	instruction
授賞	じゅしょう	giving a prize

探

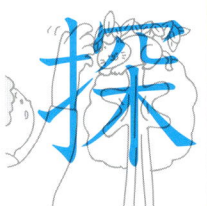

I pushed aside the leaves and found my cat hiding in the tree.

おんよみ タン
くんよみ さぐ(る)・さが(す)

いみ to search, to investigate
strokes 11画　一 十 扌 扌 扩 扩 护 捽 探 探 探

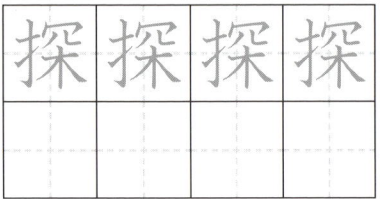

Note the similar characters!

探す	さがす	to search, to investigate
探検	たんけん	expedition
探索	たんさく	search
探査	たんさ	exploration
探知	たんち	detection

接

I was greeted by a woman at the door, through which I saw an interviewer sitting.

おんよみ セツ
くんよみ つ(ぐ)

いみ to join, to graft, to connect
strokes 11画　一 十 扌 扌 扩 扩 护 拌 接 接 接

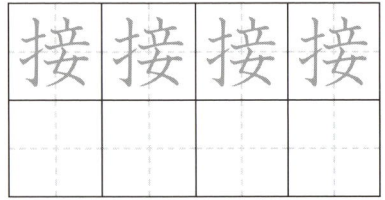

Note the longest horizontal stroke!

接ぐ	つぐ	to connect, to join
直接的(な)	ちょくせつてき(な)	direct
面接	めんせつ	interview
接近	せっきん	access, approach
接触	せっしょく	contact

払

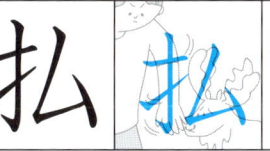

A man shooed a moose away by waving his hand.

おんよみ フツ **くんよみ** はら（う）

いみ to pay, to dust   **strokes** 5画   一 十 才 払 払

払う	はらう	to pay, to dust
払拭	ふっしょく	dispeling
支払い	しはらい	payment
前払い	まえばらい	prepayment

折

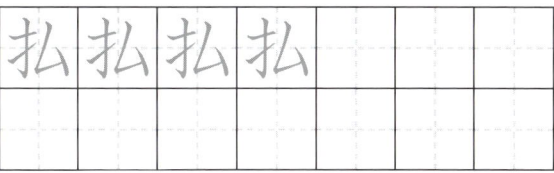

I reached my hand out and broke a branch.

おんよみ セツ **くんよみ** お（る）・おり・お（れる）

いみ to break, to snap   **strokes** 7画   一 十 才 扩 扩 折 折

Point: 折 ← Do not protrude!

折る	おる	to break, to snap
骨折	こっせつ	fracture
折半	せっぱん	going halves
挫折	ざせつ	frustration

技

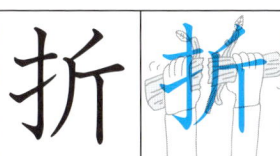

The craft worker created traditional craft art with the unique techniques.

おんよみ ギ **くんよみ** わざ

いみ skill, ability   **strokes** 7画   一 十 才 扩 扩 technique 技 技

Point: 技 ← Do not protrude!

技	わざ	skill, trick
技能	ぎのう	skill
技術	ぎじゅつ	technique
特技	とくぎ	special skill

抜

The *samurai* warrior drew a sword with his right hand.

おんよみ バツ **くんよみ** ぬ（く）・ぬ（ける）・ぬ（かす）・ぬ（かる）

いみ to pull out, to remove, to overtake   **strokes** 7画   一 十 才 扩 扩 抜 抜

Point: 抜 ×板 ×技 Note the similar characters!

抜く	ぬく	to pull out
選抜	せんばつ	selection
抜群	ばつぐん	outstanding
抜粋	ばっすい	excerpt, extract

177

投

The catcher was trying to catch a ball thrown by the pitcher.

おんよみ トウ　　**くんよみ** な(げる)

いみ to throw, to pitch　　**strokes** 7画　　一 十 扌 扌 扒 投 投

投げる	なげる	to throw
投手	とうしゅ	pitcher
投函	とうかん	posting
投資	とうし	investment

採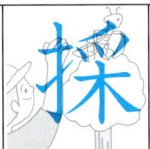

A boy caught a praying mantis on the tree with his hand for his insect collection.

おんよみ サイ　　**くんよみ** と(る)

いみ to pick, to gather, to adopt　　**strokes** 11画　　一 十 扌 扌 扩 扩 扩 抨 抨 採 採

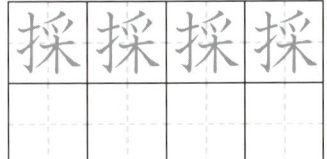

Point: Note the position of the dots!

採る	とる	to pick, to gather
採用	さいよう	adoption
採集	さいしゅう	collecting
採決	さいけつ	vote

招

A mistress beckoned a servant closer to give some orders.

おんよみ ショウ　　**くんよみ** まね(く)

いみ to invite, to summon, to cause　　**strokes** 8画　　一 十 扌 扌 扨 招 招 招

Point: Do not protrude!

招く	まねく	to invite, to cause
招待	しょうたい	invitation
招致	しょうち	invitation
手招き	てまねき	beckoning

拡

While I was playing the piano, the wall was broken down, and the extension work was started.

おんよみ カク　　**くんよみ** ―

いみ to broaden　　**strokes** 8画　　一 十 扌 扌' 扩 扩 拡 拡

Point: ×払 ×抜 Note the similar characters!

拡大	かくだい	expansion, extension
拡散	かくさん	diffusion, spread
拡張	かくちょう	extension
拡充	かくじゅう	expansion

178

People carrying protest signs joined a demonstration to criticize the government.

おんよみ ヒ　くんよみ —

いみ to appraise

strokes 7画　一 ナ 扌 扌 払 批 批

Point 批 Do not protrude!

批判	ひはん	criticism
批評	ひひょう	comment, review
批准	ひじゅん	ratification

I move both hands worshiping.

おんよみ ハイ　くんよみ おが(む)

いみ to worship, to pray

strokes 8画　一 ナ 扌 扩 扩 拝 拝 拝

Point 拝 Note the number of horizontal strokes!

拝む	おがむ	to worship, to pray
礼拝堂	れいはいどう	chapel
拝観	はいかん	having the honor of seeing
参拝	さんぱい	visit and worship

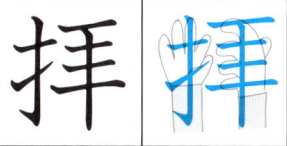

Potatoes came out of soil when I dug it with a shovel that I held in my hand.

おんよみ クツ　くんよみ ほ(る)

いみ to dig, to bore

strokes 11画　一 ナ 扌 扩 扩 护 押 捆 捆 掘 掘

Point 掘 Do not protrude!

掘る	ほる	to dig
採掘	さいくつ	mining
発掘	はっくつ	excavation

A father held his child in his arms.

おんよみ ホウ　くんよみ だ(く)・いだ(く)・かか(える)

いみ to hold, to hug, to have

strokes 8画　一 ナ 扌 扌 扚 拘 抱 抱

Point 抱 Do not connect!

抱く	だく	to hold, to have
介抱	かいほう	care, nursing
抱負	ほうふ	ambition, aspiration
抱擁	ほうよう	embrace, hug

掃

I held a broom in my hands and swept up around the palace.

おんよみ ソウ　くんよみ は(く)

いみ to sweep　strokes 11画　一 十 扌 扌 扫 扫 扫 扫 掃 掃 掃

Point
掃
Do not connect!

掃く	はく	to sweep
掃除	そうじ	cleaning
清掃	せいそう	cleaning
一掃	いっそう	cleanup

換

I traded a fish for the stone that I was holding in my hand.

おんよみ カン　くんよみ か(える)・か(わる)

いみ to exchange, to replace　strokes 12画　一 十 扌 扌 扌 护 护 抑 挽 挽 換 換

Point
換
Protrude!

換える	かえる	to exchange, to replace
交換	こうかん	exchange
換気	かんき	ventilation
変換	へんかん	change, conversion

捕

A boy held a beetle he had caught. A dragonfly that saw it ran away in a hurry.

おんよみ ホ
くんよみ と(らえる)・と(らわれる)・と(る)・つか(まえる)・つか(まる)

いみ to catch, to capture　strokes 10画　一 十 扌 扌 扩 折 拍 拍 捕 捕

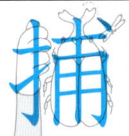

Point
捕
Note the position of the dot!

捕らえる	とらえる	to catch, to capture
捕獲	ほかく	capture
逮捕	たいほ	arrest
捕縛	ほばく	capture, arrest

操

A boy held a remote control in his hands and steered three helicopters above the tree.

おんよみ ソウ　くんよみ みさお・あやつ(る)

いみ to handle, to manage, to steer, chastity　strokes 16画

操る	あやつる	to handle
操作	そうさ	handling, operation
体操	たいそう	gymnastics
操縦	そうじゅう	handling, steering

There were people working out running or weight training inside the gym building.

おんよみ ケン・コン
くんよみ た(てる)・た(つ)

いみ to build, to construct　strokes 9画

Point

建 ← Do not connect!

建てる	たてる	to build, to construct	新しい家を建てる。
建設	けんせつ	construction	駅の近くにマンションが建設される。
建物	たてもの	building	古い建物が取り壊された。
建築	けんちく	construction	建築物をめぐる旅をする。
建造	けんぞう	construction	石で橋を建造する。
再建	さいけん	reconstruction	焼失した寺が、再建された。

I work out at the gym running and doing weight training in order to keep myself fit.

おんよみ ケン
くんよみ すこ(やか)

いみ healthy　strokes 11画

Point

健 ×律
健 ×建

Note the similar characters!

健やか(な)	すこやか(な)	healthy	子供の健やかな成長を願っている。
健康	けんこう	health	病気になって、健康の大切さがよくわかった。
健在(な)	けんざい(な)	in good health	両親は健在だ。
健全(な)	けんぜん(な)	healthy, sound, solid	健全な経営状態へと立て直す。
穏健(な)	おんけん(な)	moderate	彼は穏健な考え方をしている。
健闘	けんとう	good fight	強い相手に健闘を見せた。

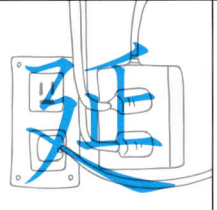

I used extension cords in the wall outlet to get electricity.

おんよみ エン
くんよみ の(びる)・の(べる)・の(ばす)

いみ to be extended, to be postponed, to extend
strokes 8画 一 丆 千 千 正 延 延 延

Point

Do not protrude!

延びる	のびる	to be extended
延長	えんちょう	extension
延期	えんき	postponement
延滞	えんたい	delay
遅延	ちえん	delay

The boy broke into a dead run on the road.

おんよみ ソク
くんよみ はや(い)・はや(める)・はや(まる)・すみ(やか)

いみ fast, quick, rapid, to hasten
strokes 10画 一 丆 冖 日 申 束 束 凍 速 速

Point

Protrude!

速い	はやい	fast, quick, rapid
高速	こうそく	high speed
速度	そくど	speed
速達	そくたつ	special delivery
時速	じそく	speed per hour

The wide road was more crowded with cars than the complicated roads.

おんよみ ―
くんよみ こ(む)・こ(める)

いみ to be crowded, to include
strokes 5画 ノ 入 込 込 込

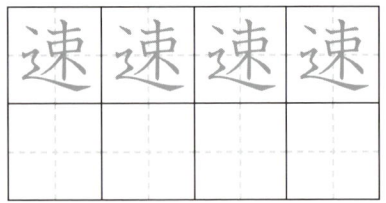

込める	こめる	to include
税込み	ぜいこみ	tax included
申し込み	もうしこみ	application
煮込み	にこみ	stew

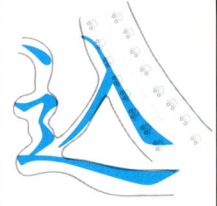
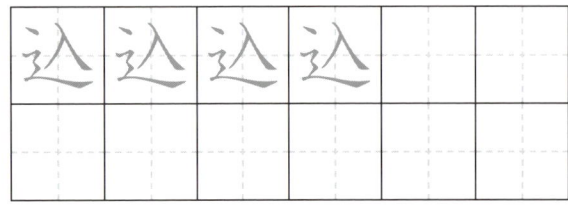

進

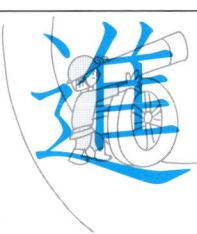

The soldier advanced, pushing his artillery.

おんよみ シン
くんよみ すす(む)・すす(める)

いみ to advance, to move **strokes 11画** ノ イ イ 亻 什 件 隹 隹 隹 進 進

Point
進 ← Note the position of the dot!

進む	すすむ	to advance, to move on	行列が前へ進み始めた。
直進	ちょくしん	going straight	直進すると突き当たりだ。
進歩	しんぽ	progress	科学技術が進歩する。
進路	しんろ	course	卒業後の進路を決める。
昇進	しょうしん	promotion	上司が部長に昇進した。
前進	ぜんしん	advance	少しずつ前進する。

返

There was a frog flipping upside down by the side of the road.

おんよみ ヘン
くんよみ かえ(す)・かえ(る)

いみ to return, to withdraw **strokes 7画** 一 厂 丆 反 反 返 返

Point
返 ←×仮
返 ←×板
Note the similar characters!

返す	かえす	to return	借りた傘を彼女に返した。
返事	へんじ	answer, reply	彼は返事をしなかった。
返信	へんしん	answer, reply	メールに返信をする。
返却	へんきゃく	return	図書館に本を返却する。
返済	へんさい	repayment	借金を返済する。
返答	へんとう	answer, reply	どう答えるか、返答に困った。

A man standing on the road saw his friend off all the way, waving both his hands.

おんよみ ソウ
くんよみ おく(る)

いみ to send, to mail　strokes 9画　、ソ ソ ニ 关 关 关 送 送

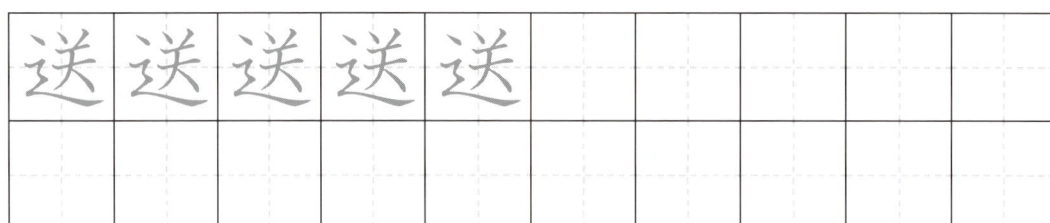

送る	おくる	to send	船便で荷物を送る。
送信	そうしん	transmission	メールを送信する。
送迎	そうげい	welcoming and sending off	空港からホテルまでバスで送迎してもらった。
発送	はっそう	dispatch	今日発送すると、いつ届きますか。
送料	そうりょう	postage	送料は、いくらになりますか。
輸送	ゆそう	transportation	石油をタンカーで輸送する。

 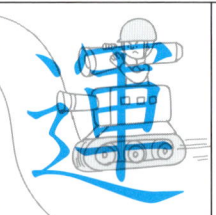

The tank went across the road carrying weapons.

おんよみ ウン
くんよみ はこ(ぶ)

いみ to carry, to transport, luck　strokes 12画　、 冖 冖 冖 冃 冒 冒 冒 軍 軍 運 運

運ぶ	はこぶ	to carry, to transport	引っ越しの荷物を運ぶ。
幸運	こううん	good luck	幸運に恵まれて成功できた。
運転	うんてん	driving, operation	彼女の運転でドライブに出かける。
運賃	うんちん	fare, freight	東京から大阪までの運賃を調べる。
運動	うんどう	exercise, movement	子供の頃から、運動が得意だ。
運命	うんめい	destiny, fate	彼は運命に逆らえなかった。

違

The woman with a hat by the roadside turned out to be different from the one I was looking for.

おんよみ イ
くんよみ ちが(う)・ちが(える)

いみ different, wrong
strokes 13画

ノ カ ヰ 产 吉 吉 吉 吉 吉 韋 韋 違 違

Point Do not connect!

違う	ちがう	different	彼とは考え方が違う。
違反	いはん	violation, offense	スピード違反で罰金を払った。
違法	いほう	illegal	違法駐車を取り締まる。
相違	そうい	difference	両者には意見の相違がある。
違約金	いやくきん	penalty, forfeit	違約金を払う。
間違える	まちがえる	to make a mistake	問題の答えを間違える。

選

Only selected people can get on the second story of the bus.

おんよみ セン
くんよみ えら(ぶ)

いみ to choose, to select, selection
strokes 15画

フ コ コ ヨ ヨ ヨ ヨ 昇 巽 巽 巽 巽 選 選

Point Do not connect!

選ぶ	えらぶ	to choose, to select	着る服を選ぶ。
選択	せんたく	choice, selection	どちらを選択するか、決める。
選挙	せんきょ	election	今日は朝から選挙に行った。
選手	せんしゅ	athlete, player	彼は現役のサッカー選手だ。
選別	せんべつ	sorting	選別してから野菜を出荷する。

逃

The couple ran away from the village holding hands along the way.

おんよみ トウ　**くんよみ** に(げる)・に(がす)・のが(す)・のが(れる)

いみ to run away, to escape, to avoid

strokes 9画　ノ 丿 丿 冫 兆 兆 兆 逃 逃

Point: Note the position of the dots!

逃げる	にげる	to escape, to run away
逃走	とうそう	escape, getaway
逃亡	とうぼう	escape
逃避	とうひ	escape

途

I take shelter in a house along the way.

おんよみ ト　**くんよみ** ―

いみ way

strokes 10画　ノ 人 ハ 会 今 余 余 余 途 途

Point: Do not protrude!

途中	とちゅう	on the [one's] way
用途	ようと	use
前途	ぜんと	future, prospects
途上	とじょう	half-way, on the way

迎

I meet a visitor and bow.

おんよみ ゲイ　**くんよみ** むか(える)

いみ to welcome, to meet

strokes 7画　ノ ヒ 幻 卯 卯 迎 迎

Point: Do not connect!

迎える	むかえる	to welcome, to meet
歓迎	かんげい	welcome
迎賓館	げいひんかん	state guesthouse

迷

A boy holding a bunch of rice stalks had lost his way and looked around.

おんよみ メイ　**くんよみ** まよ(う)

いみ to get lost, to waver

strokes 9画　丶 ソ 一 半 米 米 米 迷 迷

迷う	まよう	to get lost, to waver
迷路	めいろ	maze
迷惑	めいわく	annoyance, nuisance
迷信	めいしん	superstition

A boy stood on his hand on the roadside.

おんよみ ギャク　　**くんよみ** さか・さか(らう)

いみ reverse, opposite, to oppose　　**strokes** 9画　 丶 丷 丬 뽀 屰 屰 逆 逆 逆

Point 逆 ← Do not connect!

逆らう	さからう	to oppose
逆転	ぎゃくてん	reversal
逆境	ぎゃっきょう	adversity
逆立ち	さかだち	handstand

A police officer chased after the thief who was carrying two big bags the whole way.

おんよみ ツイ　　**くんよみ** お(う)

いみ to go after, to pursue, to chase　　**strokes** 9画　 ′ ⺅ ⺈ 白 𠂤 𠂤 𠂤 追 追

Point 追 ← Do not connect!

追う	おう	to go after, to chase
追跡	ついせき	chase, tracking
追加	ついか	addition
追突	ついとつ	rear-end collision

A camel caravan was moving forward on the road in the remote region of the frontier.

おんよみ ヘン　　**くんよみ** あた(り)・べ

いみ neighborhood, side, thereabout　　**strokes** 5画　 ⼐ ⼑ ⼒ 辺 辺

Point 辺 ← Do not protrude!

辺りに	あたりに	thereabout
周辺	しゅうへん	outskirts, the periphery
海辺	うみべ	beach, seaside
辺境	へんきょう	border, frontier

The politician raised his fist by the roadside and stated his policies.

おんよみ ジュツ　　**くんよみ** の(べる)

いみ to express, to state　　**strokes** 8画　 一 十 朮 朮 朮 朮 述 述

Point 述 ← Protrude!

述べる	のべる	to express, to state
記述	きじゅつ	description
口述	こうじゅつ	dictation
述懐	じゅっかい	recollection

遅

A sheep started to dash on the road as soon as he found himself late for the meeting.

おんよみ チ　　**くんよみ** おく(れる)・おく(らす)・おそ(い)

いみ behind, late, slowly, to be delayed　**strokes** 12画　フ コ ヨ ヨ 尸 尸 屖 屖 ｀犀 遅 遅

Point: 遅 Note the position of the dots!

遅い	おそい	slow, late
遅刻	ちこく	being late
遅延	ちえん	delay
遅筆家	ちひつか	slow writer

退

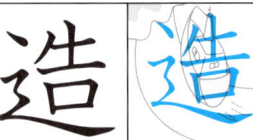

The soldier was forced to retreat from the battlefield.

おんよみ タイ　　**くんよみ** しりぞ(く)・しりぞ(ける)

いみ to withdraw, to retreat　**strokes** 9画　フ ヨ ヨ 甲 艮 艮 ｀艮 退 退

退く	しりぞく	to withdraw, to retreat
辞退	じたい	decline, refuse
退学	たいがく	leaving school
進退	しんたい	movement, one's course of action

造

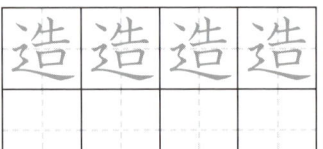

A ship built at the shipyard was transported to the sea along this road.

おんよみ ゾウ　　**くんよみ** つく(る)

いみ to make, to build, to form　**strokes** 10画　ノ 匕 牛 生 牛 告 告 ｀告 造 造

Point: 造 Do not connect!

造る	つくる	to make, to build
製造	せいぞう	production
木造	もくぞう	wooden
造船	ぞうせん	shipbuilding

遊

A girl wearing a straw hat played with a little bear by the side of a road.

おんよみ ユウ・ユ　　**くんよみ** あそ(ぶ)

いみ to play, to enjoy oneself　**strokes** 12画　丶 亠 う 方 方 ガ 苆 斿 ｀斿 游 遊

遊ぶ	あそぶ	to play, to enjoy oneself
遊園地	ゆうえんち	amusement park
遊山	ゆさん	excursion, picnic
遊泳	ゆうえい	swimming

過

As we are passing the clock tower, we will be at our destination soon.

おんよみ カ **くんよみ** す(ぎる)・す(ごす)・あやま(つ)・あやま(ち)

いみ to pass, to spend, to mistake, error

strokes 12画   丨 冂 冂 冃 冎 冎 咼 咼 咼 過 過 過

Point: Do not connect! 過

通過	つうか	passing
過労	かろう	overwork
過ぎる	すぎる	to pass
過失	かしつ	error, mistake

連

On the road there is one carriage following another.

おんよみ レン **くんよみ** つら(なる)・つら(ねる)・つ(れる)

いみ to range, to bring, to take

strokes 10画   一 厂 丙 丙 百 亘 車 車 連 連

Point: Protrude! 連

連続	れんぞく	succession, sequence
連日	れんじつ	day after day
連なる	つらなる	to range
常連	じょうれん	regular visitor

達

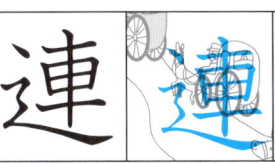

A sheep was running on the road so that she could deliver a big parcel.

おんよみ タツ **くんよみ** ―

いみ to accomplish, to reach

strokes 12画   一 十 土 士 夲 夲 幸 幸 幸 達 達 達

到達	とうたつ	arrival
伝達	でんたつ	transmission
達人	たつじん	expert, master
配達	はいたつ	delivery

適

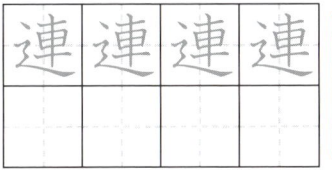 

I drew water from the well and carried it to the appropriate place.

おんよみ テキ **くんよみ** ―

いみ to match, appropriate

strokes 14画   丶 亠 さ 六 产 育 商 商 商 商 商 適 適

Point: Do not connect! 適

適正(な)	てきせい(な)	right, reasonable
適度(な)	てきど(な)	moderate
快適(な)	かいてき(な)	comfortable
適切(な)	てきせつ(な)	appropriate

189

起

It is refreshing to go for a run shortly after I get up.

おんよみ キ
くんよみ お(きる)・お(こる)・お(こす)

いみ to arise, to get up, to start
strokes 10画 一 + 土 キ キ 走 走 起 起 起

Point
起
Do not connect!

起立	きりつ	standing up
起源	きげん	origin
起きる	おきる	to arise, to get up
起動	きどう	start up, launch
起床	きしょう	getting up

超

The man ran much faster than a bird flies, or the bullet train runs.

おんよみ チョウ
くんよみ こ(える)・こ(す)

いみ to exceed, to surpass, over
strokes 12画 一 + 土 キ キ 走 走 起 起 起 超 超

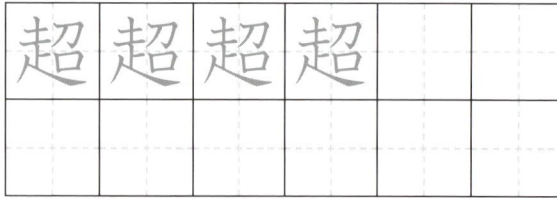

超過	ちょうか	excess
超人	ちょうじん	superman
超満員	ちょうまんいん	overcrowded
超能力	ちょうのうりょく	supernatural power
超越	ちょうえつ	transcendence

越

A bird was watching children go over the fence.

おんよみ エツ
くんよみ こ(す)・こ(える)

いみ to go over, to pass
strokes 12画 一 + 土 キ キ 走 走 起 起 越 越 越

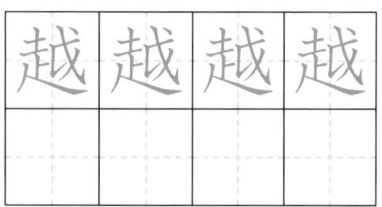

Point
越
Do not protrude!

越権	えっけん	exceeding one's authority
越える	こえる	to go over, to pass
引っ越し	ひっこし	house-moving
越境	えっきょう	border transgression
優越	ゆうえつ	superiority

均

The plot of land was equally divided by using a measure.

- おんよみ キン
- くんよみ —

いみ equal, evenly, to flatten **strokes** 7画 一 十 土 キ 圴 均 均

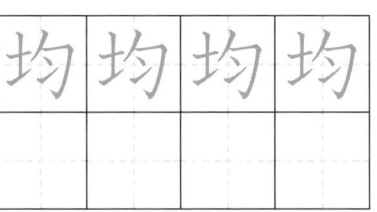

Note the position of the dots!

均一	きんいつ	uniformity
均等	きんとう	equality
平均	へいきん	average
均質	きんしつ	homogeneity
均整	きんせい	symmetry, balance

増

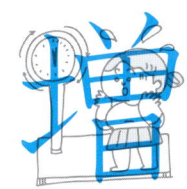

When I got on the scale, I was shocked that I had put on weight.

- おんよみ ゾウ
- くんよみ ま(す)・ふ(える)・ふ(やす)

いみ to increase, to grow **strokes** 14画 一 十 土 キ ザ ザ 护 护 垧 垧 増 増 増 増

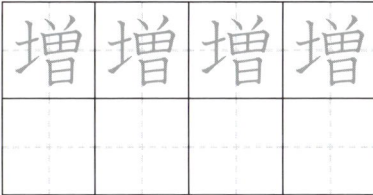

Note the position of the dots!

増加	ぞうか	increase
急増	きゅうぞう	sudden increase
増える	ふえる	to increase
増水	ぞうすい	high flow
増設	ぞうせつ	extension

境

A border guard standing on a watch tower spotted two people attempting to cross the border.

- おんよみ キョウ・ケイ
- くんよみ さかい

いみ boundary, border **strokes** 14画 一 十 土 キ ザ ザ 护 护 垃 垃 垮 垮 境 境

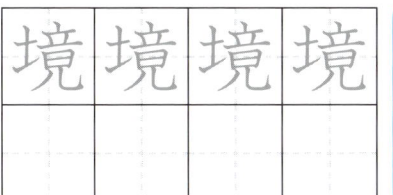

Note the number of horizontal strokes!

国境	こっきょう	national border
境内	けいだい	precincts of a temple
境目	さかいめ	boundary
境界	きょうかい	boundary, border
環境	かんきょう	environment

域

There was a 'Keep Out' sign around the construction area.

おんよみ イキ   **くんよみ** —

いみ area, level, boundary

strokes 11画 一 十 土 ュ ゴ ゴ 圹 圹 域 域 域

Point 域 ← Note the position of the dot!

地域	ちいき	area, region
区域	くいき	zone, section
職域	しょくいき	occupational field
音域	おんいき	sounding range

城

A man was meditating beside the castle.

おんよみ ジョウ   **くんよみ** しろ

いみ castle, fortress

strokes 9画 一 十 土 ュ ガ ゴ 圹 城 城 城

Point 城 ← Do not connect!

城主	じょうしゅ	lord of a castle
古城	こじょう	old castle
城跡	しろあと	the ruins of a castle
姫路城	ひめじじょう	*Himeji* Castle

塩

I used a spoon to sprinkle some salt on the steak that was on the plate on the table with a candle.

おんよみ エン   **くんよみ** しお

いみ salt

strokes 13画 一 十 土 ュ ゴ ゴ 圹 圹 圹 垆 塩 塩 塩

食塩	しょくえん	table salt
塩分	えんぶん	salinity
塩水	しおみず	salt water, brine
塩田	えんでん	salt pan

堂

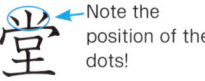

A small temple was standing quietly there.

おんよみ ドウ   **くんよみ** —

いみ temple, shrine, large building

strokes 11画 ⺌ ⺍ ⺌ 兴 尚 常 営 堂 堂

Point 堂 ← Note the position of the dots!

講堂	こうどう	auditorium, lecture hall
食堂	しょくどう	eating place
国会議事堂	こっかいぎじどう	the Diet Building
公会堂	こうかいどう	public hall

壁

A man who meditates in front of the wall, and a man who climbs up the wall are there.

おんよみ ヘキ
くんよみ かべ

いみ wall, barrier, block　strokes 16画　フ　コ　ア　尸　尸　居　居'　居゛　居゛　居゛　辟　辟　壁　壁

Point 壁 Do not connect!

壁面	へきめん	wall surface
壁画	へきが	wall painting, mural
壁紙	かべがみ	wallpaper
城壁	じょうへき	castle wall, rampart
障壁	しょうへき	barrier

型

 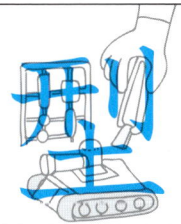

I assembled a model tank using a pair of tweezers.

おんよみ ケイ
くんよみ かた

いみ model, pattern, mold　strokes 9画　一　二　チ　开　开　刑　刑　型　型

Point 型 Note the longest vertical stroke!

原型	げんけい	prototype
模型	もけい	model, miniature
型紙	かたがみ	pattern paper
典型的(な)	てんけいてき(な)	typical
大型	おおがた	large-sized

基

A space shuttle was launched from the base while people were watching.

おんよみ キ
くんよみ もと・もとい

いみ foundation, base, basis　strokes 11画　一　十　卄　卄　甘　其　其　其　其　基　基

Point 基 Note the number of horizontal strokes!

基礎	きそ	base, foundation
基本的(な)	きほんてき(な)	basic
基	もと	base, foundation
基準	きじゅん	criterion
基金	ききん	fund

A fire was burning and ashes whirled up.

おんよみ カイ　　**くんよみ** はい

いみ ash, cinder, gray

strokes 6画　一 厂 厂 厂 灰 灰

Point 灰 ← Do not connect!

石灰	せっかい	lime
火山灰	かざんばい	volcanic ashes
灰色	はいいろ	gray
灰皿	はいざら	ashtray

 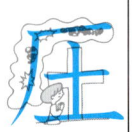

I was suffering from so much pressure that I prayed for help.

おんよみ アツ　　**くんよみ** —

いみ to press, pressure

strokes 5画　一 厂 厂 圧 圧

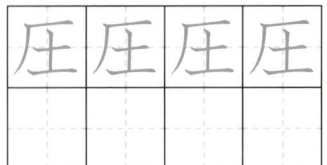

Point 圧 ← Note the longest horizontal stroke!

圧力	あつりょく	pressure
圧迫	あっぱく	oppression
血圧	けつあつ	blood pressure
威圧	いあつ	coercion

 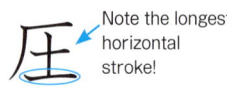

When opening the box, the child got excited to find a thick-sliced piece of bacon in it.

おんよみ コウ　　**くんよみ** あつ(い)

いみ thick, cordial

strokes 9画　一 厂 厂 厅 戽 戽 厚 厚 厚

温厚(な)	おんこう(な)	gentle
厚着の	あつぎの	heavily dressed
厚紙	あつがみ	cardboard
厚遇	こうぐう	hospitality

The old tombstone of a historic hero is surrounded by trees.

おんよみ レキ　　**くんよみ** —

いみ experience, history

strokes 14画　一 厂 厂 厈 厈 厈 厤 厤 厤 厤 歴 歴 歴 歴

Point 歴 ← Do not protrude!

歴史	れきし	history
歴代	れきだい	successive generations
経歴	けいれき	background, career
学歴	がくれき	educational background

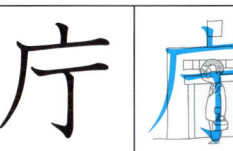

My father works at the prefectural office.

おんよみ チョウ　　**くんよみ** ―

いみ agency, office　　**strokes** 5画　　`丶 亠 广 庁 庁`

Point
Do not protrude!

官庁	かんちょう	government agency
県庁	けんちょう	prefectural office
庁舎	ちょうしゃ	government office building

 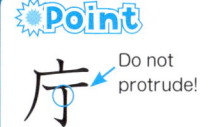

I answered the phone wholeheartedly.

おんよみ オウ　　**くんよみ** こた(える)

いみ to respond, to answer　　**strokes** 7画　　`丶 亠 广 广 応 応 応`

Point — ×忘 ×志
Note the similar characters!

反応	はんのう	reaction
応答	おうとう	response
応える	こたえる	to answer
応援	おうえん	support

  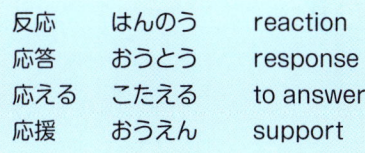

A boy is mopping the floor.

おんよみ ショウ　　**くんよみ** とこ・ゆか

いみ bed, floor　　**strokes** 7画　　`丶 亠 广 户 庄 床 床`

Point — ×庁 ×困
Note the similar characters!

起床	きしょう	getting up
床板	ゆかいた	floorboard
温床	おんしょう	hotbed

A submarine went down to the bottom of the sea.

おんよみ テイ　　**くんよみ** そこ

いみ bottom, floor　　**strokes** 8画　　`丶 亠 广 广 庐 庐 底 底`

Point
Do not connect!

底辺	ていへん	base
海底	かいてい	bottom of the sea
底力	そこぢから	underlying strength
徹底	てってい	thoroughness

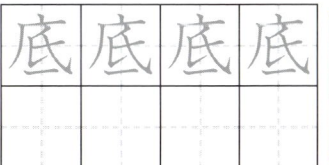 

度

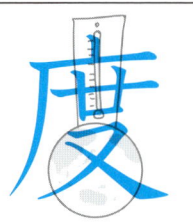

The temperature of the earth is increasing more and more each year.

- おんよみ ド・ト・タク
- くんよみ たび

いみ degree, often, to guess **strokes** 9画 丶 亠 广 户 庐 庐 度 度

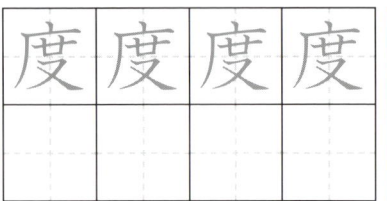

Connect!

温度	おんど	temperature
支度	したく	preparation
今度	こんど	next time, now
態度	たいど	attitude

席

Children were seated in class and took a lesson.

- おんよみ セキ
- くんよみ ―

いみ seat **strokes** 10画 丶 亠 广 户 庐 庐 庐 席 席

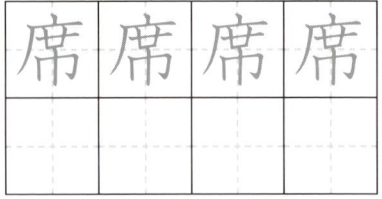

Protrude!

座席	ざせき	seat
空席	くうせき	vacant seat
出席	しゅっせき	attendance
欠席	けっせき	absence
着席	ちゃくせき	sitting down

座

A man and two women were meditating in the lotus position.

- おんよみ ザ
- くんよみ すわ(る)

いみ to sit, seat, position **strokes** 10画 丶 亠 广 产 庐 应 座 座 座

Do not protrude!

座る	すわる	to sit
講座	こうざ	course of lectures
座禅	ざぜん	sitting in meditation
星座	せいざ	constellation
座談会	ざだんかい	round-table talk

 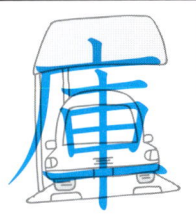

I parked my car at the carport.

おんよみ コ・ク
くんよみ —

いみ storehouse, storeroom
strokes 10画 　丶　亠　广　广　庐　庐　庐　盾　盾　庫

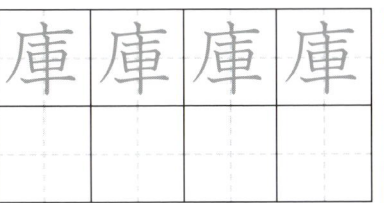

Point
庫
Protrude!

金庫	きんこ	safe, vault
車庫	しゃこ	garage, carport
在庫	ざいこ	stock
倉庫	そうこ	storehouse
庫裏	くり	priest's quarters

I regularly have health check-ups.

おんよみ コウ
くんよみ —

いみ healthy, restful
strokes 11画 　丶　亠　广　广　庐　庐　庚　庚　庚　康　康

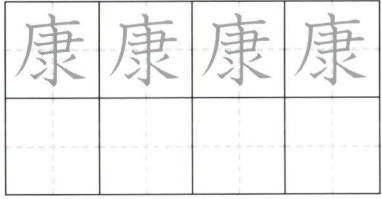

Point
康
Note the position of the dots!

| 健康 | けんこう | health |
| 小康 | しょうこう | temporary lull |

There is a pond with a bridge, and a path leading to a rest house in the garden.

おんよみ テイ
くんよみ にわ

いみ yard, garden
strokes 10画 　丶　亠　广　广　庐　庭　庭　庭　庭

Point
庭
Do not protrude!

庭園	ていえん	garden
校庭	こうてい	schoolyard
裏庭	うらにわ	backyard
家庭	かてい	home, household
庭師	にわし	gardener

関 An officer standing in front of the check point conducted a strict inspection.

おんよみ カン　くんよみ せき・かか(わる)

いみ checkpoint, to concern　strokes 14画

｜ ｢ ｢ ｢ ｢' 門 門 門 門 門 閂 閂 関 関

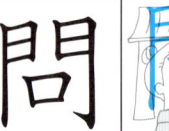 

Point 関 ← Do not connect!

玄関	げんかん	entrance
関所	せきしょ	checkpoint
関わる	かかわる	to concern
関連	かんれん	relation

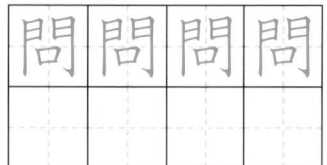 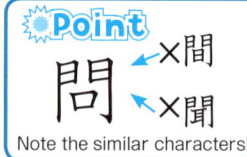

問 I asked the guard in front of the gate some questions.

おんよみ モン　くんよみ と(う)・と(い)・とん

いみ to inquire, to ask　strokes 11画

｜ ｢ ｢ ｢ ｢' 門 門 門 門 問 問

 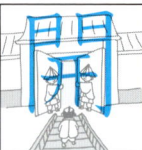

Point 問 ×間 ×聞 Note the similar characters!

問題	もんだい	problem, question
問屋	とんや	wholesaler
問う	とう	to inquire, to ask
質問	しつもん	question

 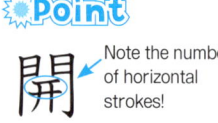

開 The gatekeepers opened the castle gate, so I crossed the bridge and went into the castle.

おんよみ カイ　くんよみ ひら(く)・ひら(ける)・あ(く)・あ(ける)

いみ to open, to undo　strokes 12画

｜ ｢ ｢ ｢ ｢' 門 門 門 門 開 開

Point 開 Note the number of horizontal strokes!

開花	かいか	flowering
開始	かいし	start
開く	ひらく	to open, to undo
開発	かいはつ	development

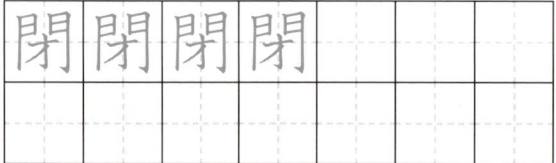

閉 I was perplexed in front of the gate because it was shut tightly.

おんよみ ヘイ　くんよみ と(じる)・と(ざす)・し(める)・し(まる)

いみ to close, to shut　strokes 11画

｜ ｢ ｢ ｢ ｢' 門 門 門 閉 閉

開閉	かいへい	opening and shutting
閉める	しめる	to close, to shut
閉鎖	へいさ	closure

岸

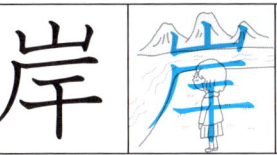

I was standing at the riverbank and had a view of the mountain range over the river.

おんよみ ガン　**くんよみ** きし

いみ shore, bank

strokes 8画　丿 山 屮 屮 岸 岸 岸 岸

Point: Note the number of horizontal strokes!

川岸	かわぎし	riverside
岸壁	がんぺき	quay
沿岸	えんがん	coast
岸辺	きしべ	shore
対岸	たいがん	opposite shore

両

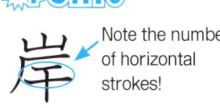

I weighed love against money and kept a good balance between both of them.

おんよみ リョウ　**くんよみ** —

いみ both, two

strokes 6画　一 ｢ 丙 币 両 両

Point: Do not protrude!

両親	りょうしん	(both) parents
両替	りょうがえ	currency exchange
車両	しゃりょう	vehicle, (train) car
両手	りょうて	both hands

島

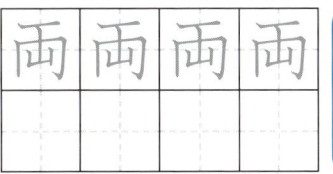

Palm trees and cactuses were growing on the island.

おんよみ トウ　**くんよみ** しま

いみ island

strokes 10画　丿 亻 忄 户 户 自 鸟 鸟 島 島

Point: Note the number of horizontal strokes!

島民	とうみん	islanders
半島	はんとう	peninsula
島国	しまぐに	island nation
離島	りとう	isolated island

去

A mother was breaking down in tears as she watched her child go away.

おんよみ キョ・コ　**くんよみ** さ(る)

いみ to leave, to go away

strokes 5画　一 十 土 去 去

Point: Note the longest horizontal stroke!

去年	きょねん	last year
過去	かこ	the past
去る	さる	to leave, to go away
消去	しょうきょ	erasure

199

芸

A *geisha* was playing the *shamisen* under the cherry tree.

おんよみ ゲイ　　くんよみ —

いみ skill, entertainment, art

strokes 7画　一 十 艹 芢 芸 芸 芸

Point
芸 ← Do not protrude!

芸者	げいしゃ	*geisha* (female entertainer)
芸術	げいじゅつ	art
園芸	えんげい	gardening
工芸	こうげい	industrial arts

私

The apples I have grown belong to me.

おんよみ シ　　くんよみ わたくし・わたし

いみ I, private

strokes 7画　一 二 千 禾 禾 私 私

Point
私 ← Do not protrude!

私立	しりつ	private
公私	こうし	public and private matters
私	わたくし・わたし	I, private affair
私語	しご	private talk

臣

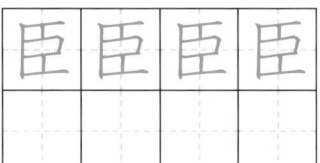

The Prime Minister was standing in front of the Diet Building.

おんよみ シン・ジン　　くんよみ —

いみ vassal, follower

strokes 7画　一 ㄧ 厂 戸 戸 戸 臣

Point
臣 ← Do not connect!

臣下	しんか	vassal
大臣	だいじん	Minister
重臣	じゅうしん	senior statesman

蔵

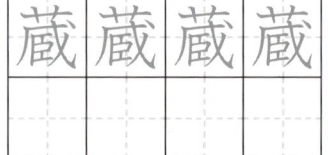

The Prime Minister enjoyed *sake* in a *sake* cellar.

おんよみ ゾウ　　くんよみ くら

いみ warehouse, to save

strokes 15画　一 十 艹 艹 艹 艹 艹 茪 茋 萐 葳 葳 蔵 蔵 蔵

Point
蔵 ← Note the position of the dot!

蔵書	ぞうしょ	collection of books
冷蔵	れいぞう	refrigeration
蔵元	くらもと	*sake* brewery
貯蔵	ちょぞう	storage

臓

The moon was worried about the Prime Minister's internal organs because he drank too much.

おんよみ ゾウ　　**くんよみ** —

いみ internal organs　　**strokes** 19画　丿 几 月 月 月 肝 胪 胪 胪 胪 胪 腔 臓 臓 臓 臓 臓 臓 臓

内臓	ないぞう	viscera, internal organs
心臓	しんぞう	heart (organ)
肝臓	かんぞう	liver
腎臓	じんぞう	kidney

参

I came over riding an elephant.

おんよみ サン　　**くんよみ** まい(る)

いみ to join, to visit, to participate　　**strokes** 8画　厶 ㄙ 宀 宀 矣 矣 参 参

Point 参 — Note the position of the dots!

参照	さんしょう	reference
参加	さんか	participation
墓参り	はかまいり	visit to a grave
参考	さんこう	reference

髪

I set my long hair with a hair brush and hair drier.

おんよみ ハツ　　**くんよみ** かみ

いみ hair　　**strokes** 14画　⼁ ⼏ ⼹ ⻑ ⻑ 長 長 長 髟 髟 髟 髪 髪 髪

Point 髪 — Note the number of horizontal strokes!

頭髪	とうはつ	hair
散髪	さんぱつ	haircut
黒髪	くろかみ	black hair
前髪	まえがみ	bangs

主

The king seated in the chair is the head of this country.

おんよみ シュ・ス　　**くんよみ** ぬし・おも

いみ lord, head, important　　**strokes** 5画　丶 亠 宀 主 主

Point 主 — Note the longest horizontal stroke!

主人	しゅじん	lord, master
坊主	ぼうず	Buddhist priest
株主	かぶぬし	shareholder
主張	しゅちょう	claim

望

The king could get anything he wished for whether it was treasure or the moon.

おんよみ ボウ・モウ　くんよみ のぞ(む)

いみ to hope, to view　strokes 11画　｀ 亠 亡 ぢ 切 胡 胡 朔 朢 望 望

Point 望 Do not connect!

望郷	ぼうきょう	nostalgia
所望	しょもう	desire, wish
望む	のぞむ	to hope, to view
希望	きぼう	hope

球

The ball that the king threw went over the castle with two guards.

おんよみ キュウ　くんよみ たま

いみ ball, sphere　strokes 11画　一 丅 Ŧ 王 王﹀ 玗 玙 圤 球 球 球

Point 球 Do not protrude!

球	たま	ball
地球	ちきゅう	earth
野球	やきゅう	baseball
球技	きゅうぎ	ball game
電球	でんきゅう	electric bulb

環

The king went out on an eco-friendly bus.

おんよみ カン　くんよみ ―

いみ circle, ring, to surround　strokes 17画　一 丅 Ŧ 王 王﹀ 玗 玙 玙 玙 玙 玙 珋 瑅 瑔 環 環 環

環状	かんじょう	annulation, circularity
環境	かんきょう	environment
循環	じゅんかん	circulation
環礁	かんしょう	atoll

珍

An elephant was presented to the king as a rare animal.

おんよみ チン　くんよみ めずら(しい)

いみ rare, precious　strokes 9画　一 丅 Ŧ 王 王﹀ 玠 珍 珍 珍

Point 珍 Note the position of the dots!

珍味	ちんみ	delicacy, dainties
珍品	ちんぴん	rare article
珍しい	めずらしい	rare
珍事	ちんじ	strange incident

202

県

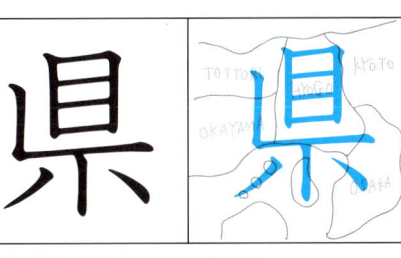

Hyogo Prefecture is located between *Okayama* Prefecture and *Osaka* Prefecture.

おんよみ ケン
くんよみ —

いみ prefecture

strokes 9画 丨 冂 冃 月 目 貝 県 県 県

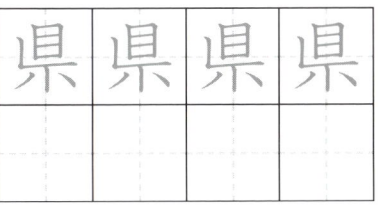

Point 県 Note the number of horizontal strokes!

兵庫県	ひょうごけん	*Hyogo* Prefecture
県民	けんみん	citizen of a prefecture
近県	きんけん	neighboring prefectures
県知事	けんちじ	prefectural governor
県庁	けんちょう	prefectural government

真

A believer, throwing himself on the floor, told God only the truth.

おんよみ シン
くんよみ ま

いみ true, real

strokes 10画 一 十 广 古 占 肯 盲 直 真 真

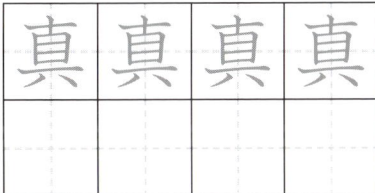

Point 真 Note the longest horizontal stroke!

真実	しんじつ	truth
真剣(な)	しんけん(な)	earnest
真心	まごころ	cordiality
真相	しんそう	truth
純真	じゅんしん	innocence

着

A woman wearing a *kimono* was waving her hand.

おんよみ チャク・ジャク
くんよみ き(る)・き(せる)・つ(く)・つ(ける)

いみ to wear, to dress, to arrive

strokes 12画 丶 ソ ソ ナ ⺷ 羊 芦 着 着 着

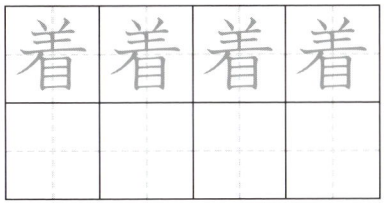

Point 着 Note the number of horizontal strokes!

着く	つく	to arrive
到着	とうちゃく	arrival
着物	きもの	*kimono*, clothes
着陸	ちゃくりく	landing
着実(な)	ちゃくじつ(な)	steady

省

While I was reflecting on my faults, my posture became like *The Thinker* by Auguste Rodin.

おんよみ セイ・ショウ　**くんよみ** かえり(みる)・はぶ(く)

いみ to reflect, to omit, to save, ministry

strokes 9画 丿 小 小 少 尐 省 省 省 省

Point  Connect!

反省	はんせい	reflection
省略	しょうりゃく	omission
省く	はぶく	to omit, to save
外務省	がいむしょう	the Ministry of Foreign Affairs

具

A blender is a useful cooking tool when you need to make fresh juice.

おんよみ グ　**くんよみ** —

いみ to have, detail, tool, ingredient

strokes 8画 丨 冂 冃 月 目 旦 具 具

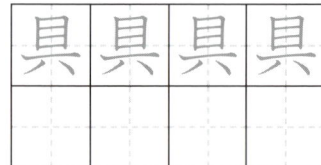

Point  Note the longest horizontal stroke!

道具	どうぐ	tool
家具	かぐ	furniture
具体的(な)	ぐたいてき(な)	concrete
玩具	がんぐ	toy

看

A nurse was holding a stethoscope and a medical record.

おんよみ カン　**くんよみ** —

いみ to watch

strokes 9画 一 二 三 チ 手 盾 看 看 看

Point  Note the longest horizontal stroke!

看護師	かんごし	nurse
看病	かんびょう	nursing
看板	かんばん	signboard
看守	かんしゅ	(prison) guard

皿

There was a delicious-looking steak on the plate.

おんよみ —　**くんよみ** さら

いみ dish, plate

strokes 5画 丨 冂 皿 皿 皿

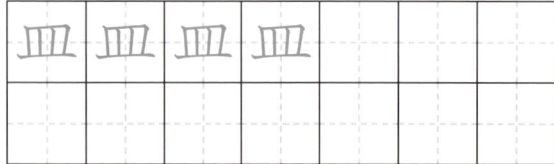

皿	さら	plate, dish
小皿	こざら	small dish
灰皿	はいざら	ashtray
受け皿	うけざら	saucer

血

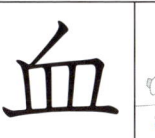 

I cut my finger with a knife and bled while I was carving the meat into slices on the plate.

おんよみ ケツ　　**くんよみ** ち

いみ blood　　**strokes** 6画　ノ 亠 厂 六 血 血

Point: Connect!

血液	けつえき	blood
血縁	けつえん	blood relation
鼻血	はなぢ	nosebleed
出血	しゅっけつ	bleeding

益

I made a profit by wrapping up steak on a plate with cloth and selling it.

おんよみ エキ・ヤク　　**くんよみ** ―

いみ profit, benefit, to increase　　**strokes** 10画　丶 䒑 䒑 䒑 䒑 益 益 益 益 益

有益(な)	ゆうえき(な)	beneficial
利益	りえき	profit
無益(な)	むえき(な)	useless

盗

A cat and two mice came to steal the delicious-looking steak.

おんよみ トウ　　**くんよみ** ぬす(む)

いみ to steal, robber　　**strokes** 11画　丶 冫 冫 次 次 次 盗 盗 盗 盗

Point: ×益 ×次 — Note the similar characters!

盗難	とうなん	theft
強盗	ごうとう	robbery, robber
盗む	ぬすむ	to steal
盗品	とうひん	stolen goods

盛

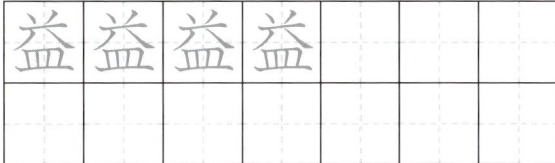 

I dished up french fries and ketchup beside the steak.

おんよみ セイ・ジョウ　　**くんよみ** も(る)・さか(る)・さか(ん)

いみ to pile, prosperous　　**strokes** 11画　ノ 厂 厂 成 成 成 成 成 盛 盛 盛

盛大(な)	せいだい(な)	prosperous
繁盛	はんじょう	prosperity
盛る	もる	to pile, to serve
盛況	せいきょう	success

曲

A violinist played a piece of music.

おんよみ キョク
くんよみ ま(がる)・ま(げる)

いみ to bend, musical piece, wrong　**strokes** 6画　一 冂 冂 曲 曲 曲

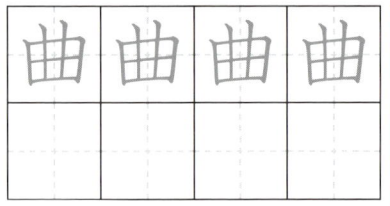

Protrude!

曲折	きょくせつ	meandering
楽曲	がっきょく	musical piece
曲がる	まがる	to bend
歪曲	わいきょく	distortion
婉曲(な)	えんきょく(な)	euphemistic

豊

Listening to music and looking after flowers helps your mind grow rich.

おんよみ ホウ
くんよみ ゆた(か)

いみ rich, abundant　**strokes** 13画　一 冂 冂 曲 曲 曲 曲 豊 豊 豊 豊 豊 豊

豊富	ほうふ	wealth
豊作	ほうさく	good harvest
豊か(な)	ゆたか(な)	rich
豊穣	ほうじょう	fertility
豊年	ほうねん	good year for crops

農

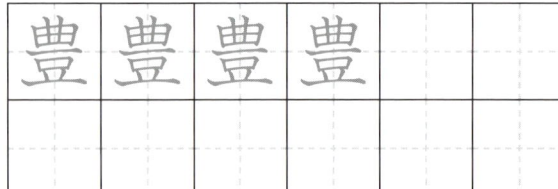

A dairy farmer was milking a cow in the pasture where you could see two forage silos.

おんよみ ノウ
くんよみ —

いみ agriculture, to cultivate　**strokes** 13画　一 冂 冂 曲 曲 芦 芦 農 農 農 農

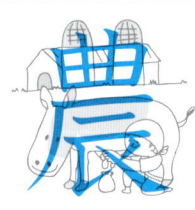

農業	のうぎょう	agriculture
農家	のうか	farmer
農場	のうじょう	farm
農具	のうぐ	farm implement
酪農	らくのう	dairy

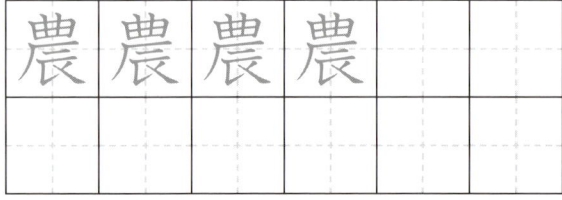

死

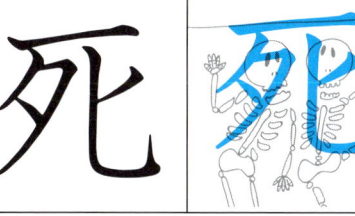

The dead bodies turned into skeletons and looked over the ground from the underground.

おんよみ シ
くんよみ し(ぬ)

いみ to die, death **strokes** 6画 一 ア 歹 歹 死 死

Point
死
Do not protrude!

死亡	しぼう	death
死者	ししゃ	the dead
死ぬ	しぬ	to die
死語	しご	dead language
死因	しいん	the cause of death

列

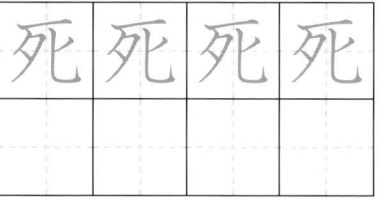

With a teacher's blow of a whistle, the children formed a line.

おんよみ レツ
くんよみ —

いみ line, queue **strokes** 6画 一 ア 歹 歹 列 列

Point
列
Note the longest vertical stroke!

行列	ぎょうれつ	procession
列車	れっしゃ	train
列席	れっせき	attendance of people
陳列	ちんれつ	display
序列	じょれつ	ranking

残

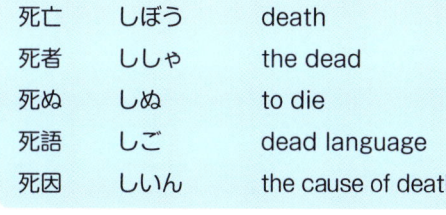

There was an unfinished drink, a fish bone and chopsticks left on the table.

おんよみ ザン
くんよみ のこ(る)・のこ(す)

いみ to remain, to leave behind **strokes** 10画 一 ア 歹 歹 歹 歹 残 残 残

Point
残
Note the number of these strokes!

残金	ざんきん	remaining money
残業	ざんぎょう	overtime work
残る	のこる	to remain
残留	ざんりゅう	residual
残雪	ざんせつ	lingering snow

者

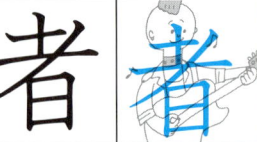

A young man was playing the guitar.

おんよみ シャ　　**くんよみ** もの

いみ person, people

strokes 8画　一 十 土 耂 耂 者 者 者

Point 者 ← Connect!

若者	わかもの	young people
役者	やくしゃ	actor
悪者	わるもの	bad person
著者	ちょしゃ	author

暑

A young man was playing the guitar even on a scorching hot and sunny day.

おんよみ ショ　　**くんよみ** あつ(い)

いみ hot

strokes 12画　丶 口 日 日 旦 早 早 昇 昇 暑 暑 暑

Point 暑 ← ×署　×若　Note the similar characters!

猛暑	もうしょ	heat wave
残暑	ざんしょ	lingering summer heat
暑い	あつい	hot
避暑	ひしょ	summering

募

I saw an advertisement looking for employees on the train.

おんよみ ボ　　**くんよみ** つの(る)

いみ to solicit, to recruit

strokes 12画　一 十 艹 艹 芍 苎 苜 莒 莫 莫 募 募

Point 募 ← Protrude!

募集	ぼしゅう	recruitment, collection
募金	ぼきん	fund-raising
募る	つのる	to solicit, to recruit
応募者	おうぼしゃ	applicant

勇

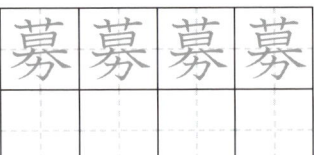

Armored warriors on horses marched up bravely.

おんよみ ユウ　　**くんよみ** いさ(む)

いみ brave, courageous

strokes 9画　フ マ マ 乛 甬 甬 甬 勇 勇

勇気	ゆうき	courage
勇敢	ゆうかん	bravery
勇み足	いさみあし	rashness
勇猛	ゆうもう	bravery, boldness

努

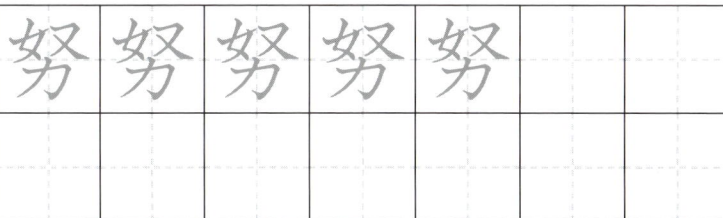

Having worked really hard, the woman graduated with top honors.

おんよみ ド
くんよみ つと(める)

いみ to try, to make efforts
strokes 7画   く 女 女 奴 奴 努 努

Point 努 ← Protrude!

| 努力 | どりょく | effort, working hard | もっと努力が必要だ。 |
| 努める | つとめる | to try | 再びミスをしないように努める。 |

勢

A rugby player holding a ball dashed vigorously avoiding the opponent's defense.

おんよみ セイ
くんよみ いきお(い)

いみ impetus, power, energy
strokes 13画   一 十 土 产 夫 去 幸 幸 幸丿 執 執 勢 勢

Point 勢 ×報 ×熱
Note the similar characters!

勢力	せいりょく	power	台風が勢力を強める。
情勢	じょうせい	situation	国際情勢によって株価が影響を受ける。
勢い	いきおい	impetus	水道管から勢いよく水が吹き出している。
運勢	うんせい	fortune	今年は運勢が良いらしい。
虚勢	きょせい	bluff	虚勢を張る。
時勢	じせい	times, trend	時勢に逆らう。

加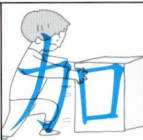

The man used his force to move a big box.

おんよみ カ　　**くんよみ** くわ(える)・くわ(わる)

いみ to add, to join　　**strokes** 5画　フ カ カ 加 加

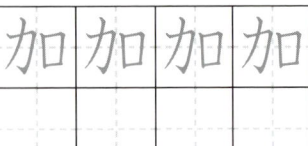

 ← Protrude!

加工	かこう	processing
加入	かにゅう	joining
加える	くわえる	to add
添加	てんか	addition

幼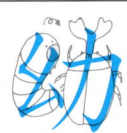

A grub turned into a big beetle.

おんよみ ヨウ　　**くんよみ** おさな(い)

いみ young, small, little　　**strokes** 5画　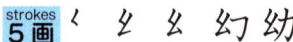

幼 ← Protrude!

幼児	ようじ	infant
幼少	ようしょう	childhood
幼い	おさない	young
幼虫	ようちゅう	grub

効

Eating eel is a good way to recover from summer fatigue.

おんよみ コウ　　**くんよみ** き(く)

いみ effect, to affect　　**strokes** 8画　 効 効

効果	こうか	effect
効力	こうりょく	efficacy
効く	きく	to affect
薬効	やっこう	drug efficacy

勉

While I was studying until late, my mother brought me a cup of coffee.

おんよみ ベン　　**くんよみ** —

いみ to work hard, to strive　　**strokes** 10画　ノ ク ク 名 各 舎 免 免 勉 勉

勉 ← Protrude!

勉強	べんきょう	study
勉学	べんがく	study
勤勉	きんべん	diligence

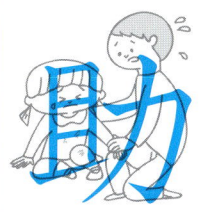

The man ran up to the child who fell over and helped her get up.

おんよみ ジョ
くんよみ たす(ける)・たす(かる)・すけ

いみ to help, to assist　**strokes** 7画　｜ 冂 月 月 目 助 助

Point
助 ← Note the number of horizontal strokes!

援助	えんじょ	assistance	父から経済的な援助を受けた。
助手	じょしゅ	assistant	彼は大学の研究室で助手を務めている。
手助け	てだすけ	help	忙しいときは、子供でも手助けになる。
救助	きゅうじょ	rescue	海でおぼれそうになり救助された。
補助	ほじょ	subsidy, subsidiary, auxiliary	起業するに当たり、補助を受けることができた。
助言	じょげん	advice	彼は的確な助言をしてくれた。

I pushed the statue really hard and moved it.

おんよみ ドウ
くんよみ うご(く)・うご(かす)

いみ to move　**strokes** 11画　一 二 〒 〒 盲 盲 亘 車 重 動 動

Point
動 ← Note the number of horizontal strokes!

動物	どうぶつ	animal	この森には野生の動物が暮らしている。
運動	うんどう	exercise, movement	運動不足なので駅まで歩く。
動く	うごく	to move	動くと痛むので安静にしている。
行動	こうどう	behavior, action	最後まで彼と行動を共にした。
移動	いどう	movement, transfer	電車で移動する。
自動	じどう	automatically, automation	機械が自動で掃除をしてくれる。

協

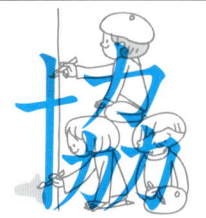

Three people worked together to paint the wall.

おんよみ キョウ
くんよみ —

いみ to work together
strokes 8画 　一 十 ナ ホ 协 协 協 協

協力	きょうりょく	cooperation
協調	きょうちょう	harmony
妥協	だきょう	compromise
協議	きょうぎ	discussion
協会	きょうかい	association

勤

Hardworking ants carried a massive piece of food to their nest.

おんよみ キン・ゴン
くんよみ つと(める)・つと(まる)

いみ to work for, to do a duty
strokes 12画 　一 十 廿 廿 芇 芇 苔 芦 堇 堇 勤 勤

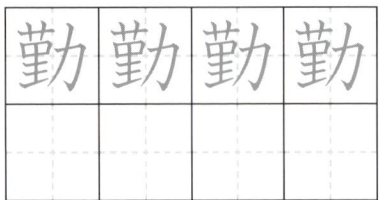
Point 勤 Do not protrude!

勤める	つとめる	to work
勤務	きんむ	duty
通勤	つうきん	commuting
転勤	てんきん	job transfer
欠勤	けっきん	absence from work

務

There were a receptionist, a computer operator and a clerk making copies in the office.

おんよみ ム
くんよみ つと(まる)・つと(める)

いみ to serve, to play a part
strokes 11画 　フ マ ヌ 予 矛 矛 矛 矛 教 務 務

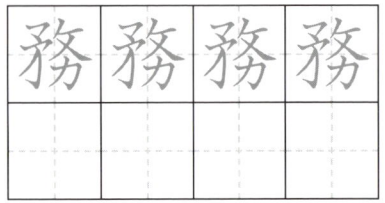
Point 務 Connect!

職務	しょくむ	duties
義務	ぎむ	obligation
務める	つとめる	to serve
事務所	じむしょ	office
公務	こうむ	public service

申

I have applied for a passport to prepare for my overseas trip that I will go on in six months.

- おんよみ シン
- くんよみ もう(す)
- いみ to say, to offer, to apply
- strokes 5画 一 𠃍 日 日 申

Point: Protrude!

申告	しんこく	declaration
申請	しんせい	application
申す	もうす	to say

神

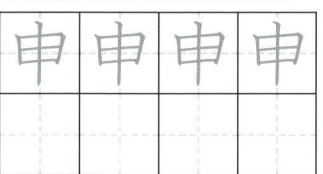

God fulfills the wishes of those who pray.

- おんよみ シン・ジン
- くんよみ かみ・かん・こう
- いみ god, venerable
- strokes 9画 ` ラ ォ ネ ネ 和 祠 袖 神

Point: ×禅 ×祝 — Note the similar characters!

神聖(な)	しんせい(な)	sacred
神社	じんじゃ	shrine
神業	かみわざ	miracle
神経	しんけい	nerve

全

The king put up an all-weather tent.

- おんよみ ゼン
- くんよみ まった(く)・すべ(て)
- いみ all, whole, entire
- strokes 6画 ノ 入 人 亼 全 全

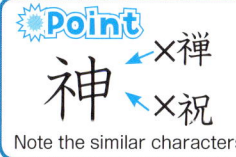

Point: Do not protrude!

全部	ぜんぶ	all, everything
全く	まったく	absolutely
全国	ぜんこく	the whole country
完全(な)	かんぜん(な)	complete, entire

余

The tent was so big that there was still enough room in it even when three people slept there.

- おんよみ ヨ
- くんよみ あま(る)・あま(す)
- いみ remainder, surplus
- strokes 7画 ノ 入 人 亼 全 余 余

Point: Connect!

余る	あまる	to be left
余分	よぶん	excess
余談	よだん	digression
余地	よち	space, room
余白	よはく	blank

213

物

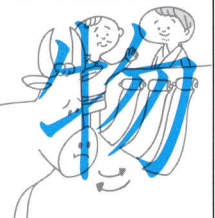

In ancient times, people made a living by bartering a cow for some cloth.

- おんよみ ブツ・モツ
- くんよみ もの

いみ thing, object, item　**strokes** 8画　ノ 匕 匕 牛 牛 牣 物 物

Point: Protrude!

生物	せいぶつ	living things	地球以外にも生物がすむ星はあるのだろうか。
書物	しょもつ	books	歴史的な書物を保存する。
物語	ものがたり	story	この物語は事実をもとに書かれている。
物質	ぶっしつ	material, substance, matter	現代は、物質に恵まれた時代だ。
物物交換	ぶつぶつこうかん	bartering	日本では昔、物物交換が行われていた。
品物	しなもの	goods	高価な品物をいただいた。

特

It is a special thing to have a cow visit the temple.

- おんよみ トク
- くんよみ ―

いみ special, especially　**strokes** 10画　ノ 匕 匕 牛 牛 牜 牜 牜 特 特

Point: Note the position of the dot!

特別	とくべつ	specially	彼が特別変わっているわけではない。
特殊(な)	とくしゅ(な)	peculiar	この製品は特殊な技術によって作られている。
特技	とくぎ	special skill	彼の特技はどこでもすぐに眠れることだ。
特集	とくしゅう	feature	この雑誌の映画特集はおもしろかった。
独特	どくとく	characteristic, unique	彼は独特のこだわりを持っている。
特急	とっきゅう	limited express	特急電車に乗る。

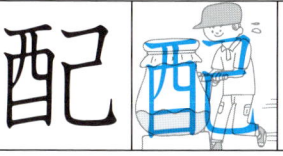

What the courier delivered was a large-sized barrel of *sake*.

おんよみ ハイ　　**くんよみ** くば(る)

いみ to deliver, to arrange　**strokes** 10画　一 丆 丌 丙 酉 酉 酉 酉¹ 配 配

Point
配 ← Do not connect!

配達	はいたつ	delivery
配色	はいしょく	color scheme
配る	くばる	to deliver
支配	しはい	domination

A mother wrapped her child in a blanket.

おんよみ ホウ　　**くんよみ** つつ(む)

いみ to wrap, package　**strokes** 5画　ノ ク 勹 匀 包

Point
包 ×抱
包 ×色
Note the similar characters!

包囲	ほうい	siege
包装	ほうそう	packing
包み紙	つつみがみ	wrapping paper
包括	ほうかつ	inclusion

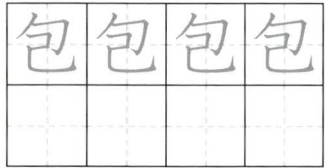

I tied the shoe lace tightly and set off for a hike.

おんよみ ハツ・ホツ　　**くんよみ** ―

いみ to start, to emit, to grow　**strokes** 9画　フ ヌ 癶 癶 癶 癶 癶 癶 発

Point
発 ← Connect!

出発	しゅっぱつ	departure
発音	はつおん	pronunciation
発端	ほったん	inception
発足	ほっそく	inauguration

The man climbed the steep mountain aiming for the summit.

おんよみ トウ・ト　　**くんよみ** のぼ(る)

いみ to go up, to climb　**strokes** 12画　フ ヌ 癶 癶 癶 癶 癶 癶 登 登 登 登

登校	とうこう	going to school
登山	とざん	mountain climbing
登る	のぼる	to go up, to climb
登録	とうろく	registration

A beautiful woman was angry and standing firmly with her legs wide apart.

おんよみ ビ
くんよみ うつく(しい)

いみ beautiful, to praise strokes 9画

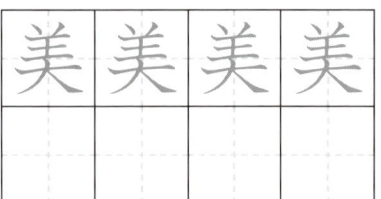

Point

Note the longest horizontal stroke!

美容院	びよういん	beauty parlor
美人	びじん	a beauty
美しい	うつくしい	beautiful
美食家	びしょくか	gourmet
美術	びじゅつ	art

 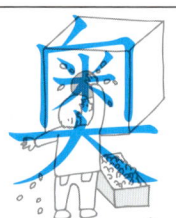

I put my hand deep inside the box so that I could collect every single grain of rice.

おんよみ オウ
くんよみ おく

いみ inner, depths, deep strokes 12画

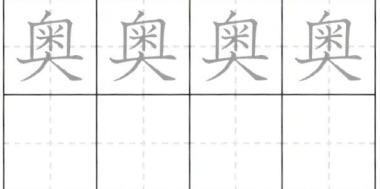

Point

Note the position of the dots!

奥義	おうぎ	arcanum
奥底	おくそこ	the depths
奥地	おくち	the backlands
奥歯	おくば	back tooth

When I opened the door, my son, who had gone to the party, had returned.

おんよみ レイ
くんよみ もど(す)・もど(る)

いみ to return, to go back strokes 7画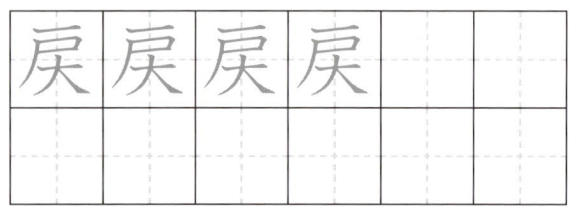

戻る	もどる	to come back, to return
返戻	へんれい	giving back
暴戻	ぼうれい	tyranny
戻す	もどす	to return

放

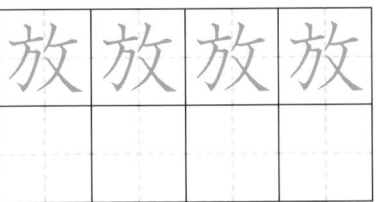

A cowboy threw a rope and caught a grazing cow.

- おんよみ：ホウ
- くんよみ：はな(す)・はな(つ)・はな(れる)・ほう(る)
- いみ：to let go, to give up
- strokes：8画　'　亠　方　方　方　方　放

Point: 放 — Do not protrude!

放牧	ほうぼく	grazing
放送	ほうそう	broadcasting
放す	はなす	to let go
追放	ついほう	expulsion
釈放	しゃくほう	release, discharge

旅

A group of tourists followed a tour guide who was holding a flag.

- おんよみ：リョ
- くんよみ：たび
- いみ：trip, travel, tour
- strokes：10画　'　亠　方　方　方　方　方　於　旅　旅

Point: 旅 — Do not protrude!

旅行	りょこう	trip, tour, travel
旅館	りょかん	inn, hotel
旅人	たびびと	traveler
旅費	りょひ	traveling expenses
一人旅	ひとりたび	traveling alone

族

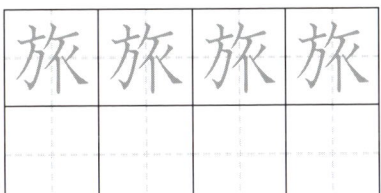

The clan led a nomadic life with bows and arrows, taking cows and horses with them.

- おんよみ：ゾク
- くんよみ：—
- いみ：tribe, clan, company
- strokes：11画　'　亠　方　方　方　方　方　於　於　族　族

Point: 族 — Do not protrude!

家族	かぞく	family
民族	みんぞく	race, tribe
皇族	こうぞく	the Imperial family
水族館	すいぞくかん	aquarium
族長	ぞくちょう	patriarch

命

In the tent, a messenger stood at attention and listened to the senior officer's order.

- おんよみ メイ・ミョウ
- くんよみ いのち

いみ life, destiny, order, command

strokes 8画 ノ 人 へ 合 合 合 命 命

Point: Do not connect!

命令	めいれい	orders	責任者の命令に従う。
寿命	じゅみょう	life span	日本人の寿命は平均して80歳を超えている。
命	いのち	life	もう少しで、命が危なかった。
運命	うんめい	destiny, fate	彼女との出会いは運命だと思う。
助命	じょめい	sparing a life	彼の助命を願い出る。
懸命(な)	けんめい(な)	hard	彼は家族のために懸命に働く。

卵

Penguins brooded their eggs while staying on their feet.

- おんよみ ラン
- くんよみ たまご

いみ egg

strokes 7画 ノ ヒ ヒ 臼 卯 卯 卵

Point: Note the position of the dots!

卵黄	らんおう	egg yolk	卵黄だけを料理に使う。
卵白	らんぱく	egg white	卵白に砂糖を加える。
産卵	さんらん	spawning	その海岸では、ウミガメの産卵が見られる。
卵形	たまごがた	egg-shaped	彼の卵形の顔がとても好きだ。
ゆで卵	ゆでたまご	boiled egg	朝食にゆで卵を食べた。
卵焼き	たまごやき	omelet	彼は卵焼きだけは作れる。

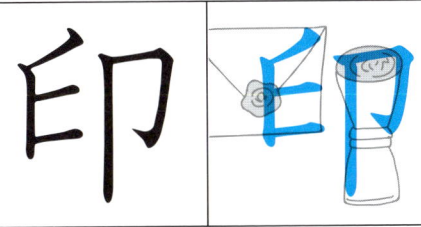

I sealed an envelop with sealing wax.

おんよみ イン
くんよみ しるし

いみ seal, stamp, guide　**strokes** 6画　

Point
印
Do not connect!

印鑑	いんかん	seal
印刷	いんさつ	printing
印象	いんしょう	impression
捺印	なついん	affixing a seal
目印	めじるし	mark

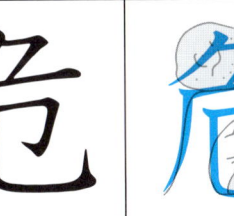

I narrowly escaped the danger from a falling rock by running quickly into a cave.

おんよみ キ
くんよみ あぶ(ない)・あや(うい)・あや(ぶむ)

いみ dangerous, to worry　**strokes** 6画　

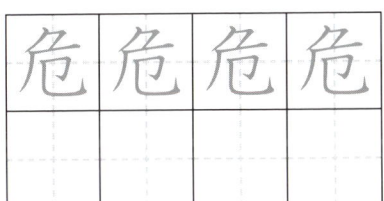

Point
危
Do not connect!

危ない	あぶない	dangerous
危機	きき	crisis, emergency
危険	きけん	danger
危篤	きとく	critical condition
危惧	きぐ	fear

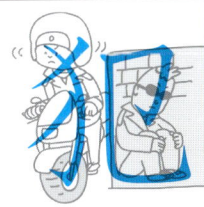

At the sight of the police officer, the criminal hid himself behind the fence.

おんよみ ハン
くんよみ おか(す)

いみ to commit, criminal　**strokes** 5画　

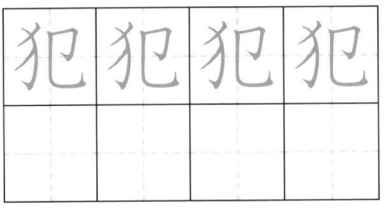

Point
犯
Do not protrude!

犯す	おかす	to commit
犯罪	はんざい	crime
犯人	はんにん	criminal
防犯	ぼうはん	crime prevention
共犯	きょうはん	complicity

様

A mother sheep and little lambs were watching the situation from behind a tree.

おんよみ ヨウ
くんよみ さま

いみ state, situation, form

strokes 14画 一 十 才 木 木 术 术 栏 栏 栏 样 样 様 様

Point
様
Note the number of horizontal strokes!

模様	もよう	pattern
様子	ようす	situation, look
様式	ようしき	style
仕様書	しようしょ	specifications
様々(な)	さまざま(な)	various

緑

A mother panda and its babies were eating bamboo leaves deep in the green mountains.

おんよみ リョク・ロク
くんよみ みどり

いみ green

strokes 14画 ⼃ ⼥ ⼥ ⽷ ⽷ ⽷ 紀 紀 紵 紵 紵 緑 緑

Point
緑
Note the longest horizontal stroke!

緑地	りょくち	green tract of land
新緑	しんりょく	fresh greenery
緑茶	りょくちゃ	green tea
緑青	ろくしょう	patina, verdigris
緑色	みどりいろ	green

暴

Above the cloud, the sun was watching the storm nearly blowing trees, houses and humans away.

おんよみ ボウ・バク
くんよみ あば(く)・あば(れる)

いみ violent, to rage, to expose

strokes 15画 ⼁ 口 日 旦 旦 早 昇 昇 昊 昊 暴 暴 暴 暴 暴

Point
暴
Note the longest horizontal stroke!

暴れる	あばれる	to rage
暴力	ぼうりょく	violence
乱暴(な)	らんぼう(な)	rough, violent
暴言	ぼうげん	violent language
暴露	ばくろ	exposure

各

The visitors came over on horseback one after another.

おんよみ カク
くんよみ おのおの

いみ each, respectively

strokes 6画　ノ ク タ 冬 各 各

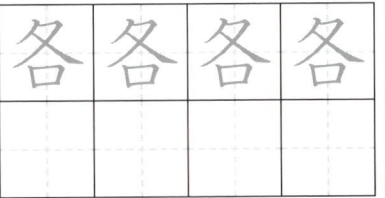

Note the similar characters!
×名
×君

各位	かくい	all, everyone
各自	かくじ	each (person)
各種	かくしゅ	various, every kind
各地	かくち	various places
各国	かっこく	each country

路

A traveler standing on the road with a stick waved her hand at the person on horseback.

おんよみ ロ
くんよみ じ

いみ road, route

strokes 13画　 一 ㇆ 口 口 ㇆ 足 足 足 趵 趵 路 路 路

Do not protrude!

道路	どうろ	road
線路	せんろ	railroad
経路	けいろ	route
岐路	きろ	crossroads
家路	いえじ	one's way home

略

A group of thieves on horses looted all the rice from the rice paddy.

おんよみ リャク
くんよみ ―

いみ to omit, to rob, omission

strokes 11画　 丨 冂 冂 用 田 田' 町 略 略 略 略

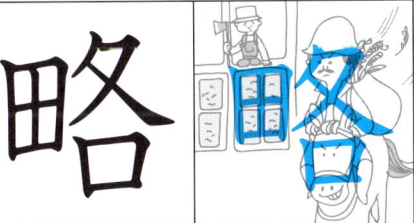

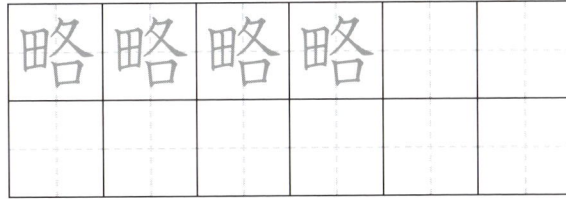

省略	しょうりゃく	omission
概略	がいりゃく	summary
略式の	りゃくしきの	informal
略奪	りゃくだつ	looting, plunder
攻略	こうりゃく	capture

絡

Because I received a letter saying that my mother was ill, I urged my horse toward home.

- おんよみ ラク
- くんよみ から(む)・から(まる)・から(める)

いみ to get tangled, to connect

strokes 12画 く 纟 幺 乡 糸 糸 紀 終 終 終 絡 絡

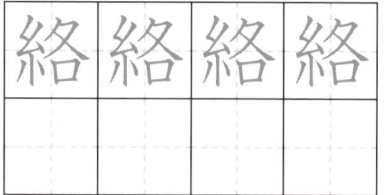

Point

Note the similar characters!

連絡	れんらく	contact
脈絡	みゃくらく	context
短絡	たんらく	short circuit
籠絡	ろうらく	cajolement
絡む	からむ	to be tangled

以

The Eastern and Western hemispheres are divided by the prime meridian.

- おんよみ イ
- くんよみ ―

いみ by, according

strokes 5画

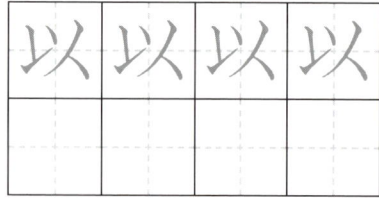

Point

Do not protrude!

～以上	～いじょう	above～, more than～, over～
～以後	～いご	after～
～以内	～いない	within～
～以来	～いらい	since～
以心伝心	いしんでんしん	tacit understanding

似

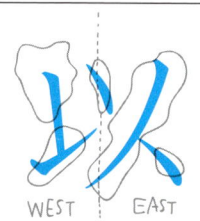

A model created by artificially copying the earth is called a terrestrial globe.

- おんよみ ジ
- くんよみ に(る)

いみ to resemble, to be like

strokes 7画 ノ 亻 亻 亻 似 似 似

似る	にる	to resemble
類似	るいじ	similarity
酷似	こくじ	close resemblance
疑似の	ぎじの	pseudo
相似	そうじ	similarity

1 Below the *Kanji*, write the Japanese reading of *Kanji* in *Hiragana*.

① 次　　② 逆らう　③ 島　　④ 命　　⑤ 庭
(　　)　(　　)　(　　)　(　　)　(　　)

⑥ 遊ぶ　⑦ 返す　⑧ 望む　⑨ 探す　⑩ 包む
(　　)　(　　)　(　　)　(　　)　(　　)

2 Choose the correct reading.

① 農業　（a　おうぎょう　b　こうぎょう　c　のうぎょう）(　　)

② 助命　（a　じゃめい　b　じゅめい　c　じょめい）(　　)

③ 座席　（a　ざせき　　b　ぜせき　　c　ざしょく）(　　)

④ 超越　（a　しょうえつ　b　もうえつ　c　ちょうえつ）(　　)

⑤ 進退　（a　しんかい　b　しんない　c　しんたい）(　　)

3 Write down the correct reading of the underlined part of the sentence.

① 番組で<u>放送</u>する。　　　　(　　　　)

② <u>環境</u>が<u>変化</u>する。　　　　(　　　　)
（へんか）

③ ドアが<u>開閉</u>する。　　　　(　　　　)

④ 薬の<u>効果</u>を<u>調</u>べる。　　　(　　　　)
（しら）

⑤ 手続きを<u>省略</u>する。　　　(　　　　)

4 After reading the *Hiragana* and English, write the *Kanji* that applies to the word in the box.

① ゆび (finger) ☐   ② さら (dish) ☐

③ かべ (wall) ☐   ④ しお (salt) ☐

⑤ し (death) ☐   ⑥ たび (trip) ☐

⑦ たまご (egg) ☐   ⑧ みどり (green) ☐

5 Choose the correct *Kanji* that corresponds to the *Hiragana* reading.

① おう(じる) (a 忘　b 応　c 志)　(　)

② あつ(い) (a 若　b 署　c 暑)　(　)

③ かみ (a 神　b 祝　c 禅)　(　)

④ かく (a 名　b 各　c 君)　(　)

⑤ いきお(い) (a 勢　b 熱　c 報)　(　)

6 In the boxes, write the *Kanji* that applies to the *furigana* reading.

① そく ど ☐☐ を守って走る。

② たて もの ☐☐ ごとに くば ☐ る。

③ [しゅっぱつ]までに[もど]ります。

④ [れっしゃ]が[ちえん]している。

⑤ [けんこう]のために[うんどう]する。

⑥ 6時に[きしょう]します。

⑦ [きゅうぎ]大会に[さんか]する。

⑧ 機械の[そうさ]を[まちが]える。

⑨ 会社に[きんむ]する。

⑩ [ち]のにじむような[どりょく]をする。

答え (answers)

❶ ①つぎ ②さか ③しま ④いのち ⑤にわ ⑥あそ ⑦かえ ⑧のぞ ⑨さが ⑩つつ

❷ ①c ②c ③a ④c ⑤c

❸ ①ほうそう ②かんきょう ③かいへい ④こうか ⑤しょうりゃく

❹ ①指 ②皿 ③壁 ④塩 ⑤死 ⑥旅 ⑦卵 ⑧緑

❺ ①b ②c ③a ④b ⑤a

❻ ①速度 ②建物, 配 ③出発, 戻 ④列車, 遅延 ⑤健康, 運動 ⑥起床 ⑦球技, 参加 ⑧操作, 間違 ⑨勤務 ⑩血, 努力

N2①

ここでは、日本語能力検定2級相当の漢字を
掲載しています。

contains the *Kanji* of the Japanese Language
Proficiency Test Level 2

訓

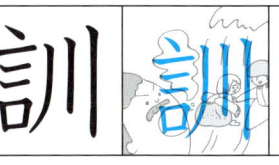

The man was giving rescue training at the river.

- おんよみ クン
- くんよみ —
- いみ teachings, the Kun reading of a kanji
- strokes 10画

Point: Note the number of horizontal strokes!

教訓	きょうくん	precept
家訓	かくん	family motto
訓練	くんれん	training
訓読	くんどく	the Japanese-style reading of Kanji

許

Because the man apologized in all sincerity, the teacher forgave him.

- おんよみ キョ
- くんよみ ゆる(す)
- いみ to allow, to forgive
- strokes 11画

Point: Do not protrude!

許可	きょか	permission
許容	きょよう	allowance
免許	めんきょ	license
許す	ゆるす	to allow, to forgive

訪

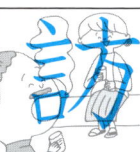

The teacher talked with his visitor at the entrance.

- おんよみ ホウ
- くんよみ おとず(れる)・たず(ねる)
- いみ to visit, to look for
- strokes 11画

Point: Do not protrude!

訪問	ほうもん	visit
来訪	らいほう	visit, call
再訪	さいほう	revisit
訪れる	おとずれる	to visit

評

The picture of a man looking at the ships and the sunset has become popular.

- おんよみ ヒョウ
- くんよみ —
- いみ to criticize, to judge, criticism
- strokes 12画

Point: Do not protrude!

評判	ひょうばん	reputation
批評	ひひょう	criticism
評価	ひょうか	evaluation, valuation
書評	しょひょう	book review

課

The teacher was tackling his task under the fruit tree.

おんよみ カ　　**くんよみ** ―

いみ to assign, section, lesson

strokes 15画

丶 亠 ニ 言 言 言 訁 訊 評 評 評 課 課

Point
課 ← Do not protrude!

課題	かだい	task
日課	にっか	daily routine
放課後	ほうかご	after school
課税	かぜい	taxation

談

The teacher was having a pleasant chat with his two friends.

おんよみ ダン　　**くんよみ** ―

いみ to talk, story

strokes 15画

丶 亠 ニ 言 言 言 訁 訁 談 談 談 談 談

Point
談 ← Note the position of the dots!

面談	めんだん	interview
雑談	ざつだん	chat
談判	だんぱん	negotiation
冗談	じょうだん	joke

調

The man prepared vegetables for cooking on the chopping board while chatting.

おんよみ チョウ　　**くんよみ** しら（べる）・ととの（う）・ととの（える）

いみ to examine, to correct

strokes 15画

丶 亠 ニ 言 言 言 訁 訊 訶 訶 調 調 調 調

Point
調 ← Do not protrude!

調理	ちょうり	cooking
調査	ちょうさ	investigation
調整	ちょうせい	adjustment
調べる	しらべる	to investigate

誤

The man chased after the garbage truck because he had mistakenly thrown away his valuables.

おんよみ ゴ　　**くんよみ** あやま（る）

いみ to mistake, error

strokes 14画

丶 亠 ニ 言 言 言 訁 訶 訶 誤 誤 誤 誤

Point
誤 ← Do not connect!

誤解	ごかい	misunderstanding
誤差	ごさ	error
誤報	ごほう	misinformation
誤る	あやまる	to mistake

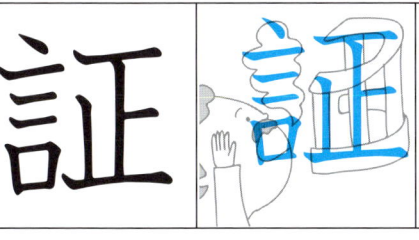

The teacher took the witness stand and gave accurate testimony.

おんよみ ショウ
くんよみ —

いみ to prove, proof　**strokes** 12画　`丶 亠 ㇉ 言 言 言 訂 訂 証 証`

Point: Do not protrude!

証明	しょうめい	proof, testimony	理論の証明がなされた。
証言	しょうげん	testimony	彼の証言により詳細が分かった。
証人	しょうにん	witness	原告側の証人として裁判に出廷した。
検証	けんしょう	verification	その問題の検証は、まだ十分されていない。
認証	にんしょう	authentication, certification	本人を指紋の認証で確認する。
証拠	しょうこ	proof, evidence	証拠を残す。

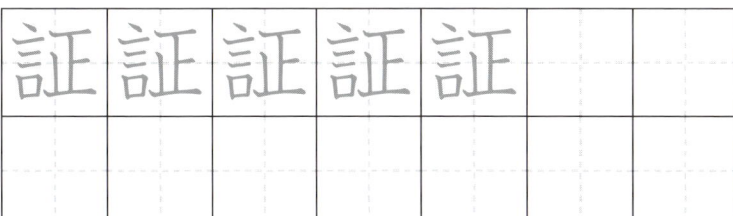

The teacher explained the importance of taxes to the people groaning under heavy taxes.

おんよみ セツ・ゼイ
くんよみ と(く)

いみ to tell, to persuade, theory　**strokes** 14画　`丶 亠 ㇉ 言 言 言 言 訁 訩 説 説 説`

Point: Note the position of the dots!

説明	せつめい	explanation	彼の説明はとてもわかりやすい。
解説	かいせつ	commentary	ニュースの解説を聞く。
説得	せっとく	persuasion	説得したが、決意は変わらなかった。
説教	せっきょう	lecture, preaching	遅刻が続き、上司から説教を受けた。
遊説	ゆうぜい	canvassing	候補者たちは選挙区の遊説に力を入れた。
説く	とく	to tell	彼は勉強の大切さを熱心に説く。

論

The father told his family to decide where to go by having a full discussion at home.

おんよみ ロン
くんよみ —

いみ to discuss, to argue, theory
strokes 15画 ｀ 一 ニ 主 主 言 言 言 診 診 診 診 論 論 論

Point
Do not protrude!

議論	ぎろん	argument, debate, discussion	激しい議論となった。
口論	こうろん	quarrel	父と母はいつも口論をしている。
結論	けつろん	conclusion	何度話し合っても結論は出なかった。
世論	よろん・せろん	public opinion	政治家の発言は世論の反発を招いた。
論理	ろんり	logic	彼の論理は破綻している。
勿論	もちろん	of course	勿論、私も一緒に行きます。

議

A man tried very hard to write down what the manager said at the meeting.

おんよみ ギ
くんよみ —

いみ to discuss, to consult, opinion, meeting
strokes 20画 ｀ 一 ニ 主 主 言 言 言 言 言 誰 誰 誰 誰 誰 議 議 議

Point
Note the position of the dot!

会議	かいぎ	conference, meeting	会議のため、席を外しています。
議会	ぎかい	parliament, the Diet	議会はその案を否決した。
議題	ぎだい	agenda	あの計画が議題にのぼった。
審議	しんぎ	deliberation	委員会で法案の審議を行う。
異議	いぎ	objection	異議を唱える者はいない。
不思議	ふしぎ	mystery, wonder	生命の不思議を解き明かしたい。

講

The teacher used a bar graph when he gave his lecture.

おんよみ コウ　　**くんよみ** ―

いみ to explain, to reconcile

strokes 17画　丶 一 ㇒ 言 言 言 言 計 計 誹 誹 誹 講 講 講 講

Point 講 ← Protrude!

講義	こうぎ	lecture
講和	こうわ	reconciliation
講習	こうしゅう	course
講評	こうひょう	criticism

詰

The teacher stuffed the canned foods into the box one by one.

おんよみ キツ　　**くんよみ** つ(める)・つ(まる)・つ(む)

いみ to stuff, to choke, to reprove

strokes 13画　丶 一 ㇒ 言 言 言 言 計 計 詰 詰 詰

Point 詰 ← Note the longest horizontal stroke!

詰問	きつもん	close questioning
難詰	なんきつ	censure
缶詰	かんづめ	canned food
詰め襟	つめえり	stand-up collar

識

While a paramedic was giving the unconscious patient a heart massage, the teacher called out to him.

おんよみ シキ　　**くんよみ** ―

いみ to know, consciousness

strokes 19画　丶 一 ㇒ 言 言 言 言 計 計 詳 詳 詳 詳 識 識 識 識 識

Point 識 ← Note the position of the dot!

知識	ちしき	knowledge
常識	じょうしき	common sense
意識	いしき	consciousness
面識	めんしき	acquaintance

認

The man was accepted as his apprentice.

おんよみ ニン　　**くんよみ** みと(める)

いみ to accept, to understand

strokes 14画　丶 一 ㇒ 言 言 言 訂 訂 認 認 認 認 認

Point 認 ← Note the position of the dots!

認識	にんしき	recognition
確認	かくにん	confirmation
認定	にんてい	authorization, recognition
承認	しょうにん	approval

231

試

The woman was trying on her wedding dress.

おんよみ シ　　**くんよみ** こころ(みる)・ため(す)

いみ to try, to test, exam　　**strokes** 13画　　丶　亠　二　亖　言　言　言　訂　訃　試　試

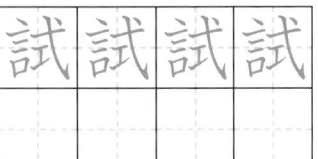

Point
試　Note the position of the dot!

試験	しけん	examination, test
試写	ししゃ	preview
試合	しあい	game, match
試みる	こころみる	to try

誌

 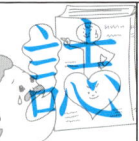

The man has a magazine that has a boy with a firm intention on the cover.

おんよみ シ　　**くんよみ** ―

いみ record, magazine　　**strokes** 14画　　丶　亠　二　亖　言　言　言　計　訐　訏　誌　誌　誌

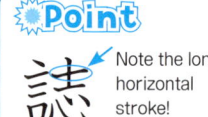
Point
誌　Note the longest horizontal stroke!

雑誌	ざっし	magazine
日誌	にっし	diary
週刊誌	しゅうかんし	weekly magazine
機関誌	きかんし	(official) organ

諸

The man spoke to the *samurai* warrior traveling around various countries.

おんよみ ショ　　**くんよみ** ―

いみ various, many　　**strokes** 15画　　丶　亠　二　亖　言　言　言　計　訐　訐　諸　諸　諸

Point
諸　Connect!

諸君	しょくん	ladies and gentlemen
諸説	しょせつ	various opinions
諸国	しょこく	various countries
諸島	しょとう	archipelago

医

The doctor examined patients on the stretchers by running to one after the other.

おんよみ イ　　**くんよみ** ―

いみ medical care, doctor　　**strokes** 7画　　一　丆　天　医　医　医　医

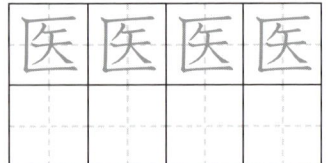

Point
医　Do not connect!

医者	いしゃ	doctor
医療	いりょう	medical care
主治医	しゅじい	doctor in charge
獣医	じゅうい	vet, veterinarian

According to the map, A ward and B ward are divided by a river, over which there is a bridge.

おんよみ ク
くんよみ —

いみ division, ward, to divide
strokes 4画 一 フ ヌ 区

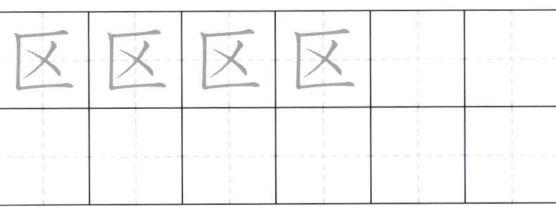

区別	くべつ	difference, distinction
区画	くかく	section, division
学区	がっく	school district
地区	ちく	area, district
区長	くちょう	ward mayor

The reason the man overslept was that he stayed up late watching TV last night.

おんよみ イン
くんよみ よ(る)

いみ cause, reason
strokes 6画 丨 冂 冃 円 囷 因

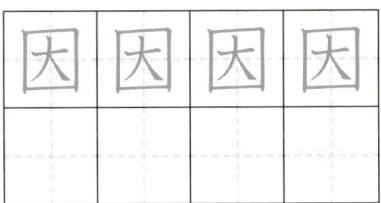

Note the similar characters!

因る	よる	to cause
因果	いんが	cause and effect
原因	げんいん	cause
敗因	はいいん	the cause of defeat
死因	しいん	the cause of death

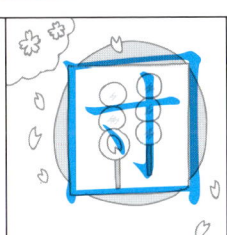

A cherry blossom petal fluttered down on *dango* (sweet rice dumpling) that was on a dish.

おんよみ ダン・トン
くんよみ —

いみ group, round
strokes 6画 丨 冂 冃 用 団 団

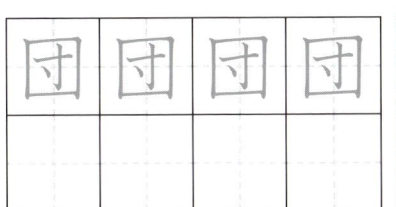

Note the position of the dot!

集団	しゅうだん	group, mass
団子	だんご	sweet rice dumpling
団結	だんけつ	unity
団地	だんち	housing complex
球団	きゅうだん	ball club, baseball team

 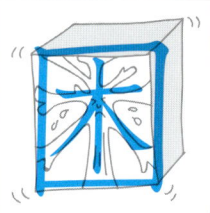

The tree that was shut into a small box was having difficulty.

おんよみ コン
くんよみ こま(る)

いみ to be troubled, poor **strokes** 7画

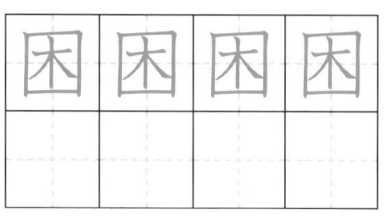

Protrude!

困る	こまる	to be worried
困難	こんなん	difficulty
困惑	こんわく	embarrassment, confusion
貧困	ひんこん	poverty
困苦	こんく	hardship

 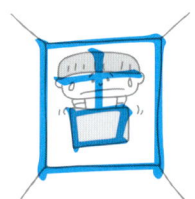

Once I put myself in the small box in the room, I was fixed.

おんよみ コ
くんよみ かた(める)・かた(まる)・かた(い)

いみ hard, firm, to harden **strokes** 8画

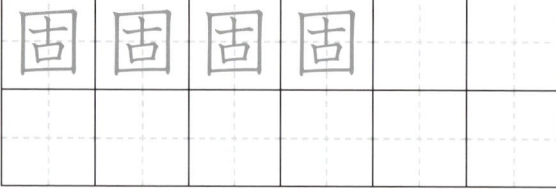

固める	かためる	to consolidate, to harden
固体	こたい	solid
固定	こてい	fixing
頑固	がんこ	stubbornness
固執	こしつ	persistence

We had a good time around the camp fire.

おんよみ イ
くんよみ かこ(む)・かこ(う)

いみ to surround, to enclose **strokes** 7画

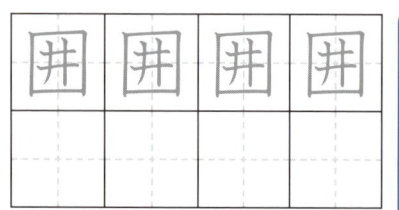

Do not connect!

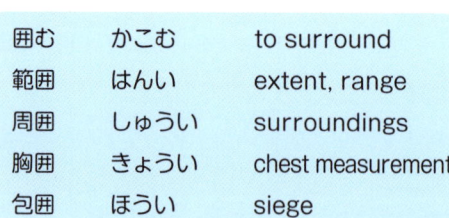

囲む	かこむ	to surround
範囲	はんい	extent, range
周囲	しゅうい	surroundings
胸囲	きょうい	chest measurement
包囲	ほうい	siege

象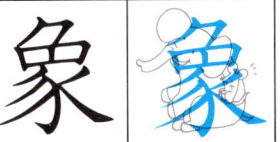

There was a mouse on the elephant.

おんよみ ショウ・ゾウ　　**くんよみ** —

いみ elephant, image　　**strokes** 12画　　ノ ク ク 产 角 角 乎 乎 罗 罗 罗 象 象

Point: Do not protrude!

印象	いんしょう	impression
対象	たいしょう	target, object
気象	きしょう	weather (conditions)
象牙	ぞうげ	ivory

像

A craft worker created a statue of the elephant with a mouse on it.

おんよみ ゾウ　　**くんよみ** —

いみ figure, image, to imitate　　**strokes** 14画　　ノ イ イ′ イ″ 伊 伊 伊 伊 伊 伊 像 像 像 像

映像	えいぞう	projected image, picture
想像	そうぞう	imagination
肖像	しょうぞう	portrait
仏像	ぶつぞう	statue of Buddha

争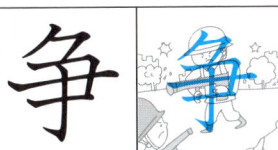

People were fighting over the territory.

おんよみ ソウ　　**くんよみ** あらそ(う)

いみ to contend, to fight, to quarrel　　**strokes** 6画　　ノ ク ク 刍 刍 争

Point: ×予 ×事 Note the similar characters!

競争	きょうそう	competition
戦争	せんそう	war
紛争	ふんそう	dispute
争う	あらそう	to fight, to quarrel

静

The moon and the alien in the UFO were quietly watching people fighting on the blue earth.

おんよみ セイ・ジョウ　　**くんよみ** しず・しず(か)・しず(まる)・しず(める)

いみ quiet, silent, to calm　　**strokes** 14画　　一 十 キ 主 丰 青 青 青 青′ 青″ 静 静 静 静

Point: Protrude!

冷静	れいせい	calmness
静寂	せいじゃく	silence
静脈	じょうみゃく	vein
物静か(な)	ものしずか(な)	quiet

235

People were groaning under the heavy taxation.

おんよみ ゼイ
くんよみ —

いみ tax　strokes 12画　ノ 二 千 千 禾 禾 禾' 禾' 利 税 税 税

Point
Note the position of the dots!

税金	ぜいきん	tax	給料から税金が引かれている。
税収	ぜいしゅう	tax revenue	景気の回復により、税収が増加する。
免税	めんぜい	tax exemption	空港の免税店でタバコを買った。
税率	ぜいりつ	tax rate	税率の引き上げが延期された。
増税	ぞうぜい	tax increase	4月から増税となった。
税務署	ぜいむしょ	tax office	税務署へ行かないといけない。

Many birds moved from the tree over there to the tree over here.

おんよみ イ
くんよみ うつ(る)・うつ(す)

いみ to move, to transfer　strokes 11画　ノ 二 千 千 禾 禾 禾' 移 移 移 移

Point
Note the position of the dots!

移る	うつる	to move, to transfer	石けんのにおいがタオルに移る。
移動	いどう	move, movement	車での移動は疲れる。
移行	いこう	shift	データの移行には時間がかかる。
移住	いじゅう	emigration, immigration	シンガポールへの移住が夢だ。
推移	すいい	transition	データの推移をわかりやすくグラフで表す。
移籍	いせき	transfer of belongings	主力選手の移籍が発表された。

和

The Olympics, symbolized by torch relays and the olive wreath, is called a Peace Festival.

おんよみ ワ・オ
くんよみ やわ(らぐ)・やわ(らげる)・なご(む)・なご(やか)

いみ peaceful, mild, to milden, Japanese　**strokes** 8画　ノ 二 千 千 禾 禾 和 和

和らぐ	やわらぐ	to milden, to soften
平和	へいわ	peace
和解	わかい	reconciliation
和音	わおん	chord
和食	わしょく	Japanese food

秒

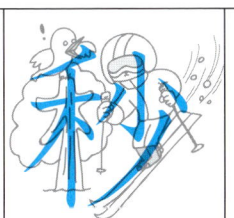

A bird flew away from the tree when a skier skied at full speed to take the lead in a second.

おんよみ ビョウ
くんよみ ―

いみ second　**strokes** 9画　ノ 二 千 千 禾 禾 利 利 秒 秒

秒速	びょうそく	speed per second
秒針	びょうしん	second hand (of clock)
毎秒	まいびょう	per second
寸秒	すんびょう	moment
秒読み	びょうよみ	countdown

程

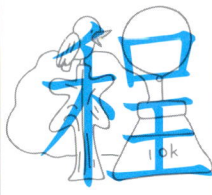

A bird on the tree watched the balloon ticd onto the weight.

おんよみ テイ
くんよみ ほど

いみ rule, degree, order　**strokes** 12画　ノ 二 千 千 禾 禾 禾 积 积 秤 秤 程 程

Point
程
Do not protrude!

十日程	とおかほど	about ten days
程度	ていど	degree, level
日程	にってい	(day's) schedule
工程	こうてい	process
方程式	ほうていしき	equation

237

積

A boy piled an alien spaceship on a shellfish and then placed an alien on the spaceship.

おんよみ セキ　　**くんよみ** つ(む)・つ(もる)

いみ to pile, to load, the product

strokes 16画　ノ 二 千 千 禾 禾 秆 秆 秆 秸 秸 秸 積 積 積 積

Point Note the longest horizontal stroke!

蓄積	ちくせき	accumulation
累積	るいせき	accumulation
面積	めんせき	area, acreage
山積み	やまづみ	heap, pile

卒

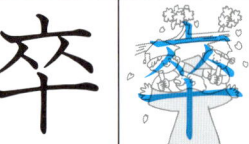

Two graduates were holding their diplomas with their teacher under the cherry tree.

おんよみ ソツ　　**くんよみ** ―

いみ to end, to graduate, soldier

strokes 8画　ヽ 亠 亠 𣥂 𣥂 㓥 卒 卒

Point Do not protrude!

卒業	そつぎょう	graduation
新卒	しんそつ	new graduate
兵卒	へいそつ	common soldier
卒倒	そっとう	faint

幸

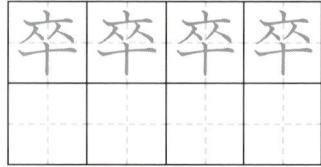

I would feel very happy if I could put a propeller on my head and fly freely in the sky.

おんよみ コウ　　**くんよみ** さいわ(い)・さち・しあわ(せ)

いみ happy, happiness, luck

strokes 8画　一 十 土 𡈼 𡈼 坴 坴 幸

Point Note the longest horizontal stroke!

幸福	こうふく	happiness
幸運	こううん	good luck
多幸	たこう	great happiness
不幸せ	ふしあわせ	unhappiness

辛

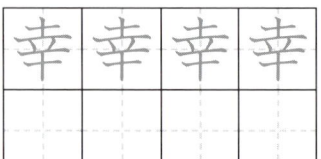

I would feel very unhappy if the propeller were gone from my head while I stayed in the sky.

おんよみ シン　　**くんよみ** から(い)

いみ hot, spicy, painful

strokes 7画　ヽ 亠 亠 立 立 辛 辛

Point Note the longest horizontal stroke!

香辛料	こうしんりょう	spice
辛苦	しんく	hardship
辛抱	しんぼう	patience
辛口(な)	からくち(な)	dry, hot, pungency

238

率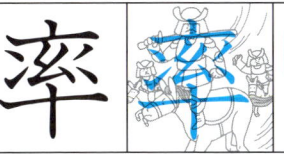

The general leading his fellow warriors launched an attack.

おんよみ ソツ・リツ　**くんよみ** ひき(いる)

いみ to lead, to head, ratio　**strokes** 11画　'　亠　亠　玄　玄　玄　㴇　㴇　㴇　率　率

Point Note the position of the dots!

引率	いんそつ	leading
率直	そっちょく	frankness
確率	かくりつ	probability
率いる	ひきいる	to lead, to head

単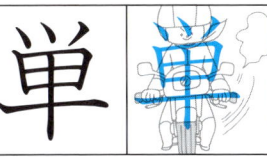

I drove a motorcycle on a motorway.

おんよみ タン　**くんよみ** ―

いみ single, only　**strokes** 9画　'　''　'''　''''　''''　当　当　当　単

Point Note the position of the dots!

単価	たんか	unit price
単身	たんしん	alone, single
単位	たんい	unit
単純	たんじゅん	simplicity

章

A reporter wearing an armband came to get coverage of the story.

おんよみ ショウ　**くんよみ** ―

いみ sentence, chapter, article, badge　**strokes** 11画　'　亠　亠　立　产　咅　咅　音　章　章

Point ×意 ×草 Note the similar characters!

文章	ぶんしょう	sentence
憲章	けんしょう	charter
勲章	くんしょう	decoration, medal
序章	じょしょう	introductory chapter

準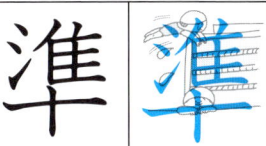

Having warmed up well, the girl dived into the swimming pool with a spray of water.

おんよみ ジュン　**くんよみ** ―

いみ standard, to conform, semi　**strokes** 13画　'　冫　シ　汁　汁　汁　汁　淮　淮　準　準

Point Note the position of the dots!

準備運動	じゅんびうんどう	warming-up
標準	ひょうじゅん	standard
準拠	じゅんきょ	conformity
準決勝	じゅんけっしょう	semifinal

239

季

Children are always energetic whatever season it is.

おんよみ キ　くんよみ —

いみ season

strokes 8画　一 二 千 千 禾 禾 季 季

Point
季 ×委
　 ×字
Note the similar characters!

季節	きせつ	season
四季	しき	four seasons
雨季	うき	rainy season
夏季	かき	summer season

孫

The child next to the old lady is her grandchild.

おんよみ ソン　くんよみ まご

いみ grandchild, descendant

strokes 10画　7 了 子 孑 孑 弥 孫 孫 孫 孫

Point
孫 Protrude!

曽孫	ひまご・そうそん	great-grandchild
子孫	しそん	descendant
初孫	はつまご	one's first grandchild

布

I had a cloth bag slung over my shoulder and held a suitcase with my hand.

おんよみ フ　くんよみ ぬの

いみ cloth, to spread

strokes 5画　ノ ナ 才 右 布

Point
布 Do not protrude!

布巾	ふきん	dish towel
毛布	もうふ	blanket
配布	はいふ	distribution
布地	ぬのじ	cloth, fabric

希

I got off at a foreign airport with a shoulder bag and a suitcase. I was full of hope.

おんよみ キ　くんよみ —

いみ rare, hope, to hope

strokes 7画　ノ メ ブ ブ 产 弟 希

希望	きぼう	hope
希少	きしょう	rarity
希薄(な)	きはく(な)	thin
希釈	きしゃく	dilution

帯

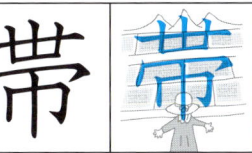

I visited the beautiful countryside.

おんよみ タイ　**くんよみ** お(びる)・おび

いみ sash, belt, to carry, to have

strokes 10画　一 十 艹 艹 丗 丗 芇 芇 帯 帯

Point 帯 ← Do not protrude!

包帯	ほうたい	bandage
携帯電話	けいたいでんわ	mobile phone, cellphone
地帯	ちたい	area
帯	おび	*obi* (Japanese sash)

師

Students were taking a class with a Japanese language teacher.

おんよみ シ　**くんよみ** —

いみ teacher, mentor, army

strokes 10画　ノ 亻 亻 亻 亇 亇 亇 師 師 師

Point 師 ← Do not connect!

教師	きょうし	teacher
師匠	ししょう	mentor
漁師	りょうし	fisherman
技師	ぎし	engineer

幅

As the wide car came down the narrow road, the man had to move his body aside.

おんよみ フク　**くんよみ** はば

いみ width

strokes 12画　丨 口 巾 帄 帄 帄 帄 帄 幅 幅 幅 幅

Point 幅 ← Do not connect!

振幅	しんぷく	amplitude
拡幅	かくふく	widening
歩幅	ほはば	stride
値幅	ねはば	price range

典

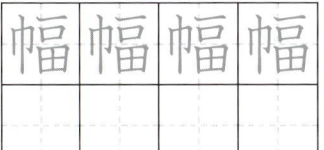

A man stood on the platform, and a memorial ceremony was performed.

おんよみ テン　**くんよみ** —

いみ book, scripture, ceremony, rule

strokes 8画　丨 口 巾 曲 曲 典 典 典

Point 典 ← Protrude!

式典	しきてん	ceremony
古典	こてん	classic
典型	てんけい	type
聖典	せいてん	Holy Scripture

241

 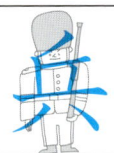

A soldier was standing wearing a gun.

おんよみ ヘイ・ヒョウ　　**くんよみ** ―

いみ soldier, army, troops　　**strokes** 7画　ノ 亻 斤 丘 丘 兵 兵

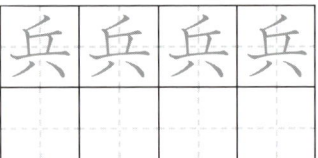

Point 兵 Do not protrude!

兵隊	へいたい	soldier, troops
兵器	へいき	weapon
兵法	へいほう	military strategy
兵糧	ひょうろう	military provisions

 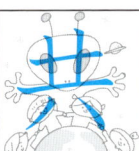

An alien was dreaming of living in peaceful coexistence with humans on earth.

おんよみ キョウ　　**くんよみ** とも

いみ together, common　　**strokes** 6画　一 十 艹 丑 共 共

Point 共 Note the longest horizontal stroke!

共存	きょうぞん	coexistence
共通の	きょうつうの	common
共感	きょうかん	empathy
公共の	こうきょうの	public

 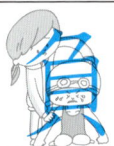

I cheered up a disappointed friend who had lost the game.

おんよみ フ　　**くんよみ** ま(ける)・ま(かす)・お(う)

いみ to shoulder, to be defeated　　**strokes** 9画　ノ ク 円 介 角 角 自 負 負

Point 負 Note the number of horizontal strokes!

負荷	ふか	load
負担	ふたん	burden
勝負	しょうぶ	game, match
負ける	まける	to lose

Two men were looking at the robot with interest.

おんよみ コウ・キョウ　　**くんよみ** おこ(る)・おこ(す)

いみ to set up, fun　　**strokes** 16画　ノ 亻 亻 旨 自 自 自 自 自 自 興 興 興 興 興 興

Point 興 Do not connect!

興奮	こうふん	excitement
振興	しんこう	promotion
興味	きょうみ	interest
興す	おこす	to set up

異

The place the alien landed was the countryside where fields of rice paddies spread out.

おんよみ イ　　**くんよみ** こと

いみ to differ, different, strange　　**strokes** 11画

一 口 四 田 田 甲 甼 昇 畀 異 異

異国	いこく	foreign country
異動	いどう	change, transfer
異常	いじょう	abnormality
異なる	ことなる	to differ

重

I balanced the scale by placing weights on each side.

おんよみ ジュウ・チョウ　　**くんよみ** え・おも(い)・かさ(ねる)・かさ(なる)

いみ heavy, important, to overlap　　**strokes** 9画

一 二 千 千 台 台 台 重 重

Point: Note the number of horizontal strokes!

体重	たいじゅう	weight
貴重(な)	きちょう(な)	valuable
二重まぶた	ふたえまぶた	double eyelid
重荷	おもに	burden

種

I used a scale to weigh the seed that was carried by a bird.

おんよみ シュ　　**くんよみ** たね

いみ seed, species　　**strokes** 14画

一 二 千 千 禾 禾 彩 秆 秆 秆 稍 稻 種 種

種類	しゅるい	kind, sort
職種	しょくしゅ	the type of job
人種	じんしゅ	race
火種	ひだね	live coal, cause

働

The president who told his employee to move the statue was satisfied with his hard work.

おんよみ ドウ　　**くんよみ** はたら(く)

いみ to work　　**strokes** 13画

ノ イ イ 亻 仟 仟 仟 佢 侑 俥 俥 働 働

Point: ×動 ×勦　Note the similar characters!

労働	ろうどう	labor
実働時間	じつどうじかん	actual working hours
稼働中	かどうちゅう	being in operation
働き者	はたらきもの	hard worker

243

不

A phoenix is a mythical creature that is said to live eternally.

おんよみ フ・ブ
くんよみ —

いみ not

strokes 4画 一フイ不

不死鳥	ふしちょう	phoenix	不死鳥は何度でもよみがえる。
不足	ふそく	shortage	彼女は経験が不足している。
不安	ふあん	anxiety	失敗に対して不安になる。
不便	ふべん	inconvenience	この辺りは駅に出るのに不便だ。
不用心(な)	ぶようじん(な)	careless, unsafe	カギをかけないと不用心な気がする。
不器用(な)	ぶきよう(な)	clumsy	不器用な父親が、心をこめて料理した。

事

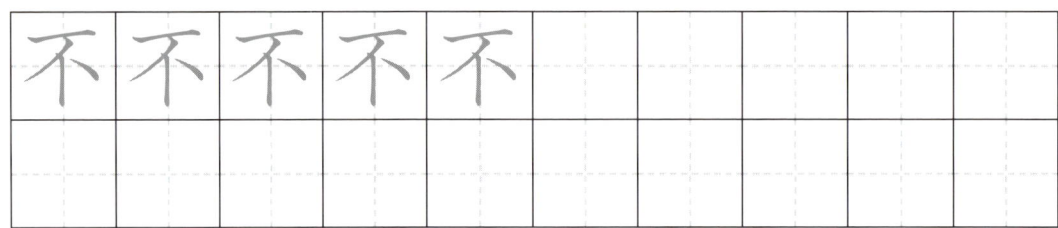

I happened to see an accident in which a car crashed into a power pole.

おんよみ ジ・ズ
くんよみ こと

いみ thing, matter

strokes 8画 一フ丆〒亘写写事

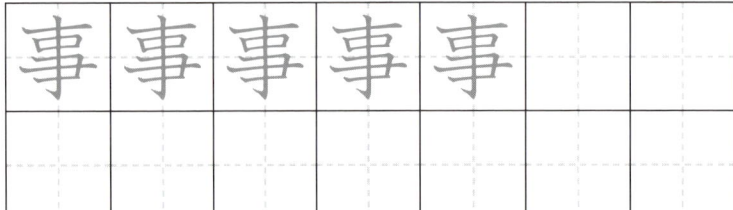

Point

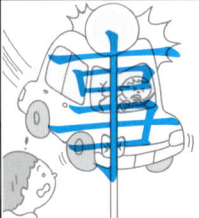

Protrude!

事故	じこ	accident, trouble	危うく事故にあうところだった。
事件	じけん	incident, case, event	事件の全てが明らかになったわけではない。
人事	じんじ	personnel matters	人事が発表された。
事実	じじつ	fact	事実を曲げるわけにはいかない。
仕事	しごと	work	彼は仕事を辞めると言い出した。
物事	ものごと	things	物事がうまくいく。

干

On a sunny day, I hang the washing such as socks on the clothesline in the garden.

おんよみ カン **くんよみ** ほ(す)・ひ(る)

いみ to dry **strokes** 3画 一 二 干

Point: Do not protrude!

干潮	かんちょう	low tide
干害	かんがい	drought disaster
干渉	かんしょう	interference
干物	ひもの	dried fish

平

There was a picture of a woman looking at the ships and the sun setting below the horizon.

おんよみ ヘイ・ビョウ **くんよみ** たい(ら)・ひら

いみ flat, even **strokes** 5画 一 ニ ア 立 平

Point: Note the position of the dots!

水平線	すいへいせん	the horizon
平日	へいじつ	weekday
平等	びょうどう	equality
平社員	ひらしゃいん	employee with no title

末

A bird perched at the end of the branch of the tree.

おんよみ マツ・バツ **くんよみ** すえ

いみ end, tip **strokes** 5画 一 ニ キ 才 末

Point: Note the longest horizontal stroke!

月末	げつまつ	the end of the month
粗末(な)	そまつ(な)	shabby
端末	たんまつ	computer terminal
末っ子	すえっこ	the youngest child

未

How large will the tree be in the future?

おんよみ ミ **くんよみ** ―

いみ not, yet **strokes** 5画 一 ニ キ 才 未

Point: Note the longest horizontal stroke!

未来	みらい	future
未定の	みていの	undecided
未成年	みせいねん	nonage
未曾有	みぞうの	unprecedented

245

束

The bouquet had a message card attached.

- おんよみ ソク
- くんよみ たば
- いみ bunch, sheaf, to bundle
- strokes 7画 　一 ／ ／ ／ ／ ／ 束

Point: 束 ← Protrude!

結束	けっそく	unity
束縛	そくばく	restriction, restraint
約束	やくそく	promise
花束	はなたば	bouquet

粉

I made rice powder by hitting the rice grains with a stick.

- おんよみ フン
- くんよみ こ・こな
- いみ powder
- strokes 10画 　、 ／ ／ ／ ／ ／ ／ ／ 粉 粉

Point: 粉 ← Note the position of the dots!

粉末	ふんまつ	powder
花粉	かふん	pollen
小麦粉	こむぎこ	flour
粉骨砕身	ふんこつさいしん	doing one's best

粒

When you cook rice well, the rice grains look upstanding.

- おんよみ リュウ
- くんよみ つぶ
- いみ grain, drop
- strokes 11画 　、 ／ ／ ／ ／ ／ ／ ／ 粒 粒 粒

粒子	りゅうし	particle
顆粒	かりゅう	granule
米粒	こめつぶ	grain of rice
雨粒	あまつぶ	raindrop

料

I made a rice meal of prawn *sushi* and placed a pair of chopsticks next to it.

- おんよみ リョウ
- くんよみ ―
- いみ material, fodder, charge
- strokes 10画 　、 ／ ／ ／ ／ ／ ／ ／ 料 料

Point: 料 ← Note the position of the dots!

料理	りょうり	cooking
燃料	ねんりょう	fuel
料金	りょうきん	charge, fare, fee
材料	ざいりょう	material, stuff

精

I polished the harvested rice with a machine.

おんよみ セイ・ショウ
くんよみ —

いみ refined, detailed, spirit
strokes 14画 　丶 ゛ ゛ ニ キ 米 米 料 籵 籵 精 精 精 精

Point
精
Note the longest horizontal stroke!

精米	せいまい	rice polishing
精製	せいせい	refinement
精鋭	せいえい	the best [pick]
精密	せいみつ	precision
精神	せいしん	spirit, mind

歯

Brush your teeth properly so that they won't go bad.

おんよみ シ
くんよみ は

いみ tooth
strokes 12画 　丨 ト 卜 歩 歩 歩 歩 歩 歯 歯 歯 歯

Point
歯
Note the position of the dots!

歯科	しか	dentistry
抜歯	ばっし	tooth extraction
乳歯	にゅうし	baby tooth
歯茎	はぐき	gums
前歯	まえば	front tooth

育

A carrot was growing rapidly underground.

おんよみ イク
くんよみ そだ(つ)・そだ(てる)・はぐく(む)

いみ to grow, to bring up
strokes 8画 　丶 亠 去 去 产 育 育 育

Point
育
Note the number of horizontal strokes!

育つ	そだつ	to grow
育児	いくじ	childcare
育成	いくせい	training, cultivation
教育	きょういく	education
発育	はついく	growth

有

The *samurai* warrior has confidence in the martial art with his daily practice.

おんよみ ユウ・ウ
くんよみ あ(る)

いみ to have, to possess, to exist　strokes 6画　ノ ナ オ 有 有 有

Point: 有 ← Protrude!

有望(な)	ゆうぼう(な)	promising	彼は将来が有望な選手だ。
有名(な)	ゆうめい(な)	famous	彼女が有名な作家だとは知らなかった。
所有	しょゆう	ownership, possession	この家は私が所有している。
有害(な)	ゆうがい(な)	harmful, injurious	有害な成分が検出された。
有頂天	うちょうてん	ecstasy, rapture	上司にほめられて、彼は有頂天になった。
有る	ある	to be, to exist, to have	彼には人を楽しませる才能が有る。

骨

A skeleton was standing with both its arms wide open.

おんよみ コツ
くんよみ ほね

いみ bone, skeleton, frame　strokes 10画　丨 冂 冂 円 円 骨 骨 骨 骨

Point: 骨 ← Do not connect!

骨格	こっかく	framework, skeleton	彼の骨格はほっそりしている。
骨折	こっせつ	fracture	腕を骨折して一週間入院した。
骸骨	がいこつ	skeleton	彼は骸骨のようにやせていた。
鉄骨	てっこつ	steel frame	建物の鉄骨が組まれ始めた。
骨子	こっし	gist, main point	計画の骨子を資料にまとめる。
背骨	せぼね	backbone, spine	姿勢が悪いので背骨が曲がってきた。

背

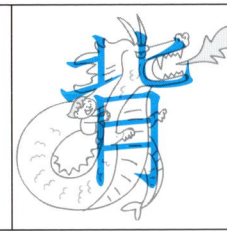

I flew in the sky on the back of a dragon.

おんよみ ハイ
くんよみ せ・せい・そむ(く)・そむ(ける)

いみ back, to betray, to go against

strokes 9画 　一 ｜ ｜ ｜ 北 北 背 背 背

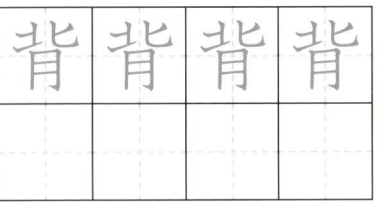

Point
背
Do not protrude!

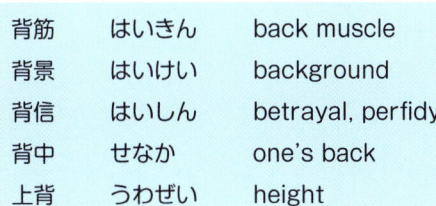

背筋	はいきん	back muscle
背景	はいけい	background
背信	はいしん	betrayal, perfidy
背中	せなか	one's back
上背	うわぜい	height

肩

A monkey was sitting on the woman's shoulder.

おんよみ ケン
くんよみ かた

いみ shoulder

strokes 8画 　一 ｜ ｜ 戸 戸 肩 肩 肩

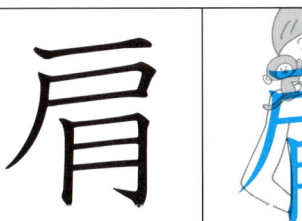

肩甲骨	けんこうこつ	scapula
強肩	きょうけん	strong throwing arm
比肩	ひけん	equality
肩章	けんしょう	epaulet
肩凝り	かたこり	stiff shoulders

胃

The stomach is connected with the small intestine and the large intestine.

おんよみ イ
くんよみ ―

いみ stomach

strokes 9画 　｜ 口 四 田 田 胃 胃 胃 胃

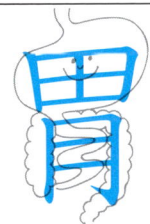
Point
胃
Do not connect!

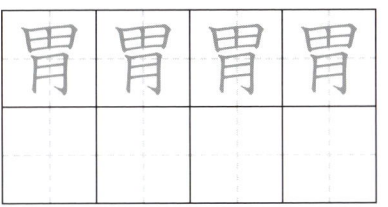

胃袋	いぶくろ	stomach
胃腸	いちょう	stomach and intestines
胃痛	いつう	stomachache
胃弱	いじゃく	indigestion
胃炎	いえん	gastritis

249

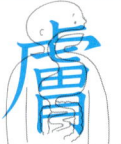

The human body consists of various organs and skin that covers whole the body.

おんよみ フ　　**くんよみ** —

いみ skin

strokes 15画　 ` ー ｒ 广 户 卢 卢 庐 庐 庐 庐 膚 膚 膚 膚

| 皮膚 | ひふ | skin |
| 完膚なきまでに | かんぷなきまでに | thoroughly |

At a certain period of time, the ladder and the moon appear side by side.

おんよみ キ・ゴ　　**くんよみ** —

いみ period of time, to expect

strokes 12画　一 十 廿 艹 甘 甘 其 其 期 期 期 期

Do not protrude!

期間	きかん	period of time
定期券	ていきけん	commuter pass
期待	きたい	expectation
期末	きまつ	the end of a term

The moon engaged in strenuous training with his teammates so it could win the game.

おんよみ ショウ　　**くんよみ** か(つ)・まさ(る)

いみ to win, to excel

strokes 12画　丿 几 月 月 月'' 肝 胖 胖 胖 勝 勝

Protrude!

勝利	しょうり	victory
決勝	けっしょう	finals
勝者	しょうしゃ	winner
勝つ	かつ	to win

At the referee's signal, the moon started arm-wrestling with the girl.

おんよみ ワン　　**くんよみ** うで

いみ arm

strokes 12画　丿 几 月 月 月' 肊 肊 肱 腕 腕 腕

Do not connect!

腕力	わんりょく	brawn
右腕	みぎうで	right arm, right-hand man
腕相撲	うでずもう	arm-wrestling
腕前	うでまえ	skill

腰

The moon helped the woman who was stretching her waist trying to reach her trunk.

おんよみ ヨウ **くんよみ** こし

いみ waist, hips

strokes 13画   ) 几 月 月 尹 尹 尹 尹 胛 胛 腰 腰 腰

Point 腰 ← Protrude!

腰痛	ようつう	low back pain
弱腰	よわごし	weak attitude
物腰	ものごし	demeanor
中腰	ちゅうごし	half-sitting posture

腹

The moon gave food to the rabbit that was so hungry that one of its ears was flopped down.

おんよみ フク **くんよみ** はら

いみ belly, stomach

strokes 13画   ) 几 月 月 尹 尹 尹 胪 胪 胪 腹 腹 腹

Point 腹 ← Note the number of horizontal strokes!

腹痛	ふくつう	stomachache, abdominal pain
空腹	くうふく	hunger
腹筋	ふっきん	abdominal muscle
蛇腹	じゃばら	bellows, cornice

脳

A patient broke into a sweat with surprise that the moon was going to perform his brain surgery.

おんよみ ノウ **くんよみ** ―

いみ brain

strokes 11画   ) 几 月 月 尹 尹 尹 胪 脳 脳 脳

Point 脳 ← Note the position of the dots!

頭脳	ずのう	brain, head
脳天	のうてん	the top of the head
脳死	のうし	brain death
首脳	しゅのう	head leader

肌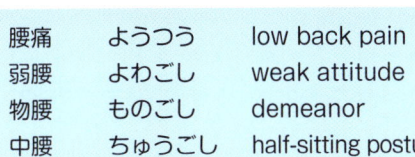

The moon applied lotion to soften the texture of its skin.

おんよみ ― **くんよみ** はだ

いみ skin

strokes 6画   ) 几 月 月 肌 肌

肌着	はだぎ	underwear
素肌	すはだ	bare skin
鳥肌	とりはだ	goose bumps
鮫肌	さめはだ	rough skin

251

The moon observed the leaf's veins.

おんよみ ミャク　　**くんよみ** —

いみ pulsation, vein　　**strokes** 10画　ノ 冂 月 月 月゛ 肝 肝 胪 脈 脈

脈拍	みゃくはく	pulsation
山脈	さんみゃく	mountain range
文脈	ぶんみゃく	context
鉱脈	こうみゃく	lode, vein

The moon's heart warmed when it saw the baby being held to her mother's bosom.

おんよみ キョウ　　**くんよみ** むね・むな

いみ chest, breast, bosom　　**strokes** 10画　ノ 冂 月 月 月゛ 肭 肭 胸 胸 胸

Point: 胸 ← Do not connect!

胸囲	きょうい	chest measurement
度胸	どきょう	courage
胸焼け	むねやけ	heartburn
胸騒ぎ	むなさわぎ	presentiment, uneasiness

The woman was wearing a national costume.

おんよみ ミン　　**くんよみ** たみ

いみ people, populace　　**strokes** 5画　フ コ ア 尸 民

Point: 民 ← Do not protrude!

国民	こくみん	nation, people
住民	じゅうみん	resident
民間の	みんかんの	civilian, private
民	たみ	people

A woman in a national dress was so tired that she fell asleep leaning against a power pole.

おんよみ ミン　　**くんよみ** ねむ(る)・ねむ(い)

いみ to sleep　　**strokes** 10画　丨 冂 冂 月 目 目゛ 昍 明 眠 眠

Point: 眠 ← Note the number of horizontal strokes!

睡眠	すいみん	sleep
不眠	ふみん	sleeplessness
冬眠	とうみん	hibernation
居眠り	いねむり	doze, snooze

252

養

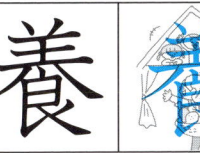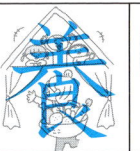

To nourish my children, I brought back a lot of food.

- おんよみ ヨウ
- くんよみ やしな(う)
- いみ to foster, to feed, to support
- strokes 15画

丶 ソ ｿ ⺷ 并 关 羊 差 美 美 养 养 養 養 養

Point: Note the position of the dots!

栄養	えいよう	nutrition
休養	きゅうよう	rest
養育	よういく	raising
養う	やしなう	to support, to nourish

良

I got a lot of food for the children who have good appetites.

- おんよみ リョウ
- くんよみ よ(い)
- いみ good, nice, fine
- strokes 7画

丶 ⺈ ⺕ ヨ 皀 皀 良

良識	りょうしき	good sense
良心	りょうしん	conscience
良縁	りょうえん	good match
良い	よい	good, nice, fine

令

The orders from the superior were absolute.

- おんよみ レイ
- くんよみ —
- いみ to command, order, law, good
- strokes 5画

ノ 人 𠆢 今 令

Point: Do not protrude!

命令	めいれい	order, command
司令官	しれいかん	commander
発令	はつれい	official announcement
令嬢	れいじょう	young lady

冷

The superior was so nervous that he broke into a cold sweat while giving his orders.

- おんよみ レイ
- くんよみ つめ(たい)・ひ(える)・ひ(や)・ひ(やす)・ひ(やかす)・さ(める)・さ(ます)
- いみ cold, chill, to cool
- strokes 7画

丶 冫 冫 冷 冷 冷 冷

Point: Note the position of the dots!

冷房	れいぼう	air conditioning
冷蔵庫	れいぞうこ	refrigerator
冷静	れいせい	calmness
冷や汗	ひやあせ	cold sweat

齢

The young superior had to put up with a toothache while giving his orders.

おんよみ レイ　くんよみ —

いみ age

strokes 17画

年齢	ねんれい	age
高齢	こうれい	advanced age
適齢期	てきれいき	marriageable age
樹齢	じゅれい	age of a tree

署

A firefighter was in front of the fire station, training to spray water.

おんよみ ショ　くんよみ —

いみ station, public office, to sign

strokes 13画

部署	ぶしょ	one's post department
警察署	けいさつしょ	police station
消防署	しょうぼうしょ	fire station
署名	しょめい	signature

置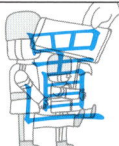

I gently put chocolates on top of the toy soldiers that were marching straight.

おんよみ チ　くんよみ お（く）

いみ to put, to set up

strokes 13画

Point: 置 Do not connect!

位置	いち	position
装置	そうち	apparatus, equipment
配置	はいち	arrangement, placement
置物	おきもの	ornament, figurine

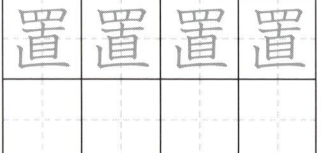

罪

The suspect pleaded guilty in court.

おんよみ ザイ　くんよみ つみ

いみ sin, mistake

strokes 13画

Point: 罪 Note the number of horizontal strokes!

犯罪	はんざい	crime
有罪	ゆうざい	guilt
謝罪	しゃざい	apology
罪	つみ	sin, crime

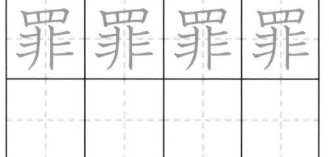

利

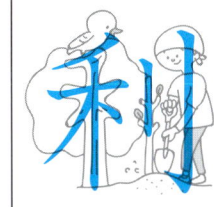

Tree planting brings benefits to both humans and birds living in the forest.

おんよみ リ
くんよみ き(く)

いみ sharp, profit, to take effect
strokes 7画 ノ 二 千 禾 禾 利 利

Point: Note the longest vertical stroke!

利益	りえき	profit, benefit	自分の利益だけを考える。
便利	べんり	convenience	駅の近くに引っ越して、とても便利になった。
利率	りりつ	interest rate	住宅ローンの利率を比較する。
利用	りよう	use, utilization	友人とよくこの店を利用する。
有利(な)	ゆうり(な)	advantageous	仕事に有利な資格をとる。
利き手	ききて	one's dominant hand	利き手は左手です。

制

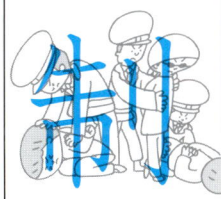

The police force kept the mob back.

おんよみ セイ
くんよみ ―

いみ to keep back, to suppress, system
strokes 8画 ノ 广 仁 仨 缶 制 制 制

Point: Protrude!

制作	せいさく	production	短編映画を制作した。
規制	きせい	regulation	道路の通行が規制される。
強制	きょうせい	compulsion	嫌いなものを食べるように強制された。
自制	じせい	self-control	食べすぎないように自制している。
制度	せいど	system	奨学金の制度について調べた。
制服	せいふく	uniform	仕事のときは制服に着替える。

刊

I read a weekly magazine after I hang out the washing on the clothesline in the garden.

おんよみ カン　　**くんよみ** —

いみ to publish, to carve　　**strokes** 5画　　一 ニ 干 刊 刊

Point  Do not protrude!

月刊	げっかん	monthly publication
週刊誌	しゅうかんし	weekly magazine
朝刊	ちょうかん	morning newspaper
夕刊	ゆうかん	evening newspaper

判

The referee showed a red card and ordered the player to get off the pitch.

おんよみ ハン・バン　　**くんよみ** —

いみ to distinguish, to judge　　**strokes** 7画　　丶 ソ ゝ 二 半 半 判

Point  Note the position of the dots!

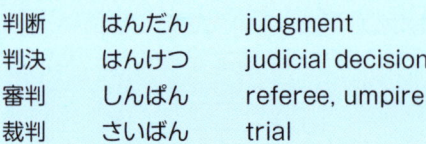

判断	はんだん	judgment
判決	はんけつ	judicial decision
審判	しんぱん	referee, umpire
裁判	さいばん	trial

別

A child felt sad along with his mother about separating from his father.

おんよみ ベツ　　**くんよみ** わか(れる)

いみ to separate, other　　**strokes** 7画　　丨 口 口 另 另 別 別

Point  Connect!

区別	くべつ	distinction
告別式	こくべつしき	funeral
別居	べっきょ	separation
別れる	わかれる	to part, to separate

刺

My arm was in pain after being stung by a bee.

おんよみ シ　　**くんよみ** さ(す)・さ(さる)

いみ to stick, to satirize　　**strokes** 8画　　一 厂 冂 市 束 束 刺 刺

Point  Do not connect!

刺す	さす	to stick, to sting
刺激	しげき	stimulation, stimulus
名刺	めいし	business card
風刺	ふうし	satire

刻

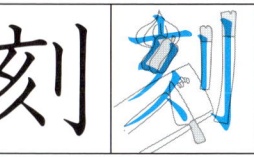

I finely chopped vegetables, such as leeks, in order to make fried rice.

- おんよみ コク
- くんよみ きざ(む)
- いみ to chop, to carve, time
- strokes 8画 　丶 亠 ナ 歹 亥 亥 刻 刻

Point: Do not protrude!

彫刻	ちょうこく	sculpture
時刻	じこく	time
深刻(な)	しんこく(な)	grave, serious
刻む	きざむ	to chop

例

A teacher and the pupils formed a line. The other teacher showed them an example.

- おんよみ レイ
- くんよみ たと(える)
- いみ to compare, example
- strokes 8画 　ノ イ イ゛ 仔 仔 伢 例 例

Point: ×列 ×倒 — Note the similar characters!

事例	じれい	case, example
定例の	ていれいの	regular
例題	れいだい	exercise, example
例える	たとえる	to compare

到

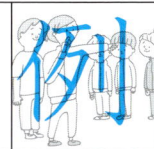

The party finally reached the camp site.

- おんよみ トウ
- くんよみ —
- いみ to reach, to arrive
- strokes 8画 　一 下 云 至 至 至 到 到

Point: ×倒 ×制 — Note the similar characters!

到着する	とうちゃくする	to arrive, to reach
到達	とうたつ	attainment
殺到	さっとう	rush
周到(な)	しゅうとう(な)	careful, scrupulous

則

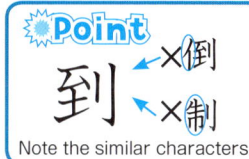

The shellfish teacher checked to see if the students wore their school uniforms properly.

- おんよみ ソク
- くんよみ —
- いみ to comfort, to rule
- strokes 9画 　丨 冂 月 月 目 貝 貝 則 則

Point: ×側 ×前 — Note the similar characters!

規則	きそく	rule
原則	げんそく	principle
反則	はんそく	foul, violation of the rules
法則	ほうそく	law

The woman continued printing after adding more paper to the printer.

おんよみ サツ　くんよみ す(る)

いみ to print, to sweep　strokes 8画　フ コ ア ア 尸 吊 吊 刷 刷

 Protrude!

印刷	いんさつ	printing
増刷	ぞうさつ	additional printing, reprint
刷新	さっしん	renewal
刷る	する	to print

The man jumped the line that had been waiting for the train.

おんよみ カツ　くんよみ わ(る)・わり・わ(れる)・さ(く)

いみ to divide, to cut, ratio　strokes 12画　 丶 ｲ 宀 宀 中 宔 宝 害 害 害 割 割

 Protrude!

分割	ぶんかつ	division, split
割合	わりあい	percentage
役割	やくわり	role
割安(な)	わりやす(な)	economical

The party finally reached the camp site and dropped on the ground with fatigue.

おんよみ トウ　くんよみ たお(れる)・たお(す)

いみ to fall, to tumble, to fall　strokes 10画　ノ イ ｲ 乍 乍 乍 佟 侄 倒 倒

 Do not protrude!

転倒	てんとう	fall, tumble
倒産	とうさん	bankruptcy
倒立	とうりつ	handstand, headstand
倒れる	たおれる	to fall, to tumble

Two tourists were overwhelmed by the magnificent theater in which a big chandelier hung.

おんよみ ゲキ　くんよみ ―

いみ drama, violent　strokes 15画　 丶 ト 广 广 卢 卢 声 卢 虎 虏 虏 豪 豪 劇 劇

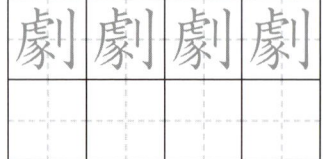

 Do not protrude!

演劇	えんげき	play, drama
劇場	げきじょう	theater
喜劇	きげき	comedy
悲劇	ひげき	tragedy

解

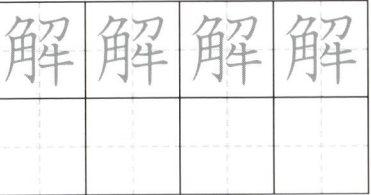

The cow understood that he couldn't be a triceratops even if he wore horns and a scarf.

- おんよみ カイ・ゲ
- くんよみ と(く)・と(かす)・と(ける)

いみ to undo, to solve, to understand

strokes 13画 ノ ク ク 角 角 角 角 解 解 解 解 解 解

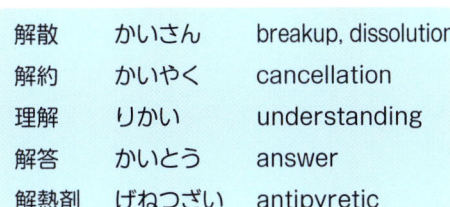

Point: 解 Do not protrude!

解散	かいさん	breakup, dissolution
解約	かいやく	cancellation
理解	りかい	understanding
解答	かいとう	answer
解熱剤	げねつざい	antipyretic

触

The worm on the leaf touched the triceratops' body.

- おんよみ ショク
- くんよみ ふ(れる)・さわ(る)

いみ to touch, to collide

strokes 13画 ノ ク ク 角 角 角 角 角 舯 舯 触 触

Point: 触 Do not protrude!

触れる	ふれる	to touch
接触	せっしょく	contact
触発	しょくはつ	stimulating
触診	しょくしん	palpation
触角	しょっかく	feeler

雑

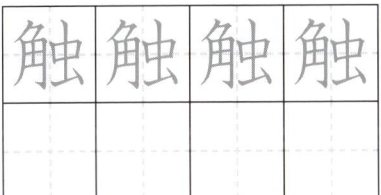

A housing complex was built in the copse that is inhabited by crows.

- おんよみ ザツ・ゾウ
- くんよみ ―

いみ mixed, unarranged

strokes 14画 ノ 九 九 卆 杂 杂 杂 剎 剎 新 新 雑 雑 雑

Point: 雑 Note the number of horizontal strokes!

複雑	ふくざつ	complexity
混雑	こんざつ	congestion
雑木林	ぞうきばやし	copse
雑誌	ざっし	magazine
雑談	ざつだん	chat

確

When a stone fell, I made sure that the housing complex and the inhabitants were unharmed.

- おんよみ カク
- くんよみ たし(か)・たし(かめる)
- いみ true, sure, to make sure
- strokes 15画 一ア丆石石石石矿矿矿碓碓碓確確

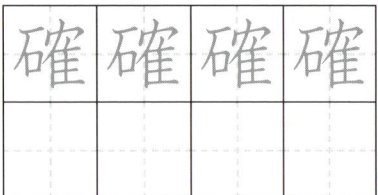

Point 確 Protrude!

確実	かくじつ	certainty
確認	かくにん	confirmation
正確さ	せいかくさ	accuracy, correctness, exactness
確信	かくしん	conviction
確執	かくしつ	discord, feud

難

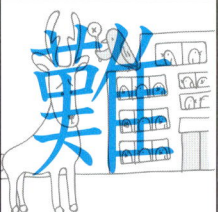

It is difficult for a deer to live in a housing complex for birds.

- おんよみ ナン
- くんよみ むずか(しい)・かた(い)
- いみ difficult, to blame, trouble
- strokes 18画 一十廾廾廿廿苩堇堇菓菓菓戴戴戴難難

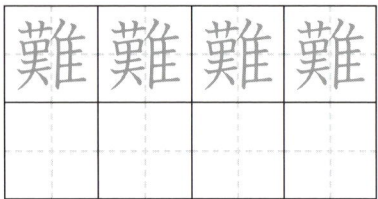

Point 難 Note the number of horizontal strokes!

難問	なんもん	difficult problem
難解(な)	なんかい(な)	difficult to solve
避難	ひなん	shelter, evacuation
災難	さいなん	disaster
無難(な)	ぶなん(な)	safe, acceptable

権

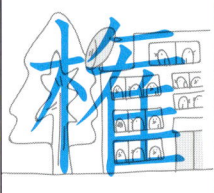

I have a right to live in the housing complex by the tree.

- おんよみ ケン・ゴン
- くんよみ —
- いみ authority, right, provisional
- strokes 15画 一十才木木术杧杧栌栌栌栌権権権

Point 権 Do not protrude!

権利	けんり	right
人権	じんけん	human rights
権力	けんりょく	power
権限	けんげん	authority
権化	ごんげ	incarnation

雇

I opened the door to become a worker employed by a company.

- おんよみ コ
- くんよみ やと(う)
- いみ to employ
- strokes 12画
- 一 二 三 戸 戸 戸 戸 戸 戸 雇 雇 雇

雇う	やとう	to employ
雇用	こよう	employment
解雇	かいこ	dismissal, layoff
雇い主	やといぬし	employer

推

I unconditionally nominated the housing complex for this year's House of the Year.

- おんよみ スイ
- くんよみ お(す)
- いみ to propel, to guess, to nominate
- strokes 11画
- 一 十 扌 扌 扩 扩 扩 拊 拊 推 推

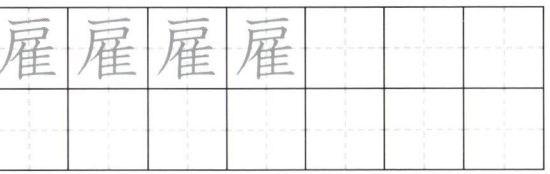

Point: 推 Protrude!

推薦	すいせん	nomination
推測	すいそく	guess
推論	すいろん	inference, reasoning
推進	すいしん	propulsion

険

Since the driver was drunk, the police officer at the check point gave him a grim look.

- おんよみ ケン
- くんよみ けわ(しい)
- いみ steep, dangerous
- strokes 11画
-

Point: 険 Do not protrude!

危険	きけん	danger
険悪(な)	けんあく(な)	grim
保険	ほけん	insurance
険しい	けわしい	steep

検

The police were checking cars by the tree.

- おんよみ ケン
- くんよみ —
- いみ to investigate, to check
- strokes 12画
-

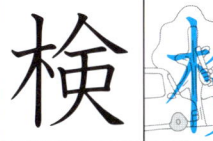

検査	けんさ	examination, check
検定	けんてい	official approval
検診	けんしん	medical examination
車検	しゃけん	automobile inspection

規

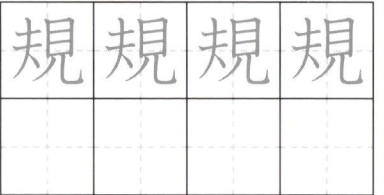

Let's lead a well-regulated life by going to bed early and waking up early.

- おんよみ キ
- くんよみ ―

いみ compass, rule

strokes 11画   一 二 ナ 夫 劧 刦 刦 規 規 規 規

Point 規 ← Note the number of horizontal strokes!

規則	きそく	rule
規格	きかく	standard
規範	きはん	norm
規制	きせい	regulation
正規の	せいきの	regular, proper

現

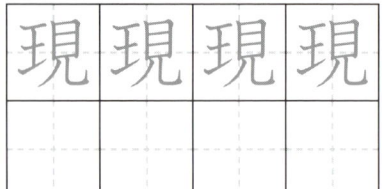

A retainer with a moustache persuaded the king to open his eyes and see reality.

- おんよみ ゲン
- くんよみ あらわ(れる)・あらわ(す)

いみ to appear, present

strokes 11画   一 T F 王 刊 邦 玥 玥 玥 現 現

Point 現 ← Do not protrude!

現実	げんじつ	reality
表現	ひょうげん	expression
現在	げんざい	the present time
現金	げんきん	cash
現象	げんしょう	phenomenon

視

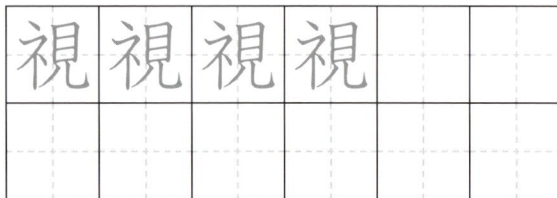

I took an eye test by covering each eye one at a time.

- おんよみ シ
- くんよみ ―

いみ to look, to see

strokes 11画   ` ラ ネ ネ ネ 初 礼 視 視 視 視

視力	しりょく	eyesight
近視	きんし	myopia, nearsightedness
視界	しかい	field of vision
視察	しさつ	inspection
無視	むし	disregard

There are many tourist attractions in *Tokyo* such as *Tokyo Tower* and *Kaminarimon* Gate.

おんよみ カン　くんよみ ―

いみ to observe, viewpoint

strokes 18画　ノ ⺊ ⺊ ヶ ⺂ 辛 辛 辛 肀 隺 雚 雚 観 観 観 観 観 観

Point
観 Do not protrude!

観察	かんさつ	observation
観光	かんこう	sightseeing, tourism
主観	しゅかん	subjectivity
先入観	せんにゅうかん	preconception, prejudice

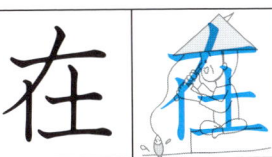 

The elderly man is in good health and goes fishing quite often.

おんよみ ザイ　くんよみ あ(る)

いみ to exist

strokes 6画　一 ナ 才 ナ 存 在

Point
在 Protrude!

健在(な)	けんざい(な)	in good health
在庫	ざいこ	stock
不在	ふざい	absence
滞在	たいざい	stay

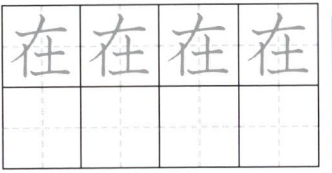 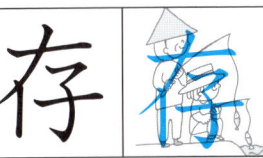

The presence of his grandchildren makes the elderly man healthy enough to go fishing.

おんよみ ソン・ゾン　くんよみ ―

いみ to exist, to preserve

strokes 6画　一 ナ 才 右 存 存

存続	そんぞく	continuation
存在	そんざい	existence, presence
保存	ほぞん	conservation, preservation
生存	せいぞん	existence, life survival

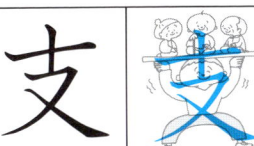  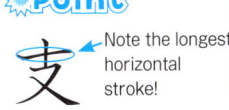

The young man supported three elderly people all by himself.

おんよみ シ　くんよみ ささ(える)

いみ to support, to direct

strokes 4画　一 十 ナ 支

Point
支 Note the longest horizontal stroke!

支出	ししゅつ	expenditure, spending
支店	してん	branch
支配	しはい	domination, rule
支える	ささえる	to support

263

枝

Thanks to a robot, the young man can support elderly people.

おんよみ シ　**くんよみ** えだ

いみ branch, twig

strokes 8画　一 十 才 木 木 村 村 枝

Point: 枝 — Do not protrude!

楊枝	ようじ	toothpick
小枝	こえだ	twig
枝豆	えだまめ	green soybeans
枝分かれ	えだわかれ	ramification

貯

The shellfish saved money by putting coins in a piggy bank little by little every day.

おんよみ チョ　**くんよみ** ―

いみ to store, to save

strokes 12画　丨 冂 冃 月 目 貝 貝 貝' 貝' 貯 貯 貯

Point: 貯 — Do not protrude!

貯金	ちょきん	savings
貯蓄	ちょちく	savings, hoard
貯蔵	ちょぞう	storage
貯水池	ちょすいち	reservoir

財

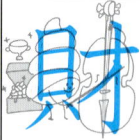

The shellfish made his fortune by taking advantage of his talent as a cello player.

おんよみ ザイ・サイ　**くんよみ** ―

いみ possessions, property

strokes 10画　丨 冂 冃 月 目 貝 貝 貝一 財 財

財産	ざいさん	property, fortune
財宝	ざいほう	treasure
財政	ざいせい	finance
財布	さいふ	purse, wallet

賛

Those holding placards expressed their approval of the shellfish's opinion.

おんよみ サン　**くんよみ** ―

いみ to admire, to assist

strokes 15画　一 二 チ 夫 夫一 夫二 夫夫 夫夫 替 替 替 替 賛 賛

Point: 賛 ← Protrude!

賛成	さんせい	agreement, approval
賛否	さんぴ	yes or no
賛辞	さんじ	praise
賞賛	しょうさん	praise

資

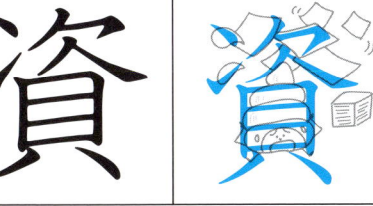

The shellfish sweated because it was overloaded with paperwork.

おんよみ シ
くんよみ —

いみ funds, to help, inborn

strokes 13画

丶 丶 冫 冫 次 次 次 咨 咨 咨 資 資 資

Point

資 ← Note the position of the dots!

資金	しきん	funds	結婚のための資金を貯める。
資産	しさん	assets	彼は事業に成功して資産を築いた。
融資	ゆうし	financing	資金を銀行に融資してもらう。
資質	ししつ	inborn trait, endowments	彼女にはリーダーとしての資質がある。
資料	しりょう	document	事前に資料をメールに添付して送る。
資本主義	しほんしゅぎ	capitalism	資本主義の世の中となる。

質

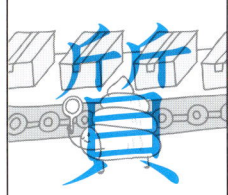

The shellfish tested the quality of the products running along the conveyor belt.

おんよみ シツ・シチ・チ
くんよみ —

いみ quality, pawn, question

strokes 15画

⺁ ⺁ ⺁ ⺁ ⺁ 斤 斤 斤 所 所 所 質 質 質 質

Point

質 ← Do not protrude!

材質	ざいしつ	material	この机は材質にこだわって作られている。
音質	おんしつ	sound quality	音質の良いスピーカーで音楽を聴く。
質疑	しつぎ	question, inquiry	質疑応答の時間です。
本質	ほんしつ	essence, nature	彼女は問題の本質がわかっていない。
質屋	しちや	pawnshop	時計を預けて質屋からお金を借りる。
言質	げんち	pledge, promise	後でもめないように、交渉では言質を取る。

賃

The shellfish received a wage as a reward for his labor.

- おんよみ チン
- くんよみ —

いみ to hire, to borrow, charge
strokes 13画 ノ 亻 亻 仁 任 任 侊 侊 侊 賃 賃 賃 賃

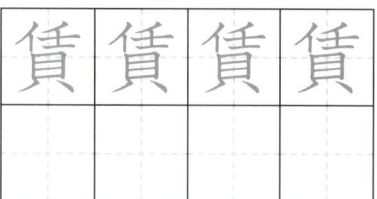

Point
賃 ← ×貨
賃 ← ×貸
Note the similar characters!

賃金	ちんぎん	wage
賃貸	ちんたい	lease, rental
家賃	やちん	house rent
運賃	うんちん	fare
駄賃	だちん	tip

員

The shellfish held his membership card high.

- おんよみ イン
- くんよみ —

いみ number, member
strokes 10画 ノ 冂 冂 丆 冃 冃 冒 冒 員 員

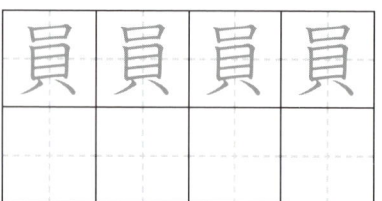

Point
員 ←
Do not connect!

定員	ていいん	capacity
会員	かいいん	member, membership
社員	しゃいん	employee, staff, member
駅員	えきいん	station staff
店員	てんいん	salesclerk

損

The shellfish waved his hand and advertised a membership card which would not cause any losses.

- おんよみ ソン
- くんよみ そこ(なう)・そこ(ねる)

いみ to spoil, to mar, loss
strokes 13画 一 十 扌 扌 扩 押 押 捐 捐 捐 捐 損 損

損害	そんがい	damage
破損	はそん	breakage
損失	そんしつ	loss
損得	そんとく	loss and gain
欠損	けっそん	deficit

貸

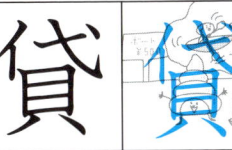

The shellfish worked for a rental boat shop at a lake. There was a bird flying over the lake.

おんよみ タイ　　**くんよみ** か(す)

いみ to lend, to rent out　　**strokes** 12画　ノ 亻 イ 亻 代 代 伐 代 代 貸 貸 貸

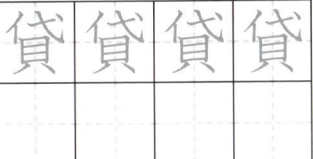

Point:  Note the position of the dot!

貸借	たいしゃく	lending and borrowing
貸与	たいよ	lending
貸家	かしや	house for rent
貸す	かす	to lend, to rent out

貨

A wolf that turned into a girl handed out a shellfish instead of a coin.

おんよみ カ　　**くんよみ** ―

いみ money, goods　　**strokes** 11画　ノ 亻 イ 化 化 作 作 作 貨 貨 貨

Point:  Do not protrude!

貨幣	かへい	currency, money
硬貨	こうか	coin
通貨	つうか	currency
百貨店	ひゃっかてん	department store

賢

The shellfish practiced for its performance together with wise animals.

おんよみ ケン　　**くんよみ** かしこ(い)

いみ wise, talented　　**strokes** 16画　一 厂 厂 厂 臣 臣 臣 臣 臣 賢 賢 賢 賢 賢 賢 賢

Point:  Do not connect!

賢い	かしこい	wise, smart
賢者	けんじゃ	sage, wise person
賢明(な)	けんめい(な)	sensible
賢母	けんぼ	wise mother

貧

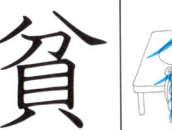 

The shellfish had financial difficulties, so they shared a small fish between the two of them.

おんよみ ヒン・ビン　　**くんよみ** まず(しい)

いみ poor, meager　　**strokes** 11画　ノ 八 分 分 分 谷 谷 督 貧 貧 貧

Point:  Do not protrude!

貧しい	まずしい	poor, meager
貧困	ひんこん	poverty, destitution
貧血	ひんけつ	anemia
貧乏	びんぼう	poverty

費

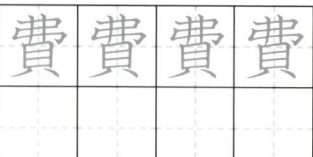 

The shellfish stood in front of a mirror which reflected the $ sign on his bag backwards.

おんよみ ヒ　　**くんよみ** つい(やす)・つい(える)

いみ to spend, to consume, cost　　**strokes** 12画　　一　　ユ　　弓　　弔　　弗　　弗　　冉　　冉　　曹　　曹　　費　　費

Point
 ← Protrude!

費用	ひよう	cost
消費	しょうひ	consumption
浪費	ろうひ	waste
費やす	ついやす	to spend

賞

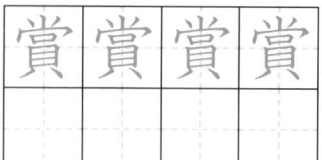 

The three people standing on the podium were given testimonials by the shellfish.

おんよみ ショウ　　**くんよみ** ―

いみ reward, to praise　　**strokes** 15画　　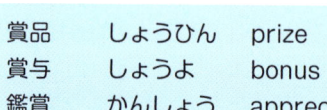

Point
賞 ← Note the position of the dots!

賞品	しょうひん	prize
賞与	しょうよ	bonus
鑑賞	かんしょう	appreciation

貿

The shellfish works for a trading company that deals with exports and imports.

おんよみ ボウ　　**くんよみ** ―

いみ trade　　**strokes** 12画　　ノ　　ト　　亡　　印　　印　　印　　留　　留　　貿　　貿

Point
貿 ← Do not protrude!

貿易	ぼうえき	(external) trade

責

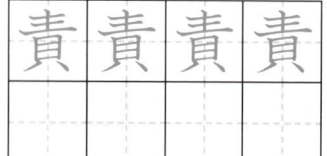 

The shellfish that is in charge of sales gave a presentation about the sales results.

おんよみ セキ　　**くんよみ** せ(める)

いみ to blame, duty　　**strokes** 11画　　一　　十　　キ　　圭　　圭　　青　　青　　青　　青　　責　　責

Point
責 ← Note the longest horizontal stroke!

責める	せめる	to blame
責任	せきにん	responsibility
叱責	しっせき	rebuke
自責	じせき	self-reproach

贈

The shellfish gave the sun a nice gift wrapped up with a ribbon.

おんよみ ゾウ・ソウ **くんよみ** おく(る)

いみ to give, to donate

strokes 18画 １ 冂 冃 冐 目 貝 貝 貝` 貝´ 貝⺈ 貝⺈⺈ 貯 贮 贈 贈 贈 贈 贈

Point
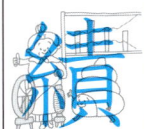
Note the position of the dots!

贈る	おくる	to give, to donate
贈呈	ぞうてい	presentation
贈与	ぞうよ	donation
贈り物	おくりもの	gift, present

績

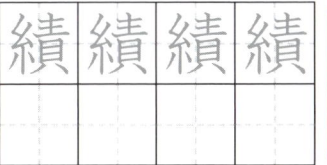

The woman spinning yarn admired the shellfish's sales results.

おんよみ セキ **くんよみ** ―

いみ to spin, feat

strokes 17画  幺 幺 纟 糹 糸 糸⺀ 紣 絓 絟 絹 績 績 績 績 績

Point

Note the longest horizontal stroke!

成績	せいせき	grade, result
業績	ぎょうせき	achievement
実績	じっせき	achievement, results
紡績	ぼうせき	spinning

約

The woman spinning yarn promised to tailor the dress by the deadline.

おんよみ ヤク **くんよみ** ―

いみ to promise, to save, approximately

strokes 9画  幺 幺 纟 糹 糸 紁 約 約

Point

Note the position of the dot!

約束	やくそく	promise
予約	よやく	reservation
節約	せつやく	saving
婚約	こんやく	betrothal

級

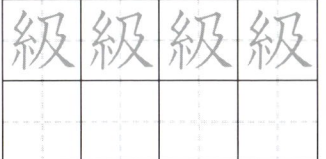

The rank of the woman who spins thread has gone up.

おんよみ キュウ **くんよみ** ―

いみ class, rank, grade

strokes 9画  幺 幺 纟 糹 糸 紀 級 級

Point
Do not protrude!

高級(な)	こうきゅう(な)	high grade
初級	しょきゅう	elementary level
学級	がっきゅう	class
同級生	どうきゅうせい	classmate

終

The woman spinning yarn told the hibernating bear that the winter would end.

おんよみ シュウ
くんよみ お(わる)・お(える)

いみ to end, to finish
strokes 11画　ノ ク タ 幺 幺 糸 糸 紅 終 終 終

Point
Note the position of the dots!

終わる	おわる	to end	いつも6時に仕事が終わる。
終了	しゅうりょう	end	試合は引き分けで終了した。
終点	しゅうてん	end point, terminal	電車で寝過ごして、終点まで来てしまった。
終日	しゅうじつ	all day	昨日は終日家にいた。
終電	しゅうでん	the last train	全速力で走り、ぎりぎり終電に間に合った。
終結	しゅうけつ	end	議論が終結する。

結

The woman spinning yarn was married to a man who loved playing chess.

おんよみ ケツ
くんよみ むす(ぶ)・ゆ(う)・ゆ(わえる)

いみ to bind, to tie, knot
strokes 12画　ノ ク タ 幺 幺 糸 糸 紅 紅 結 結 結

Point
Note the longest horizontal stroke!

結ぶ	むすぶ	to bind, to tie	不器用なので、ひもをうまく結べない。
結婚	けっこん	marriage	両親が彼との結婚に反対している。
結成	けっせい	organization	友人たちとサッカーチームを結成した。
結末	けつまつ	ending	小説の意外な結末に驚いた。
結局	けっきょく	after all	一時間待ったが、結局彼は来なかった。
凍結	とうけつ	freeze	路面が凍結していて転びそうになった。

給

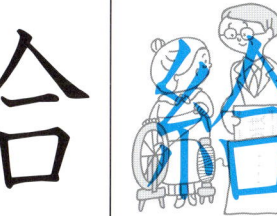

The woman spinning yarn received her salary for this month.

おんよみ キュウ
くんよみ ―

いみ to supply, to provide
strokes 12画 　く　幺　幺　千　糸　糸　糺　紒　紒　給　給

Point
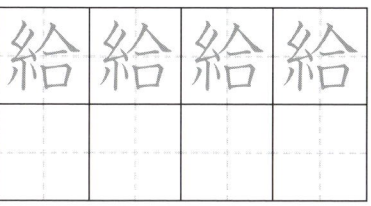
Note the similar characters!

給料	きゅうりょう	salary
給食	きゅうしょく	school lunch
給油	きゅうゆ	refueling
供給	きょうきゅう	supply
補給	ほきゅう	replenishment

経

The husband of the woman spinning yarn is an economist.

おんよみ ケイ・キョウ
くんよみ へ(る)

いみ to pass, the warp, scripture
strokes 11画 　く　幺　幺　千　糸　糸　紀　紅　経　経

Point
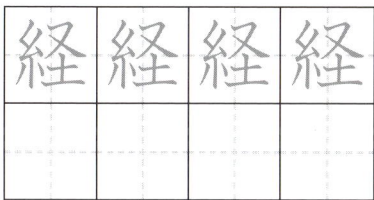
Protrude!

経る	へる	to pass, to go through
経験	けいけん	experience
経営	けいえい	management
経済	けいざい	economy

続

The cloth that they were weaving with spun yarn got very big.

おんよみ ゾク
くんよみ つづ(く)・つづ(ける)

いみ to continue
strokes 13画 　く　幺　幺　千　糸　紀　紅　紝　絲　続　続

Point
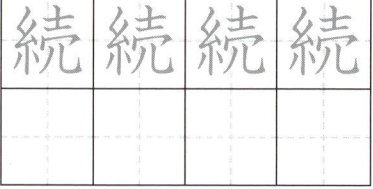
Do not connect!

続行	ぞっこう	continuation
続く	つづく	to continue
続編	ぞくへん	sequel
手続き	てつづき	procedures
接続	せつぞく	connection

271

絶

The woman spinning yarn highly praised the painter's picture.

おんよみ ゼツ
くんよみ た(える)・た(やす)・た(つ)

いみ to cease, to cut off, excellent　**strokes** 12画　く　纟　幺　幺　糸　糸　糸　糽　絆　絶　絶　絶

Point　絶 ← Do not protrude!

絶える	たえる	to cease, to lose touch	古い友人とのつきあいは絶えた。
絶滅	ぜつめつ	extinction	絶滅が危惧される生物を保護する。
気絶	きぜつ	a faint	あまりに驚いて気絶しそうになった。
拒絶	きょぜつ	rejection	面会を拒絶する。
絶景	ぜっけい	superb view	この山に登ると、絶景が見られる。
絶妙(な)	ぜつみょう(な)	exquisite	このデザートは甘さと酸味が絶妙だ。

総

Because the woman worked hard on spinning yarn, she reached her total sales target.

おんよみ ソウ
くんよみ ー

いみ all, total, to govern　**strokes** 14画　く　纟　幺　幺　糸　糸　糸　紷　紷　紷　総　総　総

Point　総 ← Do not connect!

総合	そうごう	synthesis, putting together	全員の意見を総合して結論を出す。
総括	そうかつ	summary	会議を議長が総括する。
総額	そうがく	total sum	買い物の総額は5万円になった。
総理	そうり	Prime Minister	総理が会見を開く。
総意	そうい	consensus	チームの総意で彼がキャプテンに選ばれた。

紅

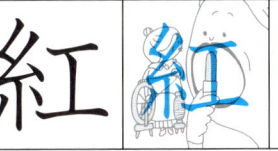

The woman spinning yarn put on lipstick.

おんよみ コウ・ク **くんよみ** べに・くれない

いみ bright red

strokes 9画 く 纟 幺 乡 糸 糸 紅 紅 紅

Point 紅 ← Do not protrude!

紅葉	こうよう	autumnal tints
深紅	しんく	deep red
口紅	くちべに	lipstick
紅	くれない	crimson

練

The woman practiced spinning yarn all night till the sun rose behind the woods.

おんよみ レン **くんよみ** ね(る)

いみ to knead, to get used to

strokes 14画 く 纟 幺 乡 糸 糸 紅 紅 紳 緬 緬 練 練

Point 練 ← Protrude!

練る	ねる	to train, to elaborate
練習	れんしゅう	practice
訓練	くんれん	training
試練	しれん	trial

納

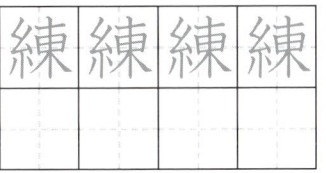

The woman spinning yarn delivered the dress she tailored to the shop.

おんよみ ノウ・ナッ・トウ・ナ・ナン **くんよみ** おさ(める)・おさ(まる)

いみ to accept, to stroke, to pay, to deliver

strokes 10画 く 纟 幺 乡 糸 糸 紅 納 納

Point 納 ← Protrude!

納める	おさめる	to pay
納入	のうにゅう	delivery
納得	なっとく	consent
収納	しゅうのう	storage

綿

The woman spun cotton into threads.

おんよみ メン **くんよみ** わた

いみ cotton, fine, to range

strokes 14画 く 纟 幺 乡 糸 糸 紅 紅 納 綿 綿 綿 綿

Point 綿 ← Protrude!

木綿	もめん	cotton
綿棒	めんぼう	cotton swab
綿密(な)	めんみつ(な)	detailed, elaborate
綿菓子	わたがし	cotton candy

273

統

The woman's family have kept the tradition and have been engaged in spinning for generations.

おんよみ トウ　　**くんよみ** す(べる)

いみ to govern, to unify　　**strokes** 12画　　く 幺 幺 糸 糸 糸 糸' 紆 紆 紆 統

Point
Note the similar characters!

統べる	すべる	to govern, to unify
伝統	でんとう	tradition
統計	とうけい	statistics
大統領	だいとうりょう	president

縮

When we wove the cloth at the inn, it shrank very much.

おんよみ シュク　　**くんよみ** ちぢ(む)・ちぢ(まる)・ちぢ(める)・ちぢ(れる)・ちぢ(らす)

いみ to shrink, to retreat　　**strokes** 17画　　く 幺 幺 糸 糸 糸 糸' 紆 紆 紆 紆 縒 縒 縮 縮 縮

Point
Note the number of horizontal stroke!

縮む	ちぢむ	to shrink
縮小	しゅくしょう	reduction
圧縮	あっしゅく	compression
短縮	たんしゅく	shortening

純

The yarn spun by the woman is pure wool.

おんよみ ジュン　　**くんよみ** ―

いみ pure, simple　　**strokes** 10画　　く 幺 幺 糸 糸 糸 糽 紂 紂 純

Point
Protrude!

純粋	じゅんすい	purity
単純	たんじゅん	simplicity
不純	ふじゅん	impurity
純金	じゅんきん	pure gold

編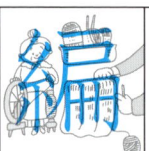

The woman knitted a muffler out of yarn she had spun.

おんよみ ヘン　　**くんよみ** あ(む)

いみ to knit, to weave, to arrange　　**strokes** 15画　　く 幺 幺 糸 糸 糸 糸 紆 紆 紆 絹 絹 編 編

Point
Do not protrude!

編む	あむ	to knit, to weave, to arrange
編集	へんしゅう	edit
前編	ぜんぺん	the first part
再編	さいへん	reorganization

紹

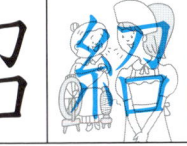

The newly employed maid introduced herself to the woman who was spinning.

おんよみ ショウ　　**くんよみ** —

いみ to inherit, to introduce

strokes 11画　く 幺 玄 幺 糸 糸 紀 紹 紹 紹 紹

Point 紹 ←Do not protrude!

| 紹介 | しょうかい | introduction |

素

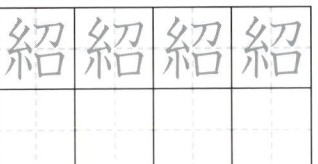

This hat is made of yarn.

おんよみ ソ・ス　　**くんよみ** —

いみ natural, element

strokes 10画　一 十 キ 主 圭 圭 去 孝 素 素

Point 素 ←Note the longest horizontal stroke!

素材	そざい	material
酸素	さんそ	oxygen
素質	そしつ	talent
素直(な)	すなお(な)	docile, obedient

系

This is my family tree.

おんよみ ケイ　　**くんよみ** —

いみ descent, series, system

strokes 7画　一 ィ 互 玄 平 系 系

Point 系 ←Do not protrude!

系列	けいれつ	series, system
家系図	かけいず	family tree
太陽系	たいようけい	the solar system
体系	たいけい	system

断

God declined to receive the rice in the box that the person delivered.

おんよみ ダン　　**くんよみ** た(つ)・ことわ(る)

いみ to cut off, to refuse, to decide

strokes 11画　、 ソ 斗 半 米 米 迷 迷 断 断 断

Point 断 ←Note the position of the dots!

断る	ことわる	to refuse, to decline
断つ	たつ	to cut off
横断	おうだん	crossing
決断	けつだん	decision

275

所

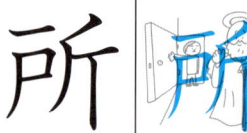

When I opened the door, I found it was the place where a god exists.

おんよみ ショ　　**くんよみ** ところ

いみ place, position

strokes 8画　一 ｜ ｜ 戸 戸 所 所 所

Point　Do not protrude!

住所	じゅうしょ	address
長所	ちょうしょ	good point, merit
場所	ばしょ	place
台所	だいどころ	kitchen

灯

 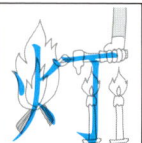

Getting fire from the bonfire, I lit candles and lined them up.

おんよみ トウ　　**くんよみ** ひ

いみ light, lamplight

strokes 6画　｜ ｜ 火 火 灯 灯

Point　Note the position of the dots!

電灯	でんとう	electric light
灯油	とうゆ	kerosene
灯台	とうだい	lighthouse
灯	ひ	light, lamplight

畑

 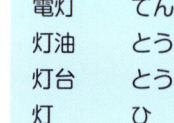

After having a bonfire in the rice paddy, a field was created.

おんよみ —　　**くんよみ** はた・はたけ

いみ plowed field, patch

strokes 9画　｜ ｜ 火 火 灯 灯 畑 畑 畑

Point　Note the position of the dots!

畑作	はたさく	farming
麦畑	むぎばたけ	wheat field
畑仕事	はたけしごと	farm work
畑違い	はたけちがい	out of one's field

焼

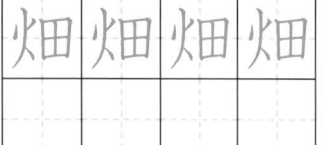 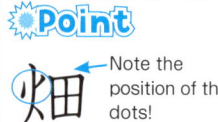

I grilled two fish on the charcoal stove using fire from the bonfire.

おんよみ ショウ　　**くんよみ** や(く)・や(ける)

いみ to burn, to grill

strokes 12画　｜ ｜ 火 火 灯 灯 灯 灯 焼 焼 焼 焼

Point　Note the number of horizontal strokes!

焼く	やく	to burn, to grill
焼却	しょうきゃく	incineration
燃焼	ねんしょう	combustion
焼き魚	やきざかな	grilled fish

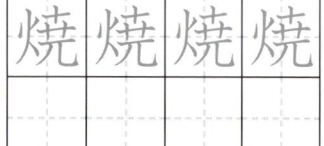

煙

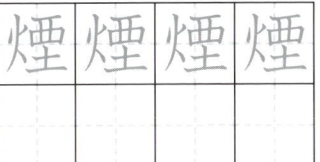

He was blowing out cigar smoke by the bonfire.

- おんよみ エン
- くんよみ けむ（る）・けむり・けむ（い）
- いみ smoke, to smoke
- strokes 13画

Point: Do not protrude!

煙突	えんとつ	chimney
禁煙	きんえん	no smoking
湯煙	ゆけむり	steam
煙る	けむる	to smoke

爆

Fire is spreading outside even though the sun is out; in the house, the fireworks are explosive and bright.

- おんよみ バク
- くんよみ ―
- いみ to burst, to explode
- strokes 19画

Point: Note the position of the dots!

爆発	ばくはつ	explosion
爆弾	ばくだん	bomb
爆音	ばくおん	explosive sound
爆竹	ばくちく	firecracker

燥

Three birds were in a panic because there was a wildfire in the dry region.

- おんよみ ソウ
- くんよみ ―
- いみ to dry
- strokes 17画

Point: Protrude!

| 乾燥 | かんそう | drying, dryness |
| 焦燥 | しょうそう | impatience |

災

Firefighters battled the big fire.

- おんよみ サイ
- くんよみ わざわ（い）
- いみ misfortune, disaster
- strokes 7画

天災	てんさい	natural calamity
災害	さいがい	disaster
火災	かさい	a fire
災い	わざわい	misfortune, disaster

1 Below the *Kanji*, write the Japanese reading of *Kanji* in *Hiragana*.

① 種　② 枝　③ 腰　④ 帯　⑤ 断る
(　)　(　)　(　)　(　)　(　)

⑥ 幅　⑦ 孫　⑧ 続く　⑨ 移す　⑩ 養う
(　)　(　)　(　)　(　)　(　)

2 Choose the correct reading.

① 貯金　(a　ざいきん　b　しきん　c　ちょきん)　(　)

② 困難　(a　いんなん　b　こんなん　c　こんざつ)　(　)

③ 期末　(a　きまつ　b　ごまつ　c　きすえ)　(　)

④ 印刷　(a　いんしつ　b　いんさつ　c　いんたつ)　(　)

⑤ 粉骨　(a　ふんこつ　b　ひんこつ　c　ここつ)　(　)

3 Write down the correct reading of the underlined part of the sentence.

① 戦(たたか)いが<u>終結</u>する。　(　)

② <u>伝説</u>が広く知られる。　(　)

③ 行動を<u>賞賛</u>される。　(　)

④ 作品の<u>講評</u>を聞く。　(　)

⑤ 外の様子を<u>確認</u>する。　(　)

4 After reading the *Hiragana* and English, write the *Kanji* that applies to the word in the box.

① みゃく (pulsation) ☐   ② たみ (people) ☐

③ ぬの (cloth) ☐   ④ はたけ (plowed field) ☐

⑤ むね (chest) ☐   ⑥ やく (to burn) ☐く

⑦ い (stomach) ☐   ⑧ つむ (to pile) ☐む

5 Choose the correct *Kanji* that corresponds to the *Hiragana* reading.

① れい　　(a 列　　b 例　　c 倒)　　(　)

② とう　　(a 統　　b 続　　c 総)　　(　)

③ きゅう　(a 拾　　b 絡　　c 給)　　(　)

④ まず(しい)(a 貧　　b 貨　　c 賢)　　(　)

⑤ あらそ(う)(a 予　　b 争　　c 事)　　(　)

6 In the boxes, write the *Kanji* that applies to the *furigana* reading.

① ちん／たい ☐☐ 住宅を見学する。

② げん／ざい ☐☐ の じ／こく ☐☐ を しら ☐べる。

③ 　はたら　き方について　ぎろん　する。

④ 　ゆうざい　の　はんけつ　が出る。

⑤ 　ねむ　っていた　そしつ　があらわれる。

⑥ 　かぜい　の　せいど　について学ぶ。

⑦ 　りえき　が　あっしゅく　される。

⑧ 　ごかい　を招いて　そん　をする。

⑨ 　ものごと　を　たんじゅん　に考える。

⑩ 　しあい　は　よ　い　しょうぶ　となった。

答え (answers)

❶ ①たね ②えだ ③こし ④おび ⑤ことわ ⑥はば ⑦まご ⑧つづ ⑨うつ ⑩やしな
❷ ①c ②b ③a ④b ⑤a
❸ ①しゅうけつ ②でんせつ ③しょうさん ④こうひょう ⑤かくにん
❹ ①脈 ②民 ③布 ④畑 ⑤胸 ⑥焼 ⑦胃 ⑧積
❺ ①b ②a ③c ④a ⑤b
❻ ①賃貸 ②現在, 時刻, 調 ③働, 議論 ④有罪, 判決 ⑤眠, 素質 ⑥課税, 制度 ⑦利益, 圧縮
　 ⑧誤解, 損 ⑨物事, 単純 ⑩試合, 良, 勝負

N2②

ここでは、日本語能力検定2級相当の漢字を掲載しています。

contains the *Kanji* of the Japanese Language Proficiency Test Level 2

 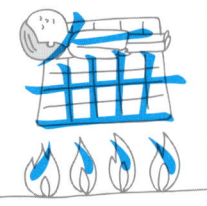

People say you can lie over a fire if you attain a state of supreme selflessness.

おんよみ ム・ブ
くんよみ な(い)

いみ not to exist, to lack　strokes 12画　ノ ー 二 仁 午 缶 無 無 無 無 無 無

Point

Note the longest horizontal stroke!

無効(な)	むこう(な)	invalid	クーポン券の期限が切れて無効になった。
無料の	むりょうの	free of charge	6歳以下の入場料は無料です。
無責任(な)	むせきにん(な)	irresponsible	彼は勝手なことばかり言って無責任だ。
無事	ぶじ	safety	電車が遅れていたが、無事会社に着いた。
無礼(な)	ぶれい(な)	impolite, rude	あいさつもしないで通り過ぎるとは無礼だ。
無私	むし	selflessness	あの人は無私の精神を持った政治家だ。

While I was rubbing pieces of wood together to make a fire, small flames spread out.

おんよみ ゼン・ネン
くんよみ ―

いみ condition, situation, such　strokes 12画

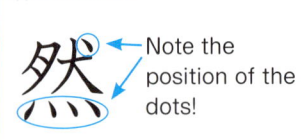

Note the position of the dots!

自然	しぜん	nature	この公園は都会の中にあるが自然が豊かだ。
当然	とうぜん	matter of course	不合格は、準備不足の当然の結果だ。
必然の	ひつぜんの	inevitable	この仕事に就いたのは必然だ。
漠然	ばくぜん	vagueness	説明が漠然としていて内容がよくわからない。
俄然	がぜん	suddenly	成績が上がり、俄然勉強する気になった。
天然	てんねん	nature	この布は天然の繊維でできている。

The sunlight is reflected on the building and is shining on the shade.

おんよみ ショウ　　**くんよみ** て(る)・て(らす)・て(れる)

いみ to shine, to blaze, to compare

strokes 13画　丨 冂 日 日 日⁷ 日⁷ 昭 昭 昭 昭 照 照

Point
照 ← Do not protrude!

照る	てる	to shine
照明	しょうめい	illumination
照合	しょうごう	collation
照会	しょうかい	inquiry

While I was rubbing pieces of wood together to make a fire, a small flame flared up.

おんよみ ネン　　**くんよみ** も(える)・も(やす)・も(す)

いみ to burn, to blaze

strokes 16画　丶 ⺍ 火 火 炏 炏 炏 炒 焖 焖 焖 燃 燃 燃 燃 燃

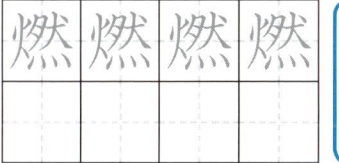 

Point
燃 ←×然
　←×熱
Note the similar characters!

燃える	もえる	to burn, to blaze
燃焼	ねんしょう	combustion
燃料	ねんりょう	fuel
不燃性	ふねんせい	incombustibility

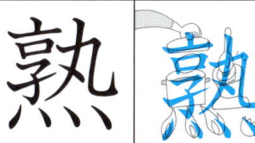

I made a soft-boiled egg by placing an egg into a saucepan and boiling it.

おんよみ ジュク　　**くんよみ** う(れる)

いみ to ripen, intently

strokes 15画　丶 亠 六 亡 古 亨 亨 享 剚 乳 乳 孰 孰 熟 熟

Point
熟 ← Do not protrude!

熟れる	うれる	to ripen
半熟の	はんじゅくの	soft-boiled
円熟	えんじゅく	maturity
熟慮	じゅくりょ	consideration

The underground heat is harnessed to generate electricity.

おんよみ ネツ　　**くんよみ** あつ(い)

いみ hot, heat

strokes 15画　一 十 土 耂 耂 走 幸 幸 刲 刲 埶 埶 熱 熱 熱

Point
熱 ← Do not protrude!

熱い	あつい	hot
熱帯	ねったい	tropics
発熱	はつねつ	fever
熱意	ねつい	enthusiasm

比

The two children compared the suppleness of their bodies with each other.

おんよみ ヒ　　くんよみ くら(べる)

いみ to compare, to match　　strokes 4画　一 ナ ヒ 比

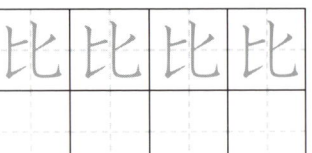

Point　比　Do not protrude!

比べる	くらべる	to compare
比較	ひかく	comparison
比率	ひりつ	proportion, ratio
比例	ひれい	proportion

疑

Chased by a guard, the man suspected of shoplifting threw away the stolen item.

おんよみ ギ　　くんよみ うたが(う)

いみ to doubt, to get lost　　strokes 14画　マ ヒ ヒ ヒ 乍 乍 갖 갖 疑 疑 疑 疑 疑

Point　疑　Do not protrude!

疑う	うたがう	to doubt, to suspect
疑惑	ぎわく	doubt, suspicion
質疑	しつぎ	question
容疑	ようぎ	suspicion

能

Talented gymnasts are sure to have a full warm-up.

おんよみ ノウ　　くんよみ ―

いみ can, able, ability　　strokes 10画　 ム 乍 甶 甶 甶 能 能 能

Point　能 ×態　×指　Note the similar characters!

知能	ちのう	intelligence
本能	ほんのう	instinct
可能性	かのうせい	possibility
芸能	げいのう	entertainment

老

An old dog was sleeping comfortably next to an old man.

おんよみ ロウ　　くんよみ お(いる)・ふ(ける)

いみ to grow old, old age　　strokes 6画　一 十 土 耂 老 老

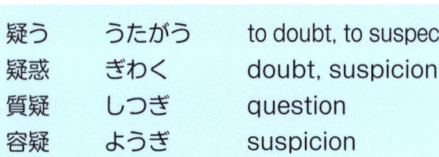

Point　老 ×考　×者　Note the similar characters!

老いる	おいる	to grow old
老人	ろうじん	elderly people
老化	ろうか	aging

独

A worm on the leaf is the only friend for the lonely cat.

おんよみ ドク　**くんよみ** ひと(り)

いみ alone, single, Germany　**strokes** 9画　ノ 丿 犭 犭 犭 狆 独 独 独

Point: 独 ← Protrude!

孤独	こどく	loneliness
独立	どくりつ	independence
独占	どくせん	monopoly
独り者	ひとりもの	single person

猫

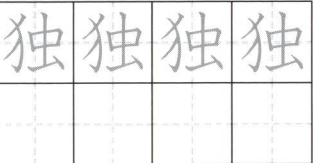 

There were two cats lying along the side of the rice field.

おんよみ ビョウ　**くんよみ** ねこ

いみ cat　**strokes** 11画　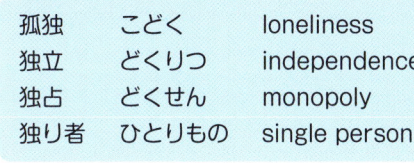

Point: 猫 — Do not protrude!

愛猫	あいびょう	pet cat
猫背	ねこぜ	stoop
野良猫	のらねこ	stray cat

変

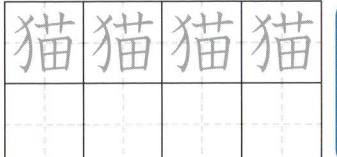 

The couple who met on a rainy day swore their eternal love to each other.

おんよみ ヘン　**くんよみ** か(わる)・か(える)

いみ to change, unusual　**strokes** 9画　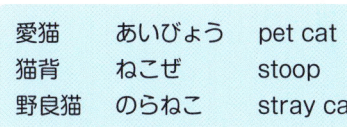

Point: 変 — Note the position of the dots!

変わる	かわる	to change
変化	へんか	change
変身	へんしん	transformation
変更	へんこう	alteration

復

 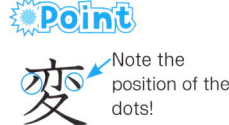

I shuttled between home and the office every day.

おんよみ フク　**くんよみ** ―

いみ to return, again　**strokes** 12画　ノ 丿 彳 彳 彳 彳 犭 狆 狆 復 復 復

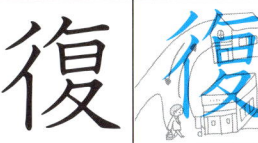

Point: 復 — Do not protrude!

往復	おうふく	round trip
復活	ふっかつ	revival
修復	しゅうふく	repair
復習	ふくしゅう	review

複

The woman photocopied some documents.

おんよみ フク　　**くんよみ** —

いみ to overlap, to become complicated

strokes 14画　　`丶 ﾌ ｪ ﾈ ﾈ ﾈ ﾈ ﾈ ﾈ ﾈ ﾈ ﾈ ﾈ 複`

Note the similar characters!

複雑	ふくざつ	complexity
複写	ふくしゃ	(photo) copy
複製	ふくせい	replication
重複	ちょうふく	overlap

服

The moon liked the clothes that were put on the table.

おんよみ フク　　**くんよみ** —

いみ clothes, to obey, to yield

strokes 8画　　`丿 几 月 月 月ﾖ 月ﾖ 服 服`

Do not connect!

服装	ふくそう	clothes, dress
和服	わふく	Japanese clothes
服用	ふくよう	dosing
克服	こくふく	conquest

報

The girl realized that she was wearing the same clothes as those that were reported.

おんよみ ホウ　　**くんよみ** むく(いる)

いみ to reward, to report

strokes 12画　　`一 十 土 キ キ 去 去 幸 幸 幸 報 報`

Note the number of horizontal strokes!

報いる	むくいる	to reward
報酬	ほうしゅう	reward, fee
報道	ほうどう	news, report
報告	ほうこく	report

較

We visited various shops by car in order to compare axes and get a top quality one.

おんよみ カク　　**くんよみ** —

いみ to compare

strokes 13画　　`一 ｢ 一ｦ 一ヨ 一ヨ 巨 車 車 車ﾞ 車ﾞ 車ﾞ 較 較`

Note the number of horizontal strokes!

比較	ひかく	comparison

転

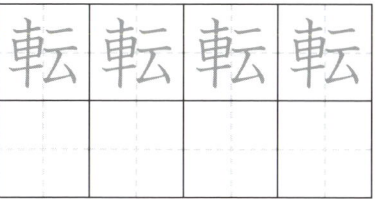 

The car that was zigzagging dangerously rolled down the mountain road.

- おんよみ テン
- くんよみ ころ(がる)・ころ(げる)・ころ(がす)・ころ(ぶ)

いみ to roll, to fall down

strokes 11画 一 厂 戶 百 亘 車 車 軒 転 転

Point
転 ← Do not protrude!

運転	うんてん	driving, operation
転換	てんかん	conversion
転向	てんこう	conversion
急転	きゅうてん	sudden change
自転車	じてんしゃ	bicycle

軽

I carried a light table in the car.

- おんよみ ケイ
- くんよみ かる(い)・かろ(やか)

いみ light, careless

strokes 12画 一 厂 戶 百 亘 車 車 軒 軽 軽 軽

Point
軽 ← Protrude!

軽食	けいしょく	light meal, snack
軽自動車	けいじどうしゃ	midget car, minicar
軽快(な)	けいかい(な)	nimble
軽薄(な)	けいはく(な)	frivolous
身軽(な)	みがる(な)	nimble, agile

輸

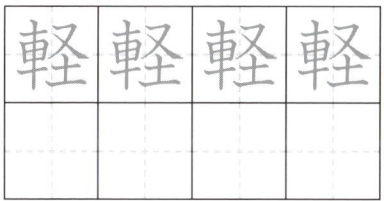 

Cars for export were lined up at the port, and were being loaded into a ship.

- おんよみ ユ
- くんよみ ―

いみ to transport

strokes 16画 一 厂 戶 百 亘 車 車 軒 軒 輪 輪 輪 輪 輸

輸出	ゆしゅつ	export
輸入	ゆにゅう	import
空輸	くうゆ	air transportation
輸送	ゆそう	transportation
禁輸	きんゆ	embargo

輪

A train was approaching a car whose wheel had come off at a crossing.

おんよみ リン　　**くんよみ** わ

いみ wheel, circle, to circle　　**strokes** 15画　一 ㇐ 亓 亓 車 車 車 軨 軨 軨 輪 輪

Point　輪　←Do not protrude!

車輪	しゃりん	wheel
輪郭	りんかく	contour, outline
年輪	ねんりん	annual ring
指輪	ゆびわ	ring

喫

I went to a café where the owner served freshly ground coffee to each customer.

おんよみ キツ　　**くんよみ** —

いみ to eat, to drink　　**strokes** 12画　丨 口 口 叮 叮 哄 喫 喫 喫 喫 喫 喫

Point　喫　←Do not protrude!

喫茶店	きっさてん	café, coffee shop
喫煙	きつえん	smoking
満喫	まんきつ	having one's fill
喫緊	きっきん	urgency

叫

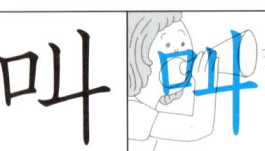

The woman shouted by using a megaphone.

おんよみ キョウ　　**くんよみ** さけ(ぶ)

いみ to shout　　**strokes** 6画　丨 口 口 叩 叫 叫

Point　叫　←Do not protrude!

叫ぶ	さけぶ	to shout
絶叫	ぜっきょう	screaming
叫び声	さけびごえ	cry, shout, yell

含

A mouse in an attic was swallowed by a snake, and included in the contents of its stomach.

おんよみ ガン　　**くんよみ** ふく(む)・ふく(める)

いみ to contain, to include　　**strokes** 7画　丿 人 𠆢 今 今 含 含

Point　含　←Connect!

含む	ふくむ	to contain, to include
含蓄	がんちく	connotation
包含	ほうがん	inclusion

288

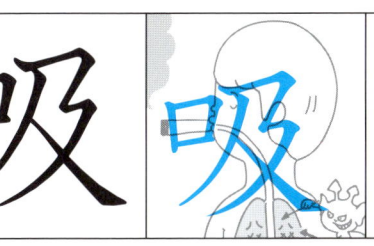

Excessive smoking is like inviting the devil into your lungs.

おんよみ キュウ
くんよみ す(う)

いみ to breathe in, to suck, to absorb **strokes** 6画 ｜ ㅁ ロ ⼝ 吸 吸

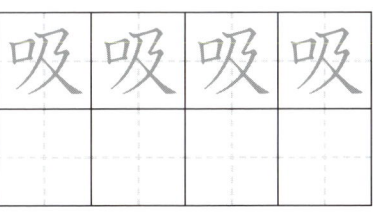

Point
吸
Do not protrude!

吸う	すう	to breathe in, to absorb
呼吸	こきゅう	breathing
吸収	きゅうしゅう	absorption
吸引	きゅういん	suction
吸入	きゅうにゅう	inhalation

I fully enjoyed tasting the seasonal food.

おんよみ ミ
くんよみ あじ・あじ(わう)

いみ taste, to savor **strokes** 8画 ｜ ㅁ ロ ⼝ ⼝ 叶 味 味

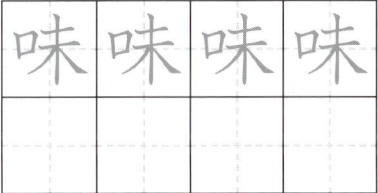

Point
味
Note the longest horizontal stroke!

味覚	みかく	sense of taste
美味	びみ	deliciousness
酸味	さんみ	acidity, sourness
意味	いみ	meaning
趣味	しゅみ	hobby

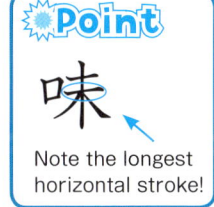

I called the waitress over, and ordered a cup of coffee.

おんよみ コ
くんよみ よ(ぶ)

いみ to call, to breathe out **strokes** 8画 ｜ ㅁ ロ ⼝ ⼝ 叮 呼

Point
呼
Note the position of the dots!

呼ぶ	よぶ	to call
点呼	てんこ	roll call
呼称	こしょう	naming
呼吸	こきゅう	breathing

器

Put the *sushi* on the divided serving dish.

おんよみ キ
くんよみ うつわ

いみ container, caliber　strokes 15画　丨 口 口 吅 吅 㗊 哭 哭 器 器 器 器

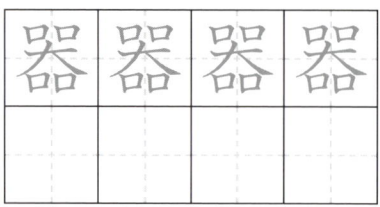 

Point 器 ← Protrude!

食器	しょっき	tableware
容器	ようき	container
陶器	とうき	pottery
器用(な)	きよう(な)	skillful
器量良し	きりょうよし	good-looking

品

I delivered three items.

おんよみ ヒン
くんよみ しな

いみ item, class, grade　strokes 9画　丨 口 口 叩 吊 品 品 品 品

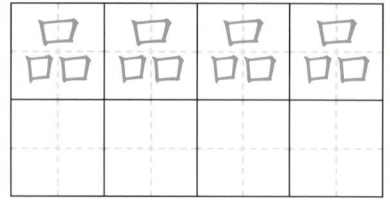 

Point 品 ← Do not connect!

食品	しょくひん	food
製品	せいひん	product
品質	ひんしつ	quality
上品	じょうひん	elegance
品物	しなもの	goods

可

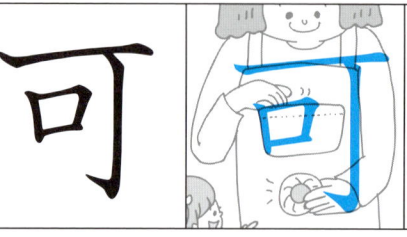

The mother was able to take anything out of her apron pocket.

おんよみ カ
くんよみ ―

いみ good, can, may　strokes 5画　一 丁 丂 可 可

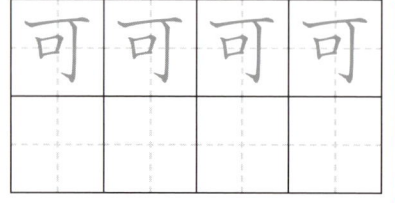 

Point 可 ← Do not protrude!

可決	かけつ	approval
許可	きょか	permission
可能(な)	かのう(な)	possible
可燃性	かねんせい	flammability
可動	かどう	mobility

寄

He was on the second floor of the building and leaning against the wall.

おんよみ キ　**くんよみ** よ(る)・よ(せる)

いみ to approach, to drop in, to give　**strokes** 11画　丶丶宀宀宀宀宏宏宏寄寄

寄る	よる	to approach, to drop in
寄付	きふ	donation
寄稿	きこう	contribution
寄生	きせい	parasitism

局

At the television station, one person is in charge of checking a lot of monitors.

おんよみ キョク　**くんよみ** —

いみ office, section, chessboard　**strokes** 7画　フコ尸弓局局局

郵便局	ゆうびんきょく	post office
局地的(な)	きょくちてき(な)	local, regional
局面	きょくめん	phase, stage
テレビ局	てれびきょく	television station

周

I cared about what the people surrounding me thought of me.

おんよみ シュウ　**くんよみ** まわ(り)

いみ circumference, to circle　**strokes** 8画　丿刀刀円円用周周

Point 周 ×同　×週　Note the similar characters!

周り	まわり	circumference
周辺	しゅうへん	periphery
周囲	しゅうい	surroundings
円周	えんしゅう	circumference of a circle

向

The window of the house faces south.

おんよみ コウ　**くんよみ** む(く)・む(ける)・む(かう)・む(こう)

いみ to face, to head for, direction　**strokes** 6画　丿亻冂向向向

Point 向 Do not connect!

向く	むく	to face, to head for
向上	こうじょう	improvement, progress
動向	どうこう	trend
意向	いこう	intention

291

告

Getting a yellow card for the foul, the player protested to the referee with his arms raised.

おんよみ コク　**くんよみ** つ(げる)

いみ to tell, to inform

strokes 7画 ノ ト 土 生 牛 告 告

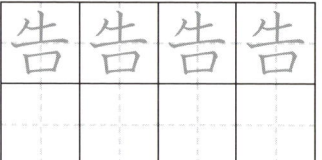

Point
Note the longest horizontal stroke!

告げる	つげる	to tell, to inform
告白	こくはく	confession
警告	けいこく	warning
予告	よこく	notice

否

You should definitely refuse a hard sell.

おんよみ ヒ　**くんよみ** いな

いみ no, to deny

strokes 7画 一 ア オ 不 不 否 否

Point
Do not protrude!

否定	ひてい	denial, negation
拒否	きょひ	denial, refusal
否決	ひけつ	rejection
否	いな	no

君

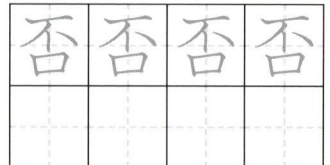

The monarch opened his mouth and talked to the common people.

おんよみ クン　**くんよみ** きみ

いみ monarch, sovereign, you

strokes 7画 フ ヲ ヨ 尹 尹 君 君

Point
Protrude!

諸君	しょくん	ladies and gentlemen
君臨	くんりん	reign
君主	くんしゅ	monarch
君	きみ	you

群

The monarch walked and was followed by a flock of sheep.

おんよみ グン　**くんよみ** む(れる)・む(れ)・むら

いみ group, flock, to gather

strokes 13画 フ ヲ ヨ 尹 尹 君 君 君' 君' 群 群 群 群

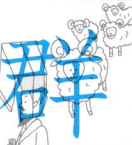

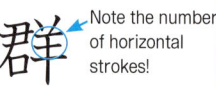

Point
Note the number of horizontal strokes!

群れる	むれる	to gather
群衆	ぐんしゅう	crowd
群生	ぐんせい	gregariousness

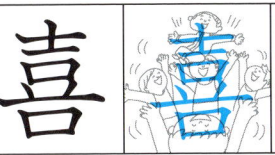

After the game, people who were full of joy started giving a victory toss.

おんよみ キ   **くんよみ** よろこ(ぶ)

| **いみ** happy, joyful, to rejoice | **strokes** 12画 一 十 土 吉 吉 吉 吉 吉 喜 喜 喜 喜 |

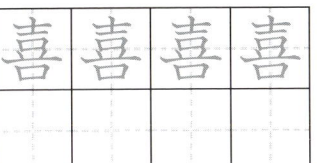

 Do not protrude!

喜ぶ	よろこぶ	to rejoice
歓喜	かんき	delight
喜劇	きげき	comedy

Plants grow very well when good people give them fertilizer.

おんよみ ゼン   **くんよみ** よ(い)

| **いみ** good, excellent | **strokes** 12画 丶 丷 丷 半 兰 羊 羊 盖 盖 善 善 善 |

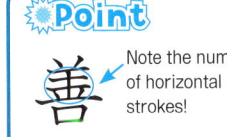 Note the number of horizontal strokes!

善い	よい	good
善意	ぜんい	goodwill
改善	かいぜん	improvement
最善	さいぜん	best

The presenter opened his mouth and started to speak.

おんよみ シ   **くんよみ** ―

| **いみ** to conduct, to administer | **strokes** 5画 フ コ 司 司 司 |

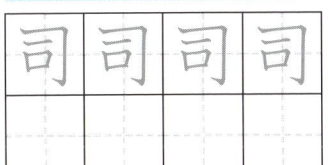

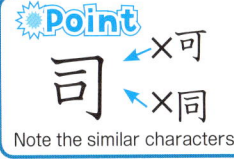 ×可 ×同
Note the similar characters!

司会者	しかいしゃ	presenter, program host(ess)
上司	じょうし	boss, superior
司書	ししょ	librarian

Everybody stopped in response to an order from the front.

おんよみ ゴウ   **くんよみ** ―

| **いみ** to shout, to call, title, number | **strokes** 5画 丶 口 口 呂 号 |

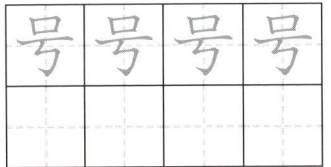

 Do not protrude!

号令	ごうれい	command, order
記号	きごう	sign, symbol
暗号	あんごう	cipher
称号	しょうごう	title

我

My house is made of sweets.

おんよみ ガ
くんよみ われ・わ

いみ I, oneself, ego

strokes 7画 ノ 二 千 手 我 我 我

Point
我 ← Protrude!

自我	じが	ego, self	成長と共に、子供に自我が芽生えてきた。
我流の	がりゅうの	self-taught	彼のダンスは我流のものだ。
我慢	がまん	patience	この一週間、酒を飲むのを我慢している。
我	われ	I, oneself	あまりにも感激して、我を忘れて泣いた。
我が家	わがや	one's home, one's house	我が家に友人を招いてパーティーをした。

成

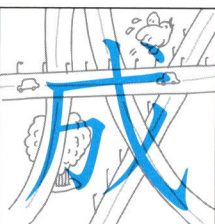

Birds lost their habitat because the motorway was completed.

おんよみ セイ・ジョウ
くんよみ な(る)・な(す)

いみ to become, to accomplish

strokes 6画 ノ 厂 厂 成 成 成

Point
成 ← Note the position of the dot!

成功	せいこう	success	失敗は成功のもと。
達成	たっせい	achievement	目標を達成する努力をしよう。
成長	せいちょう	growth	子供の成長は早い。
成人	せいじん	adult	成人して、親元を離れた。
成就	じょうじゅ	fulfillment	弁護士になるという夢が成就した。
成り行き	なりゆき	course of events	しばらくは事の成り行きを見守る。

戦

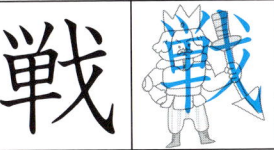

The king who is good at using spears established a position in the battle.

おんよみ セン　　**くんよみ** いくさ・たたか(う)

いみ to fight, war, to shiver　　**strokes** 13画　　`、 ゛ ヅ ゾ 肖 肖 当 当 単 単 戦 戦 戦`

Point 戦 ← Note the position of the dots!

戦う	たたかう	to fight
戦争	せんそう	war
挑戦	ちょうせん	challenge
戦慄	せんりつ	shiver

歳

In one year, the cactus penetrated the ceiling and extended through the roof.

おんよみ サイ・セイ　　**くんよみ** ―

いみ age, year　　**strokes** 13画　　`丨 丨 止 止 产 产 芦 芦 崇 歳 歳 歳`

Point 歳 ← Note the position of the dot!

歳月	さいげつ	time, years
八歳	はっさい	eight years old
歳末	さいまつ	year-end
お歳暮	おせいぼ	year-end gift

式

At the wedding ceremony, the bride was wearing a dress with a long train and a veil.

おんよみ シキ　　**くんよみ** ―

いみ ceremony, formula　　**strokes** 6画　　`一 二 テ 式 式 式`

Point 式 Do not protrude!

正式(な)	せいしき(な)	official
書式	しょしき	format
数式	すうしき	numerical formula
結婚式	けっこんしき	wedding ceremony

武

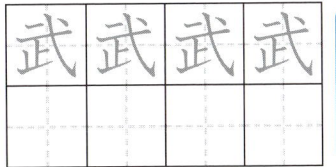

The *samurai* drew his sword and challenge the boy *Kintaro*, who was riding a bear with a broad ax, to a fight.

おんよみ ブ・ム　　**くんよみ** ―

いみ strong, robust, military affairs　　**strokes** 8画　　`一 二 テ 于 正 正 武 武`

Point 武 ← Note the position of the dots!

武勇	ぶゆう	bravery
武器	ぶき	weapon
武力	ぶりょく	military force
武士	ぶし	*samurai* warrior

When my friend suddenly fell down, I asked a passer-by for help.

おんよみ キュウ
くんよみ もと(める)

いみ to seek, to demand　strokes 7画　一 十 十 寸 寸 求 求

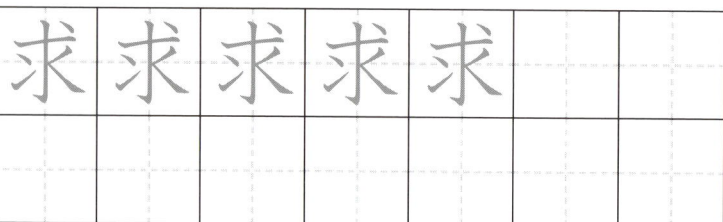

Point　Do not connect!

求める	もとめる	to seek, to demand	彼は大きな声を出して助けを求めた。
要求	ようきゅう	demand, request	そんな無理な要求に応えることは出来ない。
請求	せいきゅう	claim, demand	通信販売のカタログを請求した。
欲求	よっきゅう	desire	彼女は金に対する欲求が強い。
探求	たんきゅう	quest, search	物事の本質を探究し続ける。
追求	ついきゅう	pursuit	彼は理想を追求するばかりだ。

The rugby player desperately dashed so the ball would not be taken by his opponents.

おんよみ ヒツ
くんよみ かなら(ず)

いみ always, necessarily　strokes 5画　丶 ソ 必 必 必

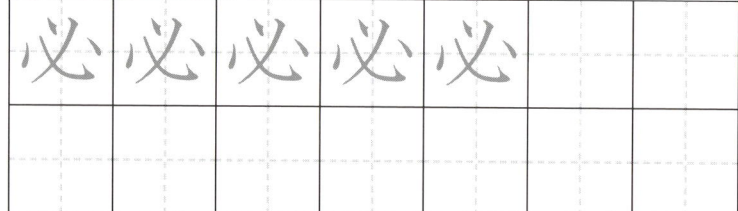

Point　Note the position of the dots!

必ず	かならず	necessarily, always	毎朝必ず犬の散歩をする。
必要	ひつよう	necessity	足りない材料を買ってくる必要がある。
必須の	ひっすの	essential, required	資格取得のためには、この知識は必須だ。
必死に	ひっしに	desperately, frantically	必死で勉強して試験に合格した。
必需品	ひつじゅひん	necessities	雨の日は傘が必需品だ。

There are two penguins, a polar bear and a bird on ice.

おんよみ ヒョウ　くんよみ こおり・ひ

いみ ice, to freeze　strokes 5画　丨 刁 氵 氺 氷

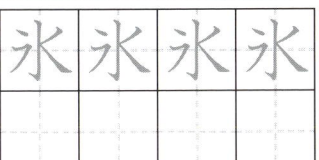

Point — Note the position of the dot!

氷山	ひょうざん	iceberg
氷点	ひょうてん	freezing point
氷水	こおりみず	ice water
氷雨	ひさめ	cold rain

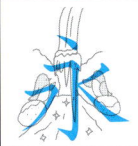

The water of the waterfall has been flowing upstream for a long time.

おんよみ エイ　くんよみ なが(い)

いみ long time, forever　strokes 5画　丶 亅 亅 永 永

永遠	えいえん	eternity
永続	えいぞく	permanence
永住	えいじゅう	permanent residence
永い	ながい	long (time)

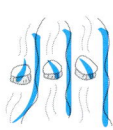

There were small islands in the middle of the river.

おんよみ シュウ　くんよみ す

いみ sandbank, country　strokes 6画　丶 丿 丿 州 州 州

州	しゅう	county, state
欧州	おうしゅう	Europe
中州	なかす	sandbank, shoal
三角州	さんかくす	delta

The woman has a good ear for distinguishing sounds. She is a cello player by profession.

おんよみ ショク　くんよみ —

いみ job, part　strokes 18画　一 丆 F F E 耳 耳' 耳 耶 耶 耶 耴 聅 聯 聵 聵 職 職

Point — Note the position of the dot!

職業	しょくぎょう	occupation
転職	てんしょく	change of job
本職	ほんしょく	(principal) profession
職人	しょくにん	craftsman

銀		The girl put the silver coins, which she earned by selling some food, in a savings box.
		おんよみ ギン
		くんよみ ―

いみ silver　　**strokes** 14画　ノ 　 　 　 　 　 　 　 　 　 　 　 　 銀

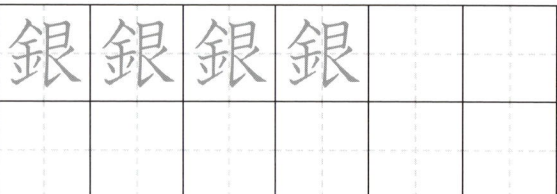

銀製品	ぎんせいひん	silverware
銀行	ぎんこう	bank
銀河	ぎんが	galaxy
銀貨	ぎんか	silver coin
銀婚式	ぎんこんしき	silver wedding

		The farmer worked really hard using an iron hoe, and he saved money.
		おんよみ テツ
		くんよみ ―

いみ iron, weapon　　**strokes** 13画　ノ 　 　 　 　 　 　 　 　 　 　 　 鉄

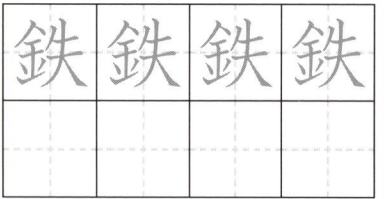

Protrude!

鉄鋼	てっこう	steel
鉄道	てつどう	railroad, railway
鉄橋	てっきょう	iron bridge
砂鉄	さてつ	iron sand
鉄則	てっそく	hard-and-fast rule

		The robot that I bought with the money I saved was made of copper.
		おんよみ ドウ
		くんよみ ―

いみ copper, bronze　　**strokes** 14画　ノ 　 　 　 　 　 　 　 　 　 　 　 　 銅

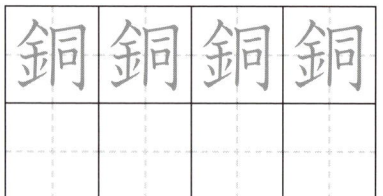

Do not connect!

銅像	どうぞう	bronze statue
銅線	どうせん	copper wire
分銅	ふんどう	(balance) weight
銅版画	どうはんが	etching

針

The boy saved money and bought a fish hook.

- おんよみ シン
- くんよみ はり

いみ needle, pin, pointer
strokes 10画 ノ 𠂉 𠂆 亽 全 全 金 金 金 針

針	針	針	針

方針	ほうしん	policy
指針	ししん	guideline
針葉樹	しんようじゅ	conifer
釣り針	つりばり	fish hooks
針金	はりがね	wire

鋭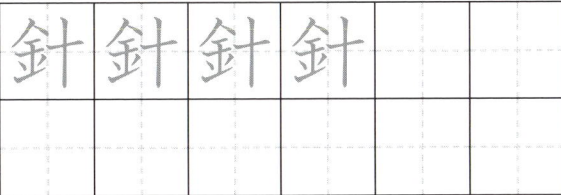

We saved money to go and see the walrus.

- おんよみ エイ
- くんよみ するど(い)

いみ sharp, keen
strokes 15画 ノ 𠂉 𠂆 亽 全 全 金 金 釒 釒 鈖 鈖 鋭

鋭	鋭	鋭	鋭

Point
Note the position of the dots!

鋭利	えいり	sharpness
鋭敏(な)	えいびん(な)	keen
鋭気	えいき	animated spirit
精鋭	せいえい	elite, the pick
鋭角	えいかく	acute angle

録

I calculated the sum of coins in the savings box, and recorded it in a notebook.

- おんよみ ロク
- くんよみ ―

いみ to write down, to record
strokes 16画 ノ 𠂉 𠂆 亽 全 全 金 金 釒 釒 鉅 鉅 鋘 鋘 録

録	録	録	録

Point
Note the longest horizontal stroke!

記録	きろく	record
登録	とうろく	registration
録画	ろくが	video recording
図録	ずろく	pictorial record
目録	もくろく	list

革

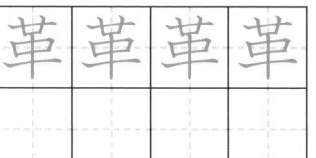

The sales assistant showed me a pair of shoes that were made of very good quality leather.

おんよみ カク　　**くんよみ** かわ

いみ leather, to change　　**strokes** 9画　　一 十 廾 廾 芦 芦 莒 革

Point 革 ← Do not protrude!

皮革	ひかく	leather
革命	かくめい	revolution
改革	かいかく	reform
革靴	かわぐつ	leather shoes

靴

A wolf that had turned into a girl came into a shoe store to buy a new pair of leather shoes.

おんよみ カ　　**くんよみ** くつ

いみ shoe, boot　　**strokes** 13画　　一 十 廾 廾 芦 芦 莒 革 革 靪 靪 靴

Point 靴 ← Do not protrude!

製靴	せいか	shoemaking
靴下	くつした	socks, stockings
長靴	ながぐつ	boots
雨靴	あまぐつ	rain shoes

巻

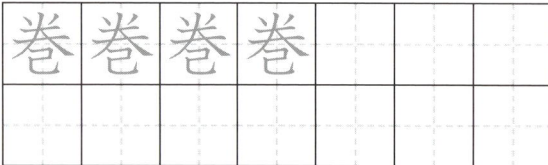

At the library, I was reading a Japanese scroll, known as *makimono*.

おんよみ カン　　**くんよみ** ま(く)・まき

いみ to wind, to roll, roll, scroll　　**strokes** 9画　　丶 ン 二 兰 半 关 夹 巻 巻

巻く	まく	to wind, to roll
巻頭	かんとう	the beginning of a book
第一巻	だいいっかん	the first volume
巻き貝	まきがい	snail, spiral shell

券

There was a long line at the ticket office.

おんよみ ケン　　**くんよみ** ―

いみ ticket, stamp　　**strokes** 8画　　丶 ン 二 兰 半 关 夹 券

Point 券 ← Do not protrude!

旅券	りょけん	passport
入場券	にゅうじょうけん	admission ticket
商品券	しょうひんけん	gift certificate
証券	しょうけん	securities

敬

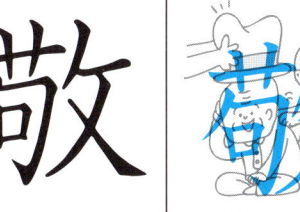

A respected elder was given a hat, and had his shoulders pounded on to remove the stiffness.

- おんよみ ケイ
- くんよみ うやま(う)

いみ to respect

strokes 12画 　一 ナ サ ヰ 芍 芍 苟 苟 苟 苟ケ 敬ケ 敬

敬う	うやまう	to respect
尊敬	そんけい	respect
敬遠	けいえん	avoidance
敬虔(な)	けいけん(な)	pious
敬称	けいしょう	honorific title

警

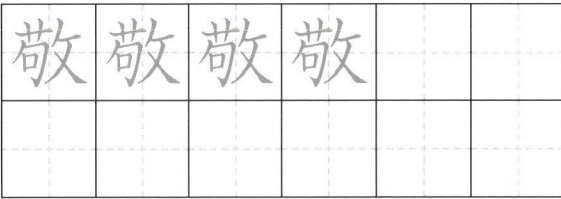

The girl told the policeman that she clapped her grandfather on the shoulder.

- おんよみ ケイ
- くんよみ ―

いみ to guard, to caution

strokes 19画 　一 ナ サ ヰ 芍 芍 苟 苟 苟 苟ケ 敬ケ 敬 敬 警 警 警 警 警

Point
Note the longest horizontal stroke!

警戒	けいかい	caution, vigilance
警告	けいこく	warning
警報	けいほう	alarm
警察	けいさつ	police
警護	けいご	guard

将

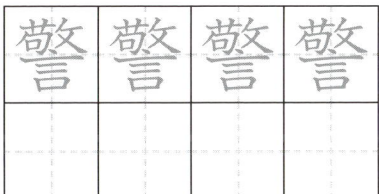

Two servants behind the sliding doors were waiting for the order from the *shogun* general.

- おんよみ ショウ
- くんよみ ―

いみ commander, to lead, to be about to ~

strokes 10画 　丨 丬 丬 圩 圩 圩 圩 将 将 将

Point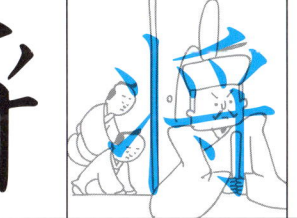
Note the position of the dots!

将棋	しょうぎ	Japanese chess
将軍	しょうぐん	general
将来	しょうらい	future
将校	しょうこう	military officer
名将	めいしょう	great commander

状

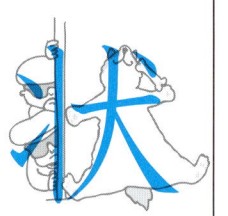

From behind the wall, two thieves were observing whether the guard dog was deeply asleep.

おんよみ ジョウ
くんよみ —

いみ situation, to express, document
strokes 7画 ノ丬丬丬壮状状

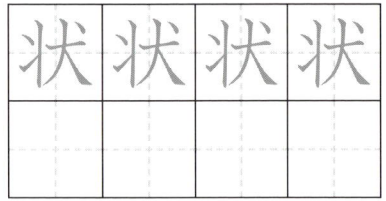

Note the position of the dot!

状態	じょうたい	state
状況	じょうきょう	situation
病状	びょうじょう	medical condition
液状	えきじょう	liquid form [state]
賞状	しょうじょう	certificate of merit

被

The woman wearing a fur coat and a fur hat was robbed of her bag.

おんよみ ヒ
くんよみ こうむ(る)

いみ to cover, to suffer
strokes 10画 `ラネネネ衤初初被被

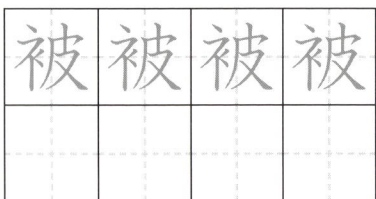

Protrude!

被る	こうむる	to suffer
被膜	ひまく	capsule, film
被害	ひがい	damage
被告	ひこく	the accused
被写体	ひしゃたい	(photographic) subject

補

The substitute players on the bench loudly cheered the batter who hit the ball.

おんよみ ホ
くんよみ おぎな(う)

いみ to supplement, to compensate
strokes 12画 `ラネネネ衤初初補補補

Note the position of the dot!

補う	おぎなう	to supplement, to compensate
補償	ほしょう	compensation
補足	ほそく	supplementation
補充	ほじゅう	replenishment
候補	こうほ	candidate

初

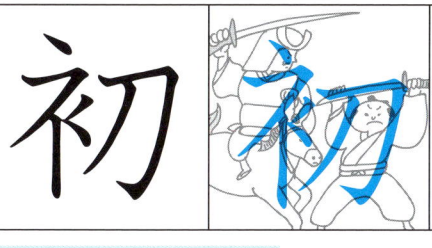

Young *samurai* warriors firmly held swords, and challenged each other to their first battle.

- おんよみ ショ
- くんよみ はじ(め)・はじ(めて)・はつ・うい・そ(める)

いみ first, to begin

strokes 7画　`ヽ ラ ネ ネ ネ 初 初`

Point
初
Do not protrude!

最初	さいしょ	the first
当初	とうしょ	at first
初めて	はじめて	for the first time
初雪	はつゆき	the first snow
初陣	ういじん	the first battle

衣

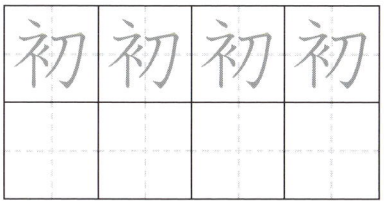

The lady was wearing a nice costume.

- おんよみ イ
- くんよみ ころも

いみ clothes, to wear

strokes 6画　`ヽ 亠 ナ 亡 で 衣`

Point
衣 ×表
衣 ×依
Note the similar characters!

衣服	いふく	clothes
衣装	いしょう	costume
白衣	はくい	white coat
救命胴衣	きゅうめいどうい	life jacket
更衣室	こういしつ	dressing room

袋

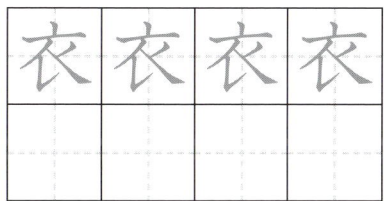

The tourist took pictures of a parrot and a kangaroo raising her baby in her pouch.

- おんよみ タイ
- くんよみ ふくろ

いみ bag

strokes 11画　`ノ 亻 亻 代 代 代 伐 伐 袋 袋 袋`

Point
袋
Note the position of the dot!

有袋類	ゆうたいるい	marsupial
手袋	てぶくろ	gloves
袋小路	ふくろこうじ	dead end
紙袋	かみぶくろ	paper bag
小袋	こぶくろ	pouch

裏

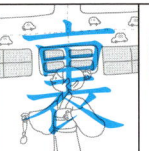

A woman in a *yukata* walked on a back road running along a rice field.

- おんよみ リ
- くんよみ うら

いみ the back, inside

strokes 13画 　一　亠　广　亩　亩　亩　审　审　重　重　寡　裏　裏

Point 裏 ← Note the number of horizontal strokes!

表裏	ひょうり	the front and back
裏口	うらぐち	the back door
裏話	うらばなし	inside story
裏道	うらみち	back road, byway

表

He was chosen to play for the Japan national football team and a new uniform arrived.

- おんよみ ヒョウ
- くんよみ おもて・あらわ(す)・あらわ(れる)

いみ surface, chart, to represent

strokes 8画 　一　十　キ　主　丰　丰　表　表

Point 表 ← Protrude!

表す	あらわす	to represent
表紙	ひょうし	book cover
代表	だいひょう	representative
表通り	おもてどおり	main street

装

A *geisha* holding an umbrella was wearing a gorgeous *kimono* and hair accessories.

- おんよみ ソウ・ショウ
- くんよみ よそお(う)

いみ to dress up, to pretend, to wrap

strokes 12画 　丨　丬　丬　キ　壮　壮　壮　壮　茾　装　装　装

Point 装 ← Note the position of the dots!

装う	よそおう	to dress up, to pretend
服装	ふくそう	clothes, dress
装備	そうび	equipment
衣装	いしょう	costume

裁

My mother, who is good at sewing, made me a clothes with a sewing machine.

- おんよみ サイ
- くんよみ た(つ)・さば(く)

いみ to cut, to judge

strokes 12画 　一　十　キ　ギ　圭　羊　羊　表　表　裁　裁　裁

Point 裁 ← Note the position of the dot!

裁く	さばく	to judge
裁つ	たつ	to cut
裁縫	さいほう	sewing
裁判	さいばん	trial

The woman wore her special apron and made special curry.

おんよみ セイ
くんよみ —

いみ to make, to produce

strokes 14画 ノ ヒ 乍 乍 缶 吿 制 制 制 製 製 製 製

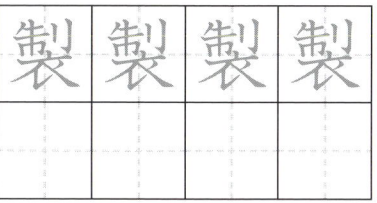

Note the similar characters!

製品	せいひん	product
製造	せいぞう	production, manufacture
製図	せいず	drafting
自家製の	じかせいの	home-made
木製の	もくせいの	wooden

The man had his chest measured.

おんよみ スン
くんよみ —

いみ (Japanese)inch, length

strokes 3画 一 十 寸

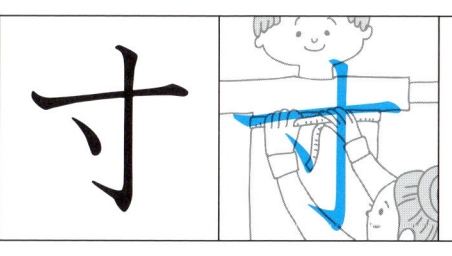

Note the position of the dot!

寸法	すんぽう	size
原寸	げんすん	actual size
寸前	すんぜん	just before
寸暇	すんか	spare moment
寸志	すんし	small present

The man had his suit tailored at a custom tailor.

おんよみ セン
くんよみ もっぱ(ら)

いみ entirely, devotedly

strokes 9画 一 丆 丏 甫 甫 甫 東 専 専

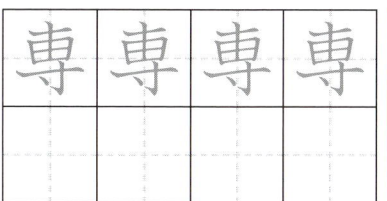

Do not protrude!

専門	せんもん	specialty, specialization
専攻	せんこう	major, main subject
専念	せんねん	devotion, dedication
専任	せんにん	exclusive duty
専用	せんよう	exclusive use

射

The man had a cold, so he got an injection at the hospital to cure it.

おんよみ シャ　　くんよみ い(る)

いみ to shoot, to emit　　strokes 10画　　′ 亻 亻 甪 甪 身 身 身 射 射

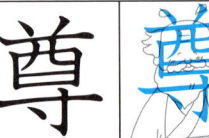
Protrude!

射る	いる	to shoot
射撃	しゃげき	shooting
注射	ちゅうしゃ	injection
反射	はんしゃ	reflection

尊

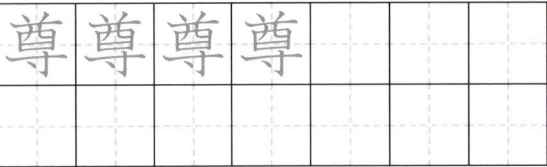

The village elder was respected by all the residents.

おんよみ ソン　　くんよみ たっと(い)・とうと(い)・たっと(ぶ)・とうと(ぶ)

いみ precious, to respect　　strokes 12画　　丶 ヽ 丷 丷 酋 酋 酋 酋 酋 酋 尊 尊

尊敬	そんけい	respect
尊大	そんだい	arrogance
自尊心	じそんしん	pride, self-esteem
尊い	とうとい・たっとい	precious, noble

等

Tourists visited the beautiful temple that was surrounded by bamboo trees.

おんよみ トウ　　くんよみ ひと(しい)

いみ equal, grade, etcetera　　strokes 12画　　′ ⺊ ⺊ ⺮ ⺮ 竺 竺 竺 笙 等 等 等

Note the position of the dots!

対等	たいとう	equality
上等(な)	じょうとう(な)	fine, superior
優等	ゆうとう	excellence, honors
等しい	ひとしい	equal

導

I followed the way that the staff instructed and found my way to the venue.

おんよみ ドウ　　くんよみ みちび(く)

いみ to lead, to guide　　strokes 15画　　丶 丷 丷 丷 酋 酋 酋 首 首 首 道 道 道 導 導

Note the number of horizontal strokes!

導く	みちびく	to lead, to guide
指導	しどう	instruction, guidance
誘導	ゆうどう	guidance, induction
主導	しゅどう	taking the lead

対

The two people confronted each other.

- おんよみ: タイ・ツイ
- くんよみ: —
- いみ: to answer, face, to opponent
- strokes: 7画

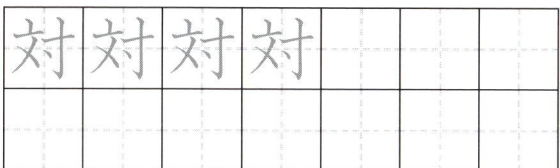

対象	たいしょう	object, target
対立	たいりつ	opposition, conflict
対策	たいさく	countermeasure
一対	いっつい	one pair

防

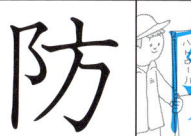

In order to prevent crime, I patrolled the area and set up security cameras.

- おんよみ: ボウ
- くんよみ: ふせ(ぐ)
- いみ: to prevent, embankment
- strokes: 7画

Point  Do not connect!

防ぐ	ふせぐ	to prevent
予防	よぼう	prevention
防備	ぼうび	defense
堤防	ていぼう	dike, levee

院

The boy made a full recovery at the Red Cross Hospital.

- おんよみ: イン
- くんよみ: —
- いみ: fence, palace, public office
- strokes: 10画

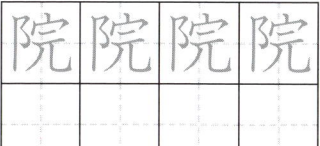

Point  Do not protrude!

病院	びょういん	hospital
入院	にゅういん	hospitalization
美容院	びよういん	beauty salon
寺院	じいん	temple

限

People occasionally need to break through their limits.

- おんよみ: ゲン
- くんよみ: かぎ(る)
- いみ: to limit, limit
- strokes: 9画

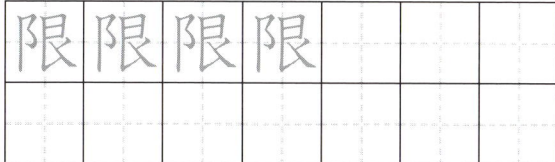

限る	かぎる	to limit
限界	げんかい	limit
期限	きげん	deadline, time limit
無限	むげん	infinity

階

The students got some training with an instructor beside a flag that fluttered in the wind.

おんよみ　カイ
くんよみ　—

いみ　stairs, storey, grade

strokes 12画　｀　｀　阝　阝‐　阝ヒ　阝ヒ　阝ヒ　阝比　階　階　階

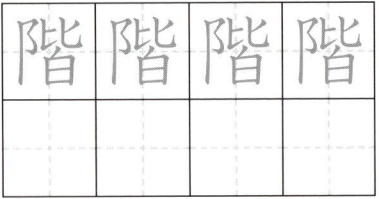

Point
階
Do not protrude!

階段	かいだん	stairs
階下	かいか	downstairs
地階	ちかい	basement
段階	だんかい	stage, phase
階級	かいきゅう	class, rank

降

The soldier surrendered by waving a white flag.

おんよみ　コウ
くんよみ　お(りる)・お(ろす)・ふ(る)

いみ　to descend, to let down, to fall

strokes 10画　｀　｀　阝　阝′　阝″　阝冬　降　降　降　降

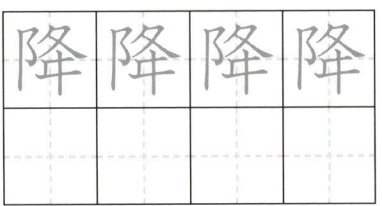

Point
降
Do not protrude!

降りる	おりる	to descend
降伏	こうふく	surrender
降下	こうか	descent
降格	こうかく	demotion
滑降	かっこう	downhill skiing

陽

The athletes marched into the Olympic venue following the flag-bearer under the sunshine.

おんよみ　ヨウ
くんよみ　—

いみ　sunshine, bright, plus

strokes 12画　｀　｀　阝　阝′　阝″　阝日　阝旦　阝昜　陽　陽　陽

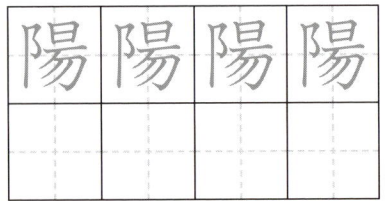

Point
陽
Do not protrude!

太陽	たいよう	the sun
陽光	ようこう	sunlight, the sunshine
陽春	ようしゅん	warm spring
陽気(な)	ようき(な)	cheerful
陽極	ようきょく	anode, plus terminal

除

I killed the germs by using a germ remover spray.

おんよみ ジョ・ジ　　**くんよみ** のぞ(く)

いみ to remove

strokes 10画 　フ　3　阝　阝　阝´　阝△　阝⌒　阝会　除　除

Point 除 ← Connect!

除く	のぞく	to remove
削除	さくじょ	deletion
除菌	じょきん	germ removal
掃除	そうじ	cleaning

陸

The drifting ship finally reached land.

おんよみ リク　　**くんよみ** —

いみ land, ground

strokes 11画 　フ　3　阝　阝−　阝+　阝土　阝圥　陸　陸　陸　陸

大陸	たいりく	continent
着陸	ちゃくりく	landing
陸軍	りくぐん	army
陸路	りくろ	land route

際

Let's hang the flag, beat a drum and dance lively when the festival is held.

おんよみ サイ　　**くんよみ** きわ

いみ border, interval, when

strokes 14画 　フ　3　阝　阝´　阝⺈　阝⺈　阝⺈⺉　阝⺈⺉⺈　阝⺈⺉⺈⺋　際　際　際　際

Point 際 ← Do not protrude!

際限	さいげん	limit
交際	こうさい	companionship
国際的(な)	こくさいてき(な)	international
瀬戸際	せとぎわ	critical moment

郵

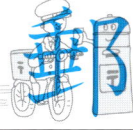

The mailman delivered the letters he picked up from the postbox by moped.

おんよみ ユウ　　**くんよみ** —

いみ post, mail

strokes 11画 　ノ　二　三　千　チ　丢　垂　垂　垂ろ　郵　郵

Point 郵 ← Note the number of horizontal strokes!

郵便局	ゆうびんきょく	post office
郵送	ゆうそう	mailing
郵送料	ゆうそうりょう	postage
郵便番号	ゆうびんばんごう	zip code

郊

The man started selling axes to people in the suburbs.

おんよみ コウ　　**くんよみ** —

いみ suburb, outskirts　　**strokes** 9画　　丶 亠 ナ 六 方 交 交′ 郊′ 郊

| 郊外 | こうがい | the suburbs, the outskirts |
| 近郊 | きんこう | the suburbs, the outskirts |

部

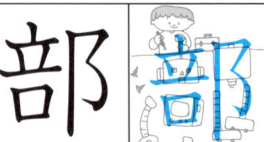

I built a robot by putting some parts together.

おんよみ ブ　　**くんよみ** —

いみ division, part, club　　**strokes** 11画　　丶 亠 ナ 立 立 咅 咅 咅 咅′ 咅′ 部

Point 部 ← Note the longest horizontal stroke!

部品	ぶひん	parts
細部	さいぶ	details
部門	ぶもん	department, division
部下	ぶか	subordinate

都

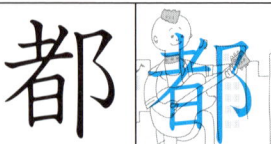

A young man came to the capital city and played the guitar.

おんよみ ト・ツ　　**くんよみ** みやこ

いみ capital city, all　　**strokes** 11画　　一 十 土 耂 者 者 者 者 者′ 者′ 都

Point 都 ← Connect!

都市	とし	city
首都	しゅと	capital city
都合	つごう	convenience
都	みやこ	capital city, metropolis

乱

The man got confused as he was given more paperwork.

おんよみ ラン　　**くんよみ** みだ(れる)・みだ(す)

いみ to disturb, to be disturbed, disorder　　**strokes** 7画　　丿 二 千 千 舌 舌 乱

Point 乱 ← Do not protrude!

混乱	こんらん	confusion, chaos
乱れる	みだれる	to be disturbed
散乱	さんらん	being scattered
乱暴	らんぼう	violence

The woman politely greeted her teacher.

おんよみ レイ・ライ
くんよみ ―

いみ courtesy, thanks strokes 5画 ` ラ ネ ネ 礼

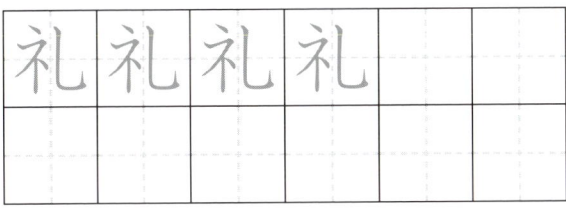

礼儀	れいぎ	courtesy, manners
礼服	れいふく	formal dress, robe
失礼	しつれい	impoliteness
婚礼	こんれい	wedding ceremony
謝礼	しゃれい	reward

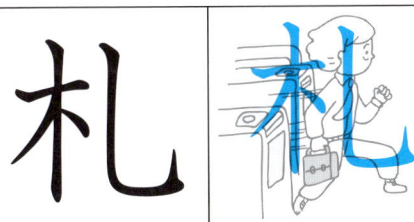

The man passed through the automatic ticket gate and headed for home.

おんよみ サツ
くんよみ ふだ

いみ label, ticket, bank note strokes 5画 一 十 才 木 札

千円札	せんえんさつ	thousand-yen bill
表札	ひょうさつ	nameplate, doorplate
改札口	かいさつぐち	ticket gate
入札	にゅうさつ	bidding
名札	なふだ	name tag

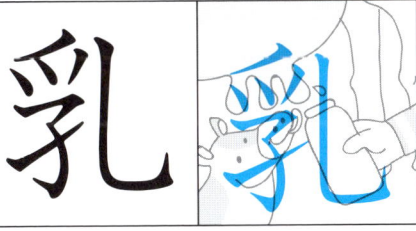

While the calf was drinking his mother's milk, I milked the cow into a bottle.

おんよみ ニュウ
くんよみ ち・ちち

いみ milk strokes 8画 ノ ⺍ ⺍ ⺍ 孚 孚 乳

Point
乳
Note the position of the dots!

乳製品	にゅうせいひん	dairy products
牛乳	ぎゅうにゅう	cow milk
豆乳	とうにゅう	soy milk
授乳	じゅにゅう	breast-feeding
乳搾り	ちちしぼり	milking

311

婚

The woman sent her friend a picture that was taken at the wedding.

おんよみ コン　くんよみ —

いみ to marry, marriage

strokes 11画　く ㄑ 女 女' 女ㄏ 女ㄈ 妒 娇 婚 婚

Point　婚 ← Protrude!

結婚	けっこん	marriage
婚約	こんやく	engagement
未婚	みこん	unmarried
離婚	りこん	divorce

婦

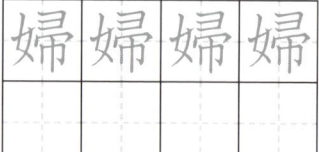

An honorable lady was standing by the palace.

おんよみ フ　くんよみ —

いみ woman, wife

strokes 11画　く ㄑ 女 女ㄱ 女ㄱ 妇 妇 妈 婦 婦

Point　婦 ← Do not connect!

婦人	ふじん	woman, lady
夫婦	ふうふ	married couple
新婦	しんぷ	bride
妊婦	にんぷ	pregnant woman

娘

The girl with the good appetite is my daughter.

おんよみ —　くんよみ むすめ

いみ girl, daughter

strokes 10画　く ㄑ 女 女' 女ㄏ 女ㄈ 妇 娘 娘 娘

娘	むすめ	daughter
愛娘	まなむすめ	beloved daughter
娘婿	むすめむこ	son-in-law
孫娘	まごむすめ	granddaughter

始

The woman was waiting for the piano performance to begin.

おんよみ シ　くんよみ はじ(まる)・はじ(める)

いみ to begin, beginning

strokes 8画　く ㄑ 女 女ㄥ 女ㄙ 始 始 始

始める	はじめる	to begin, to start
開始	かいし	start
年始	ねんし	the beginning of the year
原始の	げんしの	primitive

好

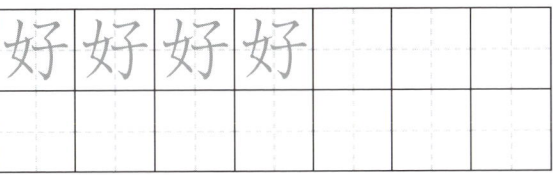

The woman loves children.

おんよみ コウ　　**くんよみ** この(む)・す(く)

いみ good, nice, to like　　**strokes** 6画　ㄑ 夂 女 女′ 好 好

好む	このむ	to like
好意	こうい	goodwill, favor
好評	こうひょう	popularity
友好	ゆうこう	friendship

委

The woman left a letter of attorney for the bird on the tree.

おんよみ イ　　**くんよみ** ゆだ(ねる)

いみ to entrust, detailed　　**strokes** 8画　一 ニ 千 手 禾 禾 委 委

Point — Note the longest horizontal stroke!

委ねる	ゆだねる	to entrust
委任状	いにんじょう	letter of attorney
委細	いさい	details
委員会	いいんかい	committee

姿

The woman couldn't take her eyes off the farmer who was planting one seedling after another.

おんよみ シ　　**くんよみ** すがた

いみ figure, aspect　　**strokes** 9画　、 ｀ ｙ 次 次 次 姿 姿

Point — Note the position of the dots!

姿勢	しせい	posture, attitude
容姿	ようし	figure, looks
雄姿	ゆうし	gallant figure
姿見	すがたみ	full-length mirror

要

The woman never looked away from the trunk which was stuffed with important documents.

おんよみ ヨウ　　**くんよみ** い(る)・かなめ

いみ pivot, to summarize　　**strokes** 9画　一 厂 戸 币 両 西 要 要 要

Point — Do not protrude!

要点	ようてん	point
重要(な)	じゅうよう(な)	important
要る	いる	to need
要石	かなめいし	keystone

313

妻

The woman became this man's wife because she submitted her marriage registration at the public office.

おんよみ サイ　くんよみ つま

いみ wife, to marry into

strokes 8画　一 ラ ヲ ヨ 事 妻 妻 妻

Point　妻　Do not connect!

夫妻	ふさい	husband and wife
妻子	さいし	wife and children
愛妻	あいさい	beloved wife
新妻	にいづま	newly-married woman

館

A girl with food greeted a police officer standing in front of a police box that was next to a mansion.

おんよみ カン　くんよみ やかた

いみ mansion, institution

strokes 16画　ノ 𠆢 ⺈ 今 今 今 亇 食 食 食' 食' 飣 飣 飣 館 館

Point　館　Do not connect!

映画館	えいがかん	movie theater
博物館	はくぶつかん	museum
大使館	たいしかん	embassy
館	やかた	mansion

飯

A girl delivered a meal to the shop assistant who had been selling rolls of cloth.

おんよみ ハン　くんよみ めし

いみ cooked rice, meal

strokes 12画　ノ 𠆢 ⺈ 今 今 今 亇 食 食⁻ 飣 飯 飯

炊飯器	すいはんき	rice cooker
赤飯	せきはん	red rice
夕飯	ゆうはん	supper
朝飯	あさめし	breakfast

介

The man introduced the two men to each other.

おんよみ カイ　くんよみ —

いみ to intervene, to help

strokes 4画　ノ 𠆢 介 介

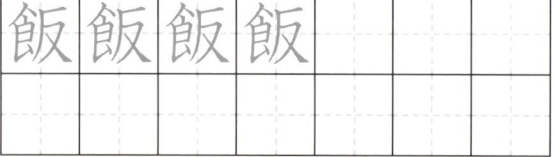

紹介	しょうかい	introduction
介助	かいじょ	help, assistance
介護	かいご	nursing care
介在	かいざい	intervention

 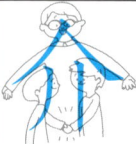
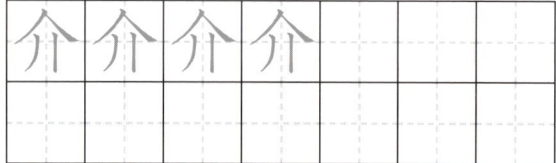

界

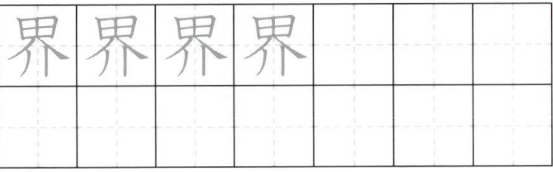

The man likes to look at the rice fields and see the way the boundaries are formed.

おんよみ カイ **くんよみ** ―

いみ border, scope, world **strokes** 9画 丨 冂 冂 田 田 尹 尹 界 界

世界	せかい	world
境界	きょうかい	boundary
界隈	かいわい	neighborhood
業界	ぎょうかい	industry, the business world

習

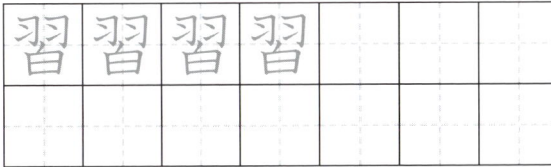

The bird learned how to fly through an online lecture.

おんよみ シュウ **くんよみ** なら(う)

いみ to learn, custom, tradition **strokes** 11画 フ ヲ ヨ 彐 羽 羽 羽 羽 習 習 習

習う	ならう	to learn
学習	がくしゅう	learning
講習	こうしゅう	lecture
習慣	しゅうかん	custom, habit

皆

All the students started to do some stretching under the command of the PE teacher.

おんよみ カイ **くんよみ** みな

いみ all, everyone, together **strokes** 9画 一 ト ヒ 比 比 毕 毕 皆 皆

 Do not protrude!

皆勤	かいきん	perfect attendance
皆無	かいむ	nothing, nil
皆既日食	かいきにっしょく	total solar eclipse
皆	みな	all

的

The boy aimed at the target on the shooting stand.

おんよみ テキ **くんよみ** まと

いみ target, accurate, -wise, -ish **strokes** 8画 ′ 丨 冂 白 白 白 的 的

 Note the position of the dot!

的確	てきかく	accuracy
知的(な)	ちてき(な)	intellectual
劇的(な)	げきてき(な)	dramatic
的中	てきちゅう	hit

暖

  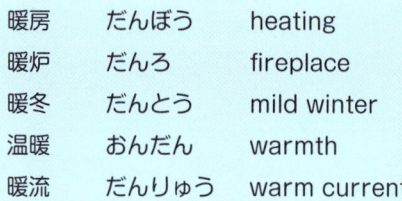

One sunny day in the winter, I took my dog out for a walk wearing warm clothes.

おんよみ ダン
くんよみ あたた(か)・あたた(かい)・あたた(まる)・あたた(める)

いみ warm, to warm　strokes 13画　｜ 冂 日 日 日´ 日゛ 日゛ 日゜ 日゜ 晄 睅 暖 暖

Point
暖
Note the position of the dots!

暖房	だんぼう	heating
暖炉	だんろ	fireplace
暖冬	だんとう	mild winter
温暖	おんだん	warmth
暖流	だんりゅう	warm current

昨

A new day started with the sunrise, and I tried to forget about something nasty that happened yesterday.

おんよみ サク
くんよみ ―

いみ yesterday, last year, last～　strokes 9画　｜ 冂 日 日 日´ 昨 昨 昨 昨

Point
昨
Do not protrude!

昨日	さくじつ・きのう	yesterday
昨夜	さくや	last night
昨年	さくねん	last year
一昨年	いっさくねん	the year before last
昨春	さくしゅん	last spring

晩

Around sunset, the mother told her child loudly that the supper was ready.

おんよみ バン
くんよみ ―

いみ evening, night, late　strokes 12画　｜ 冂 日 日 日´ 日゜ 晀 晚 晚 晚 晚 晩

今晩	こんばん	tonight
晩飯	ばんめし	supper
晩夏	ばんか	late summer
晩婚	ばんこん	late marriage
晩年	ばんねん	later years

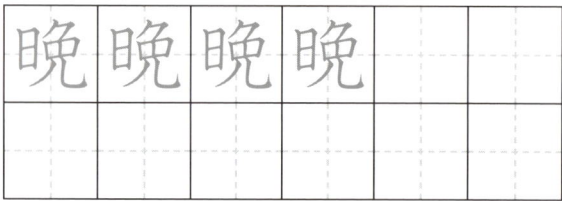

映

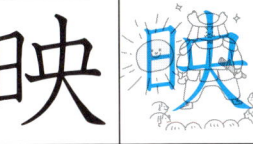

The *samurai* warrior is standing under the sun surrounded by other warriors.

おんよみ エイ　　**くんよみ** うつ(す)・うつ(る)・は(える)

いみ to reflect, to be reflected　　**strokes** 9画　ノ 冂 冃 日 日′ 日ㄣ 日央 映 映

Point  ←Protrude!

映す	うつす	to reflect
映画	えいが	film, movie
映像	えいぞう	image, picture
反映	はんえい	reflection

暗

I listened to lively music under the sun in order to wipe away my gloomy feeling.

おんよみ アン　　**くんよみ** くら(い)

いみ dark, gloomy, secret　　**strokes** 13画　ノ 冂 冃 日 日′ 日ㄣ 日立 日立 日音 日音 暗 暗 暗

暗室	あんしつ	darkroom
暗示	あんじ	suggestion
暗記	あんき	memorizing
暗い	くらい	dark, gloomy

量

I measured flour accurately with a scale to bake a cake.

おんよみ リョウ　　**くんよみ** はか(る)

いみ to measure, to weigh, quantity　　**strokes** 12画　ノ 冂 冃 日 旦 早 昌 昌 昌 量 量 量

Point 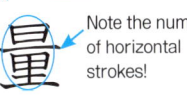 Note the number of horizontal strokes!

量る	はかる	to measure, to weigh
大量	たいりょう	a large amount
重量	じゅうりょう	weight
力量	りきりょう	competence

景

The building height in the city is limited in order to preserve the old-fashioned landscape.

おんよみ ケイ　　**くんよみ** ―

いみ scene, sight　　**strokes** 12画　ノ 冂 冃 日 旦 早 昌 昌 景 景 景

Point  Do not protrude!

景観	けいかん	view, landscape
夜景	やけい	night view
背景	はいけい	background
情景	じょうけい	sight, scene

易

I easily scooped up the sun with a net.

おんよみ エキ・イ　　**くんよみ** やさ(しい)

いみ to change, fortune-telling, easy

strokes 8画　 一 ロ 日 日 尸 号 易 易

Do not protrude!

貿易	ぼうえき	trade
簡易	かんい	simplicity
難易度	なんいど	difficulty
易しい	やさしい	easy

替

 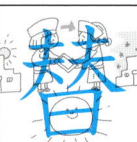

Since this hospital has a two-shift system, the two nurses changed shifts at noon.

おんよみ タイ　　**くんよみ** か(える)・か(わる)

いみ to replace, to change

strokes 12画　 一 二 チ 夫 扶 扶 扶 扶 扶 替 替 替

Protrude!

替わる	かわる	to replace
交替	こうたい	change, alternation, shift
代替	だいたい	substitute
両替	りょうがえ	currency exchange

昔

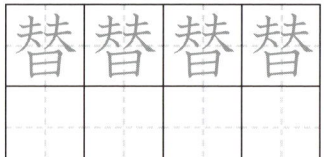

The sun has worn a hat since the old days.

おんよみ シャク・セキ　　**くんよみ** むかし

いみ the past, the old days

strokes 8画　 一 十 廾 # 昔 昔 昔 昔

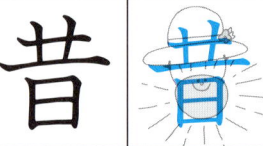
Note the longest horizontal stroke!

昔日	せきじつ	the old days
今昔	こんじゃく	past and present
昔話	むかしばなし	old story
大昔	おおむかし	ancient times

香

The sun took various kinds of perfumes from the shelf and tried them.

おんよみ コウ・キョウ　　**くんよみ** か・かお(り)・かお(る)

いみ fragrance, to be fragrant, incense

strokes 9画　 一 二 千 チ 禾 乔 乔 香 香

香水	こうすい	perfume
芳香	ほうこう	aroma
香り	かおり	fragrance
線香	せんこう	incense stick

昇

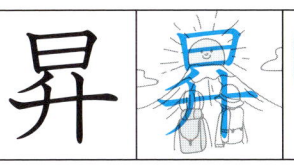

Two people were watching the sun rise around Mt. Fuji.

おんよみ ショウ　くんよみ のぼ(る)

いみ to rise

strokes 8画　丿 𠂉 𠂆 日 日 昇 昇 昇

Point: 昇 Protrude!

昇る	のぼる	to rise
上昇	じょうしょう	ascent
昇進	しょうしん	promotion
昇給	しょうきゅう	wage raise

旧

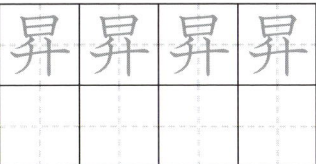

Ancient humans went out for a hunt when the sun was blazing down on them.

おんよみ キュウ　くんよみ ―

いみ old, former, to get old

strokes 5画　丨 丨丨 丨冂 旧 旧

旧式	きゅうしき	old style
復旧	ふっきゅう	restoration
旧年	きゅうねん	last year
旧姓	きゅうせい	former name

児

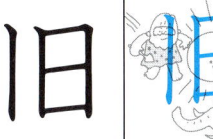

The sun saw a baby, who was crawling, watched by his mother.

おんよみ ジ・ニ　くんよみ ―

いみ child

strokes 7画　丨 丨丨 丨冂 旧 旧 尸 児

Point: 児 Do not connect!

児童	じどう	(school) children
乳児	にゅうじ	infant, baby
園児	えんじ	kindergarten children
小児科	しょうにか	pediatrics

暮

At dusk, birds were flying back to the nest and the lights were on in the houses.

おんよみ ボ　くんよみ く(れる)・く(らす)

いみ to get dark, to spend time, twilight

strokes 14画　一 十 艹 艹 莒 莒 苜 莫 莫 莫 幕 幕 暮 暮

Point: 暮 Protrude!

暮らす	くらす	to spend time, to live
暮色	ぼしょく	twilight, dusk
お歳暮	おせいぼ	year-end gift
日暮れ	ひぐれ	sunset, nightfall

普

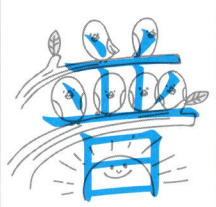

The little birds lined up on the sun as usual.

おんよみ　フ
くんよみ　—

いみ　wide, broad

strokes 12画　丶丷ᅩ产쓰並普普普普

Point
普　← Note the position of the dots!

普通の	ふつうの	common, usual	彼女はどこにでもいそうな普通の学生だ。
普及	ふきゅう	spread	インターネットが普及する。
普遍的(な)	ふへんてき(な)	universal	普遍的な美しさを追求する。
普段	ふだん	usually	普段、よくスニーカーを履く。
普請	ふしん	donations for public works, house-building	古くなってきたので、親の家を普請する。

最

As I have finished the news coverage at sunrise, my article will surely be the latest.

おんよみ　サイ
くんよみ　もっと(も)

いみ　most

strokes 12画　一口日日旦早早早早最最

Point
最　← Do not protrude!

最良の	さいりょうの	the best	彼との結婚は人生最良の選択だった。
最悪の	さいあくの	the worst	今日は最悪の一日だった。
最終日	さいしゅうび	the last day	今日が夏休みの最終日だ。
最大の	さいだいの	the maximum	今年最大の台風が近づいている。
最短の	さいたんの	the shortest	目的地までの最短ルートをたどる。
最も	もっとも	the most	野菜の中でピーマンが最も苦手だ。

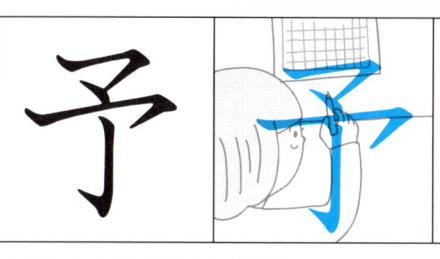

I pointed to the weekend plans on the calendar.

おんよみ ヨ
くんよみ —

いみ beforehand, oneself　**strokes** 4画　フ マ ヌ 予

Point

予 ← Do not connect!

予定	よてい	schedule, plan	週末は家族と旅行に行く予定だ。
予約	よやく	reservation	レストランの予約が取れない。
予想	よそう	expectation, forecast	予想通り、高速道路は渋滞していた。
予感	よかん	hunch, feeling	今日はいいことがありそうな予感がする。
予選	よせん	preliminary	最終予選で敗退した。
猶予	ゆうよ	postponement	3日間の猶予をもらった。

The man expressed his approval by putting his thumb up.

おんよみ リョウ
くんよみ —

いみ to finish, to understand　**strokes** 2画　フ 了

Point

了 ← Connect!

完了	かんりょう	completion	この書類を出せば、手続きは完了する。
終了	しゅうりょう	end	診察の受付は終了していた。
満了	まんりょう	expiration	仕事の契約が満了した。
魅了	みりょう	fascination	彼女の演技は観客を魅了した。
了解	りょうかい	understanding, agreement	家族に了解を求めた。
了承	りょうしょう	approval, acknowledgment	上司の了承を得る。

承

The traditional performing art has been passed down through the family.

- おんよみ: ショウ
- くんよみ: うけたまわ(る)

いみ: to undertake, to receive
strokes: 8画 　フ了了手手手承承

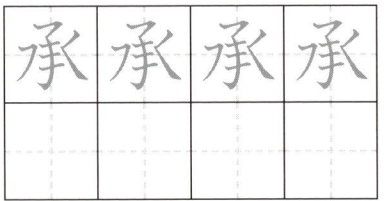

Point  Note the number of horizontal strokes!

承る	うけたまわる	to undertake
承認	しょうにん	agreement, approval
承諾	しょうだく	agreement, consent
継承	けいしょう	succession
伝承	でんしょう	lore, oral tradition

翌

In the next morning, the bird flew away from a starting stand.

- おんよみ: ヨク
- くんよみ: ―

いみ: tomorrow, next
strokes: 11画 　フヲヲヲヲ羽羽羽翠翠翌

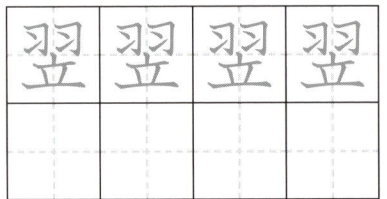

Point  Note the position of the dots!

翌日	よくじつ	the next day
翌週	よくしゅう	the next week
翌月	よくげつ	the next month
翌年	よくねん	the following year
翌朝	よくあさ	the next morning

産

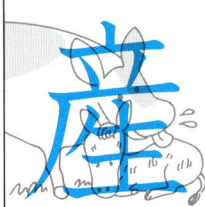

The mother cow had just finished giving birth and licked her baby calf.

- おんよみ: サン
- くんよみ: う(む)・う(まれる)・うぶ

いみ: to give birth, to produce
strokes: 11画 　、亠ナ立产产产产産産

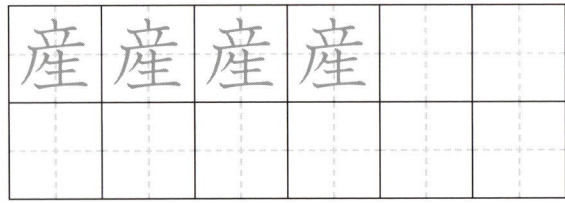

産む	うむ	to give birth
産業	さんぎょう	industry
産地	さんち	producing area
産卵	さんらん	egg-laying, spawning
出産	しゅっさん	childbirth

The fishmonger's business was prospering.

おんよみ ショウ
くんよみ あきな(う)

いみ to deal in, business, commerce strokes 11画 `、亠ᅩ产产产产商商商`

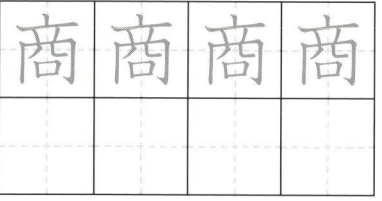

Point
商
Do not protrude!

商う	あきなう	to deal in
商品	しょうひん	product, goods
商売	しょうばい	business
商業	しょうぎょう	commerce
商人	しょうにん	merchant

Children competed with each other at the sports festival.

おんよみ キョウ・ケイ
くんよみ きそ(う)・せ(る)

いみ to compete strokes 20画

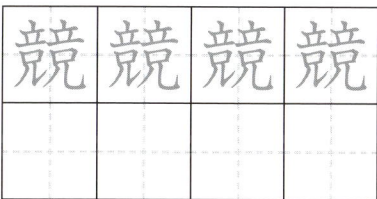

Point
競
Do not protrude!

競う	きそう	to compete
競争	きょうそう	competition
競走	きょうそう	race
競技	きょうぎ	competition, game
競馬	けいば	horse race

We have one student who is absent from our class today.

おんよみ ケツ
くんよみ か(ける)・か(く)

いみ to lack, shortage strokes 4画 `ノ ケ ケ 欠`

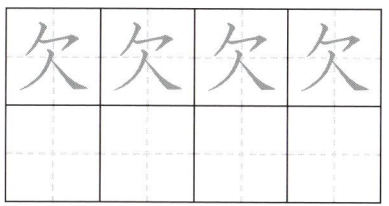

Point
欠
Do not connect!

欠ける	かける	to lack
欠席	けっせき	absence
欠陥	けっかん	defect
欠如	けつじょ	lack
補欠	ほけつ	substitute

323

欧

Oshu means "Europe" in Japanese. Many European countries use the euro as currency.

おんよみ オウ　くんよみ —

いみ Europe, European　strokes 8画　一 フ ヌ 区 区 欧 欧 欧

 Do not connect!

欧州	おうしゅう	Europe
欧米	おうべい	Europe and America
訪欧	ほうおう	visit to Europe
北欧	ほくおう	northern Europe

飲

The women ate and drank a lot.

おんよみ イン　くんよみ の(む)

いみ to drink　strokes 12画　ノ 人 个 今 今 今 食 食 食 飲 飲 飲

 Do not protrude!

飲む	のむ	to drink
飲料	いんりょう	beverage
飲酒	いんしゅ	alcohol drinking
暴飲	ぼういん	heavy drinking

欲

After taking a bath in the hot spring in the valley, I drank plenty of water.

おんよみ ヨク　くんよみ ほ(しい)・ほっ(する)

いみ to want, desire　strokes 11画　ノ ハ ク 父 父 谷 谷 谷 谷 欲 欲

 Note the position of the dots!

欲する	ほっする	to want
欲望	よくぼう	desire
意欲	いよく	ambition, will
食欲	しょくよく	appetite

吹

The man was blowing the trumpet.

おんよみ スイ　くんよみ ふ(く)

いみ to blow　strokes 7画　一 口 口 口 吹 吹 吹

吹く	ふく	to blow
吹奏楽	すいそうがく	wind music
吹き替え	ふきかえ	dubbing
吹き出物	ふきでもの	pimple, rash

軟

Snails and squids belong to the mollusk family.

- おんよみ ナン
- くんよみ やわ（らか）・やわ（らかい）
- いみ soft, weak, flexible
- strokes 11画 一 厂 戸 百 亘 亘 車 車 軋 軟 軟

Point: Protrude!

柔軟（な）	じゅうなん（な）	flexible
軟弱	なんじゃく	weakness
軟膏	なんこう	ointment
軟体動物	なんたいどうぶつ	mollusk

祖

The man paid a visit to his ancestral grave to pray.

- おんよみ ソ
- くんよみ ―
- いみ ancestor, founder
- strokes 9画 丶 ラ オ ネ 礻 初 衵 袒 祖

Point: Note the longest horizontal stroke!

祖先	そせん	ancestor
祖国	そこく	homeland
祖父	そふ	grandfather
開祖	かいそ	founder of a sect

祝

We baked a big birthday cake and celebrated our big brother's birthday.

- おんよみ シュク・シュウ
- くんよみ いわ（う）
- いみ to celebrate
- strokes 9画 丶 ラ オ ネ 礻 礻 祀 祝 祝

Point: Do not protrude!

祝う	いわう	to celebrate
祝福	しゅくふく	blessing
祝日	しゅくじつ	holiday
祝杯	しゅくはい	drinking a toast

祈

The girl prayed to the god.

- おんよみ キ
- くんよみ いの（る）
- いみ to pray, to wish
- strokes 8画 丶 ラ オ ネ 礻 礻 祈 祈

Point: Do not protrude!

祈る	いのる	to pray
祈願	きがん	prayer
祈念	きねん	prayer
祈禱書	きとうしょ	prayer book

福

They celebrated the good rice harvest and thanked the gods.

おんよみ フク
くんよみ ―

いみ happiness, fortune
strokes 13画 　丶　ラ　ネ　ネ　ネ　ネ　ネ　福　福　福　福　福

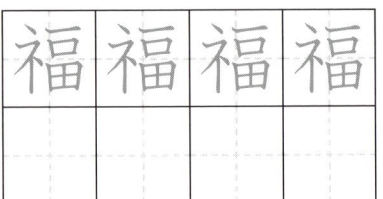

Do not protrude!

福祉	ふくし	welfare
幸福	こうふく	happiness
祝福	しゅくふく	blessing
裕福	ゆうふく	affluence, wealth
至福	しふく	bliss

示

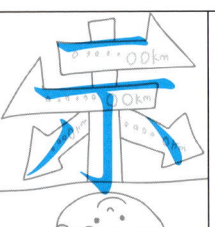

The signpost indicated which way I should take.

おんよみ ジ・シ
くんよみ しめ(す)

いみ to show, to indicate
strokes 5画 　一　二　テ　示　示

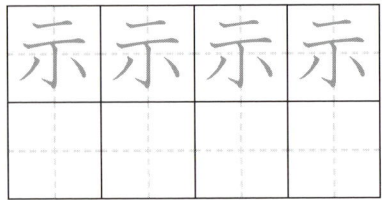

Do not protrude!

示す	しめす	to show, to indicate
指示	しじ	direction
表示	ひょうじ	display
提示	ていじ	presentation
示唆	しさ	suggestion, hint

禁

The two hikers noticed a "Keep Out" sign standing in front of the woods.

おんよみ キン
くんよみ ―

いみ to forbid, to stop, to resist
strokes 13画 　一　十　オ　木　木　村　材　林　林　埜　埜　禁　禁

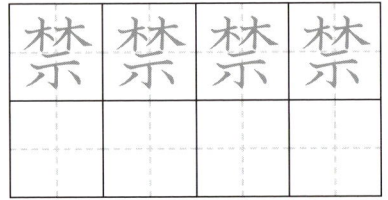

Do not protrude!

禁止	きんし	ban, prohibition
禁煙車	きんえんしゃ	non smoking car
厳禁	げんきん	strict prohibition
禁忌	きんき	taboo
解禁	かいきん	the lifting of a ban

祭

At the summer festival, the moon and fireworks shone brightly while many people looked at the night sky.

おんよみ サイ　　**くんよみ** まつ(る)・まつ(り)

いみ to enshrine, festival　　**strokes** 11画　ノ　ク　タ　タ　ダ　ダ　タ　ダ　祭　祭　祭

Point 祭 ×察 ×際 Note the similar characters!

祭る	まつる	to enshrine
学園祭	がくえんさい	school festival
芸術祭	げいじゅつさい	art festival
前夜祭	ぜんやさい	eve

航

 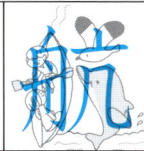

The two went on a voyage in a small ship while a sea gull and a dolphin watched them over.

おんよみ コウ　　**くんよみ** ―

いみ ship, to sail, to cruise　　**strokes** 10画　ノ　丿　冂　冃　舟　舟　舟'　航　航　航

Point 航 Do not protrude!

航海	こうかい	voyage
航空	こうくう	aviation
欠航	けっこう	suspension of a survice
航行	こうこう	sailing, navigation

処

I made a phone call to request the disposal of oversized trash.

おんよみ ショ　　**くんよみ** ―

いみ to settle, to manage, place　　**strokes** 5画　ノ　ク　夂　処　処

対処	たいしょ	coping with
処置	しょち	treatment
処理場	しょりじょう	disposal facility
処分	しょぶん	disposal

殺

A dead body and a knife were left at the murder scene; the police inspected them in detail.

おんよみ サツ・サイ・セツ　　**くんよみ** ころ(す)

いみ to kill　　**strokes** 10画　ノ　メ　夹　手　杀　杀　杀　杀　殺　殺

Point 殺 Do not connect!

殺す	ころす	to kill
殺人	さつじん	murder
相殺	そうさい	offset
殺菌	さっきん	sterilization

327

般

In general, dolphins and squids can swim faster than a row boat.

おんよみ ハン
くんよみ —

いみ sort, aspect, time
strokes 10画   ′ 丿 刀 丹 丹 舟 舟 舯 舯 般

Note the position of the dots!

一般的(な)	いっぱんてき(な)	common, general
全般的(な)	ぜんぱんてき(な)	whole, general
諸般の	しょはんの	various
先般	せんぱん	some time ago
今般	こんぱん	now

役

This is a TV program in which the main character fights against villains.

おんよみ ヤク・エキ
くんよみ —

いみ labor, service, role, war
strokes 7画   ′ 丿 彳 彳 役 役 役

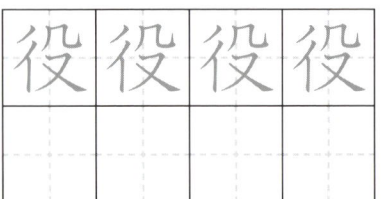

Do not protrude!

役所	やくしょ	government office
役目	やくめ	duty, role
役者	やくしゃ	actor, actress
兵役	へいえき	military service
現役	げんえき	active duty

段

I was talking on my mobile phone while walking, and I fell down the stairs.

おんよみ ダン
くんよみ —

いみ stairs, step, section
strokes 9画   ′ 丿 斤 斤 身 身 段 段 段

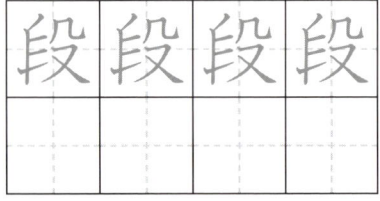

Protrude!

階段	かいだん	stairs
石段	いしだん	stone steps
段階	だんかい	stage, phase
段落	だんらく	paragraph
算段	さんだん	management

There were a lot of workers at the tall building's construction site.

おんよみ セツ
くんよみ もう(ける)

いみ to set up, to prepare **strokes** 11画 `、 ー 二 ミ ニ 言 言 言 訁 訊 設 設`

Note the number of horizontal strokes!

設ける	もうける	to set up
設立	せつりつ	establishment
設置	せっち	installation
施設	しせつ	facility, institution
建設	けんせつ	construction

 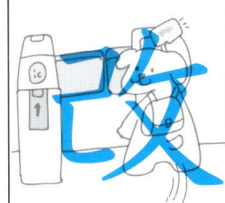

A dog touched a card and went through the ticket gate.

おんよみ カイ
くんよみ あらた(める)・あらた(まる)

いみ to alter, to correct **strokes** 7画 `フ コ 己 己 ア 改 改`

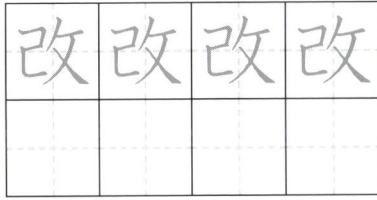 

Do not connect!

改める	あらためる	to alter, to correct
改革	かいかく	reform
改正	かいせい	amendment, revision
改良	かいりょう	improvement
改札口	かいさつぐち	ticket gate

I aimed to be a politician who could lead people in the right direction.

おんよみ セイ・ショウ
くんよみ まつりごと

いみ politics, government **strokes** 9画 `一 丁 下 正 正 正 政 政 政`

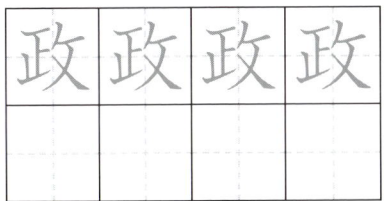

Do not protrude!

政治家	せいじか	politician
政策	せいさく	policy
行政	ぎょうせい	administration
政党	せいとう	political party
摂政	せっしょう	regent

The shellfish was defeated by the dog in the race.

おんよみ ハイ
くんよみ やぶ(れる)

いみ to lose, to be defeated   **strokes** 11画   丨 冂 冃 月 目 貝 貝 貯 貯 敗 敗

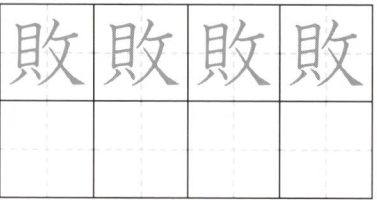

Do not protrude!

敗れる	やぶれる	to lose, to be defeated
敗北	はいぼく	defeat
敗者	はいしゃ	loser
無敗の	むはいの	undefeated
失敗	しっぱい	failure

The pet dog of the deceased man was snuggling by his gravestone.

おんよみ コ
くんよみ ゆえ

いみ old, reason, therefore, happening   **strokes** 9画   一 十 古 古 古 古 故 故 故

故事	こじ	historical fact, fable
故人	こじん	the deceased
故郷	こきょう	hometown
故障	こしょう	breakdown, trouble
事故	じこ	accident, incident

When my friend suddenly fell down, I asked a passer-by for help to call an ambulance.

おんよみ キュウ
くんよみ すく(う)

いみ to save, to rescue   **strokes** 11画   一 十 寸 寸 求 求 求 求 救 救

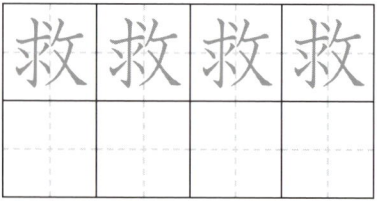

Note the position of the dots!

救う	すくう	to save
救出	きゅうしゅつ	rescue
救援	きゅうえん	relief
救命	きゅうめい	lifesaving
救急車	きゅうきゅうしゃ	ambulance

The moon wore a hat and took her dog for a walk.

おんよみ サン　　**くんよみ** ち(る)・ち(らす)・ち(らかす)・ち(らかる)

いみ to scatter, to be scattered

strokes 12画　一 十 卄 廾 芇 苩 背 背 背 散 散

Point
Note the number of horizontal strokes!

散らす	ちらす	to scatter
散歩	さんぽ	walk
発散	はっさん	diffusion, emission
散乱	さんらん	scattering

A police officer was directing traffic at the intersection, and a dog also followed him.

おんよみ セイ　　**くんよみ** ととの(える)・ととの(う)

いみ to arrange, to prepare

strokes 16画　一 ｢ 戸 戸 束 束 束 束' 敕 敕 敕 整 整 整

整える	ととのえる	to arrange, to prepare
整理	せいり	putting in order
整列	せいれつ	alignment
整備	せいび	maintenance

Three patients were waiting for their turn to come.

おんよみ ジュン　　**くんよみ** ―

いみ to obey, favorable, order

strokes 12画　丿 丿 川 川' 川" 川" 順 順 順 順 順 順

Point
Note the number of horizontal strokes!

順番	じゅんばん	turn, order
順位	じゅんい	ranking
順調(な)	じゅんちょう(な)	favorable
順応	じゅんのう	adaptation

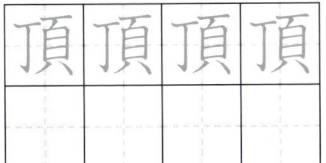

The climber put up a flag on the summit of the mountain.

おんよみ チョウ　　**くんよみ** いただ(く)・いただき

いみ summit, peak, to receive

strokes 11画　一 丁 丆 丆 丆 丁 頂 頂 頂 頂 頂

Point
Do not protrude!

頂く	いただく	to receive, to get
頂上	ちょうじょう	the summit, the top
頂点	ちょうてん	peak, apex, vertex
絶頂	ぜっちょう	climax

331

預

The man deposited cash in the bank and received interest.

- おんよみ ヨ
- くんよみ あず(ける)・あず(かる)

いみ to entrust, to take charge of
strokes 13画
フ マ ヌ 予 予 予 矛 預 預 預 預 預 預

預ける	あずける	to entrust
預かる	あずかる	to take charge of
預金	よきん	deposit
預金通帳	よきんつうちょう	bankbook, passbook
預託	よたく	deposit, commitment

領

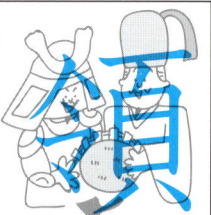

The feudal lord granted land to the *samurai* warrior as a reward for his service.

- おんよみ リョウ
- くんよみ ―

いみ to rule, to take
strokes 14画
ノ ⼈ 今 今 今 令 令 𩠐 領 領 領 領 領 領

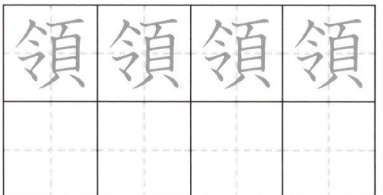

Do not protrude!

領域	りょういき	domain
領土	りょうど	territory
領主	りょうしゅ	feudal lord
占領	せんりょう	occupation
領事	りょうじ	consul

頼

I would like cash rather than a bouquet as a gift for my request.

- おんよみ ライ
- くんよみ たの(む)・たよ(る)・たの(もしい)

いみ to request, to trust, to rely, reliable
strokes 16画
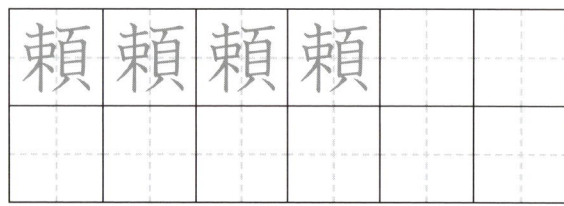

頼む	たのむ	to request
頼る	たよる	to rely
頼もしい	たのもしい	reliable, trustworthy
依頼	いらい	request
信頼	しんらい	trust

額

The clerk at the inn brought the guest a pile of towels because he was sweating while taking a foot bath.

- おんよみ ガク
- くんよみ ひたい

いみ forehead, amount

strokes 18画 　丶 丶 宀 宀 安 安 客 客 客 客 額 額 額 額 額 額

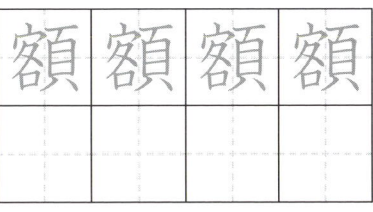

Point

Do not protrude!

額	ひたい	forehead
額縁	がくぶち	picture frame
金額	きんがく	amount of money
少額	しょうがく	small sum
差額	さがく	the difference

類

I made a variety of *sushi* using some rice and seafood.

- おんよみ ルイ
- くんよみ たぐ(い)

いみ to resemble, kind, sort

strokes 18画 　丶 丶 ゛ ュ 半 米 米 米 米 类 类 岩 類 類 類 類 類

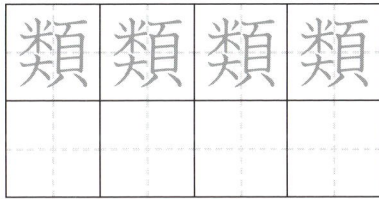

Point

Note the position of the dots!

種類	しゅるい	kind, type
分類	ぶんるい	classification
同類	どうるい	the same kind [class]
人類	じんるい	the human race
類い	たぐい	kind, sort, equal

願

A boy living in a cave wished that he could become wealthy one day.

- おんよみ ガン
- くんよみ ねが(う)

いみ to hope, to wish

strokes 19画 　一 厂 厂 厂 所 所 厉 原 原 原 原 原 願 願 願 願 願 願 願

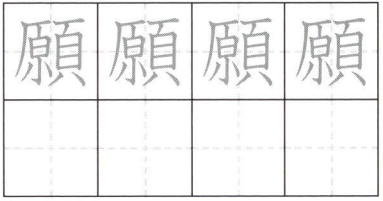

Point

Note the position of the dots!

願う	ねがう	to hope, to wish
願望	がんぼう	desire
願書	がんしょ	application form
祈願	きがん	prayer
嘆願	たんがん	plea

題

The woman tackled a large number of assignments during the day.

おんよみ ダイ
くんよみ —

いみ subject, topic, title
strokes 18画 　一 ロ 日 日 旦 早 早 昇 是 是 是 題 題 題 題 題 題 題

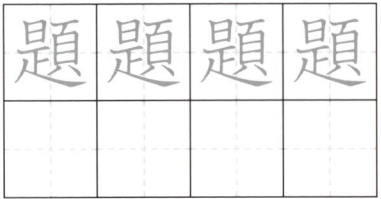 

Point: 題 Do not protrude!

題名	だいめい	title
主題	しゅだい	subject
話題	わだい	topic
問題	もんだい	problem
課題	かだい	task, assignment

駅

 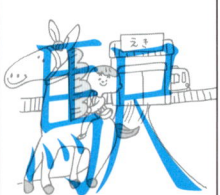

A horse took passengers from one station to another.

おんよみ エキ
くんよみ —

いみ station, stop
strokes 14画 　一 厂 冂 F F 馬 馬 馬 馬 馬 馬 駅 駅 駅

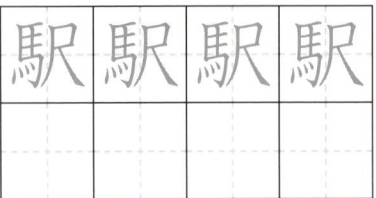 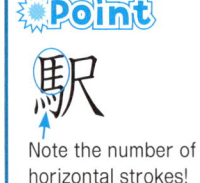

Point: 駅 Note the number of horizontal strokes!

東京駅	とうきょうえき	Tokyo Station
駅舎	えきしゃ	station building
駅員	えきいん	station staff
終着駅	しゅうちゃくえき	terminal
各駅停車	かくえきていしゃ	local train

験

The horse felt lonely because his owner was busy studying for the examination.

おんよみ ケン・ゲン
くんよみ —

いみ to examine, evidence, effect
strokes 18画 　一 厂 冂 F F 馬 馬 馬 馬 馬 駅 駅 験 験 験 験

Point: 験 Do not protrude!

経験	けいけん	experience
試験	しけん	examination, test
入学試験	にゅうがくしけん	entrance exam
実験	じっけん	experiment
効験	こうけん	efficacy

駐

The horse was waiting at the parking space for his owner.

- **おんよみ** チュウ
- **くんよみ** ―

いみ to stay, to park, to station

strokes 15画 一 厂 冂 斤 斤 馬 馬 馬 馬 馬 馬 馬` 馬‐ 馬† 駐

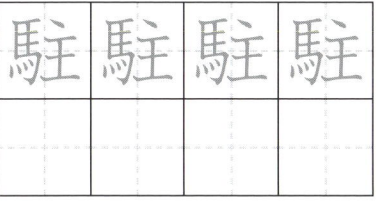

Point
駐
Do not protrude!

駐車場	ちゅうしゃじょう	parking space
駐輪場	ちゅうりんじょう	bicycle parking
駐在	ちゅうざい	residence
駐日大使	ちゅうにちたいし	ambassador to Japan
駐留	ちゅうりゅう	stationing

査

Immigration inspection was conducted in front of the tree.

- **おんよみ** サ
- **くんよみ** ―

いみ to examine, to investigate

strokes 9画 一 十 オ 木 木 杏 杏 杳 査

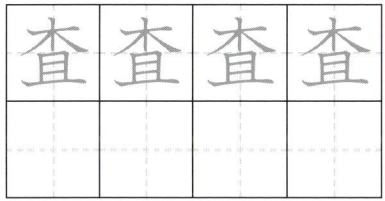

Point
査
Note the number of horizontal strokes!

審査	しんさ	examination
検査	けんさ	inspection
捜査	そうさ	investigation
監査	かんさ	inspection
精査	せいさ	close examination

再

The two met again at the old school they had graduated from.

- **おんよみ** サイ・サ
- **くんよみ** ふたた(び)

いみ again, repeatedly

strokes 6画 一 厂 冂 冉 再 再

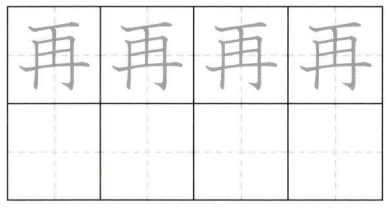

Point
再
Do not protrude!

再び	ふたたび	again
再会	さいかい	reunion
再起	さいき	comeback
再現	さいげん	reproduction
再来年	さらいねん	the year after next

並

The picture in the photo frame is of the family standing in a line.

おんよみ ヘイ　　**くんよみ** なみ・なら(べる)・なら(ぶ)・なら(びに)

いみ to line up, together, ordinary

strokes 8画 丶 丷 䒑 䒑 丷 並 並 並

Point Note the position of the dots!

並ぶ	ならぶ	to line up
並行して	へいこうして	side by side
並列	へいれつ	parallel
並木	なみき	row of trees

非

The two people both blamed each other.

おんよみ ヒ　　**くんよみ** —

いみ error, non-, to blame

strokes 8画 ノ ナ ヲ ヺ 非 非 非 非

Point Note the number of horizontal strokes!

非営利	ひえいり	non-profit
非凡(な)	ひぼん(な)	extraordinary
非難	ひなん	blame, reproach
是非	ぜひ	right and wrong, by all means

冊

 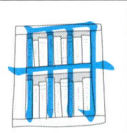

There are many books in the bookcase.

おんよみ サツ・サク　　**くんよみ** —

いみ book, booklet, copy

strokes 5画 丨 冂 冂 冊 冊

Point Protrude!

一冊	いっさつ	one book
冊子	さっし	booklet
別冊	べっさつ	separate volume
短冊	たんざく	strip of paper

甘

The girl drank a glass of sweet juice with a straw.

おんよみ カン　　**くんよみ** あま(い)・あま(える)・あま(やかす)

いみ sweet, pleasant, to pamper

strokes 5画 一 十 廿 廿 甘

Point Protrude!

甘い	あまい	sweet
甘味	かんみ・あまみ	sweetness
甘やかす	あまやかす	to pamper
甘栗	あまぐり	sweet roasted chestnuts

A frog left the rice paddy, seeking freedom.

おんよみ ユ・ユウ・ユイ　**くんよみ** よし

いみ to come from, reason

strokes 5画 ｜ 冂 冂 由 由

Point Protrude!

由来	ゆらい	origin
理由	りゆう	reason
由緒	ゆいしょ	pedigree
自由	じゆう	freedom, liberty

There were some people wearing masks at the ball.

おんよみ メン　**くんよみ** おも・おもて・つら

いみ face, mask, to face

strokes 9画 一 ァ ア 丙 而 而 而 面 面

Point Note the number of horizontal strokes!

面会	めんかい	interview
面影	おもかげ	the image, trace
細面	ほそおもて	slender face
仮面	かめん	mask

People were bathing in the Ganges River, where time is eternal.

おんよみ キュウ・ク　**くんよみ** ひさ(しい)

いみ long time, long-continued

strokes 3画 ノ ク 久

Point Do not protrude!

永久	えいきゅう	eternity, permanence
耐久性	たいきゅうせい	durability
久遠	くおん	eternity
久しい	ひさしい	long-continued

When a man passes away, his coffin is buried, and a gravestone is placed above it.

おんよみ ボウ・モウ　**くんよみ** な(い)

いみ to die, to pass away, to escape

strokes 3画 亠 亡

Point Do not protrude!

亡くなる	なくなる	to die, to pass away
死亡	しぼう	death
滅亡	めつぼう	downfall
亡者	もうじゃ	dead person

片

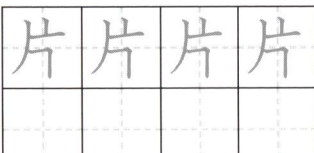

Traffic was restricted to one lane on the street because of roadwork.

おんよみ ヘン　**くんよみ** かた

いみ slice, piece, one side　**strokes** 4画　ノ ノ 广 片

Point Do not protrude!

破片	はへん	fragment
木片	もくへん	wood chip
断片	だんぺん	fragment
片手	かたて	one hand

世

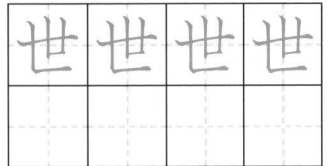

The king sitting in the chair was thinking of ruling the world.

おんよみ セイ・セ　**くんよみ** よ

いみ lifetime, age, generation, era, world　**strokes** 5画　一 十 丗 丗 世

Point Connect!

世紀	せいき	century
世代	せだい	generation
世界	せかい	world
世論	よろん・せろん	public opinion

鼻

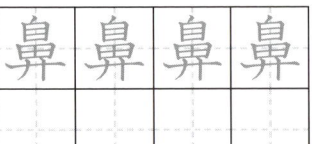

The man had a mustache under his nose.

おんよみ ビ　**くんよみ** はな

いみ nose　**strokes** 14画　ノ 丿 白 白 自 自 咅 咅 咅 咅 咅 咅 鼻 鼻

Point Note the number of horizontal strokes!

鼻炎	びえん	rhinitis
鼻	はな	nose
鼻水	はなみず	nasal mucus
鼻歌	はなうた	humming

身

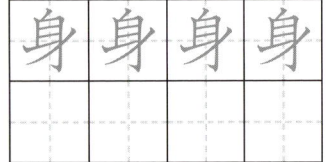

The pole vault is a sport that uses a long pole to jump over a bar.

おんよみ シン　**くんよみ** み

いみ body, oneself　**strokes** 7画　ノ 丿 亻 丆 自 身 身

Point Protrude!

身長	しんちょう	height
独身	どくしん	singles, unmarried
身分	みぶん	social standing
中身	なかみ	contents

I became short-tempered and threw away all my losing lottery tickets.

おんよみ タン　**くんよみ** みじか(い)

いみ short, defect

strokes 12画　ノ ヒ ヒ 矢 矢 矢 矢 矢 矢 短 短 短

Point 短 ← Do not protrude!

短い	みじかい	short
短期	たんき	short term
短所	たんしょ	defect
短気	たんき	short temper

A frog that had left the rice paddy took a flight to study abroad.

おんよみ リュウ・ル　**くんよみ** と(める)・と(まる)

いみ to fix, to detain, to stay

strokes 10画　 留 留 留 留

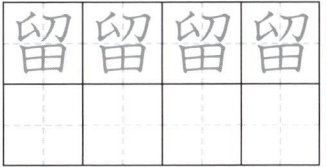 

Point 留 ← Do not protrude!

留める	とめる	to fix, to detain
留学	りゅうがく	studying abroad
保留	ほりゅう	putting on hold
留守	るす	absence

A mother gave food to her baby who was sitting on a high chair.

おんよみ ヨ　**くんよみ** あた(える)

いみ to give, to be involved with

strokes 3画　一 与 与

Point 与 ← Do not protrude!

与える	あたえる	to give
授与	じゅよ	conferment
貸与	たいよ	lending
関与	かんよ	involvement

 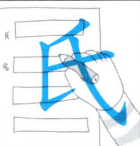

I wrote my family name on the application form.

おんよみ シ　**くんよみ** うじ

いみ clan name, family name

strokes 4画　ノ 乁 丘 氏

Point 氏 ← Do not protrude!

氏名	しめい	full name
氏族	しぞく	clan
山本氏	やまもとし	Mr. Yamamoto
氏神	うじがみ	local tutelar deity

339

辞

The man was confused with more paperwork so he handed in his resignation in anger.

おんよみ ジ　　くんよみ や(める)

いみ word, to resign, to refuse

strokes 13画　一 二 千 千 舌 舌 舌' 舌" 舌" 辞 辞 辞

Point
辞 ← Do not protrude!

辞める	やめる	to resign
辞書	じしょ	dictionary
祝辞	しゅくじ	congratulations
辞表	じひょう	resignation

史

I traced the history by reading a lot of ancient documents.

おんよみ シ　　くんよみ ―

いみ history, record

strokes 5画　丨 口 口 史 史

Point
史 ← Protrude!

歴史	れきし	history
史実	しじつ	historical fact
史跡	しせき	historic site
先史	せんし	prehistory

互

Puzzle rings were tangled up in each other.

おんよみ ゴ　　くんよみ たが(い)

いみ each other, mutual

strokes 4画　一 エ 互 互

Point
互 ← Do not protrude!

互換性	ごかんせい	interchangeability
交互に	こうごに	alternately, mutually
相互に	そうごに	each other, mutually
互い	たがい	each other

差

I stumbled over a step.

おんよみ サ　　くんよみ さ(す)

いみ difference, different, to point

strokes 10画　丶 丷 丬 爫 羊 差 差 差 差 差

Point
差 ← Do not protrude!

差す	さす	to raise, to shine
時差	じさ	time difference
格差	かくさ	disparity
物差し	ものさし	ruler

兆

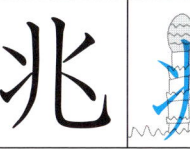

Horsetails, which tell us that spring is coming, were growing all around.

おんよみ チョウ　　**くんよみ** きざ(す)・きざ(し)

いみ sign, indication, trillion

strokes 6画　ノ ノ ナ 丬 兆 兆

Point: Note the position of the dots!

五兆	ごちょう	five trillion
兆候	ちょうこう	sign, symptom
前兆	ぜんちょう	omen
兆し	きざし	sign

毒

There are some parts of *fugu*, known as blowfish, that contain poison.

おんよみ ドク　　**くんよみ** —

いみ poison, bad

strokes 8画　一 十 キ 主 主 青 青 毒

Point: Protrude!

中毒	ちゅうどく	addiction
解毒	げどく	detoxification
消毒	しょうどく	disinfection
毒	どく	poison

飛

Two flying fish leaped into the air.

おんよみ ヒ　　**くんよみ** と(ぶ)・と(ばす)

いみ to fly, to let fly

strokes 9画　乙 乙 飞 飞 飞 飛 飛 飛 飛

Point: Protrude!

飛ぶ	とぶ	to fly
飛行機	ひこうき	airplane
飛び魚	とびうお	flying fish
飛躍	ひやく	jump, rapid progress

更

The boy changed his clothes in the dressing room.

おんよみ コウ　　**くんよみ** さら・ふ(ける)・ふ(かす)

いみ to change, to wear on, further

strokes 7画　一 厂 戸 戸 百 更 更

Point: Do not protrude!

変更	へんこう	change
更新	こうしん	renewal, update
更地	さらち	vacant lot
更衣室	こういしつ	dressing room

乾

As soon as the sun rose among the tall buildings, the clothes on the line dried immediately.

おんよみ カン　　**くんよみ** かわ(く)・かわ(かす)

いみ to dry

strokes 11画　一 十 十 古 古 古 直 卓 卓 乾 乾

Point 乾　Do not connect!

乾く	かわく	to dry
乾燥	かんそう	drying, dryness
乾電池	かんでんち	dry battery
乾物	かんぶつ	dried food

舞

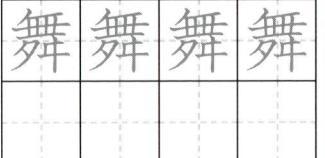

I took Japanese dancing lessons.

おんよみ ブ　　**くんよみ** ま(う)・まい

いみ to dance, to flit, dance

strokes 15画　

 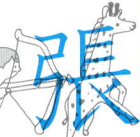

Point 舞　Do not protrude!

舞う	まう	to dance, to fly
舞踊	ぶよう	dance
舞台	ぶたい	stage
見舞い	みまい	visit, inquiry

張

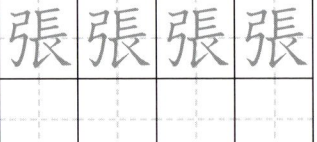

The man felt tense as he drew a bow towards the giraffe.

おんよみ チョウ　　**くんよみ** は(る)

いみ to stretch, to spread

strokes 11画　

Point 張　Note the longest horizontal stroke!

張る	はる	to stretch, to spread
緊張	きんちょう	tension
膨張	ぼうちょう	expansion
主張	しゅちょう	assertion, claim

耕

Farmers used to cultivate fields using horses a long time ago.

おんよみ コウ　　**くんよみ** たがや(す)

いみ to cultivate, to plow

strokes 10画　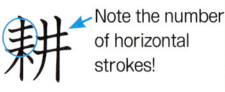

Point 耕　Note the number of horizontal strokes!

耕す	たがやす	to cultivate, to plow
農耕	のうこう	farming, agriculture
耕地	こうち	cultivated land
休耕地	きゅうこうち	fallow

1 Below the *Kanji*, write the Japanese reading of *Kanji* in *Hiragana*.

① 靴　② 氷　③ 飲む　④ 頼む　⑤ 耕す
（　）（　）（　）（　）（　）

⑥ 昔　⑦ 娘　⑧ 姿　⑨ 鋭い　⑩ 習う
（　）（　）（　）（　）（　）

2 Choose the correct reading.

① 戦争（a　せんそう　b　せんほう　c　せんとう）（　）
② 限界（a　ぎんかい　b　げんかい　c　せんかい）（　）
③ 燃焼（a　ねんしょう　b　ぜんしょう　c　えんしょう）（　）
④ 乾燥（a　けんそう　b　しっそう　c　かんそう）（　）
⑤ 婚礼（a　こうれい　b　こんれい　c　こんさつ）（　）

3 Write down the correct reading of the underlined part of the sentence.

① 映画館へ行く。　　　　　　（　　　　　　）
② 理由をたずねる。　　　　　（　　　　　　）
③ 無敗で優勝する。　　　　　（　　　　　　）
④ 尊敬の思いを抱く。　　　　（　　　　　　）
⑤ 彼は先月、辞職しました。（　　　　　　）

4 After reading the *Hiragana* and English, write the *Kanji* that applies to the word in the box.

① ねこ (cat) ☐　　② ふく (clothes) ☐

③ はな (nose) ☐　　④ どく (poison) ☐

⑤ どう (copper) ☐　　⑥ ねがう (to hope) ☐う

⑦ みやこ (capital city) ☐　　⑧ いわう (to celebrate) ☐う

⑨ ふくむ (to contain) ☐む　　⑩ ひとしい (equal) ☐しい

5 Choose the correct *Kanji* that corresponds to the *Hiragana* reading.

① ゆ　(a 輸　b 輪　c 軽)　　(　　)

② し　(a 同　b 司　c 可)　　(　　)

③ そう　(a 制　b 装　c 製)　　(　　)

④ お (いる) (a 者　b 考　c 老)　　(　　)

⑤ ねつ　(a 熱　b 熟　c 然)　　(　　)

6 In the boxes, write the *Kanji* that applies to the *furigana* reading.

① 　てつどう　の　えき　を　けいび　する。

② 　こくさいゆうびん　を送る。

③ 　かいだん　での　てんとう　を　よぼう　する。

④ 　ひょうり　が一体となる。

⑤ 大学を　じゅけん　する。

⑥ ここは　ちゅうしゃきんし　の場所です。

⑦ 　ひかく　して　さいたん　の期間を選ぶ。

⑧ 　りょうしょう　を得る　ひつよう　がある。

答え (answers)

❶ ①くつ ②こおり ③の ④たの ⑤たがや ⑥むかし ⑦むすめ ⑧すがた ⑨するど ⑩なら
❷ ①a ②b ③a ④c ⑤b
❸ ①えいがかん ②りゅう ③むはい ④そんけい ⑤じしょく
❹ ①猫 ②服 ③鼻 ④毒 ⑤銅 ⑥願 ⑦都 ⑧祝 ⑨含 ⑩等
❺ ①a ②b ③b ④c ⑤a
❻ ①鉄道, 駅, 警備 ②国際郵便 ③階段, 転倒, 予防 ④表裏 ⑤受験 ⑥駐車禁止 ⑦比較, 最短
　 ⑧了承, 必要

読み方さくいん・Reading Index

あ

読み	漢字	ページ
あ(う)	会(う)	82
あ(う)	合(う)	83
あ(かす)	明(かす)	89
あ(かり)	明(かり)	89
あ(がる)	上(がる)	32
あ(がる)	挙(がる)	149
あ(く)	空(く)	22
あ(く)	明(く)	89
あ(く)	開(く)	198
あ(くる)	明(くる)	89
あ(ける)	空(ける)	22
あ(ける)	明(ける)	89
あ(ける)	開(ける)	198
あ(げる)	上(げる)	32
あ(げる)	挙(げる)	149
あ(たる)	当(たる)	54
あ(てる)	当(てる)	54
あ(びせる)	浴(びせる)	164
あ(びる)	浴(びる)	164
あ(む)	編(む)	274
あ(る)	有(る)	248
あ(る)	在(る)	263
あ(わす)	合(わす)	83
あ(わせる)	合(わせる)	83
あい	相	119
アイ	愛	151
あいだ	間	63
あお	青	34
あお(い)	青(い)	34
あか	赤	34
あか(い)	赤(い)	34
あか(らむ)	赤(らむ)	34
あか(らむ)	明(らむ)	89
あか(らめる)	赤(らめる)	34
あか(るい)	明(るい)	89
あか(るむ)	明(るむ)	89
あき	秋	48
あき(らか)	明(らか)	89
あきな(う)	商(う)	323
アク	悪	130
あさ	朝	44
あざ	字	30
あさ(い)	浅(い)	156
あし	足	19
あじ	味	289
あじ(わう)	味(わう)	289
あず(かる)	預(かる)	332
あず(ける)	預(ける)	332
あせ	汗	165
あそ(ぶ)	遊(ぶ)	188
あた(える)	与(える)	339
あた(り)	辺(り)	187
あたい	価	106
あたい	値	106
あたた(か)	温(か)	156
あたた(か)	暖(か)	316
あたた(かい)	温(かい)	156
あたた(かい)	暖(かい)	316
あたた(まる)	温(まる)	156
あたた(まる)	暖(まる)	316
あたた(める)	温(める)	156
あたた(める)	暖(める)	316
あたま	頭	84
あたら(しい)	新(しい)	91
アツ	圧	194
あつ(い)	厚(い)	194
あつ(い)	暑(い)	208
あつ(い)	熱(い)	283
あつ(まる)	集(まる)	123
あつ(める)	集(める)	123
あと	後	50
あに	兄	47
あね	姉	47
あば(く)	暴(く)	220
あば(れる)	暴(れる)	220
あぶ(ない)	危(ない)	219
あぶら	油	163
あま	天	21
あま	雨	25
あま(い)	甘(い)	336
あま(える)	甘(える)	336
あま(す)	余(す)	213
あま(やかす)	甘(やかす)	336
あま(る)	余(る)	213
あめ	天	21
あめ	雨	25
あや(うい)	危(うい)	219
あや(ぶむ)	危(ぶむ)	219
あやつ(る)	操(る)	180
あやま(ち)	過(ち)	189
あやま(つ)	過(つ)	189
あやま(る)	誤(る)	228
あゆ(む)	歩(む)	94
あら(う)	洗(う)	165
あら(た)	新(た)	91
あらそ(う)	争(う)	235
あらた(まる)	改(まる)	329
あらた(める)	改(める)	329
あらわ(す)	著(す)	152
あらわ(す)	現(す)	262
あらわ(す)	表(す)	304
あらわ(れる)	現(れる)	262
あらわ(れる)	表(れる)	304
あ(く)	歩(く)	94
アン	行	50
アン	安	139
アン	案	143
アン	暗	317

い

読み	漢字	ページ
イ	位	104
イ	依	110
イ	偉	111
イ	意	130
イ	違	185
イ	以	222
イ	医	232
イ	囲	234
イ	移	236
イ	異	243
イ	胃	249
イ	衣	303
イ	委	313
イ	易	318
い(う)	言(う)	65
い(かす)	生(かす)	29
い(きる)	生(きる)	29
い(く)	行(く)	50
い(ける)	生(ける)	29
い(る)	入(る)	29
い(る)	居(る)	146
い(る)	射(る)	306
い(る)	要(る)	313
い(れる)	入(れる)	29
いえ	家	56
いか(る)	怒(る)	133
いき	息	135
イキ	域	192
いきお(い)	勢(い)	209
イク	育	247
いくさ	戦	295
いけ	池	58
いさ(む)	勇(む)	208
いし	石	22
いそ(ぐ)	急(ぐ)	131
いそが(しい)	忙(しい)	136
いた	板	128
いた(い)	痛(い)	155
いだ(く)	抱(く)	179
いた(む)	痛(む)	155
いた(める)	痛(める)	155
いただ(く)	頂(く)	331
いただき	頂	331
イチ	一	15
いち	市	68
いちじる(しい)	著(しい)	152
イツ	一	15
いつ	五	16
いつ(つ)	五(つ)	16
いと	糸	39
いとな(む)	営(む)	149
いな	否	292
いぬ	犬	26
いの(る)	祈(る)	325
いのち	命	218
いま	今	83
いもうと	妹	47
いろ	色	78
いわ	岩	65
いわ(う)	祝(う)	325

う

読み	漢字	ページ
ウ	雨	25
ウ	右	31
ウ	羽	52
ウ	宇	140
ウ	有	248
う(える)	植(える)	122
う(かぶ)	浮(かぶ)	166
う(かべる)	浮(かべる)	166
う(かる)	受(かる)	151
う(かれる)	浮(かれる)	166
う(く)	浮(く)	166
う(ける)	受(ける)	151
う(つ)	打(つ)	175
う(まれる)	生(まれる)	29
う(まれる)	産(まれる)	322
う(む)	生(む)	29
う(む)	産(む)	322
う(る)	売(る)	69
う(る)	得(る)	114
う(れる)	売(れる)	69
う(れる)	熟(れる)	283
う(わる)	植(わる)	122
うい	初	303
うえ	上	32
うお	魚	75
うけたまわ(る)	承(る)	322
うご(かす)	動(かす)	211
うご(く)	動(く)	211
うし	牛	74
うじ	氏	339
うし(ろ)	後(ろ)	50
うしな(う)	失(う)	115
うす(い)	薄(い)	152
うす(まる)	薄(まる)	152
うす(める)	薄(める)	152
うす(らぐ)	薄(らぐ)	152
うす(れる)	薄(れる)	152
うた	歌	74
うた(う)	歌(う)	74
うたが(う)	疑(う)	284
うち	内	64
うつ(す)	写(す)	138
うつ(す)	移(す)	236
うつ(す)	映(す)	317
うつ(る)	写(る)	138
うつ(る)	移(る)	236
うつ(る)	映(る)	317
うつく(しい)	美(しい)	216
うつわ	器	290
うで	腕	250
うぶ	産	322
うま	馬	76
うみ	海	57
うやま(う)	敬(う)	301
うら	裏	304
うわ	上	32
ウン	雲	54
ウン	運	184

え

読み	漢字	ページ
エ	絵	71
エ	会	82
エ	回	86
エ	依	110
エ	恵	132
え	重	243
え(む)	笑(む)	146
え(る)	得(る)	114
エイ	栄	148
エイ	営	149
エイ	英	153
エイ	泳	160
エイ	永	297
エイ	鋭	299
エイ	映	317
エキ	液	167
エキ	益	205
エキ	易	318
エキ	役	328
エキ	駅	334
えだ	枝	264
エツ	越	190
えら(い)	偉(い)	111
えら(ぶ)	選(ぶ)	185
エン	円	38
エン	遠	59
エン	園	67
エン	演	167
エン	延	182
エン	塩	192
エン	煙	277

お

読み	漢字	ページ
お	小	33
オ	悪	130
オ	汚	166
オ	和	237
お(いる)	老(いる)	284
お(う)	生(う)	29
お(う)	追(う)	187
お(う)	負(う)	242
お(える)	終(える)	270
お(きる)	起(きる)	190
お(く)	置(く)	254
お(こす)	起(こす)	190

お(こる)	起(こる)	190	おとうと	弟	47	か(りる)	借(りる)	108	かぞ(える)	数(える)	92	カン	完	143
お(さえる)	押(さえる)	175	おとこ	男	27	か(れる)	枯(れる)	118	かた	形	77	カン	官	144
お(す)	押(す)	175	おとず(れる)	訪(れる)	227	か(わす)	交(わす)	77	かた	方	95	カン	管	145
お(す)	推(す)	261	おな(じ)	同(じ)	64	か(わる)	代(わる)	103	かた	型	193	カン	簡	146
お(ちる)	落(ちる)	154	おのおの	各	221	か(わる)	換(わる)	180	かた	肩	249	カン	漢	162
お(とす)	落(とす)	154	おび	帯	241	か(わる)	変(わる)	285	かた	片	338	カン	汗	165
お(びる)	帯(びる)	241	おぼ(える)	覚(える)	149	か(わる)	替(わる)	318	かた(い)	固(い)	234	カン	換	180
お(りる)	下(りる)	32	おも	主	201	かい	貝	23	かた(い)	難(い)	260	カン	関	198
お(りる)	降(りる)	308	おも	面	337	カイ	海	57	かた(まる)	固(まる)	234	カン	環	202
お(る)	折(る)	177	おも(い)	重(い)	243	カイ	絵	71	かた(める)	固(める)	234	カン	看	204
お(れる)	折(れる)	177	おも(う)	思(う)	55	カイ	会	82	かた(らう)	語(らう)	66	かん	神	213
お(ろす)	表	304	おもて	表	304	カイ	回	86	かた(る)	語(る)	66	カン	干	245
お(ろす)	降(ろす)	308	おもて	面	337	カイ	械	120	かたち	形	77	カン	刊	256
お(わる)	終(わる)	270	おや	親	91	カイ	快	136	かたむ(く)	傾(く)	112	カン	観	263
オウ	王	38	およ(ぐ)	泳(ぐ)	160	カイ	灰	194	かたむ(ける)	傾(ける)	112	カン	巻	300
オウ	黄	69	おり	折	177	カイ	開	198	カツ	合	83	カン	館	314
オウ	央	116	オン	音	26	カイ	解	259	カツ	活	58	カン	甘	336
オウ	横	122	オン	遠	59	カイ	階	308	カツ	割	258	カン	乾	342
オウ	押	175	おん	御	115	カイ	介	314	ガッ	合	83	ガン	岩	65
オウ	応	195	オン	温	156	カイ	界	315	ガツ	月	12	ガン	元	69
オウ	奥	216	おんな	女	27	カイ	皆	315	かつ(ぐ)	担(ぐ)	175	ガン	顔	84
オウ	欧	324				カイ	改	329	かど	門	63	ガン	丸	96
おお	大	33	**か**			ガイ	外	73	かど	角	73	ガン	岸	199
おお(い)	多(い)	93	か	日	12	ガイ	害	139	かな	金	14	ガン	含	288
おお(いに)	大(いに)	33	カ	火	13	かえ(す)	帰(す)	68	かな(しい)	悲(しい)	132	ガン	願	333
おお(きい)	大(きい)	33	カ	花	23	かえ(す)	返(す)	183	かな(しむ)	悲(しむ)	132	かんが(える)	考(える)	97
おおやけ	公	79	カ	下	32	かえ(る)	帰(る)	68	かなめ	要	313			
おか(す)	犯(す)	219	カ	夏	48	かえ(る)	返(る)	183	かなら(ず)	必(ず)	296	**き**		
おが(む)	拝(む)	179	カ	何	49	かえり(みる)	省(みる)	204	かね	金	14	き	木	14
おぎな(う)	補(う)	302	カ	家	56	かお	顔	84	かの	彼	129	キ	気	22
オク	億	110	カ	科	68	かお(り)	香(り)	318	かぶ	株	120	き	生	29
オク	屋	147	カ	歌	74	かお(る)	香(る)	318	かべ	壁	193	キ	汽	58
おく	奥	216	カ	化	103	かか(える)	抱(える)	179	かま(う)	構(う)	121	キ	記	65
おく(らす)	遅(らす)	188	カ	価	106	かか(る)	係(る)	110	かま(える)	構(える)	121	キ	帰	68
おく(る)	送(る)	184	カ	果	122	かか(わる)	関(わる)	198	かみ	上	32	き	黄	69
おく(る)	贈(る)	269	カ	菓	125	かかり	係	110	かみ	紙	72	キ	機	121
おく(れる)	後(れる)	50	カ	仮	128	かぎ(る)	限(る)	307	かみ	髪	201	キ	起	190
おく(れる)	遅(れる)	188	カ	荷	152	カク	角	73	かみ	神	213	キ	基	193
おこ(す)	興(す)	242	カ	過	189	カク	画	85	かよ(う)	通(う)	61	キ	危	219
おこ(る)	怒(る)	133	カ	加	210	カク	格	120	から	空	22	キ	季	240
おこ(る)	興(る)	242	カ	課	228	カク	客	141	から(い)	辛(い)	238	キ	希	240
おごそ(か)	厳(か)	150	カ	貨	267	カク	覚	149	から(まる)	絡(まる)	222	キ	期	250
おこな(う)	行(う)	50	カ	可	290	カク	拡	178	から(む)	絡(む)	222	キ	規	262
おさ(まる)	修(まる)	116	か	靴	300	カク	各	221	から(める)	絡(める)	222	キ	器	290
おさ(まる)	収(まる)	117	か	香	318	カク	確	260	からだ	体	49	キ	寄	291
おさ(まる)	治(まる)	164	ガ	画	85	カク	較	286	かり	仮	128	キ	喜	293
おさ(まる)	納(まる)	273	ガ	我	294	カク	革	300	かる(い)	軽(い)	287	キ	祈	325
おさ(める)	修(める)	116	か(う)	交(う)	77	ガク	学	28	かれ	彼	129	ギ	技	177
おさ(める)	収(める)	117	か(う)	買(う)	92	ガク	楽	51	かろ(やか)	軽(やか)	287	ギ	議	230
おさ(める)	治(める)	164	か(える)	代(える)	103	ガク	額	333	かわ	川	24	ギ	疑	284
おさ(める)	納(める)	273	か(える)	換(える)	180	かこ(う)	囲(う)	234	かわ	皮	129	き(える)	消(える)	159
おさな(い)	幼(い)	210	か(える)	変(える)	285	かこ(む)	囲(む)	234	かわ	革	300	き(く)	聞(く)	63
おし(える)	教(える)	92	か(える)	替(える)	318	かざ	風	96	がわ	側	112	き(く)	効(く)	210
おそ(い)	遅(い)	188	か(く)	書(く)	89	かさ(なる)	重(なる)	243	かわ(かす)	乾(かす)	342	き(く)	利(く)	255
おそ(れる)	恐(れる)	134	か(く)	欠(く)	323	かさ(ねる)	重(ねる)	243	かわ(く)	乾(く)	342	き(こえる)	聞(こえる)	63
おそ(ろしい)	恐(ろしい)	134	か(ける)	欠(ける)	323	かしこ(い)	賢(い)	267	カン	間	63	き(せる)	着(せる)	203
おそ(わる)	教(わる)	92	か(す)	貸(す)	267	かしら	頭	84	カン	感	131	き(まる)	決(まる)	158
おっと	夫	115	か(つ)	勝(つ)	250	かず	数	92	カン	慣	137	き(める)	決(める)	158
おと	音	26	か(らす)	枯(らす)	118	かぜ	風	96	カン	寒	142	き(る)	切(る)	70

き(る)	着(る)	203	ギョウ	行	50	くる(しめる)	苦(しめる)	151	ケン	研	117	コウ	後	50
き(れる)	切(れる)	70	ギョウ	形	77	くるま	車	39	ケン	建	181	コウ	黄	69
きざ(し)	兆(し)	341	ギョウ	業	125	くれない	紅	273	ケン	健	181	コウ	光	69
きざ(す)	兆(す)	341	キョク	極	120	くろ	黒	75	ケン	県	203	コウ	交	77
きざ(む)	刻(む)	257	キョク	曲	206	くろ(い)	黒(い)	75	ケン	肩	249	コウ	公	79
きし	岸	199	キョク	局	291	くわ(える)	加(える)	210	ケン	権	260	コウ	広	79
きず(く)	築(く)	124	ギョク	玉	38	くわ(わる)	加(わる)	210	ケン	険	261	コウ	高	81
きそ(う)	競(う)	323	きわ	際	309	クン	訓	227	ケン	検	261	コウ	工	85
きた	北	45	きわ(まる)	極(まる)	120	クン	君	292	ケン	賢	267	コウ	考	97
きた(す)	来(す)	51	きわ(み)	極(み)	120	グン	軍	138	ケン	券	300	コウ	候	116
きた(る)	来(る)	51	きわ(める)	極(める)	120	グン	群	292	ケン	験	334	コウ	格	120
きたな(い)	汚(い)	166	きわ(める)	究(める)	144				ゲン	言	65	コウ	構	121
キツ	詰	231	キン	金	14	**け**			ゲン	元	69	コウ	港	161
キツ	喫	288	キン	近	60	ケ	気	22	ゲン	原	88	コウ	厚	194
きび(しい)	厳(しい)	150	キン	今	83	ケ	家	56	ゲン	厳	150	コウ	康	197
きみ	君	292	キン	均	191	け	毛	96	ゲン	減	159	コウ	効	210
キャク	客	141	キン	勤	212	ケ	化	103	ゲン	現	262	こう	神	213
ギャク	逆	187	キン	禁	326	ケ	仮	128	ゲン	限	307	コウ	講	231
キュウ	九	17	ギン	銀	298	ゲ	下	32	ゲン	験	334	コウ	幸	238
キュウ	休	35				ゲ	夏	48				コウ	興	242
キュウ	弓	52	**く**			ゲ	外	73	**こ**			コウ	紅	273
キュウ	急	131	ク	九	17	ゲ	解	259	こ	木	14	コウ	向	291
キュウ	究	144	ク	口	20	け(す)	消(す)	159	こ	子	29	コウ	降	308
キュウ	泣	164	ク	工	85	ケイ	兄	47	こ	小	33	コウ	郊	310
キュウ	球	202	ク	供	107	ケイ	計	66	こ	黄	69	コウ	好	313
キュウ	級	269	ク	苦	151	ケイ	京	76	コ	戸	78	コウ	香	318
キュウ	給	271	ク	庫	197	ケイ	形	77	コ	古	80	コウ	航	327
キュウ	吸	289	ク	区	233	ケイ	係	110	コ	個	109	コウ	更	341
キュウ	求	296	ク	紅	273	ケイ	傾	112	コ	枯	118	コウ	耕	342
キュウ	旧	319	ク	久	337	ケイ	恵	132	コ	湖	161	ゴウ	強	53
キュウ	救	330	グ	具	204	ケイ	境	191	コ	庫	197	ゴウ	合	83
キュウ	久	337	く(う)	食(う)	82	ケイ	型	193	コ	去	199	ゴウ	業	125
ギュウ	牛	74	く(む)	組(む)	73	ケイ	経	271	コ	固	234	ゴウ	号	293
キョ	居	146	く(らう)	食(らう)	82	ケイ	系	275	こ	粉	246	こうむ(る)	被(る)	302
キョ	挙	149	く(らす)	暮(らす)	319	ケイ	軽	287	コ	雇	261	こえ	声	78
キョ	去	199	く(る)	来(る)	51	ケイ	敬	301	コ	呼	289	こお(る)	凍(る)	173
キョ	許	227	く(れる)	暮(れる)	319	ケイ	警	301	コ	故	330	こおり	氷	297
ギョ	魚	75	クウ	空	22	ケイ	景	317	ゴ	五	16	コク	石	22
ギョ	御	115	グウ	偶	111	ケイ	競	323	ゴ	後	50	コク	国	67
ギョ	漁	161	くさ	草	23	ゲイ	迎	186	ゴ	語	66	コク	黒	75
きよ(い)	清(い)	167	くすり	薬	154	ゲイ	芸	200	ゴ	午	74	コク	谷	81
きよ(まる)	清(まる)	167	くだ	管	145	けが(す)	汚(す)	166	ゴ	御	115	コク	刻	257
きよ(める)	清(める)	167	くだ(さる)	下(さる)	32	けが(らわしい)	汚(らわしい)	166	ゴ	誤	228	コク	告	292
キョウ	兄	47	くだ(す)	下(す)	32	けが(れる)	汚(れる)	166	ゴ	期	250	ゴク	極	120
キョウ	強	53	くだ(る)	下(る)	32	ゲキ	激	168	ゴ	互	340	こご(える)	凍(える)	173
キョウ	京	76	くち	口	20	ゲキ	劇	258	こ(い)	濃(い)	168	ここ	九	17
キョウ	教	92	クツ	掘	179	ケツ	決	158	こ(う)	恋(う)	134	ここの(つ)	九(つ)	17
キョウ	供	107	くつ	靴	300	ケツ	血	205	こ(える)	超(える)	190	こころ	心	55
キョウ	橋	121	くに	国	67	ケツ	結	270	こ(える)	越(える)	190	こころ(みる)	試(みる)	232
キョウ	恐	134	くば(る)	配(る)	215	ケツ	欠	323	こ(す)	超(す)	190	こころざ(す)	志(す)	133
キョウ	境	191	くび	首	90	ゲツ	月	12	こ(す)	越(す)	190	こころざし	志	133
キョウ	協	212	くみ	組	73	けむ(い)	煙(い)	277	こ(む)	混(む)	162	こころよ(い)	快(い)	136
キョウ	共	242	くも	雲	54	け(む)る	煙(る)	277	こ(む)	込(む)	182	こし	腰	251
キョウ	興	242	くら	蔵	200	けむり	煙	277	こ(める)	込(める)	182	こた(え)	答(え)	57
キョウ	胸	252	くら(い)	暗(い)	317	けわ(しい)	険(しい)	261	こい	恋	134	こた(える)	答(える)	57
キョウ	経	271	くら(べる)	比(べる)	284	ケン	犬	26	こい(しい)	恋(しい)	134	こた(える)	応(える)	195
キョウ	叫	288	くらい	位	104	ケン	見	35	コウ	口	20	コツ	骨	248
キョウ	香	318	く(しい)	苦(しい)	151	ケン	間	63	コウ	校	28	こと	言	65
キョウ	競	323	く(しむ)	苦(しむ)	151	ケン	件	105	コウ	行	50	こと	異	243

348

こと	事	244	サイ	裁	304	**し**			ジキ	食	82	シュウ	集	123
ことわ(る)	断(る)	275	サイ	際	309	シ	四	16	ジキ	直	90	シュウ	宗	141
こな	粉	246	サイ	妻	314	シ	子	29	しず	静	235	シュウ	拾	173
この(む)	好(む)	313	サイ	最	320	シ	糸	39	しず(か)	静(か)	235	シュウ	終	270
こま(か)	細(か)	72	サイ	祭	327	シ	姉	47	しず(まる)	静(まる)	235	シュウ	周	291
こま(かい)	細(かい)	72	サイ	殺	327	シ	思	55	しず(む)	沈(む)	166	シュウ	州	297
こま(る)	困(る)	234	サイ	再	335	シ	市	68	しず(める)	沈(める)	166	シュウ	習	315
こめ	米	71	ザイ	材	119	シ	紙	72	しず(める)	静(める)	235	シュウ	祝	325
ころ(がす)	転(がす)	287	ザイ	罪	254	シ	止	86	しずく	滴	162	ジュウ	十	18
ころ(がる)	転(がる)	287	ザイ	在	263	シ	自	87	した	下	32	ジュウ	中	33
ころ(げる)	転(げる)	287	ザイ	財	264	シ	使	102	した(しい)	親(しい)	91	ジュウ	住	103
ころ(す)	殺(す)	327	さいわ(い)	幸(い)	238	シ	仕	103	した(しむ)	親(しむ)	91	ジュウ	従	113
ころ(ぶ)	転(ぶ)	287	さか	坂	127	シ	志	133	したが(う)	従(う)	113	ジュウ	柔	125
ころも	衣	303	さか	酒	162	シ	次	173	したが(える)	従(える)	113	ジュウ	拾	173
こわ	声	78	さか	逆	187	シ	指	174	したた(る)	滴(る)	162	ジュウ	重	243
こわ(い)	怖(い)	136	さか(える)	栄(える)	148	シ	私	200	シチ	七	17	シュク	宿	142
コン	金	14	さが(す)	探(す)	176	シ	死	207	シチ	質	265	シュク	縮	274
コン	今	83	さか(らう)	逆(らう)	187	シ	試	232	シツ	室	56	シュク	祝	325
コン	根	119	さか(る)	盛(る)	205	シ	誌	232	シツ	失	115	ジュク	熟	283
コン	混	162	さか(ん)	盛(ん)	205	シ	師	241	シツ	湿	157	シュツ	出	30
コン	建	181	さかい	境	191	シ	歯	247	シツ	質	265	ジュツ	術	113
コン	困	234	さかずき	杯	118	シ	刺	256	ジッ	十	18	ジュツ	述	187
コン	婚	312	さかな	魚	75	シ	視	262	ジツ	日	12	シュン	春	48
ゴン	言	65	さき	先	28	シ	支	263	ジツ	実	142	ジュン	準	239
ゴン	厳	150	サク	作	49	シ	枝	264	しな	品	290	ジュン	純	274
ゴン	勤	212	サク	昨	316	シ	資	265	しま	島	199	ジュン	順	331
ゴン	権	260	サク	冊	336	シ	司	293	しめ(す)	湿(す)	157	ショ	書	89
			さぐ(る)	探(る)	176	シ	始	312	しめ(す)	示(す)	326	ショ	暑	208
さ			さけ	酒	162	シ	姿	313	しめ(る)	湿(る)	157	ショ	諸	232
サ	左	31	さけ(ぶ)	叫(ぶ)	288	シ	示	326	しも	下	32	ショ	署	254
サ	作	49	ささ(える)	支(える)	263	シ	氏	339	シャ	車	39	ショ	所	276
サ	茶	56	さず(かる)	授(かる)	176	シ	史	340	シャ	社	90	ショ	初	303
サ	砂	117	さず(ける)	授(ける)	176	ジ	耳	20	シャ	砂	117	ショ	処	327
サ	査	335	さだ(か)	定(か)	143	ジ	字	30	シャ	写	138	ジョ	女	27
サ	再	335	さだ(まる)	定(まる)	143	ジ	地	62	シャ	捨	173	ジョ	助	211
サ	差	340	さだ(める)	定(める)	143	ジ	寺	87	シャ	者	208	ジョ	除	309
ザ	座	196	さち	幸	238	ジ	自	87	シャ	射	306	ショウ	生	29
さ(がる)	下(がる)	32	サッ	早	36	ジ	時	87	シャク	石	22	ショウ	上	32
さ(く)	割(く)	258	サツ	察	141	ジ	仕	103	シャク	赤	34	ショウ	小	33
さ(げる)	下(げる)	32	サツ	刷	258	ジ	治	164	シャク	借	108	ショウ	青	34
さ(さる)	刺(さる)	256	サツ	札	311	ジ	次	173	シャク	昔	318	ショウ	正	36
さ(す)	指(す)	174	サツ	殺	327	ジ	持	174	ジャク	弱	53	ショウ	声	78
さ(す)	刺(す)	256	サツ	冊	336	ジ	路	221	ジャク	若	151	ショウ	星	89
さ(す)	差(す)	340	サツ	雑	259	じ	似	222	ジャク	着	203	ショウ	少	94
さ(ます)	覚(ます)	149	さば(く)	裁(く)	304	ジ	事	244	シュ	手	19	ショウ	従	113
さ(ます)	冷(ます)	253	さま	様	220	ジ	除	309	シュ	首	90	ショウ	相	119
さ(める)	覚(める)	149	さむ(い)	寒(い)	142	ジ	児	319	シュ	修	116	ショウ	性	137
さ(める)	冷(める)	253	さら	皿	204	ジ	示	326	シュ	取	117	ショウ	笑	146
さ(る)	去(る)	199	さら	更	341	ジ	辞	340	シュ	守	140	ショウ	消	159
サイ	西	45	さわ(る)	触(る)	259	し(いる)	強(いる)	53	シュ	酒	162	ショウ	清	167
サイ	切	70	サン	三	15	し(ぬ)	死(ぬ)	207	シュ	主	201	ショウ	招	178
サイ	細	72	サン	山	24	し(まる)	閉(まる)	198	シュ	種	243	ショウ	床	195
サイ	才	86	サン	算	57	し(める)	閉(める)	198	ジュ	従	113	ショウ	省	204
サイ	菜	153	サン	参	201	し(る)	知(る)	81	ジュ	受	151	ショウ	証	229
サイ	済	165	サン	賛	264	しあわ(せ)	幸(せ)	238	ジュ	授	176	ショウ	象	235
サイ	採	178	サン	産	322	しお	塩	192	シュウ	秋	48	ショウ	章	239
サイ	財	264	サン	散	331	シキ	色	78	シュウ	週	60	ショウ	精	247
サイ	災	277	ザン	残	207	シキ	識	231	シュウ	修	116	ショウ	勝	250
サイ	歳	295				シキ	式	295	シュウ	収	117	ショウ	賞	268

349

ショウ	紹	275	ス	守	140	セイ	精	247	ソウ	宗	141	た(える)	絶(える)	272
ショウ	焼	276	ス	主	201	せい	背	249	ソウ	層	147	だ(く)	抱(く)	179
ショウ	照	283	ス	素	275	セイ	制	255	ソウ	掃	180	た(す)	足(す)	19
ショウ	将	301	す	州	297	セイ	成	294	ソウ	操	180	だ(す)	出(す)	30
ショウ	装	304	ズ	図	67	セイ	歳	295	ソウ	送	184	た(つ)	立(つ)	35
ショウ	昇	319	ズ	頭	84	セイ	製	305	ソウ	争	235	た(つ)	建(つ)	181
ショウ	承	322	ズ	事	244	セイ	政	329	ソウ	贈	269	た(つ)	絶(つ)	272
ショウ	商	323	す(う)	吸(う)	289	セイ	整	331	ソウ	総	272	た(つ)	断(つ)	275
ショウ	政	329	す(ぎる)	過(ぎる)	189	セイ	世	338	ソウ	燥	277	た(つ)	裁(つ)	304
ジョウ	上	32	す(く)	好(く)	313	ゼイ	説	229	ソウ	装	304	た(てる)	立(てる)	35
ジョウ	場	62	す(ごす)	過(ごす)	189	ゼイ	税	236	ゾウ	憎	138	た(てる)	建(てる)	181
ジョウ	乗	123	す(てる)	捨(てる)	173	セキ	夕	22	ゾウ	造	188	た(べる)	食(べる)	82
ジョウ	条	124	す(べる)	統(べる)	274	セキ	石	22	ゾウ	増	191	た(やす)	絶(やす)	272
ジョウ	情	137	す(まう)	住(まう)	103	セキ	赤	34	ゾウ	蔵	200	た(りる)	足(りる)	19
ジョウ	定	143	す(ます)	済(ます)	165	セキ	席	196	ゾウ	臓	201	た(る)	足(る)	19
ジョウ	常	150	す(む)	住(む)	103	せき	関	198	ゾウ	像	235	タイ	大	33
ジョウ	蒸	152	す(む)	済(む)	165	セキ	積	238	ゾウ	象	235	タイ	体	49
ジョウ	城	192	す(る)	刷(る)	258	セキ	責	268	ゾウ	雑	259	タイ	台	79
ジョウ	盛	205	スイ	水	13	セキ	績	269	ゾウ	贈	269	タイ	太	85
ジョウ	静	235	スイ	出	30	セキ	昔	318	そうろう	候	116	タイ	代	103
ジョウ	成	325	スイ	推	261	セチ	節	145	ソク	足	19	タイ	待	114
ジョウ	状	302	スイ	吹	324	セツ	雪	54	ソク	側	112	タイ	退	188
ショク	色	78	スウ	数	92	セツ	切	70	ソク	息	135	タイ	帯	241
ショク	食	82	すえ	末	245	セツ	節	145	ソク	測	158	タイ	貸	267
ショク	植	122	すがた	姿	313	セツ	接	176	ソク	速	182	タイ	対	307
ショク	触	259	すく(う)	救(う)	330	セツ	折	177	ソク	束	246	タイ	替	318
ショク	職	297	すく(ない)	少(ない)	94	セツ	説	229	ソク	則	257	ダイ	大	33
しら	白	34	すぐ(れる)	優(れる)	110	セツ	殺	327	ゾク	族	217	ダイ	弟	47
しら(べる)	調(べる)	228	すけ	助	211	セツ	設	329	ゾク	続	271	ダイ	内	64
しりぞ(く)	退(く)	188	すこ(し)	少(し)	94	ゼツ	絶	272	そこ	底	195	ダイ	台	79
しりぞ(ける)	退(ける)	188	すこ(やか)	健(やか)	181	セン	千	18	そこ(なう)	損(なう)	266	ダイ	代	103
しる(す)	記(す)	65	すす(む)	進(む)	183	セン	川	24	そこ(ねる)	損(ねる)	266	ダイ	第	145
しるし	印	219	すす(める)	進(める)	183	セン	先	28	そそ(ぐ)	注(ぐ)	164	ダイ	題	334
しろ	白	34	すな	砂	117	セン	線	72	そだ(つ)	育(つ)	247	たい(ら)	平(ら)	245
しろ	代	103	すべ(て)	全(て)	213	セン	船	81	そだ(てる)	育(てる)	247	たお(す)	倒(す)	258
しろ	城	192	すみ(やか)	速(やか)	182	セン	浅	156	ソツ	卒	238	たお(れる)	倒(れる)	258
しろ(い)	白(い)	34	するど(い)	鋭(い)	299	セン	洗	165	ソツ	率	239	たか	高	81
シン	森	21	すわ(る)	座(る)	196	セン	選	185	そと	外	73	たか(い)	高(い)	81
シン	心	55	スン	寸	305	セン	戦	295	そな(える)	供(える)	107	たが(い)	互(い)	340
シン	新	91				セン	専	305	そな(える)	備(える)	111	たか(まる)	高(まる)	81
シン	親	91	**せ**			ゼン	前	93	そな(わる)	備(わる)	111	たか(める)	高(める)	81
シン	信	108	せ	背	249	ゼン	全	213	その	園	67	たがや(す)	耕(す)	342
シン	寝	144	セ	世	338	ゼン	然	282	そむ(く)	背(く)	249	タク	宅	140
シン	深	157	せ(める)	責(める)	268	ゼン	善	293	そむ(ける)	背(ける)	249	タク	濯	168
シン	進	183	せ(る)	競(る)	323				そら	空	22	タク	度	196
シン	臣	200	セイ	生	29	**そ**			ソン	村	36	たぐ(い)	類(い)	333
シン	真	203	セイ	青	34	ソ	組	73	ソン	孫	240	たけ	竹	24
シン	申	213	セイ	正	36	ソ	想	135	ソン	存	263	たし(か)	確(か)	260
シン	神	213	セイ	西	45	ソ	素	275	ソン	損	266	たし(かめる)	確(かめる)	260
シン	辛	238	セイ	声	78	ソ	祖	325	ソン	尊	306	たす(かる)	助(かる)	211
シン	針	299	セイ	晴	88	そ(める)	初(める)	303	ゾン	存	263	たす(ける)	助(ける)	211
シン	身	338	セイ	星	89	そ(らす)	反(らす)	127				たず(ねる)	訪(ねる)	227
ジン	人	30	セイ	性	137	そ(る)	反(る)	127	**た**			ただ(しい)	正(しい)	36
ジン	臣	200	セイ	情	137	ソウ	草	23	た	手	19	ただ(す)	正(す)	36
ジン	神	213	セイ	清	167	ソウ	早	36	た	田	25	ただ(ちに)	直(ちに)	90
			セイ	省	204	ソウ	走	61	タ	太	85	たたか(う)	戦(う)	295
す			セイ	盛	205	ソウ	相	119	タ	多	93	タツ	達	189
ス	子	29	セイ	勢	209	ソウ	窓	134	タ	他	102	たっと(い)	尊(い)	306
ス	数	92	セイ	静	235	ソウ	想	135	ダ	打	175	たっと(ぶ)	尊(ぶ)	306

たと(える)	例(える)	257	ちぢ(らす)	縮(らす)	274	つぎ	次	173	**と**			トウ	納	273
たに	谷	81	ちぢ(れる)	縮(れる)	274	つく(る)	作(る)	49	ト	土	14	トウ	統	274
たね	種	243	チャ	茶	56	つく(る)	造(る)	188	ト	十	18	トウ	灯	276
たの(しい)	楽(しい)	51	チャク	着	203	つた(う)	伝(う)	105	ト	図	67	トウ	等	306
たの(しむ)	楽(しむ)	51	チュウ	虫	26	つた(える)	伝(える)	105	ト	戸	78	ドウ	道	59
たの(む)	頼(む)	332	チュウ	中	33	つた(わる)	伝(わる)	105	ト	頭	84	ドウ	同	64
たの(もしい)	頼(もしい)	332	チュウ	昼	44	つち	土	14	ト	徒	112	ドウ	堂	192
たば	束	246	チュウ	仲	104	つづ(く)	続(く)	271	ト	渡	160	ドウ	動	211
たび	度	196	チュウ	柱	118	つづ(ける)	続(ける)	271	ト	途	186	ドウ	働	243
たび	旅	217	チュウ	宙	139	つつ(む)	包(む)	215	ト	度	196	ドウ	銅	298
たま	玉	38	チュウ	注	164	つど(う)	集(う)	123	ト	登	215	ドウ	導	306
たま	球	202	チュウ	駐	335	つと(まる)	勤(まる)	212	ト	都	310	とうと(い)	尊(い)	306
たまご	卵	218	チョ	著	152	つと(まる)	務(まる)	212	ド	土	14	とうと(ぶ)	尊(ぶ)	306
たみ	民	252	チョ	貯	264	つと(める)	努(める)	209	ド	怒	133	とお	十	18
ため(す)	試(す)	232	チョウ	町	37	つと(める)	勤(める)	212	ド	度	196	とお(い)	遠(い)	59
たも(つ)	保(つ)	108	チョウ	朝	44	つと(める)	務(める)	212	ド	努	209	とお(す)	通(す)	61
たよ(り)	便(り)	109	チョウ	鳥	76	つね	常	150	と(い)	問(い)	198	とお(る)	通(る)	61
たよ(る)	頼(る)	332	チョウ	長	93	つの	角	73	と(う)	問(う)	198	とき	時	87
タン	反	127	チョウ	超	190	つの(る)	募(る)	208	と(かす)	溶(かす)	157	トク	読	66
タン	担	175	チョウ	庁	195	つぶ	粒	246	と(かす)	解(かす)	259	トク	得	114
タン	探	176	チョウ	調	228	つま	妻	314	と(く)	溶(く)	157	トク	特	214
タン	単	239	チョウ	重	243	つみ	罪	254	と(く)	説(く)	229	ドク	読	66
タン	短	339	チョウ	頂	331	つめ(たい)	冷(たい)	253	と(く)	解(く)	259	ドク	独	285
ダン	男	27	チョウ	兆	341	つよ(い)	強(い)	53	と(ぐ)	研(ぐ)	117	ドク	毒	341
ダン	談	228	チョウ	張	342	つよ(まる)	強(まる)	53	と(ける)	溶(ける)	157	とこ	常	150
ダン	団	233	チョク	直	90	つよ(める)	強(める)	53	と(ける)	解(ける)	259	とこ	床	195
ダン	断	275	チン	沈	166	つら	面	337	と(ざす)	閉(ざす)	198	ところ	所	276
ダン	暖	316	チン	珍	202	つら(なる)	連(なる)	189	と(じる)	閉(じる)	198	とし	年	37
ダン	段	328	チン	賃	266	つら(ねる)	連(ねる)	189	と(ばす)	飛(ばす)	341	トツ	突	144
									と(ぶ)	飛(ぶ)	341	とど(く)	届(く)	147
ち			**つ**			**て**			と(まる)	止(まる)	86	とど(ける)	届(ける)	147
ち	千	18	ツ	通	61	て	手	19	と(まる)	泊(まる)	165	ととの(う)	調(う)	228
チ	池	58	ツ	都	310	デ	弟	47	と(まる)	留(まる)	339	ととの(う)	整(う)	331
チ	地	62	つ(く)	付(く)	126	て(らす)	照(らす)	283	と(む)	富(む)	140	ととの(える)	調(える)	228
チ	知	81	つ(く)	突(く)	144	て(る)	照(る)	283	と(める)	止(める)	86	ととの(える)	整(える)	331
チ	値	106	つ(く)	着(く)	203	で(る)	出(る)	30	と(める)	泊(める)	165	とみ	富	140
チ	恥	135	つ(ぐ)	次(ぐ)	173	て(れる)	照(れる)	283	と(める)	留(める)	339	とも	友	95
チ	治	164	つ(ぐ)	接(ぐ)	176	テイ	弟	47	と(らえる)	捕(らえる)	180	とも	供	107
チ	遅	188	つ(ける)	付(ける)	126	テイ	体	49	と(らわれる)	捕(らわれる)	180	とも	共	242
チ	血	205	つ(ける)	着(ける)	203	テイ	停	107	と(る)	取(る)	117	とり	鳥	76
チ	置	254	つ(げる)	告(げる)	292	テイ	低	107	と(る)	採(る)	178	とん	問	198
チ	質	265	つ(まる)	詰(まる)	231	テイ	定	143	と(る)	捕(る)	180	トン	団	233
ち	乳	311	つ(む)	詰(む)	231	テイ	底	195	トウ	東	45			
ち(らかす)	散(らかす)	331	つ(む)	積(む)	238	テイ	庭	197	トウ	冬	48	**な**		
ち(らかる)	散(らかる)	331	つ(める)	詰(める)	231	テイ	程	237	トウ	当	54	な	名	38
ち(らす)	散(らす)	331	つ(もる)	積(もる)	238	テキ	滴	162	トウ	答	57	ナ	南	45
ち(る)	散(る)	331	つ(れる)	連(れる)	189	テキ	適	189	トウ	道	59	な	菜	153
ちい(さい)	小(さい)	33	ツイ	追	187	テキ	的	315	トウ	読	66	ナ	納	273
ちか(い)	近(い)	60	ツイ	対	307	テツ	鉄	298	トウ	頭	84	な(い)	無(い)	282
ちが(う)	違(う)	185	つい(える)	費(える)	268	てら	寺	87	トウ	党	150	な(く)	泣(く)	164
ちが(える)	違(える)	185	つい(やす)	費(やす)	268	テン	天	21	トウ	湯	163	な(げる)	投(げる)	178
ちから	力	39	ツウ	通	61	テン	点	75	トウ	凍	173	な(す)	成(す)	294
チク	竹	24	ツウ	痛	155	テン	店	80	トウ	投	178	な(らす)	慣(らす)	137
チク	築	124	つか(う)	使(う)	102	テン	展	148	トウ	逃	186	な(る)	成(る)	294
ちち	父	46	つか(える)	仕(える)	103	テン	典	241	トウ	島	199	な(れる)	慣(れる)	137
ちち	乳	311	つか(まえる)	捕(まえる)	180	テン	転	287	トウ	盗	205	ナイ	内	64
ちぢ(まる)	縮(まる)	274	つか(まる)	捕(まる)	180	デン	田	25	トウ	登	215	なお(す)	直(す)	90
ちぢ(む)	縮(む)	274	つか(れる)	疲(れる)	155	デン	電	54	トウ	到	257	なお(す)	治(す)	164
ちぢ(める)	縮(める)	274	つき	月	12	デン	伝	105	トウ	倒	258	なお(る)	直(る)	90

読み	漢字	ページ	読み	漢字	ページ	読み	漢字	ページ	読み	漢字	ページ	読み	漢字	ページ
なお(る)	治(る)	164	ニン	人	30	**は**			はた	機	121	ヒ	費	268
なか	中	33	ニン	任	104	は	羽	52	はた	畑	276	ヒ	灯	276
なか	仲	104	ニン	認	231	ハ	破	129	はだ	肌	251	ヒ	比	284
なが(い)	長(い)	93				ハ	葉	153	はたけ	畑	276	ヒ	否	292
なが(い)	永(い)	297	**ぬ**			ハ	波	160	はたら(く)	働(く)	243	ひ	氷	297
なが(す)	流(す)	161	ぬ(かす)	抜(かす)	177	は	歯	247	ハチ	八	17	ヒ	被	302
なか(ば)	半(ば)	70	ぬ(かる)	抜(かる)	177	ば	場	62	ハッ	法	167	ヒ	非	336
なが(れる)	流(れる)	161	ぬ(く)	抜(く)	177	バ	馬	76	ハツ	髪	201	ヒ	飛	341
なご(む)	和(む)	237	ぬ(ける)	抜(ける)	177	は(え)	栄(え)	148	ハツ	発	215	ビ	備	111
なご(やか)	和(やか)	237	ぬし	主	201	は(える)	生(える)	29	はつ	初	303	ビ	美	216
なさ(け)	情(け)	137	ぬす(む)	盗(む)	205	は(える)	栄(える)	148	バツ	抜	177	ビ	鼻	338
ナッ	納	273	ぬの	布	240	は(える)	映(える)	317	バツ	末	245	ひ(える)	冷(える)	253
なつ	夏	48				ば(かす)	化(かす)	103	はな	花	23	ひ(く)	引(く)	52
なな	七	17	**ね**			は(く)	掃(く)	180	はな	鼻	338	ひ(ける)	引(ける)	52
なな(つ)	七(つ)	17	ね	音	26	ば(ける)	化(ける)	103	はな(す)	話(す)	66	ひ(や)	冷(や)	253
なに	何	49	ね	値	106	は(じらう)	恥(じらう)	135	はな(す)	放(す)	217	ひ(やかす)	冷(やかす)	253
なの	七	17	ね	根	119	は(じる)	恥(じる)	135	はな(つ)	放(つ)	217	ひ(やす)	冷(やす)	253
なま	生	29	ね(かす)	寝(かす)	144	は(ずかしい)	恥(ずかしい)	135	はな(れる)	放(れる)	217	ひ(る)	干(る)	245
なみ	波	160	ね(る)	寝(る)	144	は(たす)	果(たす)	122	はなし	話	66	ひか(る)	光(る)	69
なみ	並	336	ね(る)	練(る)	273	は(て)	果(て)	122	はね	羽	52	ひがし	東	45
なみだ	涙	166	ねが(う)	願(う)	333	は(てる)	果(てる)	122	はは	母	46	ひかり	光	69
なや(ます)	悩(ます)	138	ねこ	猫	285	は(やす)	生(やす)	29	はば	幅	241	ひき(いる)	率(いる)	239
なや(む)	悩(む)	138	ネツ	熱	283	は(らす)	晴(らす)	88	はぶ(く)	省(く)	204	ひく(い)	低(い)	107
なら(う)	習(う)	315	ねむ(い)	眠(い)	252	は(る)	張(る)	342	はや(い)	早(い)	36	ひく(まる)	低(まる)	107
なら(びに)	並(びに)	336	ねむ(る)	眠(る)	252	は(れる)	晴(れる)	88	はや(い)	速(い)	182	ひく(める)	低(める)	107
なら(ぶ)	並(ぶ)	336	ネン	年	37	ハイ	杯	118	はや(まる)	早(まる)	36	ひさ(しい)	久(しい)	337
なら(べる)	並(べる)	336	ネン	念	132	ハイ	拝	179	はや(まる)	速(まる)	182	ひたい	額	333
ナン	男	27	ネン	然	282	はい	灰	194	はや(める)	早(める)	36	ひだり	左	31
ナン	南	45	ネン	燃	283	ハイ	配	215	はや(める)	速(める)	182	ヒツ	筆	145
なん	何	49				ハイ	背	249	はやし	林	21	ヒツ	必	296
ナン	難	260	**の**			ハイ	敗	330	はら	原	88	ひと	一	15
ナン	軟	325	の	野	96	バイ	売	69	はら	腹	251	ひと	人	30
ナン	納	273	の(せる)	乗(せる)	123	バイ	買	92	はら(う)	払(う)	177	ひと(しい)	等(しい)	306
			の(ばす)	延(ばす)	182	バイ	倍	109	はり	針	299	ひと(つ)	一(つ)	15
に			の(びる)	延(びる)	182	はい(る)	入(る)	29	はる	春	48	ひと(り)	独(り)	285
ニ	二	15	の(べる)	延(べる)	182	はか(らう)	計(らう)	66	ハン	半	70	ヒャク	百	18
に	荷	152	の(べる)	述(べる)	187	はか(る)	計(る)	66	ハン	反	127	ビャク	白	34
ニ	児	319	の(む)	飲(む)	324	はか(る)	図(る)	67	ハン	坂	127	ヒョウ	標	121
に(がす)	逃(がす)	186	の(る)	乗(る)	123	はか(る)	測(る)	158	ハン	版	127	ヒョウ	評	227
に(げる)	逃(げる)	186	ノウ	悩	138	はか(る)	量(る)	317	ハン	板	128	ヒョウ	兵	242
に(る)	似(る)	222	ノウ	濃	168	ハク	白	34	ハン	販	128	ヒョウ	氷	297
にい	新	91	ノウ	農	206	ハク	薄	152	ハン	犯	219	ヒョウ	表	304
にが(い)	苦(い)	151	ノウ	脳	251	ハク	泊	165	ハン	判	256	ビョウ	病	154
にが(る)	苦(る)	151	ノウ	納	273	バク	暴	220	ハン	飯	314	ビョウ	秒	237
ニク	肉	64	ノウ	能	284	バク	爆	277	ハン	般	328	ビョウ	平	245
にく(い)	憎(い)	138	のが(す)	逃(す)	186	はぐく(む)	育(む)	247	バン	番	71	ビョウ	猫	285
にく(しみ)	憎(しみ)	138	のが(れる)	逃(れる)	186	はげ(しい)	激(しい)	168	バン	万	97	ひら	平	245
にく(む)	憎(む)	138	のこ(す)	残(す)	207	はこ	箱	146	バン	板	128	ひら(く)	開(く)	198
にく(らしい)	憎(らしい)	138	のこ(る)	残(る)	207	はこ(ぶ)	運(ぶ)	184	バン	判	256	ひら(ける)	開(ける)	198
にし	西	45	のぞ(く)	除(く)	309	はし	橋	121	バン	晩	316	ひる	昼	44
ニチ	日	12	のぞ(む)	望(む)	202	はじ	恥	135				ひろ(い)	広(い)	79
にな(う)	担(う)	175	のち	後	50	はじ(まる)	始(まる)	312	**ひ**			ひろ(う)	拾(う)	173
ニャク	若	151	のぼ(す)	上(す)	32	はじ(め)	初(め)	303	ひ	日	12	ひろ(がる)	広(がる)	79
ニュウ	入	29	のぼ(せる)	上(せる)	32	はじ(めて)	初(めて)	303	ひ	火	13	ひろ(げる)	広(げる)	79
ニュウ	柔	125	のぼ(る)	上(る)	32	はじ(める)	始(める)	312	ヒ	皮	129	ひろ(まる)	広(まる)	79
ニュウ	乳	311	のぼ(る)	登(る)	215	はし(る)	走(る)	61	ヒ	彼	129	ひろ(める)	広(める)	79
ニョ	女	27	のぼ(る)	昇(る)	319	はしら	柱	118	ヒ	悲	132	ヒン	貧	267
ニョウ	女	27				はず(す)	外(す)	73	ヒ	疲	155	ヒン	品	290
にわ	庭	197				はず(れる)	外(れる)	73	ヒ	批	179	ビン	便	109

ビン	貧	267	ふと(い)	太(い)	85	ボウ	暴	220	マツ	末	245	**む**			
ふ			ふと(る)	太(る)	85	ボウ	貿	268	まつ(り)	祭(り)	327	む	六	16
フ	父	46	ふな	船	81	ボウ	防	307	まつ(る)	祭(る)	327	ム	夢	153
フ	歩	94	ふね	船	81	ボウ	亡	337	まつりごと	政	329	ム	務	212
フ	風	96	ふみ	文	37	ほう(る)	放(る)	217	まった(く)	全(く)	213	ム	無	282
フ	夫	115	ふゆ	冬	48	ほか	外	73	まと	的	315	ム	武	295
フ	府	126	ふる(い)	古(い)	80	ほか	他	102	まど	窓	134	む(かう)	向(かう)	291
フ	付	126	ふる(す)	古(す)	80	ホク	北	45	まな(ぶ)	学(ぶ)	28	む(く)	向(く)	291
フ	符	126	フン	分	70	ボク	木	14	まね(く)	招(く)	178	む(ける)	向(ける)	291
フ	怖	136	フン	粉	246	ボク	目	20	まも(る)	守(る)	140	む(こう)	向(こう)	291
フ	富	140	ブン	文	37	ほし	星	89	まよ(う)	迷(う)	186	む(す)	蒸(す)	152
フ	浮	166	ブン	聞	63	ほそ(い)	細(い)	72	まる	丸	96	む(つ)	六(つ)	16
フ	布	240	ブン	分	70	ほそ(る)	細(る)	72	まる(い)	円(い)	38	む(らす)	蒸(らす)	152
フ	負	242				ホツ	法	167	まる(い)	丸(い)	96	む(れ)	群(れ)	292
フ	不	244	**へ**			ホツ	発	215	まる(める)	丸(める)	96	む(れる)	蒸(れる)	152
フ	膚	250	ヘ	辺	187	ほっ(する)	欲(する)	324	まわ(す)	回(す)	86	む(れる)	群(れる)	292
フ	婦	312	へ(らす)	減(らす)	159	ほど	程	237	まわ(り)	周(り)	291	むい	六	16
フ	普	320	へ(る)	減(る)	159	ほとけ	仏	104	まわ(る)	回(る)	86	むか(える)	迎(える)	186
ブ	分	70	へ(る)	経(る)	271	ほね	骨	248	マン	万	97	むかし	昔	318
ブ	歩	94	ヘイ	病	154	ホン	本	27	マン	満	163	むく(いる)	報(いる)	286
ブ	不	244	ヘイ	閉	198	ホン	反	127				むし	虫	26
ブ	無	282	ヘイ	兵	242				**み**			むす(ぶ)	結(ぶ)	270
ブ	武	295	ヘイ	平	245	**ま**			み	三	15	むずか(しい)	難(しい)	260
ブ	部	310	ヘイ	並	336	ま	目	20	み	実	142	むすめ	娘	312
ブ	舞	342	ベイ	米	71	ま	間	63	ミ	末	245	むっ(つ)	六(つ)	16
ふ(える)	増(える)	191	ヘキ	壁	193	ま	馬	76	ミ	味	289	むな	胸	252
ふ(かす)	更(かす)	341	べつ	別	256	ま	真	203	み	身	338	むね	胸	252
ふ(く)	吹(く)	324	べに	紅	273	ま(う)	舞(う)	342	み(える)	見(える)	35	むら	村	36
ふ(ける)	老(ける)	284	ヘン	返	183	ま(かす)	負(かす)	242	み(せる)	見(せる)	35	むら	群	292
ふ(ける)	更(ける)	341	ヘン	辺	187	ま(がる)	曲(がる)	206	み(たす)	満(たす)	163	むろ	室	56
ふ(やす)	増(やす)	191	ヘン	編	274	ま(く)	巻(く)	300	み(ちる)	満(ちる)	163			
ふ(る)	降(る)	308	ヘン	変	285	ま(ける)	負(ける)	242	み(つ)	三(つ)	15	**め**		
ふ(れる)	触(れる)	259	ヘン	片	338	ま(げる)	曲(げる)	206	み(る)	見(る)	35	め	目	20
フウ	風	96	ベン	便	109	ま(ざる)	交(ざる)	77	みぎ	右	31	め	女	27
フウ	夫	115	ベン	勉	210	ま(ざる)	混(ざる)	162	みさお	操	180	メイ	名	38
フウ	富	140				ま(じる)	交(じる)	77	みじか(い)	短(い)	339	メイ	明	89
ふか(い)	深(い)	157	**ほ**			ま(じる)	混(じる)	162	みず	水	13	メイ	迷	186
ふか(まる)	深(まる)	157	ほ	火	13	ま(す)	増(す)	191	みずうみ	湖	161	メイ	命	218
ふか(める)	深(める)	157	ホ	歩	94	ま(ぜる)	交(ぜる)	77	みずか(ら)	自(ら)	87	めぐ(む)	恵(む)	132
フク	幅	241	ホ	保	108	ま(ぜる)	混(ぜる)	162	みせ	店	80	めし	飯	314
フク	腹	251	ホ	捕	180	ま(つ)	待(つ)	114	みだ(す)	乱(す)	310	めずら(しい)	珍(しい)	202
フク	復	285	ホ	補	302	マイ	妹	47	みだ(れる)	乱(れる)	310	メン	綿	273
フク	複	286	ボ	母	46	マイ	米	71	みち	道	59	メン	面	337
フク	服	286	ボ	募	208	マイ	毎	94	みちび(く)	導(く)	306			
フク	福	326	ボ	暮	319	マイ	枚	118	みっ(つ)	三(つ)	15	**も**		
ふく(む)	含(む)	288	ほ(しい)	欲(しい)	324	まい	舞	342	みと(める)	認(める)	231	も(える)	燃(える)	283
ふく(める)	含(める)	288	ほ(す)	干(す)	245	まい(る)	参(る)	201	みどり	緑	220	も(しくは)	若(しくは)	151
ふくろ	袋	303	ほ(る)	掘(る)	179	ま(う)	舞(う)	342	みな	皆	315	も(す)	燃(す)	283
ふし	節	145	ホウ	方	95	まえ	前	93	みなと	港	161	も(つ)	持(つ)	174
ふせ(ぐ)	防(ぐ)	307	ホウ	法	167	まか(す)	任(す)	104	みなみ	南	45	も(やす)	燃(やす)	283
ふた	二	15	ホウ	抱	179	まか(せる)	任(せる)	104	みの(る)	実(る)	142	も(る)	盛(る)	205
ふだ	札	311	ホウ	豊	206	まき	巻	300	みみ	耳	20	モウ	毛	96
ふた(つ)	二(つ)	15	ホウ	包	215	まご	孫	240	ミャク	脈	252	モウ	望	202
ふたた(び)	再(び)	335	ホウ	放	217	まさ	正	36	みやこ	都	310	もう	亡	337
フツ	払	177	ホウ	訪	227	まさ(る)	勝(る)	250	ミョウ	名	38	もう(ける)	設(ける)	329
ブツ	仏	104	ホウ	報	286	ま(じえる)	交(える)	77	ミョウ	明	89	もう(す)	申(す)	213
ブツ	物	214	ホウ	忘	133	ま(じわる)	交(わる)	77	ミョウ	命	218	モク	木	14
ふで	筆	145	ボウ	忙	136	まず(しい)	貧(しい)	267	ミン	民	252	モク	目	20
			ボウ	望	202	まち	町	37	ミン	眠	252	もち(いる)	用(いる)	97

353

モツ	物	214	やわ(らぐ)	和(らぐ)	237	ヨウ	養	253	**る**		
もっと(も)	最(も)	320	やわ(らげる)	和(らげる)	237	ヨウ	陽	308	ル	流	161
もっぱ(ら)	専(ら)	305				ヨウ	要	313	ル	留	339
もと	本	27	**ゆ**			ヨク	浴	164	ルイ	涙	166
もと	下	32	ゆ	湯	163	ヨク	翌	322	ルイ	類	333
もと	元	69	ユ	油	163	ヨク	欲	324			
もと	基	193	ユ	遊	188	よこ	横	122	**れ**		
もど(す)	戻(す)	216	ユ	輸	287	よご(す)	汚(す)	166	レイ	戻	216
もと(める)	求(める)	296	ユ	由	337	よご(れる)	汚(れる)	166	レイ	令	253
もど(る)	戻(る)	216	ゆ(う)	結(う)	270	よし	由	337	レイ	冷	253
もとい	基	193	ゆ(く)	行(く)	50	よそお(う)	装(う)	304	レイ	齢	254
もの	者	208	ゆ(わえる)	結(わえる)	270	よっ(つ)	四(つ)	16	レイ	例	257
もの	物	214	ユイ	由	337	よる	夜	44	レイ	礼	311
もり	森	21	ゆう	夕	22	よろこ(ぶ)	喜(ぶ)	293	レキ	歴	194
もり	守	140	ユウ	右	31	よわ(い)	弱(い)	53	レツ	列	207
モン	文	37	ユウ	友	95	よわ(まる)	弱(まる)	53	レン	恋	134
モン	門	63	ユウ	優	110	よわ(める)	弱(める)	53	レン	連	189
モン	聞	63	ユウ	遊	188	よわ(る)	弱(る)	53	レン	練	273
モン	問	198	ユウ	勇	208	よん	四	16			
			ユウ	有	248				**ろ**		
や			ユウ	郵	309	**ら**			ロ	路	221
や	八	17	ユウ	由	337	ライ	来	51	ロウ	労	148
ヤ	夜	44	ゆえ	故	330	ライ	頼	332	ロウ	老	284
や	家	56	ゆか	床	195	ライ	礼	311	ロク	六	16
や	谷	81	ゆき	雪	54	ラク	楽	51	ロク	緑	220
ヤ	野	96	ゆた(か)	豊(か)	206	ラク	落	154	ロク	録	299
や	屋	147	ゆだ(ねる)	委(ねる)	313	ラク	絡	222	ロン	論	230
や(く)	焼(く)	276	ゆび	指	174	ラン	卵	218			
や(ける)	焼(ける)	276	ゆみ	弓	52	ラン	乱	310	**わ**		
や(つ)	八(つ)	17	ゆめ	夢	153				ワ	話	66
や(む)	病(む)	154	ゆる(す)	許(す)	227	**り**			ワ	和	237
や(める)	辞(める)	340				リ	理	95	わ	輪	288
やかた	館	314	**よ**			リ	利	255	わ	我	294
ヤク	薬	154	よ	四	16	リ	裏	304	わ(かつ)	分(かつ)	70
ヤク	益	205	よ	夜	44	リキ	力	39	わ(かる)	分(かる)	70
ヤク	約	269	よ	代	103	リク	陸	309	わ(かれる)	分(かれる)	70
ヤク	役	328	ヨ	余	213	リチ	律	113	わ(ける)	分(ける)	70
やさ(しい)	優(しい)	110	ヨ	予	321	リツ	立	35	わ(る)	割(る)	258
やさ(しい)	易(しい)	318	ヨ	預	332	リツ	律	113	わ(れる)	割(れる)	258
やしな(う)	養(う)	253	よ	世	338	リツ	率	239	わか(い)	若(い)	151
やしろ	社	90	ヨ	与	339	リャク	略	221	わか(れる)	別(れる)	256
やす(い)	安(い)	139	よ(い)	良(い)	253	リュウ	立	35	わざ	業	125
やす(まる)	休(まる)	35	よ(い)	善(い)	293	リュウ	流	161	わざ	技	177
やす(む)	休(む)	35	よ(せる)	寄(せる)	291	リュウ	粒	246	わざわ(い)	災(い)	277
やす(める)	休(める)	35	よ(つ)	四(つ)	16	リュウ	留	339	わす(れる)	忘(れる)	133
やっ(つ)	八(つ)	17	よ(ぶ)	呼(ぶ)	289	リョ	旅	217	わた	綿	273
やど	宿	142	よ(む)	読(む)	66	リョウ	療	155	わた(す)	渡(す)	160
やと(う)	雇(う)	261	よ(る)	因(る)	233	リョウ	漁	161	わた(る)	渡(る)	160
やど(す)	宿(す)	142	よ(る)	寄(る)	291	リョウ	両	199	わたくし	私	200
やど(る)	宿(る)	142	よう	八	17	リョウ	料	246	わたし	私	200
やぶ(る)	破(る)	129	ヨウ	曜	88	リョウ	良	253	わら(う)	笑(う)	146
やぶ(れる)	破(れる)	129	ヨウ	用	97	リョウ	量	317	わり	割	258
やぶ(れる)	敗(れる)	330	ヨウ	容	141	リョウ	了	321	わる(い)	悪(い)	130
やま	山	24	ヨウ	葉	153	リョウ	領	332	われ	我	294
やまい	病	154	ヨウ	溶	157	リョク	力	39	ワン	腕	250
やわ(らか)	柔(らか)	125	ヨウ	洋	163	リョク	緑	220			
やわ(らか)	軟(らか)	325	ヨウ	幼	210	リン	林	21			
やわ(らかい)	柔(らかい)	125	ヨウ	様	220	リン	輪	288			
やわ(らかい)	軟(らかい)	325	ヨウ	腰	251						

●著者

上島 史子（かみじま ふみこ）

学習教材の編集者から転身。イギリスの大学院を卒業し、現在イギリス在住。さまざまなジャンルのライティング経験を生かし、本書では漢字の成り立ちをできるだけ生かしたイラストの案出、および短文の執筆を担当。

竹内 夕美子（たけうち ゆみこ）

大学で中学・高校英語教員免許を取得。大学院で言語学を修める。その後、大学で非常勤講師として留学生に日本語を教える。現在はフリーで日本語教育や英語教育等に携わる。

- ●イラスト　　池田蔵人
- ●本文デザイン　藤江真佐子
- ●組版　　　　アールジービー株式会社
- ●編集協力　　株式会社プランディット
- ●編集担当　　原　智宏（ナツメ出版企画）

Understanding through pictures 1000 KANJI
イラストで覚える漢字1000

2017年4月1日 初版発行

著　者	上島史子・竹内夕美子	©Kamijima Fumiko & Takeuchi Yumiko, 2017
発行者	田村正隆	
発行所	株式会社ナツメ社　東京都千代田区神田神保町1-52　ナツメ社ビル1F（〒101-0051）　電話　03(3291)1257(代表)　FAX　03(3291)5761　振替　00130-1-58661	
制　作	ナツメ出版企画株式会社　東京都千代田区神田神保町1-52　ナツメ社ビル3F（〒101-0051）　電話　03(3295)3921(代表)	
印刷所	図書印刷株式会社	

ISBN978-4-8163-6205-7　　　　　　　　　　　　　　　　Printed in Japan

　　本書に関するお問い合わせは、上記、ナツメ出版企画株式会社までお願いいたします。

〈定価はカバーに表示してあります〉〈落丁・乱丁本はお取り替えいたします〉
本書の一部分または全部を著作権法で定められている範囲を超え、ナツメ出版企画株式会社に無断で複写、複製、転載、データファイル化することを禁じます。

 日本を知るナツメ社の本

赤シート付き
CD付き 一発合格！日本語能力試験N1完全攻略テキスト＆問題集
インターカルト日本語学校＝著　B5判　240ページ＋別冊40ページ　定価:本体1800円＋税

赤シート付き
CD付き 一発合格！日本語能力試験N2完全攻略テキスト＆問題集
インターカルト日本語学校＝著　B5判　256ページ＋別冊40ページ　定価:本体1800円＋税

CD2枚付き
外国人のための英語でわかるはじめての日本語
宮崎道子＋栗田奈美＋坂本舞＝著　B5判　208ページ　定価:本体2800円＋税

原寸大（半紙大）お手本10枚付き
ここからはじめる書道入門
田中鳴舟＝著　B5判　160ページ　定価:本体1400円＋税

動画82分
DVDではじめる茶道入門
北見宗幸＝監修　B5変型判　128ページ　価格:本体1700円＋税

着物の着付けはこれ一冊で大丈夫
DVD付き ひとりで美しく着られる着付けと帯結び
花想容＝監修　AB判　160ページ　価格:本体1580円＋税

人気樹種54種を厳選
よくわかる盆栽 基礎から手入れまで
山田香織＝著　B5変型判　208ページ　定価:本体1500円＋税

写真でひもとく487色の名前
日本の色 世界の色
永田泰弘＝監修　A5判　264ページ　定価:本体2000円＋税

季節に合ったおりがみがいっぱい！
決定版！日本のおりがみ12か月
山口真＝著　A5判　384ページ　定価:本体1400円＋税

すべての作り方を写真で解説
四季を愉しむちりめん細工とつるし飾り
矢島佳津美＝監修　AB判　112ページ　定価:本体1200円＋税